Monographs of the Hebrew Union College

1. Lewis M. Barth, *An Analysis of Vatican 30*
2. Samson H. Levey, *The Messiah: An Aramaic Interpretation*
3. Ben Zion Wacholder, *Eupolemus: A Study of Judaeo-Greek Literature*
4. Richard Victor Bergren, *The Prophets and the Law*
5. Benny Kraut, *From Reform Judaism to Ethical Culture: The Religious Evolution of Felix Adler*
6. David B. Ruderman, *The World of a Renaissance Jew: The Life and Thought of Abraham ben Mordecai Farissol*
7. Alan Mendelson, *Secular Education in Philo of Alexandria*
8. Ben Zion Wacholder, *The Dawn of Qumran: The Sectarian Torah and the Teacher of Righteousness*
9. Stephen M. Passamaneck, *The Traditional Jewish Law of Sale: Shulhan Arukh Hoshen Mishpat, 189-240*

*Monographs of the
Hebrew Union College,
Number 9*

The Traditional Jewish Law of Sale

The Traditional Jewish Law of Sale

*Shulhan Arukh Hoshen Mishpat
Chapters 189-240*

*Translated and
Annotated by*

Stephen M. Passamaneck

*Hebrew Union College Press
Cincinnati 1983*

Copyright 1982 by the Hebrew Union College Press
Hebrew Union College-Jewish Institute of Religion

Library of Congress Cataloging in Publication Data

Karo, Joseph ben Ephraim, 1488-1575.
   The traditional Jewish law of sale.
   (Monographs of the Hebrew Union College, ISSN 0190-5627; no. 9)
   Translation of: Hilkhot mikah u-mimkar and Hilkhot ona'ah u-miḳaḥ taʿut, by Joseph ben Ephraim Karo.
   Includes index.
   1. Sales (Jewish law) I. Passamaneck, Stephen M.
II. Karo, Joseph ben Ephraim, 1488-1575. Hilkhot ona'ah u-miḳaḥ taʿut. English. 1983. III. Title. IV. Series.
LAW   346'.072'089924   83-4287
ISBN 0-87820-408-3   342.672089924

Designed by Noel Martin
Manufactured in the United States of America
Distributed by KTAV Publishing House, Inc.
New York, New York   10013

For My Father
Herman Passamaneck

Contents

Acknowledgments		i
Introduction		1
Abbreviations		9
A Synopsis of the Jewish Law of Sale		11
Lexicographical Notes		69
The Laws of Buying and Selling		75
Chapters:		
189	Verbal Agreement and Acquisition	75
190	Acquisition of Land by Monetary Consideration	75
191	Acquisition of Land by Instrument of Transfer	82
192	Acquisition of Land by Physical Possession	83
193	Things Attached to Land	87
194	Non-Jewish Vendor of Land	87
195	Acquisition by Symbolic Kerchief Exchange	89
196	Acquisition of a Non-Jewish Slave	93
197	Acquisition of Domesticated Animals	94
198	Acquisition of Moveable Property	97
199	Acquisition of Moveable Property by Means of Monetary Consideration	101
200	Acquisition by One's Real or Moveable Property	103
201	Purchasers' Marks on Goods; The Handshake	109
202	Acquisition of Moveable Goods as a Consequence of Acquisition of Land or Slaves	110
203	Acquisition by Exchange	114
204	Withdrawal, Condemnation, and Faithlessness	119
205	Sale Under Duress; Protested Sales	122
206	Conditional Sale to a Specific Person for a Specific Sum	127
207	Conditions, Stipulations, and Aleatory Forfeiture	128
208	Manifest Illegality in a Sale	141
209	An Indeterminate or Nonexistent Thing	141
210	Transfer of Ownership to a *Futurus*	147
211	Sale of Something Not Possessed; *Post-Mortem* Gift	148
212	Ownership of Rights; Consecration of a Nonexistent Thing	151

213	Acquisition of the Yield of a Beehive or Dovecote	156
214	An Undetailed Sale of a House	156
215	Sale of a Courtyard, Press House, Bathhouse, or City	165
216	Exceptions and Reservations in Sales of Land	169
217	Sale of an Irrigation Ditch, Roadway, or Burial Land	175
218	Sale of a Field Containing Tillable and Untillable Land	176
219	Specification of Boundary Lines	185
220	Sale of a Ship, Cart, Yoke of Oxen, Cow, Ass, or Slave-Girl	188
221	Dispute Over Price	193
222	Dispute Over Item Sold	193
223	Disputes in Barter for Animals, Fields, or Slaves	195
224	Barter for an Animal Found to Be Unfit for Use as Food by Jews	197
225	Seller's Warranties	199
226	Sale of Land Without Warranty	201

The Laws on Unfair Price as Constructive Fraud and Rescission Owing to a Fundamental Error in the Contract for Purchase

Chapters:

227	Constructive Fraud by Unfair Pricing	205
228	Misuse of Speech; Verbal Abuse; Deception; Fraudulent Practice	218
229	Refuse Material in Foodstuffs	223
230	The Sale of Wine	225
231	Weights, Measures, and Market Superintendents	227
232	Errors in Weight, Measure, and Counting	234
233	Sale of One Type of Produce Which Is in Fact Another Type	247
234	Sale of Ritually Forbidden Food	248
235	Persons of Permanent or Temporary Legal Incapacity to Buy and Sell	249
236	Extortion by Non-Jews	257

237	Acquisition of Something for Which Another Is Negotiating	263
238	The Seller's Written Record of the Sale	265
239	Replacement of a Lost Instrument of Acquisition	266
240	Multiple Instruments Relating to the Same Real Property	267
Notes		271
Index		323

Acknowledgments

This work could not have proceeded without encouragement and support. I wish to express sincerest gratitude to the Amado Family Foundation; to the B. W. Foundation; and to the Philanthropic Fund of the Rodef Shalom Temple, Pittsburgh, Pennsylvania. I am also indebted to several individuals whose assistance was most timely and greatly appreciated: Mr. Bernard Rapport of Waco, Texas; Mr. and Mrs. Morris Shapiro of Los Angeles, California; and Dr. Ronald B. Sobel, Rabbi of Temple Emanu-El, New York.

My colleagues at the Hebrew Union College-Jewish Institute of Religion have been unfailingly helpful and gracious to me in many ways both large and small. In particular, Dr. Alfred Gottschalk, President of the College-Institute, has been most understanding and ready to aid this work. This book was in part made possible through the President's Research and Academic Development Fund.

Much of the early research for this work was conducted in Oxford at the Oxford Centre for Postgraduate Hebrew Studies and in Venice. I owe a special debt of gratitude to Mr. R. May and his colleagues in the Department of Oriental Books in the Bodleian Library, Oxford. Mr. May and his staff were more than helpful. Grateful thanks are also due to Sra. Stefania Rossi of the Biblioteca Nazionale Marciana, Venice.

Professor Jacob Bazak of Jerusalem first suggested that I undertake this project. His continuing support and encouragement have been greatly appreciated. He, more than anyone else, brought me to the work and kept me at it to the end.

The skilled assistance of two distinguished scholars requires particular recognition. Dr. Bernard Jackson read the Synopsis portion of this work and offered valuable suggestions. Dr. Hanina Ben-Menachem read the translation of the text with painstaking attention to detail. I am indebted to both Dr. Jackson and Dr. Ben-Menachem for bringing to my attention various errors of omission and commission. The burden of any remaining faults and flaws is mine to bear.

Patti Holness, Cheri Burton, and Nanci Bunker worked long and

Acknowledgments

faithfully at the arduous chore of typing the manuscript. They merit particular recognition for the care they lavished on it.

Finally, I wish to express my thanks to Lawrence Martin Cohen, Esq. for preparing the Index.

Stephen M. Passamaneck
Los Angeles, California
November 24, 1982

Introduction

The *Shulhan Arukh* is the premier restatement of traditional Jewish law. It presents the richest store of talmudic and post-talmudic legislation, judicial decisions, custom, and usages in one work; and it also represents the scholarship of two of the most illustrious rabbinic jurists: R. Joseph Karo (1488-1575), the Sefardic authority who compiled the basic text, and R. Moses Isserles (ca. 1520-1572), the Ashkenazic authority who amplified and supplemented Karo's text with learned glosses. The work became the basis for scholarly legal commentary by some of the most skilled and productive rabbinic jurists of succeeding centuries.

The *Hoshen Mishpat* is the largest of the four volumes comprising the *Shulhan Arukh*. It includes the rules and usages that modern jurists would classify as both the law and the procedure for the civil, commercial, and criminal fields.

The *Hilkhoth Mekah Umemkar* and *Hilkhoth Ona'ah U'mekah Ta'uth* sections of *Hoshen Mishpat* deal with the law of sale and fraud in sales. This portion of the traditional Jewish commercial code, perhaps more than any other, still retains a measure of aptness for the modern world, because the transaction of sale is as much or more a part of the modern world as it was a part of past ages. One need not be a judge or an attorney to understand the principles and concepts of a sale. Ordinary men and women engage in buying and selling in the course of their lives and careers very frequently indeed, so that the language of the marketplace, and even the legal principles of a law of sale, are perforce far more familiar to them than the language and principles of other parts of the law. True, the Jewish law of sale and of fraud in sales developed in ages long past, and true again that these rules apply today only when litigants before a rabbinical court agree to the court's use of them. This occurs occasionally in the State of Israel, and very infrequently outside of Israel. Yet the antiquity and substantial desuetude of these laws do not render them obscure and arcane. They remain clear and comprehensible to modern men and women simply because they attempt to regulate a sort of transaction which is still familiar in modern life. Indeed, these old and unused laws serve to show us how clear and close the past may become even as we stand on the threshold of the space age. Thus, the laws of buying and selling were chosen for this translation.

This work is not the first translation of this material into English. Over sixty years ago Rabbi J. L. Kadushin wrote the *Code of Jewish Jurisprudence*, a translation of the entire *Shulhan Arukh*. Unfortunately, this work is little known. The author clearly possessed enormous erudition in rabbinic scholarship, but his familiarity with English idiom was not adequate to the task of translation of technical material.

In 1954, Dr. Chaim Denburg brought out translations of two portions of the *Shulhan Arukh* in two separate volumes. These works are excellent: clear and lucid renderings of the rabbinic Hebrew into first-rate English; and Denburg's notes to the text are equally superior. Denburg confined his work, however, to the first twenty-six chapters of *Hoshen Mishpat* in one volume and chapters 335-404 of *Yoreh Deah* in the other volume.

S. I. Levin and E. A. Boyden produced a most scholarly English translation of the laws of *terefot*, from *Shulhan Arukh, Yoreh Deah*, chapters 29-60. The work first appeared in 1940 and was reprinted in 1969. The text is thoroughly annotated and the translation is excellent. It appears under the title *The Kosher Code*. In 1977 Aryeh Kaplan brought out an English translation, and commentary, to *Shulhan Arukh, Orah Haim*, chapters 670-684, entitled *The Laws of Hanukah*. The translation is reasonably good, and the work contains footnotes to sources.

A number of rabbinic theses, written and submitted at the Hebrew Union College-Jewish Institute of Religion during the last decade, contain translations of portions of the *Shulhan Arukh*. Most of the work concerns various aspects of the law of marriage and divorce. Typescripts of the material are available only in microfilm.

Notes, References, and Notes on Style

The present translation is furnished with an apparatus of notes and references. The source references are not necessarily exhaustive, but the principal sources and cross-references given here permit the tracing of a given rule or clause to at least one other major Jewish legal work of restatement or commentary.

In some cases a commentary, e.g., that of Isserles to the *Turim*, is cited as in turn citing another authority who may be the original source for a particular decision; the commentary in these situations provides a precise and readily available abstract of the relevant opinion, but it does not always restate the precise language or context of the original source.

Occasionally some parenthetical remarks are placed in the text for purposes of amplification or clarification. While these remarks could, of course, be relegated to the apparatus of notes, their inclusion in the text is felt to be justifiable. They maintain the flow of the ideas in a particular text and preserve a more idiomatic English diction. Clearly the rabbinic sources of the *Shulhan Arukh* were not phrased with English syntax in mind, and therefore, from time to time, in order to keep the translation true to basic canons of English grammar and syntax, some paraphrasing appears. A paraphrase embodying the idiomatic sense of the Hebrew is taken to be preferable to a literal rendition of the text which might prove to be clumsy and unclear.

The Hebrew text will occasionally indicate the parties to transactions by the traditional rabbinic device of using the names of Jacob's sons: Reuben, Simeon, Levi, etc. As a rule, these names have been omitted in favor of indicating the parties by letters of the alphabet, thus, the seller A and the buyer B. This modification is an attempt at both brevity and clarity.

Further, the word order of the Hebrew is often recast into more idiomatic English, and lengthy sentences with numerous subordinate clauses are rephrased as shorter English sentences with participial or gerundive dependent phrases. Punctuation, particularly the colon, sometimes serves to remold the lengthy Hebrew clauses into more balanced English sentences.

I believe that the parenthetical insertions, the paraphrases, and the other devices of translation used here do not distort the text or render the translation untrue to the original Hebrew. These devices are intended only for the purpose of greater clarity and the

Notes on the Early Editions of the Shulhan Arukh

maintenance of reasonably correct English. In addition to source references and explanatory notes based on traditional commentary, the notes include special material on the content and development of the traditional printed text. The *Shulhan Arukh* was completed about 1555 (Denburg, *Code of Hebrew Law* [Montreal: Jurisprudence Press, 1954], p. xiv, n. 15); the first volume of it appeared in print in Venice in late 1564 and the other three volumes in 1565.

The *Shulhan Arukh* is thus unique among major Jewish legal works since it proceeded from manuscript to printed text in a relatively short time. There is no long and complex tradition of manuscript transmission of the text. It has been pointed out that the "old Venetian books...are edited and printed, in almost all cases, from good manuscripts, the early Venetian Hebrew books are true authorities..." (Joshua Bloch, *Venetian Printers of Hebrew Books* [New York: New York Public Library, 1932]). *Shulhan Arukh* was set in print during Karo's lifetime; and even the first appearance in print of the first volume with Isserles' glosses (*Orah Haim*, Cracow 1570) occurred in the lifetime of the glossator. The first printed appearance of Isserles' glosses to *Hoshen Mishpat*, however, did not come until 1580. There is no evidence that either Karo or Isserles participated in the preparation of their respective manuscripts for the printer, but certainly in the case of Isserles, it is reasonable to assume that he was at least aware of the forthcoming publication of his glosses to *Orah Haim*.

I have compared the modern editions of the *Shulhan Arukh* with the earlier editions, beginning with the Bragadini text, Venice 1565, through the Amsterdam edition of 1753-63. The early editions consulted are:

> Venice 1567, both the Griffio edition, which appeared in April of 1567, and the Cavalli edition, which appeared in July of that year.
>
> Venice 1577, 1577-78, 1593-94, 1598, and 1632.
>
> Cracow 1570-94 and 1580: the *Hoshen Mishpat* volume of the 1580 edition appeared in fact in 1580, while the *Hoshen Mishpat* volume of the 1570-94 series did not appear

until 1593. The 1580 *Hoshen Mishpat* is therefore the earlier text. This anomaly is clearly indicated by a comparison of the dates given on the respective title pages and the regnal dates of the Polish kings mentioned there.

Cracow 1593-94, 1607, 1618-19, 1670.

Amsterdam 1641-42, 1664-66, 1697-99, 1757-63.

Berlin 1717; Fuerth 1691; Hanau 1627-28; Mantua 1722-23; Prague 1628; Wilmersdorf 1671.

The modern text chosen for purposes of comparison is the Romm edition, published in Vilna, dated 1871. The anomalies in the earlier texts in comparison with this edition are mentioned in the footnote apparatus. By and large the text of the chapters under notice here appears in the Amsterdam 1661-64 edition virtually as we have it in modern editions. Some anomalies in the text, however, that were eliminated in that edition still appear unchanged in editions published after 1666 in other cities. Most of the textual peculiarities and anomalies of the earlier printed texts were, in the course of time, corrected to conform to the readings of parallel material found in the *Tur*, Maimonides, or the Babylonian Talmud. The notes on the anomalies and peculiarities of the early printed text do not constitute an attempt to construct a "scientific" text. They only demonstrate when the text was first corrected or modified, usually on the basis of parallel material, to the readings customarily found in modern editions. Although the information in the notes makes it possible to trace, at least partially, which editions were used in the preparation of which later editions, the material is not used for that purpose here.

The Synopsis of the Law of Sale

A synopsis of the Jewish law of sale prefaces this translation. The synopsis covers of course only the main features of the law. It is an attempt to map out, in orderly fashion, some fundamental ideas and concepts in the law which provide some of the principal juristic bases of the material. The synopsis includes a general sketch of the Roman law of sale and references to some aspects of medieval civil law and Roman Catholic Canon law. This material is not intended as a comparative study of the several legal systems with respect to the law of sale, although some similarities and differences among the systems do, of course, become evident. The inclusion of Roman and medieval material is only for the purpose of furnishing a measure of general background for the Jewish law in respect to other legal systems, with which it may also have shared, to some degree, a similar intellectual framework, contemporaneous history, or geographical locus. If the synopsis should suggest possible lines of research to others, that is well and good, but it is certainly not by any means a thorough technical or comparative study in and of itself, nor is it intended to be exhaustive, since that sort of undertaking goes far beyond the more modest preface required for a translation of the material.

The Jewish Law of Sale Today

It has already been pointed out that the Jewish law of sale operates today only when litigants before a rabbinical court desire that it should. These occasions are rather infrequent. Yet owing to the very nature of this material, it is not merely to be viewed as a relic of a quaint world which has passed, never to return. Since buying and selling are part of the modern world, a law of sale begins with a clearly relevant modern point of departure. Further, Jewish law, even those parts of it that grew up to regulate the shop and the marketplace, is never out of harmony with the broader moral bases of Jewish religious tradition, whose roots are often declared to be found in divinely revealed commandments. The same rabbis who as jurists framed and refined the ancient laws were also the moral preceptors and guides of the Jewish people. The influence of moral attitudes is as clearly detectable in Jewish commercial law as it is in other branches of Jewish traditional law.

Modern business ethics have come under increasing scrutiny in our society. There is a growing trend toward attack on deceitful business practice and shoddy dealing. Such trends and movements are not foreign to the traditional Jewish law of sale. Modern readers, even those without legal training, can appreciate the sustained emphasis on ethical business practice and fair dealing which characterizes this branch of the law. A careful study of this material discloses that a vigorous, functional morality need not be rejected out of hand by businessmen in pursuit of commercial advantage. Good business practice does not necessarily imply immorality or amorality. Perhaps the present work can serve to remind modern buyers and sellers of the responsibilities and duties which their commercial undertakings still involve.

Abbreviations

BaH	*Bait Hadash* commentary to *Tur, Hoshen Mishpat*
BY	*Bet Yosef* commentary to *Tur, Hoshen Mishpat*
C	Code of Justinian
CT	Theodosian Code
D	Digest of Justinian
DM	*Darkhe Moshe* to *Hoshen Mishpat*
Flor	Florentinus
Gaius	Institutes
HM	*Hoshen Mishpat*
Inst.	Justinian's Institutes
Jul.	Julian
MM	*Maggid Mishneh* commentary to *Mishneh Torah*
MP	John W. Baldwin, *Masters, Princes and Merchants* (Princeton, University Press, (Princeton, N.J.: 1970)
P. Sent	Sententiae of Paul
Pap	Papinian
Pomp	Pomponius
RLS	Francis de Zulueta, *The Roman Law of Sale* Oxford: Clarendon Press, 1945)
SMA	*Sefer Meirath Enayim* commentary to *Shulhan Arukh, Hoshen Mishpat*
U.	Ulpian
U. Mela	Ulpius Marcellus
Y.D.	*Yoreh Deah*

A Synopsis of the Jewish Law of Sale

The transaction of sale is undoubtedly the most frequent type of business undertaking in the modern world, and, for that matter, it has been so throughout the long history of commerce. The frequency of this contract gives it a special cachet. It is a part of commerce which every man understands, or believes he does, because every man is involved with it. The various systems of law which have attempted to define and regulate sale speak in words and concepts which are not remote from the ordinary course of life. No matter how antique a law of sale may be, no matter how foreign it may be to the modern marketplace, upon examination it reveals principles and points of view which are perfectly understandable to people today simply because buying and selling are very much a part of modern life.

For most of Jewish history, Jews lived in autonomous communities, and they developed their own legal system to regulate these communities in detail, including their commercial life and, specifically, the transaction of sale. Jewish jurists from the ancient period forward have stated, clarified, defined, and applied the Jewish law of sale; and we may assume that the Jewish law of sale found application wherever Jews were required to regulate and superintend their own societies. As the transaction of sale was, for the commercial world as a whole, the most frequent and common undertaking, there can be little doubt that sale (with all its attendant legal and commercial problems) was equally frequent in the Jewish community. Thus the primary assumption of this study is that we are not dealing with juristic esoterica and arcane rabbinical lore, but with a field of law that, during its periods of application, was kept fresh and vigorous, because the almost infinite variety of human needs and interests that were expressed in transactions of sale always presented new challenges and new situations to maintain its liveliness.

The present synopsis presents an overview of this particularly rich and lively field of Jewish law. It has been designed to provide a general scheme of some principal features, but by no means all features, of the Jewish law of sale. Some portions of the law are mentioned here only in passing, and some material is not included in the synopsis in the interest of brevity. Major points, however, receive some detailed and rather technical attention. Occasionally some matters are repeated in this synopsis because a specific point has to be made in more than one context. The repetitions, it is hoped, will not prove burdensome, and apology is herewith made for them. This sacrifice of brevity, it is further hoped, will yield a greater measure of clarity.

Various matters are amplified by a brief introductory overview of the Roman law of sale and by reference to medieval civil law and Roman Catholic canon law; but not every subject or matter is furnished with comparative references in another system since this synopsis is not intended to be a comparative commentary on Jewish law. A preliminary review of Roman law and medieval civil and canon law can provide particularly useful conceptual tools for examining some comparable or analogous Jewish legal institutions. A word of explanation on the choice of comparative material is in order. First, Roman law flourished during the same ancient period, roughly, that Jewish law reached its own classical peak. The two systems clearly came into contact with each other during the period of Roman hegemony and dominance in the Near East. Jewish law and Roman law, for significant periods in the history of each, shared a common time and place. The same can be said for Jewish law with respect to medieval civil law and the canon law of the Roman church. Certainly, much Jewish legal development occurred during the periods in which Jews were a small and often hard-pressed minority in Christian Europe. The methods and principles of Jewish law did not function in isolation from this sociological reality. It is therefore instructive to see, from time to time, how different yet contemporaneous and (at least in part) geographically co-existent bodies of law approach the same matter.

This study, however, is not concerned with the influence of one system upon another system, if any. Indeed, demonstration of such influence would carry us very far afield from the less ambitious task of providing an overview and general understanding of the principal elements of the Jewish law of sale. Nor is there here a concern with history as such. That, too, is a separate sort of endeavor. Occasionally, suggestions of a historical or comparative nature will be inevitable; but such matters are not by any means our primary concern. It cannot be stated too strongly that references to Roman or medieval law serve only as a means of providing some points of reference, a point of view external to Jewish law, and some technical terminology which may be useful for understanding of principles and developing a broad conceptual framework. There is no attempt at all to undertake any sort of detailed comparative study of Roman law, Canon law, and Jewish law to demonstrate influence of one system upon the other or to resolve problems of Jewish legal history. Indeed, we shall find that Roman and medieval law are quite often worlds apart on some fundamental Jewish ideas in this area. Yet, as a starting point for inquiry, Roman law and medieval law are useful and instructive despite their divergencies from Jewish law and their similarities to it, which tempt one to see cross-influences lurking here and there.

Parenthetically, it is noted that comparative materials from English law do not appear here. Jewish law and English law did not share the same time and the same place in the manner that Roman, Jewish, medieval civil law, and Roman Catholic Canon law did. The greater congruence in time and place between the Jewish, Roman, and medieval systems as well as the interests of brevity dictated the omission of comparisons with English law from these remarks.

In order to provide an overview of the Jewish law of sale, it was necessary to find a Jewish text which gave the fullest statement of the law under one heading. The *Shulhan Arukh, Hoshen Mishpat*, meets this requirement. We have in chapters 189-240 inclusive, the most comprehensive restatement of the Jewish law of sale. All relevant sources of the text up to the time of its publication are represented. The laws are rendered with all the varying views and opinions given in the text itself and occasionally with reference to some of the extensive commentary on it; the commentary, of course, may present a view or opinion which is later than the *Shulhan Arukh* text.

With these preliminary considerations in mind, we turn now to the law of sale itself. References to the *Shulhan Arukh, Hoshen Mishpat* are, when necessary, inserted into the body of the text, e.g., 189:1.

Sale is defined as the exchange of a thing for money.[1] This basic definition contemplates true sale as occurring only after money, coinage of some sort, has appeared and has become the accepted medium of exchange. The rabbis asserted a maxim in regard to money and sales, namely, that as a matter of biblical law, money effects a valid exchange;[2] that is to say that money, coinage, is declared to have functioned as a valid means of exchange from the very earliest periods of Jewish law. Therefore, Jewish law contemplates no period of history in which Jews did not use coinage and could not transact true sales, the exchange of a thing for money. Although, as we shall have occasion to see, barter remained a significant transaction in Jewish law, sale, as distinguished from barter, is perceived in Jewish law as every bit as ancient as barter and not an evolution or development from transactions of barter.

The Roman contract of sale, *emptio venditio*, does not come from the earliest periods of Roman legal development, even though Romans had certainly concluded sales and purchases by various ancient forms since time immemorial.[3] The transaction in one form or another preceded the emergence of a notion of the contract of sale *per se*. A description and discussion of the earlier Roman forms for effecting sales, *mancipatio, stipulationes*, etc., is of no particular moment in this study. But the mature contract of *emptio venditio*, the specific Roman contract of sale, furnishes us with both a vocabulary and some ideas which serve as a starting point in the examination of the Jewish law of sale.

To begin with, *emptio venditio* was a consensual contract.[4] The fundamental requisite for the contract to exist, and for its obligations to be enforceable, was the bare consent of the parties to it. There was no need for any act or form to perfect the contract; consent was sufficient. The contract was clearly bilateral, as its name suggests. Both parties have obligations, and the liability of one party depends upon the other party's having fulfilled or being ready and willing to fulfill his part of the contract.[5] The contract was often amplified or clarified by *stipulationes*, or promises, which embodied any warranties or specific conditions that affected the sale. These promises were actionable in and of themselves. In fact *stipulationes*, as an institution of Roman law, are older than the contract of sale.[6] But the point here is that these promises were unilateral in nature.[7] So we have unilateral promises, *stipulationes*, that could be incorporated into the contract, which was bilateral. It was also possible in Roman law to incorporate terms or conditions in the contract which would affect its bilateral nature;[8] but fundamentally, the contract was conceived as bilateral, and of course consensual. Even reciprocal *stipulationes* were still basically unilateral and independent undertakings of the parties.[9] We shall return to the matter of *stipulationes*, which could form the ground of legal action themselves. *Stipulationes*, as independent undertakings, were separate from the contract of sale itself; the gradual incorporation of express and implied terms into *emptio venditio* will come under notice below.

Above all, Roman law required the parties to *emptio venditio* to act and to perform in *good faith*.[10] The insistence on good faith is the heart of the matter. Good faith meant more than refraining from outright fraud; the parties had to maintain a standard of honest and decent conduct that would properly be expected of good people. Thus the parties were always subject, in case of disagreement or dispute, to having their acts measured against canons of conscience and proper behavior.[11]

In addition to the requirements of good faith, and presumably as a supplement to them, Roman law provided for express warranties to be included in the contract.[12] These warranties were either in the form of *dicta promissave* or in the form of *stipulationes*, side contracts, some of which in the course of time became customary. Customary *stipulationes* amounting to express warranties covered matters of quality of the thing and of quiet enjoyment of the thing. Since a contract of sale in any event often implied a degree of mutual trust or reliance of the parties upon each other, these customary promises might be omitted from the contract as an indication of the expectation of fair play in commerce.[13] Yet, in the course of time, Roman judges came to the view that these customary and traditional *stipulationes*, even if omitted in a particular contract, were nevertheless to operate in it and modify it where good faith required them to be presumed.[14]

We have now three basic characteristics of the Roman *emptio venditio*: consensuality, bilaterality, and good faith. The contract could accommodate many types of terms and conditions beside the express warranties already mentioned. But the contract, in order to exist and to be enforceable (*ex fide bona*), needed three elements: a thing, a price, and consent.[15]

The thing usually had physical substance, although servitudes (praedial or personal), debts, and inheritances were lawful subjects of a sale.[16] A thing which could not exist or which no longer existed at the time of the contract could not be sold.[17] One cannot sell the buyer the buyer's own property, whether the buyer is aware of his title to the goods or not. The sale of an unborn child of a female slave was licit as a conditional sale; and there was a lawful sale where the existence of the thing might never materialize: e.g., a buyer was liable to pay for next year's crop or for the haul of a fisherman's net, even if nothing was caught.[18] These references provided a sufficient outline of the Roman rules on the nature of the thing.

There must also be a price, and that price must be in money.[19] We shall comment on barter presently. This price must, in some way, be fixed and definite. If a specific sum is not included in the contract, then the particular price has to be definable by some ascertainable set of facts (e.g., a market price). Once these facts are known, the contract will not fail for want of a definite price.[20] An agreement to sell at a price to be fixed by a third party was eventually held to be licit conditional sale, provided the third party did set a price.[21] The price had to be *verum*: there had to be a real intent to pay the price set or else the transaction was a form of gift.[22] The contract created the *obligation* to pay the price; nonpayment did not invalidate the contract, and indeed the seller could later stipulate to forgive the price.[23] Roman law did not insist on the adequacy of a price, as long as it was not so low as to be derisory.[24] Parties were free to negotiate price as they wished except that in sales of land, if the price was below one-half of a just price for the property, the seller had the right to seek rescission because of *laesio enormis*.[25]

We move from price to the matter of consent, and this was the key to the formation of the contract, since the thing and the price were the subjects of the consent.[26] Roman legal texts are clear on the point that a consensual contract, like *emptio venditio*, is perfected by the actual consent of the parties, no literal or verbal formality being necessary to the formation of the contract.

While consent without formality may very well perfect the contract, the parties still may employ various means of formal behavior to demonstrate the fact that a contract has been made and obligations are thereby undertaken.[27] Merchants, following time-honored custom, may shake hands on a deal or a buyer may give some earnest to the seller, or indeed the parties may wish to have some written memorandum of their transaction. A word on each of these forms is in order.

A constitution of Justinian (dated 528) provides that, in contracts of sale, if the parties have agreed that their contract shall be put into writing, the contract shall not be in effect unless and until a final document -- not just a draft -- shall have been properly executed.[28] This is a modification of the validity of the contract as resting purely on the consent of the parties. *Arra*, or earnest, appears to have come into Roman law from Hellenistic Greek law.[29] The *arra* served as evidence of the contract; and if large enough, it also served a penal function. The penal purpose of *arra*, which persisted in some part of the Near East in the Hellenistic period, was no longer necessary in Roman law once actions were granted on consent alone as the fundamental test of the existence of the contract,[30] although it might still be occasionally useful for its penal function. A small or nominal amount of *arra* might well serve as an evidentiary token; and in classical Roman law, the giving of a coin, a ring, or even a handshake also furnished proof of the contract but was not part of the essence of the contract.[31] Of course a written memorandum was the best proof of the contract, even before Justinian's constitution made such writing crucial to the contract, if the parties wished to have a written memorandum of their deal.

It must be kept in mind that consent was the foundation stone of *emptio venditio.* The various factors that may condition or nullify consent will be dealt with when we deal with the Jewish rules on consent, conditions attached to consent, and negation of consent.

There are, however, two matters that need to be set out here: the effects of the contract, and the obligations created by the consent in *emptio venditio.*

In Roman law, property in the thing sold does not pass to the buyer by force of the contract but only by conveyance. Roman law made an important, if awkward, legal distinction between the contract of sale, which creates an obligation to do something, namely, to convey, and the actual conveyance. The contract and the conveyance are separate matters. It is the conveyance which puts the property into the possession of the buyer and obliges the buyer to pay the agreed-upon price. The contract of *emptio venditio* is manifestly executory. Roman law therefore separates the matters of title to the property and of risk for that property. Risk, which in some systems of law passes when ownership passes (since risk for the property can be seen as a criterion of ownership), passes to the buyer from the moment of consent, the time of *emptio perfecta,* even though in the absence of the conveyance, the buyer is not yet the owner of the property.[32] Unless the seller has been negligent, the buyer has to pay the full price, as set forth in the agreement, even for lost or damaged goods, and he gets whatever remains of the thing plus assignment by the seller of any rights against third parties who may have caused the loss.[33] If the seller does not deliver the goods, and has no good excuse for his omission, the seller will bear the risk of subsequent loss of the thing.[34] But if the buyer defaults, if he does not take delivery, the seller is liable for loss only in cases of gross negligence.[35] The transference of risk can, of course, be modified by the incorporation of conditions in the contract. A general principle in this matter, traceable to Roman roots, is *res perit domino,*[36] although the rule is anomalous in Roman law itself owing to the separation of contract and conveyance.

Clearly the seller has an obligation to take care of the thing until it is placed in the possession of the buyer. His duty in Roman law was to exercise the care expected of a *bonus paterfamilias.*[37] It was the seller's duty in any case to put the thing into the possession of the buyer, and in the absence of a condition to the contrary, that duty was the reciprocal of the buyer's duty to pay the price agreed upon.[38] The buyer need not pay unless he got the thing, and the seller must not give the thing unless he got his price.[39] In the absence of any other agreement, the buyer has the responsibility of fetching the thing; the seller need not send it to him.[40]

If the buyer was tardy in taking possession, the seller should give the buyer reasonable notice to come and fetch the thing away.[41] In sum, the fundamental obligations of the contract were that the buyer should pay the price and that the seller should deliver the goods. These obligations, in the absence of any condition or stipulation modifying them, were to be discharged at the same time.

The foregoing skeletal sketch of the Roman contract of *emptio venditio* provides ample detail to consider in relation to both medieval law and Jewish law. The medieval civil lawyers and canonists took over the Roman contract, subjected it to analysis, and developed detailed commentary on particular aspects of it. As we have seen, Roman contracts of sale were enforceable *ex fide bona*, and all forms of fraud were therefore excluded.[42] One direction which medieval commentary took was the further refinement of the notion of ancient Roman doctrines of fraud and error and their effects on a contract. The medieval lawyers arranged the material under two basic headings: intentional fraud, and a mistake or error of fact.[43] In the case of intentional fraud, if the sale itself had been occasioned by the fraud itself, the contract was voided.[44] If, however, the fraud was incidental to the sale -- that is to say, if the fraud did not itself cause the contract but the parties would have made a different sort of agreement had there been no fraud -- actions for damages were entertained.[45] Unintentional fraud, or mistakes in fact, had no remedy unless, in certain contracts, damages were particularly heavy.[46] This romanist analysis was adopted by canon lawyers by the beginning of the thirteenth century. How these views comport with the rulings of Jewish law on the same matters will be discussed below.

By the late twelfth century both romanists and canon lawyers had fully adopted the ancient Roman principle of free bargaining as between the buyer and the seller,[47] subject to the laws against fraud, the requirements of good faith, and the remedy for *laesio enormis* where the price was inordinately unfair.[48] Otherwise prices arrived at through the give-and-take of the marketplace were held to be in good faith. Shortly after this time, however, theologians, who had long been aware of and concerned with the canon law rules of *laesio enormis*, parted intellectual company with the romanists and canonists by demanding that a price had to represent fair value, that is to say, the just price.[49] Both the romanists and canonists on the one hand and the theologians on the other looked to the current market price when they attempted to establish the just price for a given thing; the current market price was viewed as the fair value of a commodity.[50]

What is perhaps of greater interest for us here than the romanist and canonist views of fraud and just price are the moral and social attitudes toward commercial life in the Middle Ages. The Greco-Roman world looked somewhat askance at merchants, and this negative view persisted in Western Europe during the medieval period.[51] Pope Leo I asserted that it was difficult to engage in commerce without committing mortal sin;[52] Cassiodorus observed that "merchants burden their wares more with perjuries than prices."[53] Robert of Courson warned that merchants and retailers required special attention at the confessional.[54] Theoretically, in the medieval world, each class and stratum of society had its purpose and its justification, each part of the society fitting with every other part and thus the whole of the social order achieving an internal harmony. Even the morally suspect merchants required some justification and some assignment of a positive role. Churchmen credited the merchant class with the beneficial social function of distribution of goods.[55] They took goods from an area of plenty and distributed them to places of scarcity. Since the church held that the laborer was worthy of his hire, the merchant engaged upon the useful task of distribution had a right to make his living in commerce.

We now return to Roman law for a closer look at the transaction of barter as distinguished from sale. As already suggested, barter may be viewed as the ancestor of true sale. The Roman view of barter contrasts with the Jewish view. This consideration forms a bridge to the consideration of the principal features of the Jewish law of sale.

There was a disagreement between two schools of Roman jurists concerning the distinction between sale and barter. The Sabinians held that barter was indeed a form of *emptio venditio* and, moreover, its original form.[56] The Proculians held that barter and *emptio* were distinct. They argued that in *emptio venditio* one must be able to tell the buyer from the seller. This is impossible in a transaction of barter.[57] The view of the Proculian school prevailed.[58] Further, in Roman law, barter was not a consensual contract; it was classified as an innominate contract, on the order of *do ut des*, and thus only enforceable by a party who had already performed his part of the exchange.[59] Clearly, however, both types of transactions were conducted in the marketplaces of ancient Rome.

As we have seen, Jewish law asserts the existence of a money economy, i.e., coinage as a medium of exchange, as part of biblical law. Both sales and barter are therefore ancient forms of commerce in Jewish law. Sale and barter emerge as two subheadings of one major institution of Jewish law: *acquisition*. The principal element of both sale and barter is that each is an aspect of acquisition, which will be discussed and characterized presently. In Roman law sale and barter are different contracts, which give rise to different actions. In Jewish law sale and barter are types of acquisition, and the law views acquisition as the significant and crucial feature in either type of transaction. The contrast is between the Roman distinction between sale and barter and the Jewish collocation of them as reflections of one broader principle. For Roman law, sale and barter are two distinct aspects of the vast law of *in personam* obligations, and the conveyance which gives title is a matter *in rem*. Jewish law does not employ these terms and categories; sale and barter are but two of many manifestations of the general concept of acquisition, a notion that comprehends both contract and conveyance as well as sale and barter.

The fact that the *Shulhan Arukh* and other restatements place the rules for barter among the rules for sales does not mean that there is no difference between a sale and a barter. They are clearly not the same. Separate terms are used for each. Certain rules for achieving fair value in sales do not apply in barter. But owing to the fact that these species of acquisition involve a mutual transfer of ownership of property, they resemble each other more than they resemble other types of transactions in which a formal act of acquisition is a requisite (e.g., hire, loan, etc.); they are therefore found together. Moreover, the fact that a form of symbolic barter, the so-called kerchief exchange, appears as a proper form of effecting acquisition in sales (as in other "acquisitional" transactions) tends to emphasize the similarity of barter and sale, even though each is ultimately a separate aspect of acquisition in itself.

The rabbinic term for "barter" is *halifin*, "exchange"; the rabbinic term for "sale" is *meqah umemkar*, literally, "purchase and sale." It is tempting to see in the Hebrew phrase the rendering of the Latin *emptio venditio*, but the two phrases are quite dissimilar in technical meaning. The Hebrew phrase simply describes a species of commercial transaction, buying and selling. It did not become the technical term for a type of contract. Indeed Maimonides does not use *meqah umemkar* in the title of his restatement of the laws of sale; he uses the word *mekirah*, which is simply an ancient rabbinic term for "sale."

The Hebrew terms appear to remain merely descriptive. There is no special term for a *contract* of sale as such; the rabbinic restatements of the material speak of "laws of buying and selling," etc., rather than the "contract of sale." The technical terminology in Jewish law comes from the noun and verb expressing the major concept of acquisition, which comprehends far more than buying and selling. The Latin *emptio venditio* became a highly technical term and its juristic implications go far beyond mere description. One speaks of a contract of *emptio venditio*, but not of a contract of *meqah umemkar*. The phrase does, however, suggest the notion of a bilateral undertaking, as does *emptio venditio*.

Although the role of acquisition is not limited to transactions of sale, our present concern is specifically with respect to sales, and occasionally with respect to barter or gift. In Roman law bare consent was the fundamental requisite for a contract of sale, and the obligations to deliver the goods and to pay the price for the goods were created by the contract. In Jewish law the matter is far different. No legal obligations are created by the consent of parties to buy and sell a given thing for a given price; as we shall see, moral obligations do, however, arise from bare consent.

The *Shulhan Arukh, Hoshen Mishpat,* as indeed other rabbinic law books before it, begins the restatement of the laws on sale with the assertion that no sale can be perfected by a mere verbal agreement. Even if there are witnesses to the fact that the seller promised to sell a specific thing and the buyer promised to pay a certain amount of money for it; there is still no actionable agreement, no legal obligations are present. The parties still have the legal right to withdraw from the transaction, although such withdrawal is subject to severe moral censure and condemnation. Once, however, an act of *kinyan*, a formal acquisition, has occurred, the parties no longer have a legal right to withdraw their consent to the sale. If both parties mutually renounced their bargain after *kinyan* had been performed, the act of acquisition could only be undone by the performance of another *kinyan* to effect reacquisition (189:1, 200:7). *Kinyan* is the act which validates the agreement of parties and renders it legally binding, and that agreement may include various terms and conditions (which Roman lawyers would call *stipulationes*) that might affect how, when, and where, etc., the obligations of the parties were to be carried out.

The *kinyan* does more than perfect or complete the bargain the parties agree to. It also formally transfers the lawful possession, or the outright ownership, of the goods to the buyer. Jewish law views the transaction primarily as the acquisition of the goods by the buyer, and also as the transfer of lawful possession or ownership by the seller. In terms of theory, the matter is seen more as a creation of new rights and duties occasioned by acquisition. The act of acquisition functions as a conveyance, or really as a taking over, of the thing. The buyer, pursuant to *kinyan*, becomes liable for payment of the full price, unless this requirement has been modified in some way by a condition; but the seller has already extinguished his ownership or lawful right of possession of the thing (again, unless there is some condition attached to this matter) by participating in the formal acquisition.

The act of *kinyan* has various forms. Some, as we shall see, are a sort of ritual act, while other forms may be merely delivery or the payment of the purchase price. The particular act of acquisition that the parties employ depends upon the subject of the sale. Some acts are good in regard to all types of property.

Each of the modes of acquisition and their applications will be presented, but we now anticipate that presentation in order to underscore the crucial importance of *kinyan*. Money payment is a valid *kinyan* for real estate; it is not generally a valid acquisitional act for moveable property. The reason for this distinction is restated from the Babylonian Talmud, *Bava Mezia* 47b, in 198:5: perhaps, if money payment were allowed as a valid act of acquisition for moveable property, a buyer might pay the price for something and, through no negligence of the seller, the thing might be destroyed or stolen before the buyer could take delivery. In that case, the seller, having his money and not having any ownership of the goods, might not be quick to attempt to rescue the buyer's property. One might take exception to this rabbinic reasoning and argue that one could simply withhold payment until delivery of the goods and therefore money payment need not be eliminated as a means of lawful acquisition for moveable goods. While this argument might be raised, the rabbis do not appear to question the justification for this rule as laid down in the Talmud. Perhaps a better basis for the rule, from the perspective of historical development, might be that moveable goods were of a vast and bewildering variety and were, in fact, originally exchanged principally by means of barter; thus some physical contact between the new owner and a thing acquired was fundamental. The notion that some contact between the new owner and a moveable thing perhaps persisted as somehow central to the creation of new ownership, even though the contact became purely symbolic or ritual in practice. But this is only conjecture; the rabbinic reason appears and reappears as the correct one in the traditional statements of this rule.

Since payment of price does not usually effect acquisition of moveable goods, the seller bears the loss unless the liability for such loss was fixed by some mutually-agreed-upon conditions attached to the transaction. Under Roman law the buyer had to bear the loss if there was no negligence on the part of the seller.[60] The buyer had become liable for risk from the moment of consent which perfected the *emptio venditio* even though there was as yet no conveyance; he had to pay the full price, he got what was left of the item, and he received assignments of rights (if any) against third parties alleged to have destroyed the goods. Jewish law clearly differs from Roman law in this matter: the risk does not fall upon the buyer until he has formally acquired the goods. No risk is undertaken by the force of mere oral agreement. Certainly the payment of the price does not make the goods the buyer's; and should they be destroyed, even without any fault on the seller's part, the buyer gets his money back (204:2). The act of acquisition no doubt impressed upon both parties that old duties were extinguished and new ones created, and the passing of money from hand to hand was not sufficiently important in the eyes of the rabbinic jurists to effect formal and legal acquisition for moveable goods under ordinary circumstances, perhaps because the relationship between a specific sum of money and a specific item of moveable property was not usually considered sufficiently precise. We shall come to the exceptions to this rule in due course, but as a general principle it holds good.

In Roman law, the moment of consent which was made in good faith was the genesis of a contract of sale and therefore of duties and obligations, and of the continuing demands of good faith. In Jewish law, the same chapter of *Shulhan Arukh, Hoshen Mishpat* just mentioned (204) which lays down that the buyer can get his money back if the goods are destroyed through no fault of the seller, also preserves some of the Jewish rules on good-faith dealing in sales. The fundamental rule is that good faith between the parties must also obtain prior to the act of acquisition, which generates the legal obligations consequent upon a sale. A party who chose to withdraw from a bare verbal agreement to buy or sell could indeed do so as a matter of fact, since no acquisition had yet perfected and validated the agreement, but withdrawal was clearly a breach of faith and expressly condemned. The withdrawing party was subject to a formal condemnation if a price had been paid (for moveable goods), and even if no money had changed hands, the withdrawer was still held to be morally reprobate. Anyone who withdrew from a sale of moveable goods after a price had been paid for them, but before acquisition had been formally effected, had not acted in accordance with Jewish views of decency and morality. While no legal obligations yet bound the parties, the rabbis insisted that those of ethical conduct did; one must stand by one's promise, legal act or not. Once acquisition was effected, good faith was both expected and enforceable. In Roman law, the contract itself, the oral agreement, requires a basis and context of good faith; so too in Jewish law, acquisition has to be conducted in the context of good faith, even when the law provides no penalty and there is no transaction to invalidate.

Thus we have one point of divergence and one point of convergence, as between Jewish law and Roman law, which place *kinyan* in fuller perspective. The systems diverge owing to the Jewish emphasis on formal acquisition, as opposed to the Roman emphasis on bare consent, and the manner in which risk for the goods is assigned under each system. But the systems converge in their attitudes toward the role of good faith dealing which in Roman law has to form the basis of the contract, and which is similarly demanded in Jewish law even prior to the actual onset of legal obligation.

In sum, then, *kinyan*, the formal act of acquisition, appears to function in a double role in the Jewish law of sale. First, it is a validation and confirmation of a bilateral agreement, for the Jewish transaction of sale, like the Roman *emptio venditio*, is bilateral. Second, it is, in some sense, a formal act, and the form that act takes is also quite important, e.g., the act of payment effects acquisition for land but not for moveable property. The act carries with it legal obligations. One may therefore characterize *kinyan* as a sort of "formal" contract: it takes a prescribed form and it creates legal obligations. But it is more. Third, it is the legal taking possession (as opposed, perhaps, to an actual physical taking possession, from the buyer's or acquirer's point of view) of the subject of the sale while simultaneously serving as the legal act of conveyance of the subject of the sale (from the seller's point of view). Thus *kinyan* seems to be both a form of contract and a conveyance concurrently. The contractual aspect of *kinyan* is just as important as the aspect of conveyance, since it covers matters of warranty, eventual payment of price, etc.; moreover this act was to be performed in an atmosphere of good faith bargaining and dealing, both before and after it.

As already pointed out, kinyan is applicable to many more things than sale. All types of undertakings, including the validation of marriage contracts, require kinyan to seal the matter. But our concern here is only with kinyan as it emerges in the law of sale. We proceed now to remarks on each of the several forms of kinyan in sales: those for land, those for moveables, and those which may apply to both classes of property.

Land is formally acquired by any one of four modes of acquisition: sum of money, instrument of transfer, physical possession, or symbolic kerchief exchange (190).

The payment of money can be the payment of the full purchase price, but a nominal or token payment is sufficient to effect acquisition. Moreover, the transaction is binding even if the buyer gave the seller a particular coin as a symbolic payment or token with an express condition that the seller was to return that particular coin to the buyer. The buyer, of course, is liable for the full purchase price.

Since the amount of money can be a nominal sum and the actual price is not necessarily the "money payment" in question, various other types of financial transactions or considerations can be used to effect acquisition. For instance, a seller may tell a buyer to give a sum of money to a third party, and by virtue of this gift to a third party, the buyer acquires some land of the seller (190:3). Rabbinic jurists see in this an adaptation of the law of surety (*Sefer Meirath Enayim* to 190:2). The fact that the third party would accept the gift given at the seller's order is, or could be, expressed in sufficient monetary terms to effect acquisition. One party may tell a seller that he is giving the seller a sum of money, in virtue of which the seller's field shall be sold to a third party, provided that the third party is agreeable to the transaction (190:4). In this case the text uses the verb "sold" as well as the verb "acquired." A possible implication of the verb "sold" in this text is that the gift is indeed the purchase price. Another variation of acquisition by money payment is a case in which a seller tells someone to give a sum of money to a third party in virtue of which that seller's field shall be sold to that third party; acquisition is effected when the third party accepts the money (190:5).

This case also appears to be an extension or adaptation of the rules of surety. The seller clearly enjoys some sort of financial benefit that is, or could be, expressed in cash terms and that is sufficient to effect a sale of his property to the third party, provided that the third party was amenable to the transaction in the first place. The text here again uses the verb "sold" as well as "acquired," and the possible implication of the verb is that the financial benefit is itself the whole of the purchase price, not merely a token. If the value, to the seller, of the fact that one would, at the seller's request, give a gift to a third party were merely a token value, then the third party would become liable for the purchase price. If the seller gives the buyer a sum of money and asserts that, in virtue of the buyer's acceptance of that money, the seller's field is sold to the buyer, and if that buyer is a person of importance, so that his acceptance of such a gift brings some (financially determinable) benefit or pleasure to the seller, the transaction is valid, acquisition has been effected. On the face of matters, it is possible that the value of the acceptance could easily be the whole consideration for the land; the text uses the verb "sold" rather than the verb "acquired." On the other hand, the value of the acceptance might be merely a token sum for acquisition and the important personage would be liable for a purchase price at some future time. The text allows for both possibilities, but the verb suggests the former one.

Money payment is sufficient for effecting acquisition of land, but such acquisitions are limited to transactions in places where an instrument of transfer is not also required (190:7). This rule is much older than the Roman rule mentioned above, p. 17. Both buyer and seller could place stipulations on the contract, which stipulations can specify the actual mode of acquisition to be employed: as between money payment and instrument, which one shall be the operative mode (190:8).

If a seller tenders collateral security for the purchase money, no acquisition has been effected unless the security has been given with the express stipulation that the seller shall acquire the security itself to the extent of the price due him (190:9, cf. 204:5).

A separate rule governs the situation in which a seller shows that he is willing to sell his field but to permit acquisition of that field only upon full payment of the price, of which only part has been paid (190:10, 15). In this case the seller calls repeatedly to collect the balance due. No acquisition has been effected until the full price has been paid, even if an instrument was executed for the sale and even if the buyer took possession of the land. The seller has clearly demonstrated that his consent to the transaction, which is as crucial in *kinyan* as it is in *emptio venditio* as we shall have occasion to see, was based upon the payment of the full price. Thus, no full payment means no lawful acquisition. The buyer and seller can, of course, modify this basic rule by placing conditions or stipulations on the transaction (192:16).

If a parcel of land was sold because the land is of poor quality, a partial payment will suffice to effect acquisition of the entire parcel (190:11). This rule works in favor of the seller, who can forestall withdrawal by the buyer, since the law provides for full and immediate acquisition in case of partial payment for poor land. In this case, the seller wants to rid himself of poor and unwanted property. If the buyer has, in good faith, consented to buy the poor land, the buyer cannot reconsider and claim that he has purchased only a portion of the property in consideration of the portion of the price he has paid, even if the seller calls repeatedly for the balance of the price. Ordinarily such behavior on the part of the seller means that acquisition of the entire parcel depends upon full payment of the price. The buyer in this case, and in those we will come to presently, has to stand by the bargain even if he has become thoroughly disenchanted with the barren acres he acquired.

Land is acquired by the force of an instrument of transfer (191:1). This mode of acquisition has limited application. The instrument itself is sufficient if the seller is selling a parcel of land because the land is poor (191:2). The seller writes a formula of grant and sale in favor of the buyer; once the document reaches the buyer's hand, he has acquired the poor property (191:1). The buyer is, of course, liable for the agreed-upon purchase price. No witnesses are required at the delivery of the document to the buyer (191:1). A seller may stipulate that an instrument is not an instrument of transfer but only a memorandum, of evidentiary value only (191:3). Thus in a sale, the transfer of land by instrument operates independently only for poor grades of real estate, although it is a necessary element in an acquisition of any type of land where the practice is to indite such instruments and to acquire by means of money, unless the parties have modified these provisions by their own stipulations (190:7, 8). The limitation to poor types of land works in favor of the seller in the same way that partial payment works in his favor. Since the formalities of full acquisition for poor land may be accomplished so quickly and easily, the buyer must be particularly careful in real estate transactions.

Land is acquired by an act of physical possession. If a buyer, in the seller's presence, or at his express command, enters the property and performs some act which only a lawful owner could perform or which has some perceptible positive effect on the land, even some token act, or breaks the barrier between the land and his own adjacent property, the land has been acquired by the possessive act (192:1-8). The buyer, of course, becomes liable for the purchase price. Clearly the buyer is required to deal with the property in some fashion that demonstrates the fact of possession and ownership. There is a body of opinion that mere use of the land (e.g., eating its fruit or using it for pasturage) is a sufficient possessive act; and the opposite view is also expressed: there is no valid possessive act for the land because the land itself is not benefited by the act (192:11). On this latter view, the possessive act has to be some token of improvement, which ordinarily only a lawful owner could properly perform.

If a seller sells ten real properties in ten separate locales, once the buyer has performed a possessive act with one of them, the buyer has acquired all of them, provided that the buyer has paid the purchase price for all of them. If not, acquisition is effected to the extent of the amount paid (192:12). The mode of acquisition, therefore, appears to be a combination of money payment and, insofar as applicable, possessive act. If the seller does not, by his conduct, demonstrate that his consent to the acquisition was really based upon payment of the price, the possessive act has lawfully completed the transaction. The parties are free to make their own stipulations to govern the relative significance of money payment and possessive act as modes of acquisition in their transaction (192:16).

Land can be acquired by symbolic kerchief exchange. This mode also effects lawful acquisition of moveable property (195:1-3). It appears to be a vestigial form of barter, not a formality of the marketplace, such as the offer of a nominal sum of money. In this method, the buyer gives the seller some object -- usually a witness's kerchief, which has, through technicality, become the buyer's temporary property -- and holds the object in such a manner that the seller can take a good grasp of it. A formula of acquisition -- "acquire this in exchange for your property" -- may or may not be recited by the buyer since this ceremony itself is well understood to be for the express purpose of effecting a lawful acquisition. When the seller has grasped and pulled the object, acquisition of land (or moveable goods) is completed thereby without any other formality. Neither party can withdraw from the transaction, except as we shall presently see; and it requires no witnesses as long as the parties themselves acknowledge that the ceremony of kerchief acquisition was duly performed. The buyer becomes liable for the purchase price. The owner of the kerchief will, of course, get his property back; it was given only as a conditional gift, and the condition was that it be returned to its owner.

The object used for symbolic kerchief exchange is to be a man-made article of some monetary worth that Jews are not forbidden to use or to derive benefit from; it cannot be agricultural produce, nor can it be current coinage, since this transaction is a mode of barter, in which money is an impermissible medium of exchange. The object cannot belong to the seller, for the obvious reason that he would be "acquiring" his own property and, therefore, really receiving nothing new in exchange (195:2).

The buyer need not be present when an object transferred to his temporary ownership for the purpose of his effecting symbolic acquisition therewith is thus used, but another opinion holds the acquisition from the seller to be invalid since in a purchase, as distinguished from a gift, the acquirer may not wish to obligate himself in the transaction (195:3).

When a buyer places a condition upon a symbolic kerchief exchange, to the effect that the seller acquires the kerchief now but the buyer's acquisition does not commence until some future date, there is no acquisition, since in all likelihood the seller has returned the kerchief to its former owner long before the buyer's title to the goods would commence. Therefore the transfer by the seller is either to take simultaneous effect with his acquisition of the kerchief or there is to be a stipulation of retroactivity for the acquisition of the buyer; i.e., acquisition shall commence at some future date, but retroactively to the moment of kerchief exchange. Such a condition of retroactivity will even be presumed to exist unless circumstances clearly demonstrate that it should not be presumed (195:5).

Ordinarily, neither party can withdraw from the transaction after acquisition has been effected. In the case of kerchief exchange, however, the parties are allowed a brief grace period for withdrawal (195:6, 7). As long as buyer and seller are still arranging that same transaction, they can nullify acquisition by kerchief exchange. Once negotiations are finished and the parties depart or pass on to other matters, no withdrawal is permitted. This rule may be modified by stipulation of the parties (195:8). There appears to be a presumption that the symbolic act may be performed before the full consent of the parties has been achieved -- and consent is crucial -- while the other modes of acquisition of land would not or could not occur before full consent of the parties had been achieved. Even with symbolic exchange, however, full consent to the transaction is presumed once the parties have left each other's presence or gone on to other matters.

The rules governing the acquisition of a non-Jewish slave are the same as those governing acquisition of real property (196:1). The possessive act which constitutes *kinyan* for a slave is generally the employment of the slave by the new master for the performance of some sort of personal service usually performed by slaves, e.g., the removal of the master's shoes (196:2-4).

We turn now to other modes of acquisition applicable in sales of moveable goods in addition to symbolic kerchief exchange, which operates for both moveable and real property.

The rules for the sales of large and small domesticated animals disclose that the act of pulling the beast toward oneself is the appropriate mode of acquisition for such animals. Additional opinions also permit delivery as the act of acquisition, and delivery is defined as the buyer's grasping of the animal in the presence or at the express command of the seller (197:1, 198:8). Delivery involves only the grasping of the animal; no pulling or lifting is required. The act of pulling for acquisition is appropriate only in those places where the buyer and seller both enjoy some theoretical or actual ownership of the ground on which the formal act is performed (197:2). Delivery is an effective mode of acquisition in places where neither party enjoys any theoretical or actual ownership of the location of the transaction (198:9). The act of pulling is to be performed in the presence of the seller or at his express command (197:3).

Physical lifting of an object, or animal, to a height of three handbreadths (some say one handbreadth) is a licit act of acquisition in any location; (197:2, 198:1, 2). Leading an animal with a rod or by the sound of one's voice is also an effective act of acquisition; but the act of riding a domesticated animal will be recognized as an act of acquisition only for certain types of persons and in certain specific locations (197:3, 5).

The seller may specify the mode of acquisition to be employed, and the buyer-acquirer is not to effect acquisition by some other mode, whether that mode is less or more physically demanding than the one specified (197:1).

As a rule, pulling is used to effect acquisition of some object which is too clumsy or difficult to acquire by means of lifting (198:1). The degree to which the acquirer must pull an object is specified; the amount of pulling represents a clear demonstration that the object has been entirely removed from one space and now exists in a completely new portion of space, or that the object has been moved from one type of place (e.g., a public street) to a place owned by the buyer, even though the object has not been entirely moved from its entire former position (198:3, 14).

The case of acquiring a ship is the paradigm for acquisition of a large and unwieldy item of moveable property, and special rules apply. In particular, the act of pulling will not effect acquisition if the ship is in a location where such acquisition may not be lawfully performed; should the seller stipulate acquisition by pulling, it becomes necessary to remove the ship to a place where pulling is licit. One opinion holds that a ship which is beached can only be acquired formally by *lifting* (as difficult as this may be); if it is afloat, it can be acquired by pulling. A ship standing in a public square, for example, can be acquired by delivery, but if the buyer commences to acquire by pulling, that act of pulling is taken as a sign of the buyer's intent to acquire by pulling and the act must be fully performed as required by law (198:10-13).

The buyer becomes liable for the purchase price once acquisition has been effected, whether by pulling, lifting, or delivery, as the case may be. Here again, however, if a seller demonstrates by his conduct that he is intent on collecting the full purchase price for the moveable goods, and only partial payment has been given, acquisition will really depend upon the full payment of the price. This modification of the rule that money payment effects no legal acquisition for moveable goods obtains where the items have not been sold because of their poor quality; in that case, the act of pulling, for example, is sufficient lawful act of acquisition (190:11). Other circumstances which permit acquisition of moveable property by means of money payment will be reviewed presently.

Up to this point, *kinyan*, whether of land or of moveables, has involved some act, whether payment of money or grasping or kerchief exchange, etc. There is one form of *kinyan*, however, which is an exception. This is the case in which the moveable goods to be acquired are already on, or in, the property of the buyer and under his conscious supervision or protection; in this circumstance, once there has been agreement to buy and to sell a thing for a definite price (even if that thing is as yet unmeasured or uncounted), acquisition has been effected by the buyer, who becomes liable to pay the purchase price (200:1, 3-6). The Roman parallel here is not *emptio venditio* but a form of transfer, *traditio*, specifically *traditio brevi manu*; where the transferee already holds the property to be sold. There is a change of ownership by simply handing something to someone else. The crucial element in this situation is that the goods are *already* on or in the buyer's property. Presumably no further act, demonstration, or signification of the buyer's possession, or right of possession, is necessary for valid acquisition in Jewish law. It is therefore arguable that the location of the goods comes to represent a sort of act of *kinyan* before the fact, which is perfected by the consent, instead of vice versa, owing to the special circumstances of sales *per mesuram* conducted on the seller's property, with the buyer's measure, or with a measure purchased from the seller and placed on the buyer's property, etc. (200:3-10).

Another form of acquisition of moveable goods is by means of acquiring land (202:1). If one transfers ownership of a piece of land (even a small or nominal amount of it, 202:7) by sale or gift, and acquisition of that land has been lawfully effected, moveable goods located on that land can be acquired by the same buyer (or donee) as a consequence of the formal acquisition of the land (202:1).

Even if the land were acquired as a gift and the moveables thereon as the subject of a sale, or vice versa, the acquisition of the land still suffices for the concurrent acquisition of the moveable goods. If the moveable goods are not located on the land, the seller (or donor) uses a special formula in the act of *kinyan* for the land in order to confer title to moveable goods wherever they are situate; one opinion requires this formula even if the goods are located on the acquired land (202:2). Again we see the importance of *kinyan* as the comprehensive element which functions in the creation of all types of ownership or lawful possession. Both sale and gift are specific cases of *kinyan* and causes for *kinyan*; while the rules governing each do differ in various respects, neither can occur without *kinyan* of some sort.

Under certain unusual or special circumstances, money payment alone suffices to effect acquisition of moveable goods. If a buyer offers an unweighed or uncounted sum of money to a seller, and the seller accepts that money as the purchase price of the thing, the thing has been lawfully acquired. Further, if a seller has sold moveable goods to a person for a definite sum of money, acquisition having been effected and liability for the purchase price therefore existing, and the seller and buyer then reverse roles, so that the buyer sells other goods to the seller for the price that was settled in the previous transaction, no further *kinyan* is required for this second transaction (199:1, 2). One opinion modifies this rule and lays down that the former seller has to say to the former buyer, "Sell me the items in exchange for the benefit you have from my forgiving the purchase price." Presumably some additional monetary value can be attached to the benefit, although one imagines that such value would vary from situation to situation and from person to person, but it is enough for acquisition.

Both these cases are unusual and, according to the text, the rabbis did not therefore prohibit them as contrary to the rule that money effects no acquisition of moveable goods. They are also dangerously close to cases of barter, since in the former case the money was not established as a definite money-price equivalent for the goods, and in the latter case, the price owing the seller was renounced in favor of getting goods: almost an exchange of goods for goods, except in the opinion requiring the value of a "benefit," which is a rather oblique sort of "kinyan." Nevertheless the presence of money as either a medium of exchange to some extent or as a measure of value places the transactions somewhat closer to sale than to outright barter.

The rabbis also eased the rules so that money payment alone effected acquisition when tendered as prepayment for kosher meat, on the eve of certain holy days (199:3).

Another exception was allowed: when minor orphans, or their legal guardians, have sold some of the orphans' goods, acquisition having been effected, but no price paid, and the price of those goods rises sharply (and no doubt immediately), the acquisition is voided. The rabbis, for the protection of the orphans, invoked the biblical regulation which specified money payment as the means of acquisition for moveable goods (199:4).

As we have seen above, the act of acquisition (pulling, etc.) superseded the biblical rule of acquisition by money payment because a seller, in possession of the purchase price, might not be quick to save a buyer's endangered property if money payment were sufficient to extinguish the seller's ownership and risk with respect to the goods (*B. Bava Mezia* 47b). Therefore, when the goods are actually located in the buyer's property, which was leased to the seller, the buyer is presumed to be in a good position to attempt to rescue his goods, and money payment for them is sufficient act of *kinyan*. Moreover, when the goods are in no danger of fire (or presumably flood, etc.), money payment is also held to be a sufficient act of *kinyan*. The buyer and seller are, of course, free to stipulate that, rabbinic rules notwithstanding, money payment shall effect acquisition for moveable goods (198:5).

Symbolic kerchief exchange, reviewed above, effects acquisition for moveable property.

Other forms of the act of acquisition emerged from the practice of the marketplace itself. If a buyer and a seller agree on matters of price and thing, and the buyer puts his mark on the goods, with the seller's consent, so that all will know the property is his, any withdrawal from the transaction, even before the price is paid, is liable to a rabbinic condemnation; one has not dealt in good faith (201:1, 204:6). If the use of such marks in a particular locale customarily indicated full acquisition, the rabbis acknowledge such mercantile practice as fully legal and binding for effecting it. Moreover, a handshake or any other act customary among merchants of a particular locale as a means of sealing a bargain became part of the rabbinically recognized and lawful modes of effecting acquisition (201:1, 2).

A buyer becomes liable for the purchase price when one of these customary or marketplace modes of acquisition is employed. As we shall see, the role of mercantile custom was fully recognized and incorporated into Jewish law governing sales.

A vow, an oath, or a handshake is also a licit mode of sealing a promise and effecting acquisition in respect of a unilateral undertaking. Such unilateral undertakings, similar to Roman *stipulationes*, are not, however, viewed as sales themselves. They may be special sorts of promises relating to future sales, loans, dowries, or other matters, which promises are usually invalid but are rendered lawful by an oath, etc., that confirms the good-faith consent of the promissor (207:13, 19).

A final word on the act of *kinyan* itself: In regard to symbolic kerchief exchange, it is laid down that acquisition by this mode is not to be performed on the Sabbath (195:11). If the parties transgressed the law and performed the actual act or form of acquisition, their violation of the ritual law does not invalidate their transaction. Since Jews are forbidden the use of money and other necessary appurtenances of commercial life on the Sabbath and other holy days, no transactions of sale, or for that matter of acquisition, may be performed at those times.

The transaction of sale is bilateral. This is as true in Jewish law as it is in Roman law. The transaction also rests firmly on the basis of the consent of the parties to it. Without full consent of buyer and seller, no *kinyan* can be lawfully performed. The consent in question is clearly described as a full agreement that a certain amount of property will go for a specific price (200:7). We have already distinguished between Roman law and Jewish law on the role of consent; it must be kept in mind that although in Jewish law the consent does not perfect the sale, it is absolutely crucial to the sale's perfection through *kinyan*. The consent of the parties must be full, absolute, and unconditional, in the absence of any specific condition or conditions to which the parties also give their full and absolute assent.

There are four matters to be discussed under the general rubric of bilateral consent, the complete bilateral resolve to sell and to buy: (1) who may be a party to a sale (i.e., legal capacity); (2) the definition of the thing that may be a lawful subject of sale; (3) the concept of the specific price; and (4) some matters which negate consent.

The buyer and the seller are ordinarily assumed to be adult males or females, in full command of their mental faculties. This is implicit in all the texts. Such people are free to give or withhold their consent. While many transactions of sale appear to assume that both buyer and seller are physically present at the time of the *kinyan*, this is not necessarily so, and therefore the question of the consent of the buyer can be legitimately raised (195:3). *Kinyan* fails without full consent of the parties; but the buyer can effect acquisition through his (or her) duly appointed agent for performing acquisition (200:12). In certain cases of acquisition of land in which the monetary consideration is calculated in terms of some pleasure or benefit, a third party may be the transferee of the field owing to the substantial benefit enjoyed by one of the parties to the direct negotiations. In such case the third-party transferee, or new owner, must be amenable to the transaction and demonstrate his agreement; e.g., the negotiator was his agent (190:4, 5).

Certain classes of persons are not free to transact sales because they do not have the capacity to make full lawful consent to a transaction. This incapacity may be temporary or permanent. The mentally incompetent cannot transact sales (235:20). A person who has episodes of mental incompetence and episodes of sound mental state can transact sales during his periods of sound mind, although such deals have to be carefully monitored by witnesses (235:21). An inebriated person may sell real or moveable property unless the person's state of inebriation is so far advanced that he has lost all sense of reason and decency (235:22). Slaves cannot buy or sell in their own right, but their masters can confirm and thereby legitimate such transaction if made (235:24).

Minor children are a special class of persons in regard to sales. A minor is defined as a male up to the age of thirteen or a female up to the age of twelve. The age qualification is supplemented by the requirement that the person shall also have begun to show the physiological signs of adult development (235:1). Below these age of majority, special rabbinical ordinances apply to minor children, clearly presumed to be orphans, who have no adult guardianship. From age six to age ten, an orphan who upon an examination of mental competence can demonstrate awareness of the nature of commerce, of buying and selling, may buy and sell moveable goods. From age ten to majority, an orphan who is not manifestly incompetent can engage in buying and selling moveable goods. There is a body of opinion which permits the nullification of an orphan's transaction when the orphan has clearly acted against his best interest (235:1).

A minor orphan cannot sell or buy real property. The capacity to sell or to buy real property commences with the attainment of majority (235:1); but an orphan cannot sell real property which came to him or her as an inheritance or a gift *mortis causa* until he or she has reached age twenty and is clearly physiologically mature (235:9).

Special rules apply to the lawful modes of acquisition available to male and female minor orphans (235:4-7).

Although the attainment of majority relieves the orphan from any requirement to show understanding of the nature of commerce as regards sales of moveable property, in the matter of real property, attainment of majority and the onset of puberty are not sufficient to permit a minor who does not understand the nature of commerce to engage in sales of land (235:8).

Special rules govern cases of real estate sales made by orphans between ages thirteen and twenty (235:14); special rules also provide for cases in which the orphan never exhibits signs of adult physiological development or does not exhibit them until well past the normal time for their appearance (235:11-13).

There is a difference of opinion as to whether a *futurus* can be, in some sense, a party to a commercial transaction. The matter clearly applies in cases of gift; in cases of sale, the necessity for making very special arrangements for payment of price renders the possibility of a *futurus* as a party to a sale highly unlikely. A father is permitted to transfer property to the child with which his wife is pregnant at the time of the transfer, provided that the acquisition is effected by means of pulling by someone acting on behalf of the fetus, and, according to some, provided that the father is himself *in extremis* (210:1).

While the law makes provision for parties who are, whether permanently or temporarily, unable to give the necessary consent for a *kinyan*, the general presumption is that sales are transacted by mentally competent adults who give their consent to the *kinyan*. The consent is often reached through a process of negotiation. It has already been emphasized that the process of negotiation must be conducted in good faith (204:1-7), and good-faith dealing would certainly exclude words or conduct, however innocent they may appear to be, that would tend to deceive or mislead, whether such words or conduct were on the part of the buyer or the seller (228:4, 6). Neglect or disregard of the canons of good-faith dealing is subject to condemnation (204:1), and faithlessness in bargaining (e.g., withdrawal before payment of price for moveable goods) is deemed morally reprobate (204:7). Good faith becomes especially important when it is recalled that no witnesses were required to legitimate a sale; the parties themselves were expected to acknowledge their own legal acts.

The process of negotiation and agreement could very well include the actual payment of the purchase price, even before an act of *kinyan* was performed to complete the transaction (204:1, 2; 22:4). Why precisely one would pay money before the property lawfully became one's own is difficult to say, but payment before *kinyan* is clearly contemplated as a variation of circumstance or possibility in the law of sale.

Good-faith dealing can also play a role after *kinyan*, after the new owner of property is in possession of it. Even though a seller undertook to provide no warranty against eviction, he can still sue a third party who evicted the buyer. The seller does not want the buyer to have a complaint against him, even though complaint is not grounds for a suit (226:1). Presumably the unfortunate buyer would benefit in some way if the seller were successful in his suit.

The canons of good-faith dealing allow for a brief grace period for withdrawal after acquisition by means of symbolic kerchief exchange (195:6, 7).

If a seller has agreed to sell an item at its market price, but does not own or possess the item he undertook to sell, the seller is obliged to acquire the item for the buyer (209:6). The matter of market price can affect the manner in which good-faith bargaining is interpreted in a given situation. A fluctuating market price could be used to justify a party's withdrawal from a transaction without prejudice of any kind (204:11).

The parties to a sale had to come to agreement on the thing to be sold, its amount or quality, etc., as well as the price for the thing. This aspect of consent corresponds to the Roman concept of *res certa* (cf. 200:7). No doubt most sales were for a specific item offered in the marketplace, and therefore no problem arose concerning the certainty and identity of the thing sold. A thing for sale may be made sufficiently specific by reference to a set price for the thing, even though the amount of the thing itself is not yet known; e.g., a certain heap of wheat for ten *dinars*. The set price can also function as the specific measure of amount; e.g., wheat for ten *dinars* -- the buyer is to be supplied with the amount of wheat the ten *dinars* will fetch in the open market.[61] If, however, a seller merely offers all the contents of a building or a box for a set price, and the buyer consented and performs an act of acquisition, the acquisition is a nullity because the law does not recognize the existence of a full and informed resolve on the part of the buyer to enter the transaction. The buyer does not know the type or amount of the goods he is acquiring (209:1-3). This regulation is a limitation on the right of the parties to bargain freely; more on this matter appears below. It is clear, therefore, that the subject of a sale had to be specific and certain before a lawful acquisition of it could be effected.

Obviously an item for sale among Jews had to be an item which Jews could lawfully possess.[62] The appurtenances of idolatry were not licit subjects of a sale. Jews could not sell nonkosher meat to other Jews for use as food, etc. Special rules cover sales of ritually unfit meat and other items (234:1-4).

A nonexistent thing cannot be bought and sold under Jewish law. Nor will Jewish law tolerate the sale of anything which does not, in some sense, have actual physical substance.

One cannot sell the unborn offspring of a slave or of a cow, or the as yet ungrown yield of a tree. If the fruit on a tree is fully ripe, it can be sold; but the unborn offspring of a pregnant slave-girl, for example, cannot be sold. One can, however, sell the tree itself for its yield of fruit or the slave herself for her offspring. In these latter cases, an existing thing is sold -- for a specific purpose (209:4). Some opinions hold that a nonexistent thing may be lawfully sold on the condition that at some point it will exist (209:4).

If a seller does not possess what he undertakes to sell, the thing is deemed to be nonexistent for the purpose of that transaction. Yet should the seller acquire the thing, the transaction becomes valid. The seller has clearly acted in good faith and the buyer must also show good faith. We have also noted the requirement that a seller who undertakes to sell something at its market price is obliged to acquire that thing if he does not already possess it (209:5, 6).

Just as a nonexistent thing cannot be sold, so too we recall that property cannot be transferred to a nonexistent person, except when a father transfers property to the fetus of his pregnant wife through the agency of a third party acting for the fetus. There is an opinion that this rule applies only when the father is in extremis (210:1).

The rules against the sale of a nonexisting thing are relaxed in two cases. First, an impoverished heir is permitted to sell a portion of his moribund father's estate, which of course has not yet become the heir's property and is nonexistent for his use. This sale is permitted for the purpose of defraying the costs of the impending funeral. Second, in order to secure some meager sustenance, a poor fisherman may sell his catch, i.e., whatever his net brings up from the sea, in advance (211:2). While Roman law holds that such a contract implies an absolute risk and the buyer is liable to pay even if the fisherman catches nothing, the Jewish rule contemplates the fisherman's catch for the whole day, and the implicit hope is that something of value will be wrested from the sea during the day's labor. The Roman rule speaks of the fisherman's "next haul" as being sold; the matter appears to rest on the fruit of a single cast of the net.[64] The contract appears to be more aleatory than the one in which a whole day's catch is offered.

In Jewish law a right to do something or to enjoy something is not subject to a sale. It has no physical existence. As we saw earlier, an unborn calf cannot be sold. The desire of parties to transfer rights to use and to enjoy various things is accomplished by selling the thing itself (e.g., a house, a tree, or a slave) for a particular purpose, use, or enjoyment (212:1). In this fashion the thing along with rights to it is acquired. Presumably this rule answered a specific technical and philosophical problem in the development of the law. Sale no doubt originally meant the exchange of one physical thing, money, for another physical thing. Sales contemplated tangible items. Yet a person might wish to have an intangible right. There would have been in that case an anomaly: how can something tangible be exchanged for something intangible? There would appear to be no solid substance to satisfy both parties. The notion of selling the *thing* for a purpose preserved the concept of exchange of one tangible thing for another.

A seller can reserve for himself rights in the property he is selling. This is particularly clear in sales of real property (212:3). But here, too, the reservation is understood as applying to something physical (e.g., an apartment in which to live).

Airspace is not held to be a tangible object and cannot in and of itself be sold (212:2).

The law devotes a great deal of time and attention to the description of various things, particularly types of real property, but also types of large or specialized classes of moveable property. Every effort is made to detail what would normally be included in a sale of a house, or even of a village, a ship, a yoke of oxen, a beehive, a burial plot, etc. (214-220 inclusive). These specifications permit both buyer and seller to know precisely what is and what is not included in a sale of a certain type of thing. Methods of measuring boundary lines and allowing for untillable areas of farmland in a larger tract of land are presented in detail. The rules are subject, of course, to modification by conditions, reservations, and stipulations placed upon the transactions by the parties themselves. Moreover, the descriptive terminology for specific things and the modes of establishing boundary lines, etc., are subject to further modification by the existence of any well-known commercial customs in the place of the transaction. The basic rule is laid down that Jews are to rely on the prevalent commercial custom obtaining in their locales in matters of sales of real or moveable property and that they are to use the local terminology to describe things and their contents or appurtenances (215:8, 218:19, 220:15).

There are also detailed regulations governing the sizes, construction, materials, and types of measuring devices, scales, and weights used by merchants. The rabbinical court was strictly charged with the duty of providing supervision of market weights, measures, and prices (231). The laws requiring accurate weights and measures are of biblical origin.

Roman law also provided for supervision of the marketplace to ensure fairness in commercial dealings.[65]

From the time of Charlemagne, both civil and ecclesiastical authorities in Western Europe had undertaken the inspection of weights and measures.[66] There were, at various times and places, attempts to standardize units of measure. Roman Catholic theologians condemned gains derived from fraudulent weights and measures;[67] this was a commonplace for them -- and indeed biblical and rabbinic insistence on justice in the marketplace had been a commonplace for centuries.

Just as agreement on the thing sold was a prerequisite for lawful acquisition, so too was agreement on the price for that thing (200:7). The price may be rendered certain either by the express agreement of the parties to it, or by references to a fixed market price, if any, for that item, or by the appointment of a third party to set a price for the transaction -- if the third party does in fact nominate a price (206:2, 3).

The purchase price is to be distinguished from money given for the purpose of effecting acquisition in sales of real property and, under special circumstances, in sales of moveable goods. A sum of money given for *kinyan* need not be the whole of the purchase price (190:2). If land is sold because of its poor quality and a part of the price has been paid, the seller, by calling repeatedly to collect the balance of the purchase price, demonstrates by such conduct that the perfection of acquisition rested on the full payment of the price (190:10). If a seller does not keep calling to collect the full price, the acquisition is complete and the unpaid balance is charged to the buyer as an ordinary debt; if the part-payment was earnest money, then acquisition of the poorer portion of the land has been effected up to that value, unless the parties stipulated otherwise (190:10).

There is one opinion which appears to relax the element of certainty in the price in a specific situation. In that case (199:2), A has sold goods to B, who has not yet paid for them; A turns to B and says, "Sell me your goods for the purchase price you were to pay for my goods." One opinion permits this transaction in just those terms, but another opinion holds that there is lawful acquisition only if it is declared by A to be for "the benefit accruing to you by my forgiving you the previous purchase price." Upon close inspection, we see that the fixed and certain nature of the purchase price has not been changed. The additional benefit, to which some nominal value at least could be assigned, was the value for which acquisition was effected; it was not the purchase price itself.

If a buyer nominated one price for a thing and the seller nominated another price for it, and they reached no agreement, the later conduct of the parties determined which price was to be the fixed and settled one (221:1). If the buyer returns to the seller and effects acquisition without further ado, the seller's price is to be paid. If the seller summons the buyer and gives him the thing, the buyer's price is to be paid.

The texts give no indication or hint that any other consideration beside money may be tendered as a purchase price in a transaction of sale.

In Roman law adequacy of price was not necessary, and therefore both buyer and seller enjoyed a rather broad freedom of bargaining.[68] Naturally the laws against fraud and the canons of good faith supplied limits to this freedom; and, for sales of land, the rules of *laesio enormis* protected the seller when a price amounted to half, or less, of the fair price for his property. In Jewish law, a complex series of rules, in addition to the laws against fraud and the canons of good faith, restrained both buyers and sellers from taking unfair advantage of each other in sale of most types of moveable goods; and an analogous restriction was applied, in the Middle Ages, to sales of land. We turn now to the principal features of those laws, which functioned, in effect, as a mechanism for keeping prices for goods within a reasonable range of a theoretical *pretium iustum* for them.

The Jewish laws are those against the violation called *ona'ah*, a term examined in the Lexicographical Notes. They deal with adjustments in a price that is one-sixth above or below a correct price for the item in question, and with prices which are either less or more than that one-sixth in overpricing or underpricing.

The Jewish laws against *ona'ah* applied originally to sales of all moveable goods except for slaves, notes of debt, and consecrated objects (227:29).

In Roman law, a seller has the right to void a sale of land if the purchase price he received was only one-half of the *pretium iustum;* the buyer, of course, could pay the difference and then the seller would have no need to rescind.[69] There is no textual authority for extending this rule, known as *laesio enormis*, to sales of moveable goods or to give a buyer a similar remedy if he overpaid by fifty percent of the *pretium iustum*. On the other hand, there is no logical reason for not making both extensions. The medieval romanists did make both of these extensions. There is some body of opinion in medieval Jewish law that extends a rule similar to that of *laesio enormis* to sales of land; a purchase price in excess of the just price by more than twice the latter price rendered the sale voidable (227:29). The reason or reasons why the rabbis originally excluded land sales from these rules is a special question in the history of Jewish law which would draw us far afield, but we shall come to one possible reason for this exclusion presently.

The remedy for *laesio enormis* was carried over into medieval civil and canon law, under which the remedy applied to moveable goods and was available to the buyers. Twelfth-century Roman Catholic theologians were not satisfied with a state of affairs in which a manifestly unfair price had to exceed a just price by fifty percent of the latter before any remedy was available. They asserted that divine law required restitution for any amount of unfair price. The canonists and romanists took a strict view of this matter, but the theologians espoused a broader view of what constituted improper and unlawful pricing.[70]

Why the Roman law appears to have limited *laesio enormis* to land while Jewish law developed special rules on unfair pricing with reference to most classes of moveable goods is a separate and absorbing question. The Jewish exclusion of land from these rules is based on an interpretation of Scripture (*B. Bava Mezia* 56a). But apart from the exegetical basis for such a rule, quite sufficient for the talmudic legislative process, it may be suggested that land purchases represented a much more significant and serious undertaking. Therefore buyer and seller were possibly expected to have a rather full knowledge of the quality, etc., of the land and to bargain much more precisely and carefully. Moreover, land was perhaps available for inspection and measurement, etc., by the purchaser or his agents. The chance of a grossly incorrect price was less.[71] In the case of moveable goods, including foodstuffs, their variety and quality covered a broad range from excellent to terrible.

No one person could be expert in the quality, etc., of all types and varieties of moveable goods, and thus the occasions for fraud and deceit were infinitely more numerous. Hence the special rules to remedy unfair pricing with regard to moveable goods.

The Jewish rules assume that the correct, or just, price of the item is known or could be ascertained in a rather short time. The correct price is the base in terms of which three situations are proposed. If a price is too much, or too little, by less than one-sixth of the correct price, the sale is lawful and the excess is not returnable; it is deemed forgiven (227:3). These rules and remedies protect both the buyer and the seller (227:1). If a price is precisely one-sixth over or under the correct price, the sale is valid and the excess amount is to be returned. There is a difference of opinion as to whether an excess of one-sixth, if in fact it represents only one penny or less, is returnable (227:2, 5). If the price is more than one-sixth above or below the correct price, the victim in the situation has the option of rescinding or confirming the transaction. Some opinions hold that the perpetrator can withdraw from the transaction, cancel it, unless the victim wishes to confirm it or has not sought recission during the grace period allowed for seeking it (227:4). Obviously a price in excess of one-sixth above or below the correct price may be deemed to negate consent to the transaction, *ipso facto*, and therefore withdrawal without prejudice is a real option.

The buyer enjoys a grace period for seeking return of excess payment of one-sixth or for voiding a sale for excess of more than one-sixth. The length of this period varies, but it is to be sufficient for a buyer to show the item to another merchant or to a relative whose opinion he trusts; the buyer's right is not extinguished even if an illness or accident prevented him from ascertaining the correct price quickly (227:7).

The seller may always sue for his money in case of a buyer's underpayment of one-sixth, or for rescission if the underpayment is greater. The seller is subject to the limitations of a grace period only when an item similar to the one sold comes into his possession or the item sold is something of a known uniform quality. If the seller, thus becoming aware of the error in price, does not then take immediate advantage of his remedy, he loses his right to do so later (227:8).

Neither buyer nor seller may take unfair advantage of fluctuations in market prices in order to claim return of an overcharge or an undercharge or to seek rescission (227:9-13).

The parties may stipulate to waive the remedy for overprice or underprice, if the amount of overprice or underprice has been made specific and the stipulation is not inherently deceitful (227:21, 22).

In the case of sales of coins, the grace period for seeking return of the sixth or for seeking rescission depends on the location of the transaction. In villages, the period extends to the eve of the Sabbath, when the coin would normally be spent; in cities the period is the reasonable time to get the opinion of a banker, a qualified expert on coins, on the coins' value. It is, however, a mark of special piety to take back a coin which, though lawful currency, has lost some of its weight (227:17). This is also an example of good-faith dealing.

A minor who is qualified to engage in commerce is not exempt from the rules governing unfair price (235:3).

Two classes of persons are exempt or partially exempt from the rules governing unfair price. If a householder sells his personal goods, his prices are exempt from the rules of unfair price up to but not beyond one-sixth, whether his prices were inflated or he sold cheap because of his own need for cash (227:23, 24). Some opinions state that the exemption does not hold if the buyer was unaware of the fact that the seller was acting as a private person selling his personal goods or if an agent acted for the buyer. Merchants who conduct their business on trust comprise a second class of persons enjoying exemption. Such merchants declare to the buyer what their cost was and what profit they are charging, and the buyer accepts the honesty of these declarations on trust. A merchant of this type is not permitted to take advantage of a buyer by averaging prices (227:27, 28).

These rules on unfair price apply only in the matter of price. If there is a discrepancy, either too much or too little, in the amount of a thing which requires weighing, measuring, and counting, the shortage or surplus can be made good, or returned, at any time. The matter of price in terms of monetary value is also distinguished from the number of coins actually paid. If the number of coins paid was more or less than the number of coins agreed upon, and if, in the case of surplus, a counting error is indicated, the surplus is to be returned. This rule holds irrespective of any unfair-price remedy that may obtain. If the surplus of coins is such that the number of extra coins does not suggest an error in counting, the surplus need not be returned (232:1, 2). Clearly this rule providing for the return of coins according to their number, as distinguished from their value, is an additional safeguard for both buyer and seller. The rule tends to reduce the occasions of suits on an unfair price.

If a third party, at the request of the buyer and the seller, has set the purchase price, and that price is unfair to the extent that return of the excess amount or rescission could be sought, the rules governing unfair pricing apply. The third party, if he served as a price arbitrator without pay and was an expert appraiser, is not liable to make up any discrepancy to the buyer or the seller, nor is he liable for any damages (227:25).

The implication of the last rule is most important for this entire body of regulations. Unfair price need not be based on any intent to defraud. Clearly, if either the buyer or the seller suspected the third party of a partiality that could involve them in a fraud, that third party would not have been chosen to set the price. Indeed, in no case of unfair price is there necessarily any intent to defraud. Nor is there any necessary intent to cheat or to engage in sharp practice. For the protection of both buyer and seller, however, the law will construe a fraud to be present, irrespective of intent, if the pricing was unfair to the extent of one-sixth or more. There is, in effect, a rule of constructive fraud, and that rule exerts powerful leverage against the abuses of price that are possible when rights to bargain as freely as the traffic will bear exist without regulation. Moreover, these rules tend to ensure that buyers and sellers arrive at an adequacy of price, at some sort of equivalent fair value in their dealings. Roman law left adequacy of price to the parties themselves.

In Roman Catholic canon law, the just price was presumed to be the actual market price. Canon lawyers did not attempt to correlate their theories of profit with the method of arriving at a just price.[72] The theologians as well accepted market price as fair value. The correct price, in terms of which constructive fraud was determinable in Jewish law, was also the market price, or some known fixed price for certain commodities. But the Jewish law provides specifically for the rabbinical court actually to enter the marketplace and curb both prices and profits. We shall see how prices for moveable goods, in particular, basic foodstuffs are carefully protected from manipulation that may be grossly unfair. The court is also charged with the duty of appointing officers to superintend market prices (231:20). This power goes far beyond the power to regulate weights and measures. The texts specify that superintendents of prices are to see to it that individuals do not profit as they might greedily wish.

Wholesalers in wine, oil, and grain are permitted a profit of one-sixth (231:20). A small shopkeeper dealing in these goods may charge a profit of one-sixth in addition to overhead, unless the market price is high enough so that a one-sixth profit will amply cover both fair profit and overhead (231:20). The court must superintend the prices of all merchants evenhandedly.

A rabbinical court is empowered to impose flogging or other penalties on merchants who disrupt the market with inflated prices (231:21). But a merchant is free to sell at a low price in order to encourage trade (228:18).

Speculation and hoarding of foodstuffs are prohibited wherever Jews form the majority of the population, presumably because they can significantly affect market prices by hoarding, etc., and the prohibition is laid down with specific reference to the Land of Israel (231:23-26).

The residents of a city may come together and lawfully regulate the market prices in their community (231:27). This regulatory power requires the advice and consent of the rabbinic authority of the community, when such authority has been appointed over the community.

The thrust of these rules is that, clearly with reference to food, merchants are to serve their community under the watchful eye of the rabbinical court. Excess profits, hoarding, and disruption of the market prices are strictly outlawed. The fair price and the just price might be arrived at through negotiations between buyer and seller, but only up to a point: only as long as neither the parties nor their fellow citizens were hurt by their transaction. The rabbinical court was a silent partner to the setting of market prices -- and the silence could be broken to protect individuals or the community as a whole when necessary.

We have reviewed regulations touching on consent, thing, and price. Full consent can be deemed to be missing in a sale transaction if the purchase price was in excess of one-sixth of the correct price. But there are other circumstances or factors that negate consent.

Justinian drew broad boundaries for the Roman notion of *dolus*, "cunning, deceit, or contrivance used to cheat another;"[73] and *dolus* was ground for rescission of a sale. Moreover, *emptio venditio* was enforceable in terms of good faith.[74] Clearly, then, if a party to a sale claimed that he had been defrauded or cheated, and could prove his claim, the sale was voidable. His consent to the contract was erroneous and there had really been no consent.[75] Medieval romanists distinguished two types of fraud: intentional fraud and a mistake or error in fact. If consent to a sale was rooted in intentional fraud, the contract was nullified. If an intentional fraud was incidental to the sale, so that the parties would have contracted with different terms if the true nature of the situation been known, there was a remedy for damages.[76] In Roman law, it was contrary to *bona fides* for a seller not to disclose a defect of which he had knowledge but the buyer did not, if the knowledge clearly *would* change the buyer's attitude toward the contract.[77] After all, *emptio venditio* was enforceable *ex fide bona*. An unintentional fraud, a mistake in fact, had no legal remedy except in exceptional cases where damages were high.

In the Jewish law of sale, there was a remedy for unintentional, or constructive, fraud in price; it follows *a fortiori* that intentional cheating in this matter also had a remedy.

Beyond the matter of price, a general prohibition forbade all types of intentionally fraudulent or deceptive practices in sales, including adulteration of goods and the failure to reveal defects in goods (228:6-17). In the absence of a superseding local custom or ordinance, the law even specifies how much refuse material a seller may lawfully include in sales of foodstuffs (229:1, 2). If a person was victimized by some fraudulent or deceptive practice, he was not without recourse. The victim of a fraud could obviously claim that he gave no consent to a transaction rooted in intentional fraud. Incidental fraud and mistake will be dealt with presently.

Ordinarily, consent given under duress is not lawful and binding consent. If, however, a person has been placed under duress, even extreme physical duress, for the purpose of forcing him to sell something, and in fact an adequate price was paid for the thing, the sale is lawful. The seller's consent is deemed present owing to the payment of an adequate price. In the case of land, if no price is given, or the price is substantially less than value of the property, there is no sale; in the case of moveable goods, however, the seller has the remedy for constructive fraud in price available to him and the sale is not void, *ipse iure*. The person who has been forced to sell can, prior to the sale, make a witnessed declaration that the sale is under duress and is a nullity. The sale is voided by this declaration. The witnesses are required to have independent knowledge of the duress and they may not rely on the seller's bare declaration that he is under duress. The law also provides for the contingency that the seller may be put under duress to rescind a declaration of protest. If, however, it is clear that the seller has fully and completely canceled any and all declarations of protest, the sale is valid (205:1, 2, 6, 7, 9-11). A seller's personal pressing need to liquidate his assets is not duress; the duress must be exercised for the specific purpose of forcing the seller to sell something. If the duress was for the purpose of extortion of money, and the seller has sold goods to raise the money, there is no sale under duress under this rule (205:12).

If one is placed under duress in order to force him to purchase something, no lawful acquisition can be effected under these circumstances. Obviously, the buyer does not really consent to the purchase; but a seller may give consent to a sale under duress if a sufficient price is paid for the property (205:12).

In a transaction for land, a situation may arise in which a buyer has already acquired the land formally and lawfully but has not yet made *any* use of the property, and third parties come and raise legitimate or plausibly legitimate complaints concerning the buyer's legal title. The buyer can withdraw from this sale, even after acquisition, and the sale is voided without prejudice. A dispute of this type is clearly not to the buyer's liking; he gets his money back if he paid for the land. The buyer has in these circumstances withdrawn his consent to the transaction.

At times a seller may intentionally mislead a buyer about the quality of the goods for sale. Those cases are covered by the rules on fraud. There are other situations which correspond to the medieval notion of incidental fraud and to mistake in fact. The Jewish law appears to be far more rigorous than medieval civil law in these matters.

Some cases which could be incidental fraud can be resolved under the rules of constructive fraud. For instance, a silver object presumed to be pure silver turns out to be alloyed with base metal. The sale is valid, but the excess of one-sixth is returnable; presumably if the excess in price was more than one-sixth, the sale would be voidable (233:1).

On the other hand, if one sells a defective item, and that defect reduces the value of the item by a specific amount, the seller cannot refund that amount. The buyer can void the transaction because he has a right to receive an item without defects for his money. Here, too, one can imagine that there could have been some intentional fraud incidental to the sale and the parties would have come to different terms without the presence of the fraudulent element. But the buyer, contrary to medieval civil law, could void the sale. The matter of damages is not discussed in the text, but presumably the buyer could sue for them, if any (232:4).

A buyer cannot void a sale because of a temporary defect (e.g., damage by vandalism) for which the seller is not responsible and for which he is willing to adjust the price (232:5).

Apart from the matter of fraud and deceit, the Roman law (and the medieval law) had a doctrine of error which functioned as a means of negating consent. An error *in re* was a mistake as to the identity of the thing itself.[78] Many errors of this type were no doubt precluded in Jewish law because of the specific rules for identifying and describing various types of things noted above. The Roman doctrine of error in the matter of sale included an error *in substantia*, where the mistake concerns the material of the thing sold.[79] Here, too, an error negates consent. In Jewish law there is a corresponding rule. If one sells wine that turned out upon delivery to be vinegar, there is no lawful sale; either party can withdraw from the transaction without prejudice (233:1). There is, however, no error *in substantia* when there is a difference in the quality of the thing, as in the matter of the silver alloy mentioned above as a possible case of incidental fraud. We saw there that the matter could possibly be resolved under the rules of constructive fraud in price (233:1). The matter of the silver alloy could be either a case of incidental fraud or a case involving the wider conception of error *in substantia*, which was more broadly interpreted in later Roman law itself.[80]

In Jewish law, a defect in property, real or moveable, of which the buyer is unaware, is ground for voiding the sale even after some years have elapsed since the transaction. The transaction is deemed to have been rooted in fundamental error. Clearly the buyer's consent can be negated by the defect. The buyer must, in order to void the sale and get his money back, refrain from using the land or goods, for which he is liable with respect to theft or loss. The seller absorbs the loss caused by the defect in the item, even if it is stolen from the buyer, provided that the buyer did in fact inform the seller of the defect in a timely manner (232:3, 22; cf. 216:5).

Every buyer, in the absence of a specific stipulation to the contrary, has a right to except defect-free goods from the seller. In Justinian's law, a seller was held to give an implied warranty that a thing was free of serious defects existing at the time of the contract. He was not, however, responsible for patent defects.[81] In Jewish law, a stipulation to renounce a right of rescission for defects must either be based upon the seller's full explanation of any and all defects in the item or be a buyer's undertaking of acceptance of defects which would reduce the item's value up to a specified amount of money. The buyer has to know what the defect is or declare the amount of financial loss he will absorb (232:7). A seller cannot require a buyer to accept a refund of the value of a defect nor can a buyer demand such a refund (232:4).

The residents of a particular place can agree among themselves what is and what is not to be a defect for which rescission of a sale may be sought. This local custom shall prevail in all cases of dispute unless it is expressly set aside by a stipulation of the parties to waive it in their particular transaction (232:6).

When the proper use of an item involves damaging it (e.g., the cutting of cloth), and such damage is caused before a defect in the item is detected, the buyer may seek rescission and is not held liable for the damage to the goods (232:13; cf. 232:14). The buyer is liable for damage other than that caused by normal use of the thing when he seeks rescission because of a defect.

It is clear that the seller had a duty to inform the buyer of any defects in the land or goods or face the distinct possibility of a lawsuit. The concealment of defects is fraud. The seller is required by law to inform the buyer of any defects in what he is selling (228:6; cf. 222:4). In Roman law the distinction is drawn between patent and latent defects. The seller was presumed to warrant his goods free of the latter, but not of the former. The Jewish law does not appear to work with this distinction.

The texts use, in this regard, the example of a cattle dealer who declares that certain discernible (i.e., patent) defects are present in an animal (232:8, 9). It would seem, therefore, that the requirement for a seller to mention all defects in goods includes both latent and patent ones. This is supported by the text that declares that a buyer has a right to expect his purchase to be free of *all* defects; and no distinction between latent and patent is drawn (232:7). Certainly much buying and selling was transacted in the marketplace where the buyer could see and examine the thing he wanted to purchase. But it is possible to effect acquisition of things that the buyer has no knowledge of except by description or sample. If a buyer receives goods purchased on the basis of a sample and those goods are patently defective, Jewish law would allow the buyer a remedy. Indeed certain large-scale purchases or purchases of rare or special commodities might only be conducted on the basis of the buyer's inspection of the seller's sample. It is reasonable that a patent defect is as much ground for rescission as a latent defect in this case.

But the buyer must also protect himself, when it is clearly possible for him to do so, against patent defects. If one sold another an item of wood and told him it was made of gold, and the buyer was present to inspect the item, the seller can claim that he intended no fraud but said that the item was "good as gold" (232:7). A buyer, after all, must bear some responsibility for what he does, and if he can inspect wood and think it gold, *caveat emptor*. Here is a clear error *in substantia*, but the sale is not voided; the mistake is too glaring and the seller denies offering wood as gold. The fault here is the buyer's. In the sale of slaves, a defect on a visible portion of the slave's body, which defect does not affect the performance of the slave's duties, gives no right of rescission; if the defect is manifest (e.g., a severe skin condition), the right of rescission is apparently not renounced if the defect prevents the slave from doing his assigned duties (232:10). In this situation a patent defect is a matter of *caveat vendor*. There is a similarity to the Roman law on the matter of a sale of a slave whose bodily defects interfere with the discharge of his duties.

Aside from the case of the foolish buyer of the wooden item just mentioned, there is another situation in which a seller is not held liable for a defect. A cattle broker, who does not retain his stock long enough to determine the presence of latent defects in his animals, will not be held liable if he sells an animal and it dies because of a latent defect. The law lays down that the buyer should have been more careful in examining the animal (232:18).

Our review of the principal rules on the negation of consent in the Jewish law of sale has brought us to the possible consequences of a sale of defective goods. The subject of defects and the responsibility for bringing them to light in a transaction of sale leads naturally to the subject of warranties, stipulations, and conditions. Some reference to this matter has already been made, but a closer look is now in order.

A warranty may be expressed or implied; it may be limited or unlimited. The warranties of interest here are those against eviction and those of quality. In Roman law, buyers and sellers used *stipulationes* and *dicta promissave* to provide warranties of various types.[82] There was no liability for defects so obvious that the buyer ought to have known them; this idea may correspond to the Jewish case of the seller who inspected the goods and still thought wood was gold. Express warranties or descriptions of the goods, the *dicta promissave*, were included as terms of an *emptio vendito*. Apart from the Roman insistence on good faith as a basis for *emptio venditio*, the *stipulatio*, a unilateral side promise, enforceable at law, was the most useful means of providing for a warranty. As one might imagine, *stipulationes*, warranties of quality, covered an enormous range of matters.[83] The warranty against eviction first became customary in *emptio veditio*, then compulsory, and eventually a warranty against eviction became implied as a matter of course in *emptio venditio*.[84] The warranty could be altered or eliminated altogether by express agreement of the parties.[85]

In Jewish law as well, a seller was held to provide the buyer with a warranty against eviction, whether the item sold was land, slaves, or moveable goods. The warranty need not have been expressly made, and its omission as a provision in an instrument of transfer or a bill of sale was taken to be a mere notarial error (225:1). This warranty against eviction was limited. In the absence of an express warranty against any eventuality that might disturb the buyer's quiet enjoyment of the property, the warranty covered seizure of the goods, owing to some prior act or omission of the seller, by means of Jewish legal process. The seller was not, however, liable if the seizure was through non-Jewish legal or governmental process: these were deemed unavoidable constraints and the seller was not ordinarily liable for them (225:2). If the seller did warrant against any incident or circumstance affecting quiet enjoyment of the property, the buyer was protected even in case of non-Jewish legal or governmental seizure owing to some act or omission by the seller. Even that warranty was not unlimited, since the seller was not held to have warranted against unpreventable natural disasters; indeed, it is laid down that an express warranty may be reviewed in case of a dispute in an action for indemnity, damages, etc. That review is to establish the reasonable limits of the warranty (225:3).

Warranties of quality could no doubt cover as broad a range of possibilities in Jewish law as they did in Roman law. We have already looked at the matters of fraud and of defective goods as factors which negate consent. The warranty of quality is a sort of converse to the rules concerning defective goods and consent. The Jewish law provides that, in the absence of a stipulation to the contrary, every buyer has a right to expect to receive defect-free goods (232:7). The law also specified implied waranties of quality, which a buyer, in the absence of an express stipulation or local custom to the contrary, may rely upon in purchases of various foodstuffs (229:1, 2) and wine (230:1-6). In the case of purchase of wine, the circumstances of the buyer's storage of the wine may affect any warranty for it (230:5, 6).

In addition to the basic warranties, parties can attach various other stipulations or conditions to their common agreement which is prerequisite to lawful acquisition. A few examples of these will suffice to suggest some types of possible stipulations.

A stipulation may make a particular mode of acquisition a requirement for the transaction (190:8, 192:16). A stipulation may alter the right of withdrawal in kerchief acquisition (195:8). The specifications of what is included in a sale of a house or a field, etc., function as conditions or terms of the sale in the absence of stipulations to the contrary; and of course local mercantile custom functions as a term or condition of a sale where such custom obtains (213-217).

Other kinds of conditions which affect the existence of the transaction itself require some preliminary remarks. In Roman law, a conditional contract means that the contract itself, by express or implied agreement of the parties to it, will depend on some future event which may or may not in fact occur.[86] The word "condition" can refer to the event or to the clause of the contract providing for the entire contract to hinge upon that event. There are two types of conditions: suspensive and resolutive. In a suspensive condition, the contract itself is inoperative, suspended, until the fulfillment of the condition; no legal rights or obligations are as yet created by the contract conditioned suspensively.[87] If the condition, in the sense of the future event, does not materialize, there is no contract. In *emptio venditio* the contract is truly conditional only when the condition is suspensive. The resolutive condition is another matter. In this case the transaction is nullified or canceled if a certain future event occurs.[88] In Roman law, the sale is complete and perfect, with all lawful obligations and rights operative, while the condition has not yet materialized.[89]

Jewish law knows both suspensive and resolutive conditions although that terminology does not appear. A suspensive condition can be annexed to a sale of either land or moveable goods (207:1). The condition must be capable of fulfillment. If the condition is fulfilled, the acquisition of the item, which had to be formally effected, is complete. If the condition (i.e., the event) does not materialize, there is no sale (207:1). A body of opinion holds that the condition is lawful when acquisition of the item has been effected (conditionally) and the condition becomes one's responsibility to fulfill (207:2). Presumably this requirement precludes purely aleatory conditions. Moreover, the acquisition itself cannot be put off until the fulfillment of the condition. The acquisition must be effected in such a fashion that it becomes, upon realization of the condition, retroactive to the time of the acquisition itself; e.g., acquisition shall become effective in thirty days, as from now. If retroactivity of acquisition is not part of the transaction, the acquisition is deemed aleatory and no ownership or title passes to the acquirer (207:2). The requirement of immediacy of acquisition, through a retroactive operation, suggests that a sale originated in an immediate exchange of goods for money and that the rabbinic jurists preserved this concept as fundamental to a sale. Moreover, the retroactivity requirement for acquisition can also be seen as a method of fixing the point of consent to the transaction, as validated by *kinyan*, to the time of *kinyan* itself, since *kinyan* needed consent for its validity. The mental resolve of the parties was already present at *kinyan* and it did not depend upon the future event for its existence, only for its retroactive operation.

A type of resolutive condition in Jewish law required an express formulation by the seller that he was selling something for the specific purpose of applying the proceeds of the sale to the purchase of desperately needed food, for example, or to the costs of travel to settle elsewhere. If the specific purpose declared by the seller could not be realized, the sale was canceled, money was returned, etc. During the time of the sale, the buyer was legal owner. This rule is deemed to apply to sales of real property; in sales of moveable goods, the seller must clarify his intent by setting forth his purpose under highly formal rules for proposing conditions (207:3; cf. *Even Haezer*, chaps. 38, 44). Strictly speaking, the sale is complete, while the ultimate resolution of the contract is the doubtful or conditional factor; this is similar to the view of resolutive conditions found in Roman law.

Either a buyer or a seller could stipulate that goods were to be sold on condition that they be returned to the seller at a specific time or that they be returned when the seller had the money to buy them back. These are lawful conditions. In the case of a sale of real estate, however, only the buyer can freely stipulate that the seller has an option to repurchase the land. Should the seller place such a condition on the sale, the transaction appears to be a loan rather than a sale, and the buyer is forbidden to enjoy the yield or benefit of that land, since the value of such enjoyment amounts to usury on the loan. In this case, the buyer gives back the land he never enjoyed in return for his purchase price. The buyer, however, can freely undertake to sell back to the seller, without risk of tainting his enjoyment of the property with usury (207:5-7).

We have already seen that one cannot transfer ownership of a nonexistent thing. A conditional sale of something not yet in existence is a nullity (209:4).

There is a maxim in Jewish law that every stipulation, every condition, in money matters is valid (225:5). The maxim is, of course, subject to certain restrictions. The stipulation cannot be aleatory in the sense that the consent of the parties inherent in the making of *kinyan* would be held in suspense until the occurrence or nonoccurrence of some future event, for in that case there is no real consent at the time of *kinyan*; the acquisition in a transaction involving an aleatory stipulation must be declared to take effect as from the time of the *kinyan* itself (i.e., retroactive to the time of *kinyan*); the stipulation must be capable of fulfillment, etc. But within the ample boundaries of the law, this maxim emphasizes the rights of sellers and buyers to stipulate, to warrant, to set aside warranties, and to make their transactions conditional as suits their mutual purpose.

When a buyer and seller arrive at agreement as to the thing to be sold and the price to be paid, and they have effected formal acquisition of the thing, one supposes that the ownership of the thing has passed from the seller to the buyer. The nature of this ownership, however, calls for some comment.

In Roman law, the result of a sale was not necessarily to make the buyer an absolute and unconditional owner of a thing.[90] The seller was obligated to warrant against eviction; but this is not the same as making someone the sole and absolute owner of a thing. The seller had to do whatever would transfer ownership, if he had it to transfer; but if the seller only had a defective title to pass on, the buyer had no claim against the seller in this matter until the buyer suffered because of the defective title.[91]

In Jewish law, the texts do not mention ownership as an absolute institution. Indeed the notion of ownership does not imply an absolute exclusion or denial of rights which others may enjoy in the thing: to take one general example, one may purchase an apartment building, but the tenants of the apartments retain their rights in the property. The term often rendered as "ownership" is *reshuth*, which can also mean "authority" and "control." The word is taken in the translation of the text to mean "lawful control and ownership" or "lawful authority and control," or some other phrase of the same import. But the word "ownership" does not necessarily imply that the seller transfers an absolutely clear title to the property to the buyer. This matter, for all practical purposes, appears to be substantially the same in Jewish law as it is in Roman law. The seller is to give the buyer full ownership of the thing if it can be lawfully transferred by the seller. This is, of course, one sense of putting something "in the buyer's *reshuth*." The Jewish law is clearly aware that a web of rights may be spun about some property and not all those rights may belong to the seller to transfer or extinguish. A classic case of this appears in 226:3. The seller sells land to the buyer and does not expressly warrant the buyer against eviction. The seller is still deemed to have guaranteed the buyer that the seller will not sue to retake the property under any right the seller may enjoy at the time of the transaction. If the seller acquires a new right to the property after the sale, he may sue under the new right; e.g., if the buyer was a debtor of the seller's father, and the seller inherits his father's rights against the buyer, the seller could sue to retake the field in payment of the debt. Further, a lessee may enjoy property during the term of his lease irrespective of the fact that ownership of the property has changed hands during the period of the lease. The fact that Jewish law requires the seller to provide warranty against eviction for the buyer (unless this warranty is expressly set aside) gives us clearly to understand that the ownership contemplated in Jewish law might not always be without some proper lawful challenge. To put a thing in another's *reshuth*, or to have something in one's *reshuth*, was to give or to have a thing under one's lawful authority and control, to enjoy the thing as owner and to dispose of it as owner, even though the "ownership" might not be beyond all legal question. To put something in another's *reshuth* as a result of a transaction of sale appears to correspond to the Roman seller's duty *vacuam possessionem tradere*: the seller is to put the thing under the buyer's lawful control.

Risk is an index of lawful authority and ownership because the new owner assumes the risk of loss or damage in regard to the property he has purchased. In both Roman law and Jewish law risk passes to the buyer when the sale is perfected: for Roman law, the time of consent; for Jewish law, the time of *kinyan* (provided in both cases that there is no suspensive condition attached to the transaction). As we have remarked earlier, the rabbinical ordinance of *kinyan* for moveable goods had to do with possible risk to the property (198:5). The risk which passes to the buyer is, of course, risk which is not covered by an express or implied warranty. Further, *kinyan* provides a specific moment when risk as an aspect of lawful ownership falls to the buyer; and, as we have seen, the risk commences irrespective of actual physical delivery although ordinarily many, if not most, types of moveable goods were often in fact acquired by a *kinyan* which amounted to a physical delivery: delivery itself, lifting, pulling, etc.

Special rules govern the incidence of risk when the buyer informs the seller that goods purchased are to be transported and they are eventually found to be defective. These rules, generally, require the seller to reassume risk once the defect has been detected (232:21, 22).

In the case of barter of one animal for another, if one party pulls the animal of the other party, acquisition of the animals is mutually effected. Yet if one of the animals is found dead before the party acquiring it can lead it away, or such animal is found to be ritually unfit for Jewish consumption, there may be doubt as to which party actually exercised lawful control and ownership of the beast at the moment of its death. There are specific rules, and conflicting opinions, concerning which party has the duty to prove the animal alive or dead at the moment of acquisition. A butcher who purchased a meat animal which, upon postslaughter inspection, proves to be ritually unfit as Jewish food, bears the burden of proof that the defect in the animal originated prior to his purchase of it, since the defect did in fact appear while he was clearly the animal's owner (224:1, 2).

A special rule governs the matter of risk when a person takes an object from an artisan for inspection, or perhaps on approval (200:11). If the item was destroyed while the prospective buyer had it, and the item had a set price, and the prospective buyer's act of lifting would have effected lawful acquisition of the whole object, the prospective buyer becomes liable for the purchase price, provided that the item was in fact attractive to the prospective buyer. Goods which are not attractive, or which the seller wishes to get rid of, remain at the seller's risk until a price is set and an act of lifting to effect acquisition is performed. If a buyer declares that he does not want a particular item he had been inspecting, and that item is lost or stolen before he can return it to the seller, one view holds the buyer liable as an unpaid bailee, another, as a paid bailee. The act of lifting, of taking, the item, which is an act of *kinyan*, is held to be *kinyan* for the purpose of bailment only, not for the purpose of sale. These rules substantially preserve the requirement of buyer's consent, express or implied, to the transaction before the buyer is liable to pay a purchase price for the goods. If, after all, a buyer would not have consented to the acquisition as a requisite of purchase, because the seller simply wanted very much to dispose of the goods, the buyer's consent is not implied and he is treated as a bailee, not a purchaser, of one kind or another in case of theft or loss. A paid bailee is held liable to indemnify in cases of theft and loss; an unpaid bailee is not.

In Roman law, the risk for an item taken by a buyer on approval is the seller's if the right of approval was framed as a suspensive condition; but a right of approval was more often couched in terms of a resolutive condition, and so the risk fell to the buyer because of *emptio perfecta*.[92] If the risk was covered by a seller's warranty, the risk was, of course, borne by the seller.[93]

This synopsis began with the tacit assumption that the Jewish law of sale was intended to regulate sales among members of a Jewish community. That is by and large an accurate assumption, since this body of law functioned within the autonomous or semi-autonomous Jewish enclave. This community, however, was surrounded more often than not by the non-Jewish community, and the Jewish law had perforce to recognize that beyond its own confines there stretched another vigorous and productive community, with its own rules and regulations. Jewish merchants came into regular contact with non-Jews. It is not therefore surprising that the Jewish law makes some provision for, or attempts accommodation with, non-Jewish legal systems and procedures.

In the matter of sales of land between Jews and non-Jews, irrespective of which party is the buyer and which party the seller, acquisition of land is effected by an instrument of transfer, with payment of the purchase price (194:1). This provision bears a strong resemblance to Justinian's ruling that a contract of sale was not to take effect until a final written memorandum of the transaction had been prepared, provided the parties agreed that the contract should be in writing.[94] Clearly a written contract would clarify matters for both the Jew and the non-Jew. The Jewish emphasis on the document may reflect a comparable non-Jewish emphasis on written contracts for sales of land.

The crucial importance of the written document prompted the Jewish jurists to frame special rules for the case where one Jew purchased land from a non-Jew, and paid for it, but did not take possession of the land before another Jew came along and seized it (194:2). In such a circumstance the second Jew has taken lawful title to the land if his seizure occurs before the instrument of transfer reaches the first Jew. The view taken is that the first Jew does not contemplate acquisition until he receives the instrument of transfer, while his payment of the purchase price to the non-Jew has extinguished the ownership of the non-Jew. Since the non-Jew no longer owns the land and the Jew does not yet own the land, the Jewish third party could lawfully take the property by act of possession. This ruling appears to operate on the assumption that payment is sufficient to discharge the contract under non-Jewish law, but not sufficient for acquisition under Jewish law in this case, a clear departure from the rule that obtains among Jewish buyers and sellers (190:1). The importance of the writing, perhaps a reflection of non-Jewish practice, works to the disadvantage of the Jewish buyer who paid too soon. In practice the law requires that parties protect themselves by delaying payment until the instrument is written (and delivered, in practice no doubt at the same time payment occurs) (194:3). A transaction in which one ownership can cease some time before another ownership commences places a buyer in jeopardy. The Jewish law does provide, however, that the Jew who takes possession of the land is to reimburse the Jewish purchaser for the money he paid to the non-Jew.

This rather complicated rule, with its inherent disadvantage for the Jewish buyer, applies only when the non-Jewish government has no rules or procedures governing sales of land. The absence of such rules or procedures is hardly likely to have obtained anywhere in the Roman world or in medieval Europe. Where the non-Jewish government provides that only the person paying the purchase price, or the person named as buyer in the written contract, shall be the lawful buyer, Jews are to adopt these rules in their land dealings with non-Jews (194:2, 3).

When a Jew and a non-Jew transact a sale of moveable goods with each other, a simple payment of purchase price effects acquisition. This is a departure from the usual rules governing acquisition of moveable goods among Jews (194:3).

A non-Jew has no standing in Jewish law to sue for the return of an underprice or overprice of one-sixth under the rule of constructive fraud (227:26). But a Jew, presuming the effective jurisdiction of a rabbinical court, can sue a non-Jew for return of the one-sixth overprice or underprice under Jewish law. This latter remedy is allowed so that, if the non-Jew had a Jewish partner and they both sold the overpriced item to a Jew, the Jewish partner would not be liable for the whole of the refund.

An entire chapter (236) lays down rules and procedures under which a Jew can regain land extorted from him by a non-Jew who then sold the extorted land to another Jew. One provision of this chapter is of especial interest for the matter of the Jewish view of non-Jewish governments and legal systems. When a Jew could avail himself of non-Jewish legal process to recover land extorted from him by a non-Jew, and does not do so, the Jew is deemed to have despaired of getting his land back. The presumption is that the Jew has some standing in the non-Jewish court and could use it to regain his property (236:9). Moreover, confiscation of land or goods by a king or nobleman, acting in his royal or noble capacity, is not unlawful. Such confiscation is presumably provided for under the law of the land, and Jews are required by their own legal system to adhere to the law of the land whenever such laws are not repugnant to the Jewish religion or hostile to Jewish religious practice and usage.[95]

Finally, the Jewish law of sale has emphasized at great length and in detail the importance of local mercantile custom in regulating sales among Jews. Such custom, unless expressly set aside by the parties to a sale, supersedes the traditional Jewish law. Of course the custom must itself be well known and regularly observed. There is nothing in the law of sale which requires that a mercantile custom be the exclusive development of Jewish usage and practice. It is quite possible for the custom of a trade or a marketplace or a particular mercantile endeavor to have non-Jewish roots. As long as the custom, be it Jewish or non-Jewish, is not flagrantly contrary to Jewish law (as would be, e.g., the charging of interest), Jews are bidden to transact their business according to its provisions. The recognition and reception of mercantile custom reflect the real and distinct probability that non-Jewish commercial practice formed a legitimate part of the Jewish law of sale.

Lexicographical Notes

The language of the law of sale is often technical. Specific words and terms in the lexicon of Jewish law denote institutions and concepts that have no precise counterpart in the technical language of other systems of law. Therefore part of the challenge of translation has been to analyze the terminology customarily used in translating ancient and medieval Jewish legal material and then to determine whether or not that terminology is as accurate as it could be. Occasionally during the process of translation, it became clear that some of the standard renderings of some Hebrew and Aramaic technical terms were not altogether satisfactory, and thus it was necessary to develop new renderings that appeared to convey the sense of the text with greater precision. This brief section discusses the specific renderings used here and the reasons they are preferred over some more customary renderings.

The technical term *ona'ah* is commonly rendered in English as "overreaching," which is defined in Webster's *Third New International Dictionary* (1971) as "to get the better of, especially by sharp, unfair, tricky, or deceitful means." This definition appears to fit the meaning of the noun, based on the Hebrew verbal root, 'NH, which Jastrow defines as "to press, wrong, oppress, to impose, *to overreach* in dealing" (Marcus Jastrow *Dictionary of the Targumim*, etc. [New York: Parkes, 1950], p. 84). Webster's definition of "overreaching," however, implies an element of intent to outwit or to cheat. The element of intent is not necessarily present in the Hebrew term "*ona'ah*. Indeed *ona'ah* may be present even when the buyer and seller choose a third party to set the price for their transaction. Certainly, if either the buyer or the seller suspected the third party of intent to defraud, he would not have agreed to the price that person set. Moreover *ona'ah* is also used in reference to insulting, deceptive, or abusive speech; while intent is almost certainly present when one verbally abuses or insults another, there is not necessarily any apparent sense of outwitting or cheating or deceiving in regard to any quantifiable amount of money, etc. (For an analysis of *ona'ah* from the point of view of economic theory, see Aaron Levine, "The Just Price Doctrine in Judaic Law -- An Economic Analysis," *Dine Israel*, vol. VIII [Tel Aviv University Faculty of Law,].)

The term *ona'ah* therefore required more than one mode of translation. When the word occurs in the context of a sale, it is rendered by the phrase "constructive fraud." Since the term has the specific connotation of an overcharge, or undercharge, of one-sixth of the correct price of moveable property (not real property), whether there has been intent to defraud or not, the phrase suggests accurately that the fraud, which is clearly a violation of law, is construed to exist in the event of such an overcharge or undercharge. The phrase is often supplemented in the translation with the further phrase "by unfair price" or by a similar phrase. This supplement is intended to convey the notion that unfair price is involved, without specific reference to either vendor or purchaser as the witting or unwitting culprit, since the unfairness can indeed be, intentionally or unintentionally, caused by the purchaser if the bargaining results in an undercharge to the vendor's disadvantage. Although one may properly assume that the seller would most often be at fault in a case of *ona'ah*, it is by no means far-fetched that a clever purchaser can out-bargain a merchant who may not be fully aware of the value of the goods he offers for sale. A younger businessman, or perhaps one who is just learning the intricacies of a particular line of merchandise, could be victimized and beguiled into undercharging for his wares. Lastly, the idea of constructive fraud in cases of the one-sixth over (or under) charge allows the court to assume deceit, even when a party involved in the transaction can justly claim that he was merely using his hard-won skills of commerce to drive a hard bargain, without meaning to cheat or to do anyone wrong. The presence of a constructive fraud is, of course, taken to be an abuse of one party by the other, and this notion of abuse, which lies behind the concept of fraud, is the link to the original root meaning of the term. The element of abuse appears more clearly when the word *ona'ah* appears in the context of the spoken word of abuse or insult intended to harm or endanger another. The rendering employed in that case is "unfair advantage by means of abuse of speech," or simply "abusive speech," or a version of such a phrase as the context may require. This context of *ona'ah* need not involve any substantive fraud or deception, even in a constructive sense, but it certainly carries the meaning of wronging a person. Here there is intent to do hurt, to shame, embarrass, or even to deceive; but there is no actionable fraud, no taking of another's money or goods.

The term *aharayuth*, from the Hebrew verbal root 'HR, has a variety of meanings and connotations in legal texts; "surety," "security," "liability for risk," "insurance risk," "insurance," "responsibility," or simply "risk." In the context of some provisions of the law of sale, the word reveals to us yet another facet of meaning. A seller may undertake *aharayuth* with respect to the thing he sells. He agrees to hold the buyer harmless against eviction from the property owing to some act of omission or commission on the part of the seller. This undertaking apparently became so common that its omission as an express undertaking in the bill or instrument of sale was assumed to be a mere notarial error and the undertaking was presumed to exist unless specifically excluded by the parties.

Given the terms of definition or description of *aharayuth*, as found in these laws, the proper rendering seems to be "warranty against eviction," or occasionally "warranty," with the qualification "against eviction" understood from the context.

Another specialized term in the law of sale (and in the law of loans and debts as well) is the word *asmakhta*. The word is a noun form based on the Hebrew and Aramaic verbal root *SMKh*, "to lean on, to rely on," and, by extension, "to lay on hands." The *asmakhta* connotes some sort of aleatory contract, a wager, or, most often, a contingent promise to give or to do something for another, for example as a penalty, without receiving any benefit or value for that promise. Such a promise effects no lawful acquisition of the thing promised, because the law presumes that, without proof to the contrary, the promise does not represent a sincere resolve to give or to do the thing promised. The promise is dependent on something that may or may not occur. Since the promise is contingent, the promissor is presumed to harbor the hope that the contingency will not occur and thus that the promise will not require fulfillment. Unless there is some proof that the promissor has indeed resolved to fulfill the promise should the stipulated contingency come to pass, this contingent promise has no legal effect and cannot be used as grounds for a suit to have the promissor give or do what was promised. In the words of the Talmud, an *asmakhta* effects no acquisition; it confers no right *in personam* or *in rem*.

The rendering of *asmakhta* used here is, therefore, "aleatory forfeiture." This phrase conveys the notion that the promise amounts to a mere forfeiture, conditioned by an uncertain future event, of property, (or perhaps, of time and effort, which clearly have a monetary value) for which forfeiture no value has been received.

The verbal root *BTL* gives us the stative and participial forms of *batel* and *b'telah*, generally rendered as "null" or "void." In some cases, however, the context requires that the word be taken as "voidable" rather than simply "void." When a buyer or seller wishes to annul a sale, the sale itself is technically voidable, not void.

The common meanings of the Hebrew verbal root *QNH* are "to buy," "to acquire," and "to possess." The root therefore often appears in a treatise on the law of sale. A noun based on this root, *kinyan*, is a crucial technical term in the law of sale. The noun conveys, variously, the notions of purchase, acquisition, or an item acquired, or ownership, possession, and acquisition of ownership by some symbolic act.

As a technical term in the law of sale, two meanings of *kinyan* given below are most often intended; the use of the verbal root in this context usually indicates the same two meanings. A third meaning of the noun will be mentioned presently, as will a less technical use of the verbal root. The term *kinyan* denotes the concept of the lawful getting of some tangible thing. The notion is not limited to the law of sale. The concept applies to, and is used in reference to, gift, hire, let, and any other form of lawful acquisition. Simultaneously, the term denotes the formal act which validates and makes binding an agreement to buy and sell, to give, to hire, etc., and by means of which lawful ownership or possession passes from one party to another. The word *kinyan* occasionally reflects the more specific meaning of one type of such a formal act, which act is performed by the buyer and seller (or their agents) using a kerchief, the symbolic kerchief acquisition, *kinyan sudar*. The verbal root, when found in the *qal* conjugation, bears the meaning of effecting the lawful acquisition, both in regard to the concept of acquiring or getting in order to hold as one's own, and in regard to the act of validation, confirmation, etc., performed to make the agreement to sell, or to deed, binding and lawful. Therefore the noun *kinyan* is rendered and understood as acquisition in its formal and legal sense or as an act of acquisition, again in its formal and legal sense. The verbal form of *QNH* in the *qal* is usually rendered here as "to effect acquisition." While this translation is not as clear and simple as "to buy" (which less technical meaning is employed in certain contexts), it does have the virtue of conveying both the assertion of the concept of acquisition and the performance of the act which make the concept manifest. Moreover, it suits contexts of lease and gift as well as purchase. A third, and less common, meaning of *kinyan* is the thing lawfully acquired itself.

When the verbal root *QNH* appears in the causative inflection, the meaning conveyed, and the rendering generally used here, is "to transfer ownership" (or lawful possession).

The Laws on Unfair Price as Constructive Fraud and Rescission

189: The rule that no purchase is completed by mere verbal agreement. One paragraph.

1) A purchase is not completed by mere verbal agreement.[1] Should one say to another, "How much (need I pay that) you give me this object," and the other reply, "For thus and thus much," and both of them are satisfied and they have fixed the price -- either party can still withdraw from the transaction. This is so even if there had been witnesses (to their negotiations as to thing and price); and the parties had (even) said to the witnesses, "Be witness to the fact that this one has sold and the other one has purchased." (The verbal agreement) has no legal force (as a valid sale) until the purchase is completed according to the proper lawful and appropriate mode (of formal effecting of acquisition): and according to its appropriate mode; animals according to theirs; moveables according to theirs.

After a purchase is completed by its appropriate mode of effecting acquisition, neither buyer nor seller can withdraw from the transaction, even if there were no witnesses to the transaction.[2]

> GLOSS: And even if buyer and seller both renounced the sale after the formal act of acquisition, such renunciation is not valid. The buyer must formally transfer the item to the seller by the appropriate mode of effecting acquisition.[3]

190: The rules governing acquisition of land by monetary consideration. Eighteen paragraphs.

1) Land is acquired by one of four formal means:[1] by a sum of money, by instrument of transfer, by physical possession, or by symbolic kerchief-acquisition.

> GLOSS: The rules governing the means of formal effecting
> of acquisition in the case of a lease of real property
> are the same as the rules for formal acquisition in a
> sale of real property; cf. infra end of ch. 195.

2) In the case of money:[2] If A has sold B a building or a field and B has given A money in the sum of one *perutah*, B has formally effected acquisition of the property. Neither party can withdraw from the transaction. No withdrawal is permitted, even if the money were given on the express condition that the seller would return the particular coin, or coins given, to the buyer: the acquisition has been effected.[3]

3) If A says to B,[4] "Give a *maneh* to C, and effect acquisition thereby of my land for yourself," once he has given the money to C, the acquisition of the land by B has been effected.

4) There is an opinion[5] that an acquisition has similarly been effected in the following case: A says to B, "Here is a *maneh*, (in consideration of which) your field is sold to C"; once B has received the money, the acquisition of the land by C has been effected.

> GLOSS: Provided that C is amenable to that transaction;
> e.g., C appointed A an agent (to perform such transac-
> tions) or C has declared to B, "I have acquired your
> field in consideration of the money A gives you."[6]

5) Similarly, there is an opinion[7] that an acquisition has been effected in the following case: A says to B, "Give a *maneh* to C, (in consideration of which) my field is sold to that same C." Once C has received the *maneh* from B, the acquisition of the field by C has been effected (provided that the buyer is amenable to the transaction as provided above in para. 4).[8]

6) Similarly there is an opinion[9] that an acquisition has been effected in the following case: A says to B, "Here is a *maneh* for you. My field is sold to you for it." Once B has taken possession of the *maneh*, his acquisition of the field has been effected, provided that the purchaser is an important personage, so that the seller derives pleasure from the fact that the buyer would accept a gift from him.

> GLOSS: A owed B a *maneh*. The time for repayment arrived. B said to A, "I shall sell you land for a *maneh*." A was agreeable to that transaction and gave B the *maneh*. B cannot claim that he has collected the *maneh* for the previous debt owed by A. Rather, the land has been acquired by A, and B may collect the debt afterwards.[10]

7) Acquisition by money alone[11] is valid only where it is not the practice to indite an instrument of transfer. Where it is the practice to indite an instrument of transfer, no acquisition has been effected until one indites such an instrument of transfer.

8) (If) the buyer makes the following stipulation:[12] "If I wish I shall acquire (the land) by a sum of money, and if I wish I shall acquire (the land) by instrument of transfer." If the buyer has given the money payment on this condition, the transaction is valid and the seller cannot withdraw from it because of the condition (i.e., the instrument has not yet been executed); the buyer can withdraw until one writes the instrument of transfer for him. Similarly, if the seller has stipulated in this matter, the resolution of the matter depends upon him (i.e., his wish).[13]

9) If one is acquiring land[14] from another, and they have set the price, but the buyer has given collateral security for the money (not the money itself), no acquisition has been effected.[15] Either party may withdraw from the transaction.

> GLOSS: If, however, the buyer said, "Take lawful acquisition of the collateral security to the extent of your money (i.e., the sum you are owed)," acquisition of the land had been effected.[16]

10) If one is selling[17] a field to another for the sum of one thousand *zuz*, and the buyer has paid some of the (mutually agreed) price, and the seller has repeatedly called to collect the balance of the purchase price, even if the outstanding sum is only one *zuz*, the buyer has not effected acquisition of the entire property.[18] This holds good even if one has indited the instrument of transfer or one has taken possession of the property.

If the buyer withdraws[19] under such circumstances, the seller shall enjoy the advantage: the seller can say to the buyer, "Here is your money," or "Effect acquisition of an amount of land valued at the sum you have already paid"; and the seller provides such land from the poorest portion of that parcel of land, (at the current market price for such land).[20] If the seller withdraws under such circumstances, the buyer shall enjoy the advantage: the buyer can say to the seller, "Either give me back my money or provide me with an amount of land valued at the sum I have already given"; the seller is to provide such land from the best portion of that parcel of land.[21]

If the seller has not repeatedly called to collect the balance of the purchase price,[22] the buyer has effected acquisition (by the sum already paid) of the entire property. Neither party can withdraw from the transaction. The balance of the purchase price is charged to the buyer as an ordinary debt.

> GLOSS: Similarly: If the seller has charged the balance of the purchase price to the buyer as a loan,[23] even if the seller has called repeatedly to collect the balance due, the buyer has effected acquisition, if indeed the partial payment had been tendered as partial payment of the price.
> If, however, the partial payment was given as a pledge or as earnest money (to be forfeit should the buyer withdraw from the transaction),[24] then even if the seller did not repeatedly call to collect the balance due, acquisition has been effected only for an amount of land valued to the amount of the earnest unless the buyer should stipulate that the earnest given is for formal acquisition of the entire parcel of land.[25] Both parties can withdraw from such a transaction; and acquisition has not been effected by the earnest except in regard to the poorest grade or quality of land in the parcel.[26]

11) When one sells his field because it is of poor quality,[27] and has received only part of the purchase price, even though the seller calls repeatedly to collect the balance of the purchase price,

acquisition of the entire parcel of land has been effected. The buyer has no right to withdraw from such a transaction. The fact that the seller repeatedly seeks the balance of the purchase price is not because he had not yet finally resolved to sell the land (as might be the case with a more desirable parcel of land) but because he wants to forestall a withdrawal by the buyer.

The law is similar in the case of a seller of moveable goods:[28] even though the buyer of moveable goods has physically drawn them into his control[29] (which would normally effect legal acquisition) -- and the seller calls repeatedly for the balance of the purchase price (only partial payment having been given), no acquisition has been effected; and whichever party withdraws from the transaction is at the disadvantage: unless the seller sold the goods because of their poor quality, in which case acquisition of the entire lot of goods has been effected (even with partial payment of the purchase price).

12) When one sells his property because he wishes to move and take up residence in another city, he is deemed to be the same as one who sells property because of its poor quality.[30]

13) If one purchased[31] a field worth one hundred *zuz* for two hundred *zuz*, paid part of the purchase price, and the seller called repeatedly to collect the balance of the purchase price, there is an unresolved doubt in the Talmud whether or not such a seller is deemed to be analogous to one who sells property because of its poor quality. Therefore neither party is permitted to withdraw from the transaction; if the seller retakes a portion valued to the amount of the balance of the price outstanding, he cannot be sued for recovery of that property.

14) If one sought to sell[32] a field for one hundred *zuz* and did not find a buyer for a field worth that sum, and it therefore became necessary for him to sell a field worth two hundred *zuz* and he received a portion of the purchase price from the buyer and called repeatedly to collect the balance of the purchase price, no acquisition has been effected; and either party can withdraw from such a transaction.[33] If, however, the seller could have found a buyer for the field valued at one hundred *zuz* if he had wished to put in the effort required to do so, but did not extend himself and chose

rather to sell the property valued at two hundred *zuz*, there is an unresolved doubt[34] whether or not such a seller is deemed to be analogous to one who sells property because of its poor quality. Therefore neither party is permitted to withdraw from the transaction, and if the seller retakes a portion of this property he sold, a portion valued to the amount of the balance of the price outstanding, he cannot be sued for return of that property.

15) The assertion[35] that when the seller calls repeatedly to collect the balance of the purchase price no acquisition has been effected refers to a situation in which we know that there would be no sale except for the seller's (immediate) need for cash money. Even if the seller fixed a time for payment, and the seller pressed the buyer for payment when that time arrived, but the buyer put him off; and it is clear to the judge (reviewing the case) that the seller is in sore need of the money and calls for it repeatedly, no acquisition has been effected.

16) There is an opinion[36] that the matter of repeated calling for payment from the buyer, by the seller, means that the seller has gone to the buyer twice to seek his money. It is all the same whether the seller actually found the buyer on those visits and sought the money from him or did not find him -- but clearly indicated that his purpose in the visit was to seek his money from the buyer. Specifically (the rule on repeated calls requires that the) visits be made on the day they set for the (actual money) transaction, or the day close to it (just prior to it).[37] But if he did not call on the day of the transaction, even if he called the next day, the seller cannot withdraw. If the seller did call (later) on the day of the transaction, even if he was silent then (i.e., did not assert his claim to the balance verbally), and after several more days he withdraws from the transaction, the seller has exercised a lawful option of withdrawal. If the seller called twice on the day of the transaction and the buyer did not give him the balance of the price outstanding, yet before the day was over the buyer brought him the balance of the price due, acquisition has been effected. The seller cannot withdraw. Payment on the same day is tantamount to immediate payment.

GLOSS: Similarly when we say that acquisition of land has been effected up to the amount of money already given, there is one opinion that this rule can apply only in places where money payment without instrument of transfer, effects acquisition. Where the instrument is also required, that instrument does not effect a partial acquisition. Any form of acquisition that is not valid for effecting, in and of itself, acquisition of the whole property in question does not have validity for a part of that property.[38]

If, however, the parties have stipulated (otherwise), their stipulation shall govern the transaction.[39]

17) In this matter, the rule covering moveable property[40] is the same as the rule governing land: even if the buyer of the moveable goods has physically drawn them into his control (which would normally effect legal acquisition) and the seller has called repeatedly for the balance of the purchase price, no acquisition has been effected.

There is, however, a distinction to be made with regard to moveable goods: If the item is not properly divisible, e.g., an animal (which as a living thing cannot be divided as inanimate objects might be), and the buyer has given part of the price, while the seller has called repeatedly for the balance of it, the purchase is entirely void, since (a) the item cannot be divided, and (b) the seller does not wish to be a partner with the buyer in regard to the item. (But if the buyer specifically said that his earnest money or pledge should effect acquisition, acquisition to the extent of the money given has been effected.)[41]

Where the item can be divided (without destroying it), the purchase is void only to the extent of the unpaid price owed the seller.

18) When one has effected acquisition of an item and has paid the price, but has erred in the counting out of money, and the seller later asserts that the one hundred *zuz* supposedly paid were in fact only ninety *zuz*, the purchase has been lawfully acquired. The buyer pays the additional ten *zuz*, even if a number of years have elapsed

since the contract. This is the rule for both real and moveable property.[42]

> GLOSS: Where a person has been victimized by false charges and in order to prevent seizure of his lands (as a consequence of the calumny)[43] sold his lands for cash: when the accusations are withdrawn, the purchase is void, even if the parties afterwards are content with the earlier sale, since the instrument of transfer for the original sale is voided because that sale was prompted by the necessity for protecting the property. The original instrument bears a date prior to the actual agreement of the parties to the sale; it is therefore invalid as a predated instrument of transfer.[44]

191: The rules governing acquisition of land by instrument of transfer. Four paragraphs.

1) In the case of the instrument of transfer: The seller[1] writes on paper, on a clay shard, or on a leaf, "My field is given to you; my field is sold to you." Once this document reaches the hand of the buyer, acquisition has been effected, even though there are no witnesses at all there (to this delivery of the instrument).

2) This above-stated rule[2] holds good when one sells his field because of its poor grade or quality. In other real estate transactions (where the land is not sold because it is poor), acquisition has not been effected until the purchase price is paid, even though the instrument of sale was delivered to the buyer before witnesses.

3) Instruments (of transfer) indited by Jews (nowadays) are instruments for effecting acquisition.[3]

> GLOSS: Land is acquired by means of such instruments. If the seller has explicitly written that he did not sell the land by means of the instrument of transfer and that the instrument has evidentiary value only, acquisition is not effected by the document.[4]

4) When one has effected acquisition of land by means of a

certain sum of money,[5] and the seller says he has not received the money, while the buyer says, "I have given it to you": If this situation arises in a place where they pay the money and write the instrument of transfer afterward, and one has written in the instrument that he (the seller) acknowledges receipt of the money, the buyer is thereby lawfully confirmed (in his assertion).

> GLOSS: When one has sold land by means of an instrument of transfer or by means of money and has said to him -- the buyer -- "Acquisition shall be effective[6] after thirty days," and the instrument is destroyed or the money lost in that thirty-day period, if the seller said acquisition shall be effective retroactively from today and after thirty days have passed, acquisition does become retroactively effective. There is, in this case, no acquisition if the seller did not specify the element of retroactivity, (by using) the phrase "from today." The same rule applies in a case of acquisition by means of physical possession."[7]

192: The rules governing acquisition of land by physical possession. Sixteen paragraphs.

1) In the case of physical possession:[1] When one has sold or given a house or field, once the buyer has placed a lock on the property, or has, to some extent, constructed a fence around it, or has broken through a fence (to create a new access route), and the buyer's acts have some perceptible positive effect (on the land), acquisition has been effected.

2) This rule holds good[2] when such possessive act is performed in the presence of the seller or of the donor. If it is not performed in the presence of the seller or the donor, no acquisition has been affected unless the seller or donor shall have declared to the buyer, "Go, possess, and effect acquisition." If the seller delivers the key to the property to the buyer, that act is tantamount to the declaration of "Go, possess, and effect acquisition."[3] Similarly, if one sells a well, the delivery of the bucket for that well to the buyer is tantamount to the declaration of "Go, possess, and effect

acquisition."

3) In the case of placing a lock on the property, if one has sold or given a house or courtyard, the entrance to which was open, and the buyer has locked the entrance and then opened it, acquisition has been effected.[4] There is an opinion that the locking process must be done with a key. There is an opinion that acquisition has been effected if the buyer has made a bar for a door or placed doors on the property.[5]

4) The appropriate minimum amount of fencing is held to be as follows: A preexistent fence was easily climbed; the buyer added something to it, bringing it up to a height of ten handbreadths (there is an opinion that even less than ten handbreadths is satisfactory), so that the barrier could be climbed only with difficulty.[6] This addition has brought about the necessary perceptible effect; and acquisition has been effected.

5) The necessary extent of clearing an access through a fence is held to be as follows:[7] a preexisting passage through the fence was too narrow for easy access; the buyer widened the breach for easy access. This act has brought about the necessary effect and acquisition has been effected.

6) If the buyer has placed a small rock[8] on the property and thereby has effected some benefit for the land, e.g., he has retained [and conserved][9] the water already on the land, or has removed a small rock which similarly effected some benefit for the land, e.g., he thereby allowed water to flow into the land, acquisition has been effected. If, however, he saw a stream of water about to damage the land and he placed a stone to divert it (or he removed a stone -- to allow a potentially damaging watercourse to run off that land), no acquisition has been effected, since the achievement of some positive benefit for the land, not existent before, effects acquisition, not the removal of an existing source of potential damage to the land.[10]

7) If A sells or gives a field to B,[11] and that property is situated next to a field which B already owns, once B has knocked down the barrier between the two fields and made them a single parcel of land, acquisition has been effected. If, however, B enters the new field and walks off its length and width,[12] such walking on it has

no legal effect. If A has sold a vineyard pathway to B, since it exists for the purpose of walking on it, acquisition thereof is effected by such walking.

The extent of the area legally acquired by walking is construed as follows: If the path is bounded by walls, acquisition has been effected for a space large enough to take a step with one's foot and bring the other foot up beside it[13] (i.e., a comfortable step). If the path is not bounded by walls, acquisition has been effected for a space wide enough for a person, walking and carrying a bundle of twigs on his head, to turn around in. (There are those who say just the reverse: that where there are *no* walls, the space acquired is sufficient for a comfortable step, and when there are walls, the space acquired is sufficient for the person with the bundle on his head to turn around in.)[14]

8) If the land sold was barren rock,[15] with neither (inadequate) fence nor opening (in need of widening), unfit for sowing seed, the possessive act which effects acquisition thereof is the spreading of one's fruit thereon to dry or the placing of one's animals thereon, and any like use of such land.

9) If one has made up a bed[16] in a house or in a field and slept upon it, or set a table (in a house or a field) and taken a meal thereat,[17] or moreover, even if one has put his belongings there or heaped up his produce, which is properly stored in a heap, there, acquisition of the property has been effected.[18]

10) If A sells a field to B, who then enters the property[19] and sows it with seed, or tills it, or collects fruit from the trees therein, or trims (those trees), etc., acquisition has been effected.

11) Similarly, if the seller has gathered a basket of fruit from that property[20] and given it to the buyer, acquisition has been effected.

> GLOSS: There is a contrary opinion that some of the above-mentioned possessive acts do not effect acquisition -- neither the eating of the fruit of the property nor placing one's animals therein, etc., brings any benefit to the land itself, and such indeed is the more logical view of the matter.[21] If there was a mound

of dirt on the field and the buyer removed it, or a pit which he filled, this would constitute an act of possession, it seems to me, if in fact such acts benefited the field. If, however, one simply dug a small hole, one has not effected acquisition unless the field was ready for plowing.[22]

12) If A sells B ten fields in ten different countries,[23] once a possessive act has been performed with one of the properties, acquisition of all of them has been effected, even if one of them is a high mountain and another one is a deep crevasse,[24] where the appropriate uses of these parcels are clearly not the same.[25] This rule holds good if indeed the buyer has paid the purchase price for all the parcels of land. If, however, he has not paid the purchase price for all the parcels, acquisition has been effected only to the extent of the amount of money actually paid.

Therefore if all the parcels of land were a gift,[26] the donee has acquired all of them. (There is a differing opinion on the matter of a gift.)[27]

(This rule applies equally to ten separate buildings or to a house in one place and a field in another place.)[28]

13) Similarly in a case of lease[29] (of ten parcels in ten separate places), once a possessive act has been performed with one of them, the lessee has effected acquisition of them all for the term of the lease.

> GLOSS: In lease there is no requirement that the full amount of rental has to be given conjointly with the performance of the possessive act, since the full amount of the rental is not due until the end of the term of the lease.[30]

14) If a few parcels[31] of land were transferred by sale and a few parcels of land were transferred by a lease, once a possessive act has been performed with any single parcel, whether of the lot sold or the lot leased, acquisition of them all has been effected.

15) The rule governing the possessive act with respect to the property of a convert will be explained in Ch. 275.

16) A possessive act,[32] without a money payment and without instrument of transfer, effects acquisition where the seller does not repeatedly call upon the buyer for full payment (even where the custom is to write the instrument of transfer; but if the parties have made their own stipulation in this matter their stipulation shall govern their transaction).[33]

193: Whatever is attached to land is treated as land. One paragraph.

1) Everything attached to land,[1] which is dependent upon the land, is like land, and acquisition thereof is formally effected by a sum of money, by instrument of transfer, or by physical possession. Even if one did not intend[2] to effect acquisition of land, but performed a possessive act on the land in order to effect acquisition of something attached to the land, or gave money for the land in order to effect acquisition of something attached to the land, one has effected acquisition thereof even though one has not acquired the land.

If, however, the item is not dependent upon the land: e.g., grapes ready for the vintage, they are treated as moveable property in matters of effecting acquisition and the law of unfair advantage by constructive fraud in pricing[3] applies to them. (There is a differing opinion which holds that even an item not dependent upon the land is treated as land.)[4]

194: The matter of the non-Jew who sells land to a Jew, has received the purchase price, but has not written an instrument of transfer. Three paragraphs.

1) A non-Jew[1] cannot effect acquisition (of land from a Jew) either by possessive act (or by money payment).[2] Acquisition is effected by the non-Jew by instrument of transfer, along with payment of the purchase price. The Jew who acquires from a non-Jew does so under the rules which govern acquisition by a non-Jew; acquisition is effected by an instrument of transfer only (with the payment of the purchase price).

> GLOSS: In the case of a lease from a non-Jew, however, acquisition is effected by money payment alone. Similarly, if a buyer has stipulated that he shall effect acquisition by money payment alone, he has effected acquisition immediately (upon such payment).[3]

2) Since a non-Jew acquires land from a Jew and transfers acquisition of land to a Jew only by an instrument of transfer,[4] if A has purchased a field from a non-Jew and paid the price therefor, but before A could perform a possessive act with the land, B comes and in fact performs a possessive act with that land, which act would be deemed to effect lawful acquisition in respect to the property of a deceased convert to Judaism (without heirs), B has legally taken title to the land.[5]

(There is an opinion that even if A has performed a possessive act, B still takes lawful title to the land by his possessive act) because A, in such a transaction, does not contemplate the acquisition as effected except by means of the instrument of transfer,[6] and thus does the law appear to me. If, however, A performed his possessive act before he paid the money price, he has effected ownership (on all Jewish legal views).[7]

In this situation,[8] B gives A the money (that A paid to the non-Jew), because once the non-Jew had taken that money, the land ceased to be under his control, while A had not effected acquisition until he took possession of the instrument of transfer. Consequently such property ranks as wilderness, which falls to the ownership of whoever performs a possessive act with it.

The warranty (against eviction) remains the responsibility of the non-Jewish seller.[9]

> GLOSS: B is termed wicked (for dealing this way).[10] In any event, if A attempts to use non-Jewish assistance to take the property from B, A is termed a traitorous informer against a fellow Jew, since B is to give A his money.[11]

These rules apply when the non-Jewish government[12] has not promulgated a law governing such transactions. If, however, the non-Jewish government has established the law and procedure that only the person named in the deed of transfer, or the person who shall pay the purchase price (to the previous owner), etc., shall come into ownerership of the land in question, (this law is valid) and the parties shall act according to the non-Jewish rule governing this matter.

> GLOSS: When a non-Jew had placed a pledge or a deposit (i.e., moveable property) with A, a Jew, and then made that property over to B, a Jew, in a deed of transfer, A assumes ownership of that property which he actually possesses. On the one hand, once the non-Jew has given the written instrument to B, the non-Jew's ownership has ceased; on the other hand, B has effected no acquisition until he shall have performed a possessive act, i.e., pulled the (moveable) property to himself. Therefore the property is like ownerless property; and A becomes the owner thereof, as he would become the owner of any ownerless property -- which he lawfully seized.[13]

3) There is an opinion that even if the non-Jew wrote the instrument of transfer for A before B shall have performed a possessive act with the land (but after the non-Jew had received his money), such a document is a nullity.[14] Since (with the payment of the money) the non Jew's ownership has ceased, the non-Jew no longer has any relationship to the property. Thus it is necessary that the instrument of transfer be indited before the non-Jew receives the money). (All this applies only to sales of land; with moveable goods, acquisition is effected by means of the money payment.)[15]

195: The rule governing acquisition of land or moveables by symbolic exchange. Eleven paragraphs.

1) In matters of acquisition, symbolic exchange is conducted as follows:[1] The one who wishes to acquire the property shall give some small object to the one who transfers the ownership and shall say, "Acquire this in exchange for the land -- or the moveable property -- which you sold -- or gave -- to me." (The acquirer does not customarily recite this formula, since without any further speci-

fication or information, the acquirer is presumed in fact to be giving the object to the transferor with the intent of effecting acquisition.)[2] Once the transferor has grasped and pulled upon the object,[3] acquisition of the land or moveables has been effected by the buyer or donee, wherever the property may be, even though he has neither performed a possessive act with the property nor paid the purchase price, nor written an instrument of transfer, nor pulled moveable property toward himself (to effect acquisition thereof). Neither party can withdraw from the transaction even if there are no witnesses to it, if the parties mutually acknowledge the facts of the case.[4]

> GLOSS: Similarly, if the parties (gave and) received (by such a form of) acquisition in the presence of persons unfit to give testimony in a Jewish court, the acquisition is valid, since they mutually acknowledge that acquisition has been effected.[5]

2) Acquisition (of this type) is effected only with some object, even though such object may be valued at less than a *perutah*[6] (provided that the object be made of some valuable material, i.e., not made of (worthless) animal droppings).[7] Acquisition (of this type) is not effected with an object that is forbidden for Jews to use or to benefit from, nor with agricultural produce, nor with current coinage.[8] (An animal is deemed an object and acquisition is effected therewith. Other moveable goods that are not (fabricated) objects are not valid for effecting acquisition. A coin that is completely unfit for use as current money is deemed an object with which acquisition can be effected.)[9]

Acquisition (of this type) is not effected with the utensils of the transferor.[10]

3) If one has transferred ownership[11] of an object to the seller, in order that a buyer shall effect acquisition of property for sale therewith, the buyer has become the owner of that property: even though[12] the transfer of ownership of that object was not done in the presence of the buyer; and even though one transferred the ownership of the object on the express condition that the object be transferred to its former owner, acquisition of the purchase has

been effected.[13]

> GLOSS: Thus the practice of effecting acquisition with a kerchief belonging to one of the witnesses to the transaction has become common -- even if the person acquiring the property is present -- since most formal acts of acquisition (of this type) are not done in the acquirer's presence.[14] The rule that acquisition is effected outside the presence of the acquirer applies to matters of gift, etc., where the recipient is certainly pleased to make the acquisition. But with a purchase, where it is possible that one does not desire to make the acquisition, no acquisition has been effected and both parties are free to withdraw from the transaction.[15]

4) Even though the person transferring the lawful acquisition has grasped only part of the object,[16] and part of it remains in the grasp of the acquirer, acquisition has been effected: provided that the transferor shall have grasped a portion of the object equal to three fingerbreadths (square). If he grasped less[17] than that amount, he must grasp the object in such a fashion that he could tear away the entire object (from the grasp of the acquirer) and bring it to himself.

> GLOSS: There is an opinion that acquisition is *not* effected if the transferor has grasped less than three fingerbreadths of the object.[18]
> The seller is not permitted to retain or to cut off a bit of the object, because the acquisition is commonly taken to involve a stipulation to return the object used for symbolic exchange to its owner or owners.[19]
> An object can be used for symbolic exchange only with the agreement of its owner or owners. Thus one who has taken a kerchief without the owner's consent, and has effected acquisition therewith, has not effected valid acquisition. There is a further opinion that even if the object was lawfully borrowed by a person and he effected acquisition therewith, no acquisition has in fact been effect-

ed unless the object was borrowed for that specific purpose, and thus does the law appear to me.[20]

5) There is an opinion[21] that acquisition (of this type) is not effective unless the transferor does in fact transfer the property sold or given immediately. If, however, the acquirer said, "Acquire this kerchief (now) and my acquisition of your property will be effected thirty days hence," no acquisition has been effected. When the time comes for the acquisition of the property to commence, the transferor has long since returned the kerchief (of symbolic exchange) to the purchaser. If, however, the acquirer said,[22] "Acquire this kerchief (now) on condition that my acquisition of your property shall commence retroactively as from now once thirty days have elapsed," acquisition has been effected.

> GLOSS: In the absence of indications to the contrary, we hold that an acquirer has included an effective stipulation of retroactivity, since surely the acquirer is not merely trifling[23] (but has entered the transaction seriously and soberly).

6) Even though a transaction involving acquisition by symbolic kerchief exchange[24] has been concluded, both parties can withdraw as long as they are still involved with that same specific transaction. If they have broken off their dealing with that specific transaction (and moved to other matters, or separated), neither party can withdraw from that transaction.

7) In the other modes of effecting acquisition,[25] neither party can withdraw from the transaction after the first moment succeeding the transaction.

8) One authority has written[26] that if one has explicitly stated at the time of transacting symbolic kerchief acquisition that no withdrawal shall be allowed, or if they have written an instrument of transfer, or if they have accepted certain persons as arbitrators in a matter of acquisition, even though the parties are still involved with that specific transaction (of symbolic kerchief), neither is permitted to withdraw after the first moment succeeding the transaction.

9) The same modes of acquisition valid for sale of land[27] are valid to effect both lease and borrowing of land.

> GLOSS: This holds even where money payment does not effect acquisition without an instrument of transfer, cf. supra ch. 190:16; in any case money alone is sufficient in a matter of lease of land.[28]

And there are those who say that lease and borrowing of land are not effected by symbolic kerchief exchange.[29]

10) A lease (treated as a sale for a term) and a pledge of land[30] are not acquired by the redefinition of a loan, owed by the seller to the buyer, (into a "purchase price," i.e., a rental).

> GLOSS: This is so because both lease and pledge of land are treated as sales; and acquisition in sale is not effected by the redefinition of a loan (as a price) -- even if (one redefines it) as monetary consideration.[31]

11) Acquisition by means of symbolic kerchief exchange is not to be effected on the Sabbath. If parties have effected such acquisition, it is valid even though they have committed a transgression.[32]

196: The rule governing acquisition of a non-Jewish slave. Five paragraphs.

1) The rule governing the acquiring of a non-Jewish slave is the same as the rule governing the acquisition of land:[1] acquisition of such a slave is effected by money payment, by written instrument of transfer, by performing a possessive act with the slave, or by symbolic kerchief exchange.

> GLOSS: Such a slave is also acquired by the act of pulling; e.g., the acquirer has seized such a slave and brought him toward himself, as will be explained infra.[2]

2) A possessive act by which acquisition of a non-Jewish slave is effected is demonstrated by making use of the slave, in the presence

of his master, to perform for oneself a personal service customarily performed by slaves.[3] If such an act is performed outside the presence of the master,[4] it is necessary that the master shall have said to the acquirer, "Go, perform a possessive act, and acquire thereby."[5]

3) A personal service[6] may consist of taking off the shoe from the master's foot, or putting a shoe on the new master's foot, or walking behind the new master and carrying his personal gear to the bathhouse, or undressing the new master, or oiling the new master's body, or scraping oil from the new master's body, or dressing the new master, or lifting the new master: acquisition is effected by means of any one of these possessive acts. There is an opinion[7] that acquisition has been effected also if the new master lifts up the slave.

4) If the slave has performed a service which is not part of the physical care of the body, e.g., he sewed the master's torn garment, etc., the master has effected acquisition thereby;[8] there is also the opinion that the master has not effected acquisition thereby.[9]

5) If a master has seized a slave[10] and brought him to himself, acquisition of that slave has been effected. If, however, the master called to him and he came over to the master, or the former master said, "Go to the buyer," and he went, no acquisition has been effected. If the slave is a minor and the master called him -- and he went to him, acquisition has been effected.[11]

197: The rule covering acquisition of both large and small domesticated animals. Seven paragraphs.

1) Whether a domesticated animal is large or small, it is not acquired[1] by delivery (of the animal to the new owner); rather, acquisition is effected by the act of pulling the animal toward oneself. It is not necessary to lift the animal physically.

> GLOSS: There is an opinion that delivery effects[2] acquisition in the case of large animals, and there is an opinion that delivery effects acquisition even with a small animal,[3] if it is conducted in the presence of the seller. See infra 198:8-13, *re* rules governing delivery: if a

seller has said that acquisition is to be effected by the
act of pulling, but the buyer changed the mode to one less
legally advantageous (see next paragraph), e.g., to simple
delivery, or to one more legally advantageous, e.g.,
actual lifting, no acquisition has been effected except
by the act of pulling as the seller had stated.[4]

2) Physical lifting effects acquisition in any location,[5] but
pulling effects acquisition only in a recessed alcove directly off
the public area or in a courtyard jointly owned by the transferor
and the acquirer[6] -- but not in a public area or in a courtyard not
jointly owned by the transferor and the acquirer.

3) In regard to a domesticated animal,[7] one need not belabor the
point that acquisition is effected if one has pulled the animal, and
it follows that it is effected by mounting the animal and riding it,
but acquisition is effected[8] even if one called to the animal and it
came to one or if one struck the animal with a rod (or led it by the
sound of one's voice)[9] and it ran on in front of the acquirer: once
the animal has lifted its feet[10] in a walking motion, acquisition
has been effected.

The pulling of the animal for purposes of acquisition is to be done
in the presence of its (former) owner,[11] and if done outside that
owner's presence, it is necessary that the owner shall have stated
prior to such pulling, "Go, pull, and effect acquisition thereby."

4) If one sells a flock of domesticated animals[12] to another, or
has given the flock as a gift, once the seller or donor has delivered the lead animal of the flock, i.e., the animal which all the
others follow, it is not necessary to say, "Pull and effect acquisition." If one did perform the acquiring act of pulling with the
(remainder of the) flock, even outside the presence of the (former
owner of the flock), acquisition has been effected, since delivery
of the lead animal is tantamount to the statement "Go, pull, and effect acquisition thereby."

> GLOSS: If one has sold a book which is published in two
> volumes, and has given the buyer half of it, i.e., one of
> the two volumes, and the buyer goes and pulls or lifts
> the second volume (without the consent of its owner),[13]

no acquisition has been effected, because the part of the book which the seller gave is not like a leading animal in a flock.[14]

If the seller did not deliver a leading animal and sold only ten animals (out of the flock), if acquisition was effected by the act of pulling, only the animal actually pulled has been acquired. If acquisition was effected by delivery, if the transferor delivered them in one act of giving possession and the acquirer gave the purchase price for all the animals, acquisition has been effected. If he did not give the full price, acquisition of animals has been effected to the extent of the money value paid, as has been explained above in respect to land, ch. 192, end.[15]

5) If one sells or gives an animal to another[16] and says, "Effect acquisition after the fashion that people use to effect acquisition," if he pulled the animal, or lifted it, acquisition has been effected. If, however, he rode on the animal: if such riding was in a field (or in a recessed alcove directly off the public area),[17] acquisition has been effected. If such riding occurred in a city (in a public area),[18] no acquisition has been effected, since people do not ordinarily ride within the city. Therefore[19] if the acquirer was a well-known personage, who would customarily go mounted in the city; or a person of no consequence or standing at all, who does not care in the slightest about his transportation in the city, e.g., one who professionally tends to the care of animals, or slaves, or a woman;[20] or the riding occurred in a very crowded public area, acquisition has been effected by the act of riding the animal, provided it will go with him.

6) If A says to B, "Pull, and you shall effect acquisition,"[21] or, "Perform an act of possession and you shall effect acquisition," etc., and B goes and does pull or performs the possessive act, no acquisition has been effected, since the connotation of *you shall effect acquisition* is for the future, at some future time, and as yet, presently, no acquisition has been transferred. This same interpretation applies if A says to B, "Pull this object to acquire it." (It is necessary to say, "Pull and acquire," or, "Perform a

possessive act and acquire.")[22]

7) If A says to B, "Pull this cow, but you shall not effect acquisition thereby until thirty days hence,"[23] and B does pull the cow toward him, no acquisition has been effected. If A says to B, "Effect acquisition retroactively as from today, once thirty days have elapsed,"[24] acquisition has been effected. Even if the cow was standing in a swamp on the thirtieth day (i.e., not in the acquirer's property), the acquisition has been effected,[25] for A is like one who transferred acquisition of the cow, from the present moment, conditionally. Once the condition has been satisfied, the acquisition is fully effected. Anyone who uses the language *on condition* is deemed to have used the language of retroactivity, i.e., "from now on."

198: The rule concerning acquisition of moveable property: which types are acquired by the act of pulling and which are acquired by delivery. The rule concerning the purchase price when a party withdraws from the transaction. Fifteen paragraphs.

1) According to biblical law, the payment of the purchase price effects acquisition.[1] The rabbinical sages, however, have ordained that acquisition of moveable goods shall not be effected except by physical lifting of the goods, or by the act of pulling in regard to something which is not ordinarily lifted.[2] (Once the acquirer has pulled or lifted [as the case may be], acquisition has been effected, even though the purchase price has not been paid.) This concept is amplified as follows: when one collects a load of sticks or of flax, etc.,[3] and gathers the sticks or the flax into a huge load that could not be lifted, it is not acquired by pulling, because it is possible to untie the load and lift it, e.g., stick by stick. If, however, the load were of nuts, peppercorns, or almonds, etc., which one could not lift, it is acquired by pulling. (There are those who disagree and reason as follows: even the load of sticks can be acquired by pulling, since the effort required to untie the bundle and lift each stick is excessive.) (See infra 200:7.)[4]

2) In regard to lifting:[5] one view holds that one must raise the

object three handbreadths, and another view holds that one handbreadth is sufficient.

3) In regard to pulling:[6] it is necessary that one pull the entire object and remove it from the entire space which it formerly occupied.

4) If one does lift objects which are not usually lifted (in order thereby to effect acquisition), one has effected acquisition.[7]

5) The reason why the rabbinical sages ordained that payment of the purchase price does not effect acquisition[8] is that perhaps a buyer might in fact pay the price for something and yet prior to his taking possession of it the thing might be destroyed in some accident, e.g., fire, or brigands might carry it off. If the thing were deemed to be under the legal control of the buyer, the seller might not be quick to attempt to rescue the thing. Therefore the rabbinical sages deemed the thing to have remained under the legal control of the seller, so that he might indeed attempt to rescue it.

Therefore,[9] if the thing sold was located in a building belonging to the buyer, which building was leased to the seller, the rabbinical sages invoked the biblical law that the payment of the price effects acquisition, since the thing is in fact conveniently located on the buyer's property and he is able (to attempt) to rescue it. Similarly,[10] when one is the lessee of property, such lease having been validated by a mode of acquisition appropriate to a lease, cf. 195:9, the lessee has effected acquisition (by payment of price alone) of things sold (to him) when those things are located on that leased property. Neither party can withdraw from the contract of sale (relating to these items located where the buyer is in a position to protect the things) -- provided[11] that the courtyard (i.e., the leased property) is in fact under the guardianship of the lessee, who is aware that he is exercising such guardianship, or that the lessee is himself located adjacent to that place of storage of the goods sold to him.

> GLOSS: There is an opinion[12] that if the goods are stored in a place where there is no danger of fire, the payment of the purchase price effects acquisition; similarly, if the parties explicitly stipulated that payment of the

purchase price shall effect acquisition, it is effected thereby.

6) There is an opinion[13] that in regard to the lease of moveable goods, such lease is effected by a money payment, since there is no cause to be apprehensive that the lessor would say, "*Your* wheat has been burned in the loft"; since the lessor's ultimate ownership of the goods has not been extinguished, he would indeed take pains to rescue the goods in case of fire.

7) Since a ship cannot be physically lifted[14] (by an individual), and pulling it requires enormous effort and can be accomplished only by a large number of people, pulling was not required for effecting acquisition thereof. Delivery alone will effect acquisition. This rule holds good similarly for all large objects.

If the seller said[15] to the buyer, "Go, pull, and effect acquisition thereby," acquisition has not been effected until the buyer shall have pulled the vessel completely and removed it from the place it formerly occupied.[16] The seller (in this case) has shown himself most particular that pulling shall be the only means whereby acquisition shall be effected.

8) The delivery of which the rabbinical sages spoke[17] need not be delivery which passes directly from the hand of the seller to the hand of the buyer. Once the buyer has grasped the object in the presence of the seller, or at his express command, delivery has been effected.

9) Delivery effects acquisition only in a public area[18] or in a courtyard which belongs to neither party (which they entered without the consent of the owner of the courtyard). Pulling effects acquisition only in the recessed alcove directly off a public area, or in a courtyard belonging to the parties jointly. Lifting effects acquisition in any location.

> GLOSS: If a seller has told the buyer to effect acquisition by delivery or by pulling in a location where neither mode of acquisition is valid, such a statement is invalid and no acquisition has been effected (should either mode be employed).[19]

10) Thus, if a ship was in a public place[20] or in a courtyard belonging to neither party, and the seller has explicitly shown himself to be most particular concerning the mode of acquisition he wishes employed and says to the buyer, "Pull and effect acquisition thereby," it then becomes necessary to pull the vessel completely and remove it entirely from that location where pulling does not effect acquisition and bring it into a location where pulling does effect acquisition.

11) If the ship was standing in a recessed alcove[21] off the public area or in a courtyard belonging to the parties jointly, acquisition is effected only by pulling, not by delivery.

12) If the ship was standing in a public place and the seller made no explicit statement regarding the mode of acquisition to be employed,[22] and the buyer went and pulled (the vessel), no acquisition has been effected until the pulling has been accomplished as required by law: from a public area to a recessed area off such a public area. Even though the vessel is lawfully acquired by delivery in a public area, which delivery need not pass directly from the hand of the seller to the hand of the buyer, even so, once the buyer has commenced the process of pulling, he has forthwith demonstrated his intention that he wishes to effect acquisition by pulling and not by the act of seizing and holding it.

13) There is an opinion that a ship is not acquired by pulling it except if the pulling be done after the normal fashion of such an act with reference to a vessel;[23] e.g., the ship is fully afloat in water, or it is in very shallow water close to deeper water, located in a recess adjacent to a public area or in a space which belongs to the parties jointly. If, however, the vessel is on dry land, acquisition is not effected until one lifts it.

14) With reference to an object which is acquired by the act of pulling,[24] if the object is in a public area or in a courtyard which does not belong to the parties jointly, and the buyer pulls it to his property or to a recessed alcove adjacent to the public area, once he has removed it partially from the public area, or the courtyard not jointly possessed, acquisition has been effected since he has in fact pulled the entire object and removed it from the whole space it formerly occupied (in the public area, etc.).[25]

15) When a buyer has paid all or part of a purchase price for

moveable goods[26] (acquisition not having been formally effected), and he withdraws from the transaction, and the seller says, "Come, take back your money," the buyer's money in the seller's possession ranks as a deposit, so that if it is stolen or lost, the seller bears no responsibility for it. If, however, the seller withdraws from the transaction and says to the buyer, "Come, take back your money," the funds are deemed to be under his control, and he is held responsible for them, even in the case of major unavoidable mishaps,[27] until the seller shall accept the formal rabbinic condemnation of "He who punished" and shall afterwards say to the buyer, "Come, take back your money." Then, if in fact the very same currency or coins paid by the buyer are still physically in the possession of the seller, the seller is relieved of liability. If, however, the seller spent them and designated other monies instead of them, and he accepted the formal rabbinic condemnation in regard to the money, there is one opinion[28] that the money goes back to the buyer as if it had been a loan, and (thus) the seller is liable for the funds, even in the case of unavoidable mishaps and accidents, until they come into the effective control of the buyer once again; there is another opinion[29] that even if the seller had spent the monies, once he accepted the formula of rabbinical condemnation, and he gives them back (i.e., albeit *other* coins, etc.), he is relieved of responsibility -- even if the buyer did not wish to accept them.

199: There are modes and occasions in which the payment of money does affect acquisition (of moveable goods). Four paragraphs.

1) Money (alone) may effect acquisition[1] (of moveable goods) when a buyer holds in his hand a certain sum of money which has neither been counted nor weighed, and the buyer says, "Sell me your item for this money I have in my hand," and the seller takes it but does not take care to count it; the item has been acquired by the buyer. Neither party can withdraw from the transaction. Since this is an unusual type of transaction, the rabbinic sages did not declare a prohibition regarding it.

> GLOSS: Even if the buyer knew how much money he had in his hand, but he simply said, "Sell me them for these (coins)," and the seller did not take care to count them, there are some who would hold that acquisition has been effected.[2]

2) Similarly: when A sells moveable goods to B[3] for a *maneh*, and B effects acquisition of the goods and becomes liable for their purchase price, and afterwards B has other goods for sale and A says to B, "Sell them to me for the money of the purchase price, which money you still possess from the previous sale," and B agrees, A has effected acquisition of the goods, wherever they may be located, even though he has neither pulled nor lifted them. This is also an unusual type of transaction which the rabbinic sages did not declare to be prohibited.

If, however, B owed money to A because of some transaction other than the previous sale of goods by A to B (e.g., a loan), and A said, "Sell me the goods for the debt which you owe me," and both parties have agreed to this transaction, no acquisition has been effected.

> GLOSS: But there is an opinion that[4] acquisition is effected in such a transaction only when A says, "Sell me the goods in exchange for the *benefit* accruing to you by my forgiving you the previous purchase price." If, however, A simply said, "Sell me the goods for the money of the purchase price, which money is mine but you still possess it," no acquisition has been effected. See infra 204:10.

3) There are specific occasions[5] on which money alone effects acquisition for moveable goods, because the rabbinic sages ordained that the biblical rule on acquisition of moveables shall hold good in regard to the purchase of meat on four occasions during the year:[6] the eve of the last day of Sukkot; the eve of the first day of Pesah; the eve of Shavuoth; the eve of Rosh Hashanah.

If the butcher had an ox valued at one hundred *dinars*, and that butcher took from the buyer one *dinar* as payment for fresh meat when the butcher shall slaughter that ox, but the butcher did not receive sufficient prepayment for all the value of the meat animal to be slaughtered, the butcher can be required to slaughter the animal even though he does not wish to do so, in order to furnish the *dinar's* worth of meat to the buyer. Therefore, if the ox should die prior to its slaughter, the buyer has lost his *dinar*.

> GLOSS: One authority has written[7] that this rule also applies to prepayment for Sabbath kiddush wine on the eve of Sabbath; i.e., acquisition has been effected, since in any situation analogous to the case of the prepayment for the meat on the occasions specified, the rabbinic sages ordained that the biblical rule on acquisition of moveable goods shall apply.

4) Orphans or their legal guardians who have sold moveable goods,[8] which the buyer has pulled but not yet paid for, and which goods have sharply increased in value in the marketplace, may withdraw from the transaction. This type of transaction is governed by the biblical rule under which money, not pulling, effects acquisition (but in any event the buyer, who is presumed to be in possession of the goods, is responsible for them as though he were a paid bailee for them[9]).

The law for orphans (in regard to sales) is distinguished from the law for other classes of persons in this one particular only.[10] In other matters of sales the law for orphans is the same as that for all other (Jews).

> GLOSS: This rule (that orphans are on a par with all others except for the one distinction specified) applies only to orphans[11]; but sacred and charitable institutions effect acquisition of moveable property by means of money. Thus, if one gave money to a sacred institution to purchase an item, which rose in value, that institution cannot withdraw from the transaction.

200: The rule concerning effecting acquisition of moveable goods by means of one's property – real or moveable. Twelve paragraphs.

1) (If) moveable goods (to be acquired) are located on the real property of the buyer and that location is under the conscious supervision of the buyer:[1]

> GLOSS: There are those who disagree and reason that in a sale or a gift, it is sufficient if the location, where the goods are, is under the conscious supervision of the seller or the donor (i.e., he has leased it from the buyer). This appears to me as the better course of decision.[2] But if the seller has leased that location to the buyer, and the moveable goods to be sold are still stored there with other movable goods of the seller, so that one cannot tell what is to be sold from other goods, the location is not deemed to be under conscious supervision.[3]

Or if the buyer is standing at the side of his real property,[4] where the goods are (there is an opinion that he must be within the real property -- but not outside it),[5] once the seller has undertaken to sell these goods,[6] the buyer has effected acquisition, even though one has not yet measured out the goods, provided that a purchase price has been set.[7] (There are those who hold that the acquisition of moveables is effected if they are located within the immediate four square cubits within which a man is standing, as is the case with found goods.)[8]

2) If the moveable goods to be sold were located on the real property of the seller or of a third party[9] with whom they were deposited, the buyer has effected no acquisition until he either lifts the goods or pulls them, as has been explained.

> GLOSS: If, however, the buyer was the lessee of the location[10] where the moveable goods to be sold were stored, or the place had been given him as a gift, acquisition of such lease or gift having been made by an act of acquisition or (in the case of a depositee's location) even by mere oral declaration of such lease or gift, the buyer has effected acquisition of the goods.
> The location is deemed to be his and it effects acquisition for him.[11] The validity of the oral declaration

applies in the case that the goods are on the property of a third party. If they were on the seller's property, and the seller said, "Let my courtyard effect ownership on behalf of the buyer in regard to the goods he purchased from me," no acquisition has been effected until the seller shall lease the place to the buyer and acquisition thereof be effected by one of the lawful modes of acquisition.[12] If the goods were deposited on the property of a third party, it is not sufficient that the third party shall say, "My courtyard shall effect acquisition for the buyer," until he shall so declare with the consent of the seller.[13]

3) A man's utensils effect acquisition for him[14] in any location where he enjoys the right to place those utensils. Once moveable goods have been put in such a utensil, neither party (in the sale of these moveable goods) can withdraw from the transaction. This matter is the same as placing the goods in the man's house.

> GLOSS: There are those who differ and hold that if they are not on the buyer's property, but in a recessed alcove adjacent to a public area, etc., utensils do not effect acquisition unless (the seller) measured out the goods (to be sold) or until (the seller) shall have said, "Go, effect acquisition."[15]
> Therefore one's utensils do not effect acquisition in public areas or on the seller's property[16] unless the transferor of ownership has said, "Go, effect acquisition with this utensil." Then acquisition has been effected if one is on the seller's property.[17]

4) Thus, if one has purchased a utensil from the seller and lifted it,[18] and afterwards placed it down on the seller's property, and then went back and purchased produce from that same seller, once the produce is in that utensil, acquisition of the produce has been effected. The seller does not care or mind that the utensil was on his property, because of his own benefit in the sale of that utensil.

5) Just as the buyer's utensils do not effect acquisition for him

on property of the seller,[19] so the seller's utensil does not effect acquisition for the buyer even though it is on the property of the buyer. (There are those who say this holds good even if the seller said to the buyer, "Go, effect acquisition": no acquisition has been effected.)[20]

6) Acquisition by pulling is validly effected with the utensils of the seller if the seller has measured the goods out and put them into his utensil,[21] whereupon the buyer pulls that utensil in the presence of the seller: acquisition has been effected even if the seller has not said, "Pull the utensil to effect acquisition of what is in it."

7) Neither one's real property, nor one's utensil, nor the act of pulling, nor the act of lifting effects acquisition unless it has first been settled that a specific amount of goods will go for a specific price.[22] As long as amount and price have not been agreed upon, there is no mode by which one can effect acquisition.[23] As long as amount and price have not been settled, neither party is deemed to have agreed with full resolve to the transaction: perhaps they may not concur as to price.

If the item is something which has a known fixed price,[24] even though the parties have not settled the matter of price, acquisition has been effected (by one of the modes of acquisiiton, if performed). Similarly if A says to B, "I shall sell you the item for the price that shall be set for it by a group of three appraisers," acquisition has been effected (if performed) even if the item has no known fixed price.[25]

If produce was in a recessed alcove off the public area or in a courtyard belonging to both parties jointly,[26] or even if it was on the property of the buyer, but in the utensil of the seller, if then the seller undertook to sell the goods and began to measure them out into his own utensil: if the seller said, "I sell you a *kor* at thirty *selas*,"[27] the seller can withdraw from the transaction even at the last *seah* (one *kor* equals thirty *seahs*), since the goods are still in *his* utensils, and the measurement of the full amount to be sold has not been completed. The utensils of the seller do not effect acquisition for the buyer, even on the buyer's property.

The Laws of Buying and Selling

GLOSS: There is an opinion that if one expresses the intent to sell only one entire *kor* of produce altogether, even if it was on the property of the buyer, or the buyer pulled or lifted it, no acquisition has been effected unless the seller has measured out the entire *kor*.[28]

If the seller said, "I am selling you a *kor* at thirty *selas*, (each) *seah* for a *sela*," the buyer effects acquisition of them one by one: once they have agreed on the price of each *seah*,[29] each *seah* that the seller lifts and empties (from his measuring instrument) is the subject of a completed sale, since the produce is not on the seller's property, nor in a public place. If the produce had not been in the utensil of the seller, the buyer would have effected acquisition after amount and price had been settled, even without the measuring out of the goods, since they were on the buyer's property, as has been explained in para. 3.

GLOSS: There is an opinion that the acquisition of each *seah*, one by one, is by reason of physical possession by the buyer;[30] therefore if he has not paid the price for the goods, the buyer may withdraw from the transaction (he is also in continuing possession of the money).
A seller opened a barrel of wine for a buyer. When the seller had measured out half of it, the buyer wanted to withdraw and not take any more. The seller said that the remainder would keep. The buyer in this case had to accept the entire barrel or accept liability for the remainder, should it spoil: he would make full payment to the seller for the whole barrel according to its value when he effected acquisition of it (i.e., the wine he purchased).[31]
There is an opinion that this ruling applies only when the seller has measured the wine; if the buyer has measured the wine, he has effected acquisition of the entire barrel because his act of measurement perforce involved pulling it.[32] There are those who differ with this latter view.[33]
In every case where acquisition of the subject of the sale has been effected, neither buyer nor seller can withdraw from the transaction even though differences of opinion

concerning it emerged and the seller refused to deliver the goods to the buyer. They must go to law over their differences.[34]

8) If a buyer has brought donkeys,[35] carrying crops, into a building of his, that pulling (of the donkeys) has no legal effect (regarding the crops), even if a price had been set and the seller measured out the crops loaded onto the donkeys: no acquisition of the crops has been effected. There is an opinion that even if the buyer measured out the crops for loading on the donkey, no acquisition has been effected, since (any) pulling (in the process) was not performed with the intent (of effecting acquisition of the crops), nor was the act of measuring (the crops) performed with the intent (of effecting acquisition) -- it was intended merely as a simple measuring out of the crops. (There are those who differ with this view and hold that if the buyer has measured the crops, acquisition has been effected, as has been explained.)

9) If one sells wine or oil to another in a recessed alcove off a public area,[36] or in a courtyard which belongs to the parties jointly, or on the property of the buyer, and the measuring vessel belonged to a middleman (i.e., an agent or a broker): until the measuring vessel is full, the item belongs to the seller; once it is full, it passes to the ownership of the buyer; and neither party can withdraw from the transaction. So too with produce:[37] if it was heaped in the recessed alcove off the public area, or in a courtyard belonging to the parties jointly, and the measuring vessel does not belong to either party, and the seller measured out the produce: until the measuring vessel is full, the goods are under the ownership of the seller; once the measuring vessel is full, the goods are under the ownership of the buyer.

(10) If the measuring vessel belonged to one of the parties,[38] and it was calibrated to show quantities of one-fourth measure, one-third measure, one-half measure, etc.; as the vessel is filled to each calibration mark, that portion of the whole is acquired, even though the entire vessel is not yet full. Each calibration mark is considered a measure unto itself: each portion is a separate measure. And one relies on the calibration marks (as both accurate and

sufficient for effecting acquisition).

(There are those who say that if the measuring instrument belongs to the seller, no acquisition has been effected until the seller empties the measuring vessel.)[39]

11) When one takes an object from an artisan for the purpose of examining it[40] (for quality, workmanship, etc.), if it had a set price and it was destroyed while in the examiner's possession,[41] the one who took it is liable for that set price. From the moment he lifted it, it was (legally) under his control, and the seller could not withdraw from this transaction, provided that such lifting would be in order to effect acquisition of the whole of the object, and that the object for sale was attractive to the buyer.[42] But merchandise which the seller does not care for and tries very hard to sell remains under the legal control of the seller until a price is settled upon for the object and the buyer lifts it after the price has been settled upon. If the buyer expressed himself to the effect that he does not want the item (he is examining) and it is lost or stolen before he can return it, one opinion deems the buyer a paid bailee in regard to the item and another opinion deems him a gratuitous bailee in regard to the item.[43]

12) If one has himself pulled, lifted, or performed a possessive act[44] (to effect acquisition of an item) or has told another to lift, pull, or perform the possessive act on his behalf, he has thereby affected acquisition. This holds good also for the other modes of effecting acquisition.

201: The rule governing a purchaser's mark put on a barrel and the legal significance of shaking hands on a transaction. Two paragraphs.

1) If a vendor has made a verbal agreement to sell,[1] and the parties have settled the matter of price, and the buyer has put his mark on the goods in order that he have it as a specific symbol that the merchandise is his, even though he has not yet paid any of the agreed-upon price, whoever withdraws from this type of transaction, receives the formal rabbinic condemnation of "He who punished."[2] If it is the prevalent custom of that country that such buyers' marks shall effect full acquisition, the object is deemed

fully acquired by the buyer thereby. Neither party can withdraw from the transaction; the buyer is liable for the purchase price. All this holds good provided that the mark has been made in the presence of the seller or the seller has said, "Mark your purchase."[3]

2) Similarly, all means by which businessmen customarily effect (and validate) acquisition[4] (in sales), e.g., the buyer gives the seller a token coin, or a handshake,[5] (or in a place where the prevalent custom among merchants is the delivery of the key [to where the goods are stored] to the buyer)[6] and all other such means (are deemed valid for effecting acquisition).

202: The rule governing acquisition of moveable goods as a consequence of acquisition of land; or land and slaves; and coincident acquisition of a slave and moveable goods; or a domesticated animal and the utensils on it. Fifteen paragraphs.

1) When one transfers ownership of one's land and moveable goods as one block of property,[1] once the transferee has effected acquisition of the land by one of the modes of acquisition appropriate thereto, acquisition of the moveable goods has also been effected. This is so whether both land and moveables were sold or given as a gift;[2] or the moveables were sold and the land was given as a gift, or the land was sold and the moveables given as a gift; once acquisition of the land has been effected, acquisition of the moveables has been effected thereby. (There is an opinion that even if the land was leased to the acquirer, and the moveables were given as a gift, acquisition of the moveables is effected by the acquisition of the land.)[3]

2) The above rule applies when the moveable goods are located on the land to be acquired.[4] If, however, the moveables were located elsewhere, the transferor must say, "Acquire the moveable goods as a consequence of acquiring land." Even if the moveables were in another country and the transferor said, "Acquire them as a consequence[3] of acquiring a particular parcel of land," once acquisition of the land has been effected, acquisition of the moveables has been effected, even though the moveables are not located on that land. If the transferor did not speak the formula "Acquire as a consequence

of acquiring the land," no acquisition of moveables has been effected if they are not located on that land.

> GLOSS: There is an opinion which holds that even if the moveable goods are located on that land, the transferor must use the formula "Acquire as a consequence of acquiring the land";[5] this opinion appears to me to be the essentially correct one. There is an opinion which holds that the language "as a consequence of" is required in the transaction; the word "with" is insufficient: there are those who disagree on this point.[6]

3) If one transfers ownership of the piece of land to A and the moveable goods to B,[7] even though the transferor said, "Acquire the moveable goods as a consequence of the acquisition of the land," and A took possession of the land, B has not effected acquisition of the moveable goods. If B seizes those goods after the transferor has withdrawn from the transaction (in regard to moveables), the goods are not to be taken away from B by Jewish judicial process, because he did seize them after A had effected acquisition of the land, as a consequence of which the goods were to be acquired. (There are those who disagree and reason that the goods may be taken away from B, under the rule which provides that when a doubt arises as to the legal ownership of property, seizure of the property does not resolve the doubt or cure a defective title.[8])

4) If one transfers ownership of the land to the guardian of an orphan and the moveable goods to the orphan,[9] acquisition (of the moveables) has been effected. (The same rule applies to a collector of funds for Jewish charitable causes.)

5) Domestic animals are deemed moveable property in (the interpretation of) these rules.

6) Land is not acquired as a consequence of the acquisition of (other) land.[10]

7) The smallest piece of land may be used to effect the acquisition of a large amount of moveable goods.[11]

> GLOSS: The requirement specifying the smallest piece of real property is to preclude (the validity of such a

transaction) if we have certain knowledge that the transferor has no amount of real property. When, however, we have no knowledge that he does not own real property, and he does transfer as a consequence of real property, that is satisfactory. It is not necessary to specify the land, as a consequence of whose acquisition by another, he transfers ownership of moveable goods. This one may transfer in consequence of acquisition of land of a mere four cubits square space, even though we do not know that he owns such land,[12] cf. supra ch. 113. One may transfer ownership of moveable goods as a consequence of transferring ownership of one's seat in a synagogue; even though those seats are in a public area, each person takes one place, and it is as though that place were borrowed (by the transferor and thus his lawful property for the purposes of this rule): and we transfer (moveable goods) as a consequence of transferring such seats in the synagogue.[13]

8) If one transfers ownership of slaves and a piece of land as one lot of items,[14] when the acquirer has performed a possessive act with the slaves, he has not effected acquisition of the land. If the acquirer performed a possessive act with the land, and the slaves were present on that land, acquisition of the slaves has been effected. If the slaves were not present at that location, no acquisition of them has been effected[15] even if the transferor says, "Effect acquisition of them as a consequence of acquiring the land."

9) If one transfers ownership of slaves and moveable goods as one lot of items, when the acquirer pulls the moveable goods to effect acquisition, no acquisition of the slaves has been effected;[16] when the acquirer has performed a possessive act with the slaves, no acquisition of the moveable goods has been effected unless the moveable goods were on the slaves,[17] and the slaves were immobile in stocks. There is an opinion that holds that the slaves must also be asleep.

10) If A owned an earthenware planter,[18] with a hole in it (so that the earth in the planter was in direct contact with the ground), and B owned the seeds in that planter, if A transferred

ownership of the planter to B, once B has pulled the planter, acquisition has been effected.

11) If the owner of the seeds in the planter transferred ownership of those seeds to the owner of the planter, no acquisition of the seeds has been effected until the owner of the planter shall perform a possessive act with the seeds themselves.[19]

12) If A owned both the planter and the seeds in it, and A transferred the ownership of both items to B,[20] if B performed a possessive act with the planter for the purpose of acquiring the seeds in it, B has not even effected acquisition of the planter. If B performed a possessive act with the seeds, he has effected acquisition of the planter.[21] (There is an opinion to the effect that a wooden planter requires a perforation so that the earth in it is in contact with the ground beneath it; but an earthenware planter, even unperforated, is considered as if perforated;[22] and there is an opinion which maintains exactly the opposite view.[23])

13) If A transfers ownership of an animal and the utensils on it as one lot of items, even though B pulled the animal and effected acquisition of it, he has not effected acquisition of the utensils until he shall lift them, or pull them if they are not subject to lifting.[24] The animal is deemed a "moving courtyard," and the contents of such a location are not acquired by the owner of that location in virtue of being present there. Therefore, if the animal was tethered, B has effected acquisition of the utensils.[25]

There is an opinion to this effect: with regard to found property, if one says, "I pull this animal for the purpose of acquiring it and the utensils on it," acquisition has been effected even if the animal is not tethered.[26]

14) If a seller says to a buyer, "Pull this animal and effect acquisition of the utensils on it," since he did not transfer ownership of the animal itself, even though the buyer of the utensils pulled it, and it is tethered, no acquisition of the utensils has been effected.[27]

15) If a seller said to a buyer, "Pull this strongbox, and by pulling it, effect acquisition of whatever is in it," (the pulling) has effected acquisition of the contents of the box, even though acquisition of the box is not effected.[28]

203: Acquisition of all moveable goods is effected by exchange; acquisition of coins is not effected by exchange. Ten paragraphs.

1) All moveable goods can be used to effect acquisition with respect to each other by means of exchange.[1] It goes without saying that this rule applies when a transferor does not particularly care to know the value of the object which he takes in exchange; as when acquisition is effected by exchange of the kerchief,[2] which effects a completely valid acquisition for all things, whether real or moveable (except for documents, see above ch. 66) or livestock; or even agricultural produce, even though it cannot itself be used to effect acquisition, it can be acquired by means of exchange.[3] The exception is coinage, which can neither be acquired nor be employed to effect acquisition, by means of exchange;[4] also a thing which does not have physical substance cannot validly be the subject of acquisition,[5] e.g., a formal act of acquisition was performed regarding a promise that A shall acccompany B to a particular place, or that A and B should divide a piece of real estate between them (see above, 157:2), etc., since these are really acquisitions of mere words (i.e., intangible) and the acquisition affects nothing of physical substance.

> GLOSS: The value of a favor or a particular advantage conferred by A upon B does not rank as money value, and a right thereto cannot be acquired by exchange.[6] See below ch. 245: If A says, "I shall give a thing to B," whether such an assertion is merely an acquisition of an intangible thing (i.e., words). If A performs a formal act effecting acquisition for B to the end that A shall indite a document forgiving some financial obligation, this too is an acquisition of an intangible thing, because such a document is merely the extinguishing of an obligation (not a specific tangible object of commerce). We do not have acquisition of an intangible if A performs the formal act effecting acquisition with B to the end that A return all evidences of his rights against B.[7]

Even if the transferor takes particular care to know the value of the object which he takes in exchange, which object is now analogous to a sum of money, even here, acquisition is effected with the exchange.[8] This is demonstrated in the following example:[9] A has a cow and B has a donkey. They mutually assess the value of each animal and agree to exchange them, one for the other. Once the owner of the cow has pulled the donkey, acquisition of his cow has been effected for the owner of the donkey, wherever that donkey may be located. Neither party can withdraw from the transaction. (There is an opinion to the effect that if the two parties have set the values of two agricultural products, one in terms of the other, acquisition can then be effected even by means of [exchange of these] agricultural products; there are those who hold a contrary opinion.)[10]

2) If one was to exchange a donkey for a cow and a lamb, and pulled the cow but not the lamb, no acquisition has been effected, since there has been no complete act of pulling[11] (with reference to both animals). There is an opinion to the effect that only in the circumstance just described[12] has no acquisition taken effect; since the donkey cannot be divided (without destroying it altogether), a portion of it corresponding in value to the cow cannot be acquired in this transaction. If, however, one was to exchange a cow and a lamb for a *kor* of wheat, and the transferee pulled the cow but not the lamb, acquisition of wheat has been effected for the transferor of the cow up to the value of the cow. (There is an opinion to the effect that if A exchanged goods with B and C, and either B or C withdrew from the transaction, the acquisition is entirely void.)[13]

3) Bars of gold, silver, and other metals are like other moveable goods;[14] acquisition thereof may be effected by exchange, and acquisition of one type of metal may be effected by exchange for another type of metal. Coinage in silver or gold or copper ranks as money with regard to all moveable goods.[15] If one gives a coin as the price of moveable goods, no acquisition of the goods has been effected;[16] no coin is acquired through exchange as a mode of acquisition; nor may a coin be used to effect acquisition by exchange.

> GLOSS: Therefore when A designates a given, specific, and particular set of coins and is to transfer ownership of them to B by means of exchange of moveable goods,

> since acquisition of the money has not been effected for B, A has not effected acquisition of the moveable goods. This is so even if A has pulled the moveable goods. This rule is specifically in regard to the rule on exchange, when A has designated a given, specific, and particular set of coins (to be exchanged for moveable goods); but with money tendered as a purchase price, once the buyer has pulled the object, he is immediately obligated to pay the price set for it.[17]

4) The above rules apply when one sells other moveable goods for one of the above-mentioned types of metal.[18] But if one sells a coin for a coin, the gold *dinar* is held to be analogous to agricultural produce in respect to silver coinage.[19]

> GLOSS: If one transferred ownership of silver money as the purchase price, i.e., he did not specify a given, particular set of silver coins (as an exchange), once the buyer has pulled the gold coin (effecting acquisition), the buyer is liable for the purchase price in silver which was mutually[20] set.

Similarly copper money is deemed to be analogous to agricultural produce in respect to silver coinage.[21]

For example: A gives B a gold *dinar* valued at twenty-five silver *dinars*. Once B has pulled the gold *dinar*, he is liable for the twenty-five silver *dinars*, the agreed upon price: if (payment is to be made in) new coinage, then in new coinage; if in old coinage, then old coinage.[22] If however A gives B twenty-five silver *dinars* as a price for one gold *dinar*, A has not effected acquisition until he shall have taken the gold *dinar*.

5) If A gives B thirty copper *issars* for a silver dinar,[23] B is obliged to give A the silver *dinar*, the agreed upon price: if (payment is to be made in) new coinage, then in new coinage; if in old coinage, then old coinage. If however A gives B a silver *dinar* for thirty copper *issars*, A has not effected acquisition until he shall have taken the copper *issars*. (Our present) coinage is an alloy of silver and copper; it is deemed money in regard to silver coinage.[24]

6) As regards the status of copper money[25] in relation to gold coinage, one opinion holds that copper ranks as money in reference to gold; another opinion holds that copper ranks as agricultural produce in reference to gold.

7) All metal coinage ranks as money in reference to other types of moveable property;[26] each metal coinage ranks as money in reference to itself; for example, one sells a gold *dinar* for a gold *dinar*, or a silver *dinar* for a silver *dinar*, or a copper *dinar* for a copper *dinar*, all the respective coins are deemed to be coins for the purposes of this rule.

8) Bad coinage which a government has withdrawn from circulation,[27] or coinage which is not legal tender in a given locale and is not used for commercial purposes there until it is minted into different coinage,[28] ranks as agricultural produce in every respect. Acquisition of such coinage may be effected by means of performing an act of acquisition with it; and pulling it (for the purpose of effecting acquisition) makes one liable for the purchase price set for it. If one takes good coinage in exchange for them (intending thereby to confer acquisition of the bad coinage), no acquisition has been effected (i.e., they rank as moveable goods and acquisition is not effected by an exchange of good coinage for them).

> GLOSS: There is an opinion to the effect that even if coinage is not entirely defaced, but it does not openly circulate, it is deemed moveable goods (not money); this appears to be the fundamental rule.[29]

9) In regard to coinage, (therefore) there is no way that one who is not in control of the coins can assume ownership thereof (when the money is *not* given as a purchase price) except in consequence of an acquisition of land.[30] For example: one effects acquisition of coinage in consequence of an acquisition of land; or one becomes the lessee of the location of the coinage: once one has become the owner of the land, either by money payment, instrument of transfer, possessive act, or acquisition (by symbolic act of exchange), one has become owner of the coinage. This is so provided that the monies physically exist; for example, they were on deposit in another location and the depositary did not deny the deposit.[31] But in a case

where A was the creditor of B[32] and A transferred to C ownership of land, in consequence of which transfer, A transferred the debt to C, C has not effected acquisition of the monies of the debt. One may, however, transfer ownership of a debt owing (from a Jew) in the presence of the three involved parties (creditor, debtor, and prospective creditor), as explained in ch. 126; similarly one may transfer ownership of the debt to him by selling or giving him the note of indebtedness, as explained in ch. 66.

10) If one exchanges land for land, or moveable goods for land, or land for moveable goods,[33] once one party has assumed ownership of property received in the exchange, he is obliged to provide the specified property for exchange.

> GLOSS: If one has exchanged money and moveables or money and land, as a single block of property, one opinion holds that the entire transaction is void since exchange does not effect acquistion of money; a second opinion holds that the acquisition is entirely valid; and a third opinion holds that acquisition has been effected with regard to the land and moveables, but not with regard to the money.[34]
> The same rules hold (i.e., the three opinions just cited) if acquistion has been effected with regard to something to which acquisition applies and with regard to something intangible, which is an acquisition of mere words, to which acquisition does not lawfully apply.[35]
> In a case where A and B have made a formal act of acquisition in regard to a mutual exchange of all their property, one opinion holds that an act of acquisition has no validity in this situation; another opinion holds that the act of acquisition is valid but that each one retains his own property. Whichever party shall have more property shall give that additional property to the other until their relative worths are exactly the opposite of what they were before the exchange; their basic intent is deemed to be to make a profit, not to effect an actual exchange.[36]

204: The circumstances under which a party who withdraws from a transaction receives the formal rabbinical condemnation of "He who punished"; the circumstances under which a buyer or seller is deemed faithless. Eleven paragraphs.

1) When one has paid a purchase price, but not pulled the moveable goods[1] (in order to effect acquisition), even though acquistion of the goods has not been effected, as has been explained, whoever withdraws from the transaction, whether buyer or seller, has not behaved as a Jew should[2] and is obliged to take upon himself the formal rabbinical condemnation of "He who punished." This holds good even if only part of the price was paid.[3]

2) When one has paid a purchase price for an item and the item is accidentally destroyed before the buyer could take possession of it,[4] and the buyer seeks either the item or the return of his money, even though there are witnesses to the fact that the item was destroyed accidentally, that the seller was powerless to save it, and that there was no negligence on the part of the seller, the seller is to return the buyer's money. This situation requires no undertaking of the formal condemnation of "He who punished," cf. para. 4. There is an opinion that the same rule of noncondemnation applies to a buyer who withdraws from the transaction because he is afraid that the item will become a total loss for him.[5]

3) The rule concerning a seller who sets a price with a buyer according to the prevailing market price for that item, accepts the buyer's money, and does not in fact have the item specified, for which the price was agreed upon is explained in 209:6.

4) One undertakes the formal condemnation in the following manner:[6] They condemn him before the rabbinical court, saying, "He who punished the generation of the Flood, and the generation of the Tower of Babel, and the men of Sodom and Gomorrah, and the Egyptians who drowned in the sea, shall exact punishment from whoever does not stand by his word." (There is an opinion to the effect that they say, "He shall exact punishment from you if you do not stand by your word";[7] there is an opinion to the effect that they recite the condemnation to him in public.[8])

5) If one buys land or moveable goods, and buyer and seller have mutually agreed upon the purchase price,[9] and the buyer has given

something in pledge for that price, no acquisition has been effected; whichever party wishes to retract can do so; no one is obliged in this situation to undertake the formal rabbinical condemnation.

6) If parties have made a verbal agreement to sell (something), and the parties have settled the matter of price,[10] and the buyer has put his mark on the goods in order that he have it as a specific symbol that the merchandise is his, even though he has not yet paid any of the agreed-upon price, whoever withdraws from the transaction after the mark has been put on the merchandise receives the formal rabbinical condemnation of "He who punished."

If it is the prevalent custom of that country that such buyers' marks shall effect full acquisition, the object is deemed fully acquired by the buyer thereby. Neither party can withdraw from the transaction. All this holds good provided that the mark has been made in the presence of the seller or the seller has said, "Mark your purchase" (see above ch. 201).

7) When one conducts and concludes commercial transactions using words only[11] (the negotiation and agreement not being completed by a formal act of acquisition), that person should stand by his word, even though none of the purchase price has been taken, nor a buyer's mark made on the goods, nor a pledge given (for the price): whoever withdraws from this type of transaction, whether buyer or seller, is deemed a faithless person. Rabbinical sages are not well disposed toward him, even though he is not obliged to receive a formal condemnation.

8) Similarly, if A said to B that he intended to give B a gift, and A did not give that gift, A is deemed a faithless person. This rule holds good[12] with a gift of small value, since the donee entertains a genuine expectation of receiving such a gift if it is promised. But with a gift of great value,[13] no faithlessness is deemed to exist (if the gift is not given). The prospective donee is not in this case deemed to have entertained a genuine belief that he would receive the gift unless acquisition of the gift has been effected by an appropriate mode of acquisition.[14]

9) There is an opinion to the effect that if several people express an intent to give one person a gift, they cannot withdraw from this transaction even if the gift is of great value.[15]

10) If A was the creditor of B, and A said to B, "Sell me these

goods for the debt you owe me," and the seller agreed to do so, there is an opinion[16] to the effect that A is analogous to one who has paid a purchase price. Whoever withdraws from this type of transaction receives the formal rabbinical condemnation. There are those who hold a contrary opinion (and assert that acquisition is not effected[17] except by the value that can be assigned to the benefit accruing to the debtor by remission of the debt or the granting to the debtor of an extension of the time in which to repay the debt: if the creditor says to the buyer, "Let acquisition of your item be effected for me in consideration of this benefit [i.e., forgiveness or extension]," the creditor is analogous to one who has paid a purchase price).

11) A owed B a *maneh*.[18] The creditor B said to the debtor A, "I shall sell you this moveable item for a *maneh*." A gave B the *maneh*. B may say, "I collect this *maneh* for the debt you owe me." But if the debtor A said to creditor B, "Here is (another) *maneh* besides (the one I owe you), give me the item," B must give him the item or receive the formal rabbinical condemnation.

> GLOSS: Even though in a transaction which is conducted and concluded by means of words only, where no money is tendered, one can withdraw from such a transaction and does not receive the formal rabbinical censure, in any event, a person should stand by his word even though no act of acquisition has been performed, only mere words have passed between the parties: the rabbinical sages are not well disposed toward whoever withdraws from this type of transaction, whether buyer or seller. This opinion holds when the item has a steady price; if its price fluctuates, one who withdraws in this situation is not deemed faithless.[19] Whoever expresses intent to give another a gift of small value and does not give that gift is deemed faithless. There is an opinion to the effect that even if the price of the item fluctutates, one is not permitted to withdraw from the verbal agreement; and if he does so, he is deemed faithless:[20] this appears to be the essence (of these rules).

205: The rule governing sales made under duress and the declaration of protest nullifying such a sale.
Twelve paragraphs.

1) If one had been placed under duress[1] until he sold something, and he had taken a (reasonable) purchase price for it, even if he had been hanged, suspended in air (to force the sale), the sale is valid, whether of real or moveable property,[2] because he did in fact resolve to transfer ownership because of the duress, even though he did not take the purchase price in the presence of witnesses.[3]

> GLOSS: There are those who differ on this matter and reason that we do require witnesses to see the paying over of the purchase price.[4] But the seller's declaration that he received the purchase price is insufficient. There is an opinion that we specifically require that the buyer pay over the money of the purchase price; if, however, he presented a promissory note for the purchase price, no acquisistion takes effect. There are those who differ with this opinion.[5]

Therefore if one has issued a declaration of protest before selling the item, and he asserts to two witnesses,[6] "Know ye that I make this sale of such and such moveable property, or such and such real property, to such and such person under duress," the sale is null. Even if the buyer has had possession of the property for a number of years, the rabbinical court takes it from him and the seller returns the money paid for it. The witnesses must have definite knowledge[7] that the sale is made under duress and that the seller is in fact under duress; they are not to rely on the seller's verbal declaration of such duress. Any declaration of protest in which it is not written, "We the witnesses know that this person was under duress (in regard to the sale)," is not a valid declaration of protest.[8]

2) These rules hold good with reference to a sale. With regard to a gift, or to the forgiving of some obligation, however, the witnesses need not observe or be acquainted with the duress.[9]

3) The rules governing sales are the rules which govern a compromise settlement[10] (consequent to a dispute); the rules governing

gifts are the rules which govern the forgiving of an obligation. (If a deed of gift contains a clause in which the donor assumes a warranty [against eviction] regarding the goods given, the gift is governed by the rules on sales.[11])

4) There is an opinion which holds that what has been asserted above, i.e., that when one has not transmitted a declaration of protest the sale (made under duress) is valid, (aplies) if the transaction is for land, even if the buyer did not give the seller its full value,[12] since the rule of constructive fraud in pricing (and the remedy of a postsale price adjustment) does not apply to real property. But with moveable goods, since there is a possible situation of constructive fraud (and a later price adjustment) or of voiding the sale (because of a grossly excessive purchase price), there is in this case no valid sale. This view applies when the buyer has put pressure on the seller[13] to make the sale itself, but has not forced the seller to accept a less than adequate price. If, however, the buyer forces the seller to sell for (far) less than the worth of the property, there is no lawful sale even in respect to real property. The situation is as if the seller were forced to give the property as a gift; and a gift made under these circumstances is not a lawful gift. (But if a man is forced to sell for an inadequate price, the matter retains the character of a sale in that, if he transmits a declaration of protest, we require that the witnesses to the declaration have their own definite knowledge of the duress, as in a sale.[14])

5) There is an opinion which holds that even if a seller said (to at least two men), "Write for me that I transmitted a declaration of protest in your presence,[15] so that when the duress that I have suffered is made known by competent testimony, your attestation may be combined (with theirs) to void the sale," we do not listen to him (i.e., this form of protest is not allowed). (But if the protest has already been indited and the seller brings proof afterward that he was under duress, the sale is void.)[16]

6) The requirement that the witnesses must have their own definite knowledge of the duress applies in the case of a sale or a compromise settlement[17] (consequent to a dispute). In the case of a gift or of the forgiving of an obligation, however, if a declaration

of protest has been transmitted prior to the transaction, even though the donor or forgiver is not in fact under duress, the (e.g.) gift is void, because in gifts we only follow the manifest intent of the donor. If he does not wholeheartedly wish to transfer ownership, the donee has not effected acquisition of the gift. The forgiving of an obligation is tantamount to a gift.

7) A person is considered under duress when someone strikes him,[18] or when someone hangs him, until he resolves to sell (the property), or when someone terrorizes him with (the threat of) something that may possibly be inflicted on him:

> GLOSS: Whether the threat is of bodily harm or of violence directed against his property. There are, however, those who disagree; they reason that a mere terrorizing threat is not sufficient to constitute duress since one may make the most dire threats and not carry them out.[19]

Whether such duress, or the threat thereof, is carried out by Jews or non-Jews: duress is held to exist.

There is a case in which A leased an orchard from B for ten years.[20] The lessor did not possess the lessee's note on the transaction. After the lessee had enjoyed the property for three years (the lawful term for possession of land to ripen into ownership if the possession is supported by some claim of prior lawful acquisition), the lessee said, "If you do not sell the property to me, I will suppress the document of lease and claim this land is in fact in my possession by right of purchase." The rabbinic sages held that this, and similar circumstances, constitutes constraint tantamount to duress.

Therefore if the lessor brought him before the rabbinical court,[21] and the lessee denied the lessor's claim, asserting that the orchard was his, and afterward the lessor transmitted a declaration of protest, and after that sold the property to the lessee who had denied the lessor's claim, the sale is void. The lessor has witnesses to the fact that he was under constraint, i.e., those who witnessed the denial of the lessor's claim in court: these are witnesses to a declaration of protest (to the subsequent sale to the lessee).

8) The above rules apply when the duress or constraint is inflict-

ed by the perpetrator of the violence,[22] who compels the seller to sell against his own wishes. But when one robs another of property, and the robber has taken possession of it, and afterward purchases the field which he robbed, the seller is not required[23] to transmit a declaration of protest (against the sale), as will be explained.

9) The witnesses to a declaration of protest (against a sale under duress) may themselves sign the document concerning that same sale concerning which[24] a declaration of protest was transmitted to them. There is no objection to their signatures appearing on both documents. Even if the seller asserted to the witnesses, in the presence of the perpetrator of the violence,[25] "I have made the sale of my own free will, without constraint," the declaration of protest remains valid: just as the seller was under duress to sell against his will, so too he was under constraint until he declared, "I sell of my own free will."

> GLOSS: A written declaration of protest, which bears no date, and whose witnesses are not present, so that we do not know if the protest was indited before or after the sale, is deemed valid and nullifies the sale; since we do have knowledge of the fact of duress; without further information, we presume that the protest was made prior to the sale.[26]

10) Similarly, if the seller declared before them (i.e., the witnesses to the declaration of protest) that he had in fact taken the purchase price[27] after he had transmitted the declaration of protest on the sale, the seller is not obliged to return any money, since the perpetrator of the violence has forced him to make such a statement and the witnesses already had knowledge that the seller was under duress. If, however, that money was counted out to the seller in the presence of the witnesses, the seller must return it.

11) If the witnesses to the sale testify that the seller canceled the declaration of protest, that declaration is null and void.[28] If the seller said to the witnesses of the declaration of protest, "Know ye that any formal act of acquisition which I take for the purpose of canceling my protest is itself entirely null; and I make this statement (of cancellation) only because of the duress, of

which you have knowledge; and it is not my wish to transfer ownership to this violent person,": the sale is nullified, even though a formal act of acquisition was made to validate the cancellation of protest.[29]

> GLOSS: If, however, the seller went back and voided all his protests which he had made hitherto, there is an opinion which holds that such retraction of all protest is valid.[30] Therefore the prevalent custom is to write into documents (e.g., bills of sale) language to nullify "any protest of mine which arises because of protest of mine, forever."[31] This view is valid only in regard to sale. In the matter of gift, as long as we have knowledge of the duress, even though there be a cancellation of protest by the donor, there is no gift. If, however, we have no knowledge of the duress, the cancellation of protest is valid even in the case of a gift.[32] Similarly, if one declared in regard to some matter that he is under no obligation (to part with something), the case is treated like a gift in all respects.[33]

12) The duress or constraint which the sages said nullifies a purchase is a duress or constraint which comes through persons other than seller;[34] but a constraint which arises because of the seller's personal circumstances, e.g., one who sells because he is in need of ready money, is no duress or constraint. Even if the constraint arose through other persons, the constraint or duress must be exercised for the immediate and specific purpose of forcing the seller to sell something. If the constraint or duress was not exercised in order to force a sale, but in order to extort money, which the victim did not have and therefore sold property to raise the money, this is not deemed a sale under constraint and the sale is valid. (All this refers to a situation in which the seller is under constraint to sell, where we say that owing to the duress the seller has in fact firmly resolved to sell the property in question; if one is, however, forced to make a purchase, no acquisition is effected [under duress].)[35]

206: The rule when A says, "When I shall sell this thing, I shall sell it to you (B) for one hundred zuz," but A later sells it to C for more money; or when A says, "I shall sell this thing to you (B) for the price a court of assessors shall fix for it." Four paragraphs.

1) If A says to B, "When I shall sell this field, it shall be sold to you as from now for a *maneh*" (one hundred *zuz*), and a formal act of acquisition is made for the transaction, and later on A sells the field to C for a hundred *zuz*, B (is the lawful acquirer and) has purchased the field.[1] (If A did not mention the purchase price but said only, "When I shall sell it, I shall sell it to you[B]," but sold it instead to C[2]), B has not effected lawful acquisition. Similarly, if A sold it to C for more than a *maneh*, C has effected acquistion; because A only said to B, "When I shall sell," i.e., (B acquires) should A maintain the intention of selling it for the originally (stated price); but A did not wish to sell (on those terms) and made the sale only because of the additional money paid by C. Consequently A is analogous to one who sold under constraint.[3]

> GLOSS: This (latter) rule refers to the case in which A spoke to B using the language, "When I shall sell . . . I shall sell to you"; but if B said, "You shall sell only to me,"[4] or A stipulated explicitly that even if others would pay more than the price set with B, A would still sell to B, that stipulation is valid (and B is the lawful purchaser).[5]

2) If A says to B, "When I shall sell the item, you have effected lawful acquisition of it as from now according to the price which a court of three assessors shall set for it,"[6] (a majority decision of) two out of the three assessors (will be sufficient to set the price). If A said to B (that the price shall be whatever) three assessors fix, (the price is not set) until the three assessors agree (upon a proper purchase price).[7]

3) Similarly, if A said to B, "(When I shall sell, I shall sell to you as from now) for the purchase price which a court of four as-

sessors shall fix," (the price is not set) until all four assessors shall agree upon a proper purchase price.[8] Should A sell to C for the price fixed by the assessors, B subsequently effects lawful acquisition (and becomes the lawful owner).

4) If three or four assessors have assessed the item, and the seller says (he does not accept the price thus fixed) until three or four other assessors shall assess the item, we do not listen[9] to the seller in this matter, because acquisition was originally effected, so that the sale takes effect as of now (retroactively once the assessors announce their agreed-upon price).

> GLOSS: But if A did not sell as of now (i.e., with a retroactive element in the sale), even though a symbolic acquistion was effected with the seller, that, when he should sell the item, he would sell it to B, no acquisition has been effected. This is an example of an acquisition of mere words, cf. above ch. 203; it is, moreover, by way of being a type of aleatory forfeiture, as explained below, ch. 207.

207: Sales with conditions and with stipulations; the rules of aleatory forfeiture; the person who undertakes an obligation in a matter in which he would normally have no obligation. Twenty-one paragraphs.

1) When one transfers ownership of either land or moveable goods to another, and either the transferor or the transferee has placed conditions on the transaction,[1] which conditions are susceptible of fulfillment:[2] (But there is an opinion to the effect that if the seller has made a condition which amounts to a special favor for the buyer, this is not viewed as a condition of the transaction but only as a good-humored encouragement for the purchaser. This view applies when the sale has first been negotiated without any conditions, but before the transaction has become final, the seller has instituted this condition beneficial to the buyer. If, however, the seller first said, "On such and such a condition do I sell you . . .," even though the condition amounts to a special favor for the buyer, in

any event, the buyer has not effected acquisition except in contemplation of the fulfillment of the condition, and the condition is taken to be a completely operative condition. Similarly, if the parties stipulated conditions, and afterward indited an instrument which did not in fact specify the conditions of the transaction, they [are presumed] certainly to have indited the instrument in contemplation of the fulfillment of the previously stated condition[s][3]): If the conditions are fulfilled, the item, acquisition of which had been formally effected, is deemed purchased; if the conditions are not fulfilled, no sale has occurred.

The rules concerning conditions are explained in *Tur, Even Haezer*, ch. 38, and ch. 144; see also infra ch. 241.

2) There is an opinion[4] which holds that the previous rule applies when acquisition has been effected by means of one of the appropriate modes for effecting it; and it becomes one's responsibility to fulfill the condition. If, however, no acquisition has been effected now, and a condition is made with the purchaser, to wit, "If this condition is fulfilled, acquisition shall be effected, and if it is not fulfilled, acquisition shall not be effected": even though the condition be fulfilled, no acquisition has been effected, for this transaction amounts to an undertaking of aleatory forfeiture, which effects no acquisition unless the seller said, "Effect acquisition as from now," and they performed an act of acquisition (perfecting a retroactive transfer of ownership).

3) When one has sold his courtyard[5] or his field and stated explicitly at the time of the sale that the sale is made in order that he be able to remove to a particular place,[6] or because of drought he needs funds in order to buy (costly) wheat, the seller is deemed to be selling the property conditionally. Therefore, if the rain should fall directly after the sale, or wheat become available at a reduced price, or the route to that place is closed,[7] or he did not in fact succeed in making the journey there,[8] or for some reason had no success in purchasing the wheat, the seller is to return the purchase price paid (for the land) and the buyer is to return the land, because the seller specifically stipulated that he was selling the property only for the purpose of applying the proceeds of the sale to a specific thing, and that thing was not accomplished. Similar

cases are treated in a similar manner.

> GLOSS: This rule applies specifically to sales of land. When one sells moveable property, however, the declaration of the specifically intended application of the proceeds has no legal effect (to render the sale conditional) until one makes one's intent clear by stipulating (precisely) according to the formal rules of stipulation.[9]

4) If one merely sold property[10] (i.e., land), even though the seller entered upon the transaction because he mentally contemplated applying the proceeds of the sale to a specific purpose, and there is strong indication that he did in fact enter upon that transaction only to effect that particular purpose, and the project purposed was not carried out, there shall be no right of rescission, because the seller's intent and purpose (i.e., the condition) were not explicitly stated. Mere mental reservations or conditions have no legal weight. Even though the seller announced[11] the intent and purpose of the sale prior to the transaction, since he did not do so at the time of the sale, there can be no rescission (on the ground of an unfulfilled condition).

> GLOSS: If, however, there is something that gives a clear and unequivocal estimate (of the seller's intent, short of his actual statement), the sale is voided. There is an opinion that mental reservations have legal force in matters of gift.[12]

5) If A transferred ownership of something to B,[13] and A made the transfer of ownership subject to the condition that B (within a certain period of time) give or sell the thing to C,[14] if B does in fact give or sell it to C, B has effected acquisition. If B does not fulfill the condition and sells (or gives) it to D or neither sells nor gives it (to C) in the time period fixed for him to do so, B has not effected acquisition.

Similarly, if the seller or the buyer[15] has stipulated that an item purchased shall be returned at a certain time or when (the seller) shall give the money for it, the sale is valid and the return of the item is to be made according to the stipulation made. (If the return of the item was done against the seller's will, see *Hoshen Mishpat* 120 as to whether or not this returning satisfies the stipulation.)

6) If one sold real property and stipulated that the buyer should return the property when the seller should have the money[16] (to redeem it), the buyer must give the property back when the seller shall bring him the money. Therefore the buyer is forbidden to enjoy the produce of that land, because the money paid (as purchase price) was tantamount to a loan to the seller (and to enjoy value over and above the amount of the loan is usury).

7) If one sold (land) unconditionally, and the buyer, of his own volition,[17] said to the seller, "When you have the money, you may bring it to me and I shall return this land," this condition is valid,[18] and the buyer may enjoy the produce of the land (while it is his). There is no element of usury here because the buyer, of his own free will and volition, made himself subject to this condition.

8) There is a case of a woman[19] who sent an agent to effect acquisition of land from her relative, A. A, the seller, said to B, the agent, "If I shall have the money (to buy the land back), will this woman, my relative, return it?" B answered and said to him, "You and this woman are related, you are as close as brother and sister"; i.e., the likelihood is that she will return the land (for the money) and not raise an argument over it. These facts came before a rabbinical court, which held that the agent had effected no acquisition of the land because, owing to the equivocal response of B, A, the relative, did not form the mental resolution (to sell) based upon the words of B. Consequently, A had not resolved to transfer ownership.

9) If A has loaned B one hundred gold pieces[20] on (the security of) a field, and the land is worth more than one hundred gold pieces (there is an opinion that the stipulation described below is an aleatory forfeiture even if the land is not worth more than one hundred gold pieces[21]), and the creditor says to the debtor, "If you do not pay me back within three years, the land shall be mine as from now,"[22] acquisition (of the land in case of nonpayment) has been effected.

> GLOSS: There is an opinion that if originally, when the debtor pledged the parcel of land, he took pains to

pledge only that particular land, acquisition has been effected even without the stipulation of retroactivity.[23] Similarly, if the debtor said to the creditor, "If I do not repay you, you shall have no right to repayment except from this particular parcel of land," a hypothec has been created, acquisition of the land (in case of nonpayment) has been effected, and the debtor cannot remove that land from the possession of the creditor except through repayment.

10) Wherever one has not effected acquisition of land owing to the fact that such acquisition would be an aleatory forfeiture,[24] that person subtracts the value of all the produce of that land which he has enjoyed (the land being held in pledge for a debt, as above, para. 9) (from the amount of the loan) because the value of that produce amounts to usury (on the loan) as prohibited by biblical ordinance. There is an opinion which holds that the produce enjoyed by the creditor during the three-year term (of the loan) is not subtracted (from the amount of the loan) because such value represents only the dust of usury[25] (i.e., indirect usury, as defined by rabbinical, not biblical, ordinance).

> GLOSS: But whatever value the creditor may have enjoyed (in terms of produce from the pledged land) after the expiration of the three-year term of the loan, must be returned (to the debtor).[26] Similarly, with every thing where no acquisition thereof has been effected owing to the fact that such acquisition would be an aleatory forfeiture, even though such a thing comes into the possession (of the creditor), he must return it because he holds it by virtue of an error (committed in the lawful disposition of the landed security). There are those who hold a differing opinion and assert that if the thing comes into the possession of the acquirer, acquisition thereof has been effected: There is no case of renunciation nor of gift made in error. Only the value of produce of the pledged land enjoyed by the creditor after the three-year term of the loan must needs be returned to the

debtor; it is tainted with usury since (the original transaction) was a loan; without the presence of that circumstance, acquisition has been effected lawfully.[27]

11) If A (a buyer) gives a thing as security to B (a seller) and says to B, "If I withdraw (from the contract of sale) my security will be forfeited to you," and B says to A, "If I withdraw (from the contract of sale), I shall double the amount of your security (and give it to you),"[28] if A withdraws, acquisition of the security has been effected since it is (already deemed legally transferred and) in the possession (of the seller). If the seller withdraws, he is under no obligation to double security (and forfeit it), for this (undertaking on the part of the seller) would be an aleatory forfeiture, and as such no acquisition thereof has been effected.

> GLOSS: There are those who differ and reason that even if the buyer withdraws, the seller has effected no acquisition (of the security): even though it is in the possession of the seller, an aleatory forfeiture confers no acquisition.[29] This is all the more applicable when the security has been deposited with a third party.

12) Similarly, when A has paid off part of an obligation to B and deposits the document evidencing his debt with C[30] and says to C, "If I have not paid off the balance to you by such date, give him his document," and in fact the specified time arrives and no further repayment has been made, C shall not give the document (to B) because A's statement amounts to an aleatory forfeiture.

13) Similarly, (there are) stipulations which people make among themselves, even before witnesses[31] and even embodied in writing, (of this nature): "If such will be the case or if you do such and such, I shall give you a *maneh*, or I shall transfer ownership of this building to you, and if such will not be the case or you do not do such and such, I shall not transfer the ownership of the building, or I shall not give you a *maneh*." Even though the person performed as required or the circumstances was as indicated, no acquisition has been effected. Anyone who says, "If it shall be" or "If it shall not be" (as a condition governing a gift or a sale, etc.)

has not in fact mentally resolved to transfer any ownership of property, because he is still mentally of the opinion that only *perhaps* it shall be, or only *perhaps* it shall not be (i.e., there is no mental resolve to enter upon a binding transaction).

> GLOSS: There are authorities who hold that there are three distinctions which are properly made in the rules concerning aleatory forfeiture.[32] (1) (There is aleatory forfeiture) whenever the performance or fulfillment of the contract does not depend upon the efforts of the party who has undertaken to perform or fulfill a specific task, but rather the performance or fulfillment depends upon the acts of other parties. For instance: A says to B, "Purchase wine for me at such and such a place, and if you do not purchase it you will be liable to pay me such and such a sum." The fulfillment of this contract does not rest with the prospective buyer; perhaps no one will wish to sell him the wine. (The liability to pay the sum of money) amounts to an aleatory forfeiture in any event, and no acquisition (of the money) has been effected. (2) (There is no aleatory forfeiture) whenever the performance or fulfillment of the stipulation does depend upon the party who has undertaken to perform a specific task, if the forfeiture is commensurate with the loss sustained by nonperformance. For instance, A said to B, "If I leave the field (which I rent from you on a share-crop basis) fallow and I do not work the land, I shall repay you with the best (I can offer)." There is no aleatory forfeiture here, and acquisition (of the "best") has been effected. If, however, the share-cropper has stipulated a pecuniary penalty which is not commensurate with the loss sustained by nonperformance, i.e., he said, "If I leave the field fallow and I do not work the land, I shall pay you one thousand *zuz*," such stipulation amounts to an aleatory forfeiture, and no acquisition (of the one thousand *zuz*) has been effected. Therefore[33] when a seller transfers ownership to a buyer on the following condition, "If you do such and such a thing for

me, you shall acquire," there is an aleatory forfeiture (and there is no acquisition of the subject of the sale) since the fulfillment of the condition does not rest with the seller, but with the buyer. (3) If, however, the fulfillment of the stipulation does not rest in the power of the stipulator, or in the power of others, to accomplish, e.g., the case of a gambler, etc., who does not know whether or not he will be succcessful in his wager, and that person has even so made the stipulation (to pay in case of losing the wager), that person, owing to the doubtful outcome of the subject of the wager, is deemed to have resolved firmly to transfer ownership (e.g., of the money) in case he loses the wager. This rule on gambling applies when the parties play for ready cash money. If, however, they are playing on credit, the loser cannot be required by the rabbinical court to pay such losses.[34] There is an opinion which holds that even if the gambler (who sustained losses on credit) has given security to cover the amount of cash money lost, there is no lawful debt (satisfaction of which could be required by the rabbinical court): when the cash money is not to hand, the security given for it has not been lawfully acquired (and no lawful debt recognized by the rabbinical court exists, see above 190:9). But when the cash money is on the gaming table, wagering is permissible and does not constitute an aleatory forfeiture.[35] There is an contrary opinion which prohibits gambling in any event.[36] There is an opinion which holds that gambling is permissible only when the gaming table, upon which the wagered money rests, is owned jointly by the gamblers:[37] see infra ch. 370, an aleatory forfeiture exists only when the transaction depends essentially upon performance of a specific stipulation; but if A places himself under obligation to B and says that if B is alive he (A) shall give the money to B, if he is not alive he (A) shall give the money to B's heirs, this is not deemed an aleatory forfeiture (as contemplated in rabbinical law) because in

any event he is obligated to give the money: and similarly any analogous case is not aleatory forfeiture.[38]
There is an opinion which holds that wagering is not aleatory forfeiture for this reason: whereas both gamblers stipulate (outcomes of the game which are mutually exclusive) as against each other, and each runs the risk of losing (his wager), since each wishes to acquire (the other's money) each has firmly resolved to transfer ownership (of his own money in case of loss). Similarly when two people (wagering) have exchanged (valuables) with each other, they have effected acquisition (for the as-yet-unknown winner of their wager) if they have performed an act of acquisition mutually; this applies to the situation where the outcome of the wager is also not dependent on either one of them; where it is in either's power to accomplish, it does not apply, as explained above, para. 11, in the matter of giving security.[39]
There are those who disagree even in this (i.e., they hold that aleatory forfeiture does exist when there are mutually exclusive stipulations between the wagerers and neither one has the power to fulfill or perform the stipulation). They are required[40] to offer other reasons (for the legality of) wagering, and of penalty clauses in proposals of matrimony, infra, para. 16.

14) If one says, "Effect acquisition as from now,"[41] no aleatory forfeiture can be said to apply at all, and acquisition has been effected. If the person had not firmly resolved to transfer ownership, he would not have made the transfer retroactive, "as from now." For example, if one says, "If I come by such and such a date, acquisition of this building is effected (for you) as from now," and they have performed the formal act of acquisition to complete the undertaking, the acquirer has indeed effected acquisition if the person arrives in the time limit specified: and so too all analogous cases (are not aleatory forfeiture).

> GLOSS: There are those who hold the opinion that the assertion of retroactive acquisition, "from now," is not by

itself sufficient to remove the element of aleatory forfeiture, but we require also that the parties effect acquisition at a rabbinical court of high standing *and* the assertion of retroactivity, "as from now",[42] (of the acquisition). There are those who hold the opinion that for the purposes of (eliminating the element of) aleatory forfeiture, one who uses the formula "on condition" is deemed as one who uses the formula "as from now"[43]; there are those who hold a contrary opinion, that if the forfeiture is by way of being a penalty (for not refraining from something), the "on condition" formula is not tantamount to the "as from now" formula.[44]

15) An aleatory forfeiture does effect acquisition when the parties thereto have performed an act of acquisition validating it before a recognized rabbinical court of high standing:[45]

> GLOSS: Any three men expert in the laws concerning aleatory forfeiture are considered a court of high standing in this matter.[46] There is an opinion to the effect that we require the rabbinical court of high standing in the particular community or a distinguished person publicly recognized as having the requisite legal qualifications to hear this matter.[47] If one (i.e., the stipulator) ordered a document indited to the effect that acquisition had been effected (for the possible aleatory forfeiture) in a rabbinical court of high standing, even though such acquisition had not been effected, that document suffices to purge the aleatory forfeiture of illegality, because the suitor's declaration (as to the facts in this sort of case) have the weight of one hundred witnesses as to those facts. Even if (the stipulator) did not explicitly command the writing of such a document but ordered a note of debt[48] to be drawn up (for the possible aleatory forfeiture), such document is as adequate[49] (to this purpose of purging the aleatory forfeiture of illegality) as one which he specifically ordered (for that purpose).

(All of the above) applies provided that the party who undertakes to forfeit something (if he does not fulfill a stipulation) deposits his papers evidencing his rights[50] with a rabbinical court (and declares his rights to be void if he does not return within a stipulated time) and he is not unavoidably prevented (from fulfilling his stipulation). For example:[51] one deposits his note or his receipt with a rabbinical court and the formal act of acquisition is made to validate an undertaking that if he not return by a certain date, his note be given to his adversary suitor (e.g., his debtor). If the specified date arrives, and the person has not arrived, the court gives the document (to the appropriate party), provided that all this is accomplished before a court of high standing (as defined above). (There are those who hold the opinion that even though the documents evidencing rights are not deposited with the court, there has been effective (validation of the aleatory forfeiture) since the formal act of acquisition validating the forfeiture was performed before a court of high standing. R. Asher b. Yehiel wrote that such is the prevalent custom[52] (i.e., not to deposit the documents with the court).

If an impassable river or an illness[53] prevented the person from arriving on the specified date, the court shall not give the document (to the appropriate party), and so with all similar cases of non-fulfillment due to constraint. Cf. supra chs. 21 and 55.

> GLOSS: There is an opinion to the effect that if the parties have both deposited security (for the fulfillment of some undertaking, the security to be forfeit in case of non-performance, etc.) according to non-Jewish law and attested by a note drawn up in a non-Jewish court, they have lawfully and mutually effected acquisition, under the rule that the law of a non-Jewish government is also the law for Jews[54] (in nonritual and nonmatrimonial matters).

16) When the rabbinical authorities of Spain wanted to provide for lawful transfer of ownership in a case of aleatory forfeiture, they used to do as follows:[55] They had A perform an act of acquisition to validate a (fictional) debt of (e.g.) one hundred *dinars*,

which A declared he owed to B. After A had obligated himself in that fashion, they had B perform an act of acquisition to validate an undertaking that as long as such-and-such should be the case or that A should do such-and-such, the debt would be forgiven as from now; if such-and-such would not be the case or A should not do such-and-such, B could file suit to collect the debt to which A had made himself liable.

They operated in this fashion in all cases of stipulations between men and women in matters of matrimonial proposals and all similar matters.

We also adopt their usage.

> GLOSS: This usage is valid (for purging illegality from aleatory forfeiture) in any cause or matter.[56] There are places where the practice is to indite two completely separate notes of debt, both of which are deposited with a third party. If either side should withdraw or not perform, the third party would hand over both notes to the other side.

There is an opinion to the effect that the penalty which is instituted in matrimonial proposals to punish whichever side might withdraw from a proposed marriage is not an aleatory forfeiture.[57] It is proper that the withdrawing party should be obliged to pay a penalty for the public humiliation suffered by the other party. (This is the prevalent custom in all these districts [of Poland]; but a formal act of acquisition is necessary[58] [to validate the penalty and thus also is the prevalent custom].)

Similarly if a teacher undertakes, at the time he is hired, to pay a penalty if he should withdraw from his contract, and there is no other teacher available (to assume his duties, such a penalty) is not an aleatory forfeiture.[59]

17) Two people who have mutually stipulated to achieve a particular end,[60] and who have each put up security as a penalty -- that the security of a party withdrawing from the enterprise shall be forfeit to the other party, shall not use the following formula, "If I withdraw from the enterprise, I shall give you so-and-so much, and this (security) is a pledge for the money I am liable to pay should

I withdraw." But each should transfer ownership[61] (of the amount to be forfeit) by symbolic kerchief exchange, which act of transfer, purging the transaction of the taint of aleatory forfeiture, is to be performed before a rabbinical court of high standing, in order that each party become liable (to forfeiture) as a matter of law in case of withdrawal from the enterprise. Then each should give the other an item as a pledge. Thus the obligation (to forfeit) may be legally satisfied from the pledge since each has become liable to the other for a lawful penalty in case of withdrawal. Or, each should say (at the time of the act of transfer), "If I shall withdraw from the enterprise, you shall become owner of such-and-such an amount of money (payable) from this object (presented as security)."

18) A document which contains the statement "If A does not pay by a certain date,[62] A shall become liable to (forfeit) such-and-such a sum of money," and that document concludes with the declaration that (the forfeiture) is not (inserted) as an aleatory forfeiture or as a mere meaningless form of words, does not suffice to purge the forfeiture of the taint of aleatory forfeiture, and such a document effects no acquisition (of the proposed forfeited sum). (This appears to be the correct rule to follow in this matter, but there are those who disagree and assert the rule that if one wishes to claim money or property from someone else, that claimant bears the burden of proof to show that his plea is just and such property is to be surrendered [if seized].)[63]

19) A vow, an oath, or a handshake (as an unequivocal sign of individual consent, or agreement between parties) suffices (to validate and effect acquisition) even in a matter of aleatory forfeiture.[64]

> GLOSS: See infra 209:4. Similarly, this rule applies to a document in which a party has undertaken to oblige himself by the formula "under grave pain of excommunication and by biblical oath." Cf. above, this chapter, para. 15, in the matter of (a declaration that the transaction was conducted before) a court of high standing (whether it was or not, where such declaration was deemed sufficient to purge a forfeiture of its aleatory element) -- this

matter (of oath, etc.) seems the same to me (i.e., the fictitious declaration is valid), even though there is an authority who disagrees.[65] If one vows anything, in the form of an aleatory forfeiture, to charity, or to other sacred purposes, acquisition is effected (for that charity, etc.). See *Yoreh Deah* 258:10.

20) If A unconditionally makes himself liable to B, even though A heretofore owed no obligation to B, A shall be held liable to B, as explained in ch. 40; no aleatory forfeiture is deemed to exist.

21) If one undertook liability in a matter which involves payment of an as yet unknown sum of money, e.g., he said, "I am liable to pay for the cost of your food or your clothing for five years," Maimonides held that no liability was created, but all later authorities disagreed with him.[66]

208: A sale flawed by a manifest illegality. One paragraph.

1) When a sale is contracted (in spite of) a manifest illegality (in it):[1] for instance, the price has been inflated because the buyer has received an extended period in which to pay; or a price was fixed before the market price (e.g., of an agricultural commodity) was known, and the seller did not in fact have that commodity on hand to sell (and similarly if the seller vowed or took an oath that he would not sell an item and he did in fact transgress by selling it[2]), and such a sale was validated by a formal act of acquisition by kerchief exchange, or by one of the other appropriate modes of effecting acquisition, the sale is valid.[3] But the buyer is to pay the permissible market price. Neither party can void the sale (because of the illegality), but the buyer can withdraw from the transaction so as not to pay the higher (unlawful) price.[4] (In this matter, no distinction is made among the transactions of sale, gift, forgiving an obligation, or other [like] cases.[5])

209: The rule concerning transfer of ownership of an indeterminate amount of a thing or a thing which does not yet exist. Ten paragraphs.

1) A transfers ownership of an indeterminate amount of a thing to B:[1] if the type of the thing is known, though its weight or measure is not known, acquisition of the thing has been effected; if the type of the thing is not known, no acquisition has been effected. For example: (if one says, "This heap of wheat do I sell to you for such-and-such a price," or, "I sell you the wine in this wine cellar for such-and-such a price," or, "A sack of figs do I sell you for such-and-such a price," even though the exact measured amount of the heap of wheat, or the number of wine jars, or the weight of the figs is not known, this is a valid sale,[2] even though the exact measure, number, or weight may be more or less than buyer and seller estimated it to be. (The remedy for) constructive fraud by unfair pricing practice is available to them (for eliminating inequity in the price) on the basis of the market price (of the goods at the time of the sale).

2) But if A says to B, "I sell you everything in this building for such-and-such a price;"[3] or "I sell you everything in this box, or everything in this sack, for such-and-such a price," and B was willing to buy and effected acquisition by pulling, no acquisition has been effected, forasmuch as the buyer is not (deemed to have) formed the mental resolve (to purchase), since he does not know the contents of the building, box, or sack: whether it is straw or gold. This, and similar cases, are tantamount to a mere gamble (on the part of one party, but not both).

> GLOSS: There are those who hold the opinion that this same rule applies when two people have contracted to exchange all their property;[4] see above ch. 202, end, see also 241:4 on the rule for the seller of an indeterminate amount of goods.

3) If A sells to B wheat for ten *dinars,* but did not specify how many measures of wheat he sold,[5] he gives the buyer an amount of wheat according to the market price at the time of the sale (i.e., the amount of wheat the *dinars* would fetch at the time of the sale). If either party withdraws from the transaction after the price has been paid, and is not willing (to accept) the market price that obtained at the time of that payment, he receives the formal rabbini-

cal condemnation of "He who punished."

4) One cannot transfer ownership of a thing not yet in existence,[6] whether such transfer is by way of sale, gift *inter vivos*, or gift *mortis causa*.[7] Such a transaction would be as follows: (one says) "Whatever this field will yield is sold to you"; "Whatever this tree will yield is yours as a gift"; "Give the offspring of this animal to such-and-such a person"; or one says, "The offspring of my cow",[8] or "of my slave-girl is sold to you," or "is yours as a gift": such a statement is nullity in law. Even if the cow or the slave-girl was pregnant,[9] no acquisition has been effected. (But with regard to the tree, if this fruit has fully ripened on the tree, such is deemed in existence[10] [and a proper subject of a sale].)

One can withdraw from a sale (of an as yet nonexistent thing) even after the cow or slave-girl shall give birth,[11] or the fruit of the tree has grown and matured, and come into existence. If the buyer has gone ahead and taken possession of the fruit,[12] the rabbinical court cannot require him to surrender such items. (This same rule applies to other goods not yet in existence: even if the buyer has not seized them but (the seller) has written an instrument of transfer (for the buyer) and delivered it to him the buyer is deemed to be one who has in fact seized the goods[13]), (the goods having, of course, come into existence, the instrument then having been delivered, neither party having withdrawn from the transaction).

If one has sold a tree for the fruit it might yield,[14] or a cow or slave-girl for their offspring, acquisition thereof is effected immediately, and neither party can withdraw from the transaction.

> GLOSS: If A says to B that B shall acquire from A the proceeds from a sale of wine to be made by A, such proceeds are deemed a nonexistent thing.[15]
> There are those who hold the opinion that this entire rule applies when one transfers ownership of a thing simply, without any further specification (regarding its existence); but if A says that B shall acquire the thing when it will exist, acquisition has been effected even though the item does not exist at the moment of the transaction.[16] There are those who differ with this opin-

ion.[17]

Even though one cannot transfer ownership of something not in existence, one can in any event pledge (or mortgage) it;[18] but there are those who disagree with this ruling.[19]

But one can undertake an obligation upon himself (concerning the as-yet-nonexistent thing). Cf. supra 60:6.

If A transfers ownership of something not yet in existence, along with something that does exist, to B, there is an opinion which holds that such a transaction is similar to one in which A says to B, "You and the donkey effected acquisition"[20] (i.e., the person, who can acquire, becomes owner of the part of the property that exists; the donkey clearly has no power to effect acquisition); cf. infra 210:3.

If a person swore an oath to carry out a sale fully, even though the subject of the sale was not in existence at the time of the oath, that person must fulfill the terms of that oath, cf. supra 7:19 and 73:8; but the acquisition (of the nonexistent item) is not effected by an act of acquisition, i.e., kerchief exchange. Thus if we are not able to enforce the person's fulfillment of the oath, e.g., he died, any formal act of acquisition (in this case of oath) is a nullity. Similarly if one made inquiry at a rabbinical court concerning his oath and received leave to rescind the oath,[21] (any formal act of acquisition that may have been performed is a nullity).

Just as one cannot transfer ownership of a thing which does not exist, so too one cannot renounce something which does not exist.[22]

5) If something exists, but (the seller) does not exercise lawful possession and control of it, it is deemed to be like a nonexistent thing. No acquisition thereof is effected. Either party can withdraw from a transaction (concerning such a thing), cf. ch. 211.

GLOSS: In any event, if the seller has taken the trouble to go and acquire the item which he sold (but did not possess at the time of the sale), the transaction is to be carried through to completion, since it was for the specific purpose of carrying out the sale lawfully that he took the pains to acquire the item: to establish his good faith[23] (as a merchant).

6) If A has undertaken to sell an item at its market price,[24] and accepted B's money for it, but does not possess the item, the seller is obliged to acquire the item and give it to the buyer according to the undertaking regarding price. If he withdraws from the transaction he is liable to receive the formal rabbinic condemnation.

> GLOSS: If, however, the undertaking was before the market price had become known, the sale was unlawfully entered upon, and he can withdraw from it without being required to accept the formal rabbinical condemnation.[25]

7) Just as one cannot transfer ownership of something nonexistent, so too one cannot reserve something nonexistent from the sale of an item.[26] How does this emerge in practical terms? If A sold a field to B, and reserved for C a specific, particular yearly amount of the yield from that field, C has acquired none of that yield. If, however, A reserved that specific, particular yearly amount for himself, he has indeed reserved it for himself and has done so with a degree of liberality[27] (toward himself).

> GLOSS: There is no distinction to be made in this matter as among a sale, a gift *inter vivos*, or a gift *mortis causa*; there are those who disagree in regard to a gift *mortis causa*.[28]

And we say that one has reserved for himself the space occupied by that yield of produce, even though the seller did not explicitly stipulate such reservation of space. Even if the buyer (B) sold the field to C,[29] the portion reserved by A is not sold to C, and C is to give A whatever A reserved. If, however, A reserved a portion of the harvest with a stipulation that it be reserved as long as B should own the field,[30] when B sells the field to C, A's power to reserve is negated. Even if B should repurchase the field from C later on, B does not give A any of the harvest. If A dies, his heirs have no claim for the reserved portion[31] of the harvest against B, even if A dies while the field is owned by B, by virtue of the sale directly from A, unless A had explicitly made such reservation for himself and for his heirs.

> GLOSS: There are those who hold the opinion that (this last provision concerning heirs) applies specifically when one does not reserve something definite and well-defined, since then the reservation is only like a simple condition of the sale, and thus in such a case it is necessary for A to state explicitly "for myself and for my heirs." But if the reservation is made with regard to something definite, e.g., a house, and A says, "(The sale is) on condition that an upper chamber in the house shall be mine," his children inherit his rights thereto.[32]

8) Even though it is required to give a person the produce which that person has reserved for himself, if the buyer does not give it to him, the sale is not therefore void.[33] If, however, the sale had been made conditional upon the yearly gift of the reserved portion of the harvest to himself or to another, then the validity of the sale is dependent upon the gift. If the buyer does not make that gift, according to the stipulation placed upon the sale, the sale is void.

> GLOSS: (To this last point:) Even though one cannot transfer ownership of a nonexistent thing, in any event one can make a stipulation concerning an as-yet-nonexistent thing,[34] or remove himself or his authority over an as-yet-nonexistent thing, since he has in fact not yet become owner of it. (This can be done without a formal act to validate such transfer or relinquishment.[35]) Cf. *Even Hazer*, ch. 92.
> There are those who hold the opinion that although a man cannot transfer ownership of a nonexistent thing, in any event, if (he also[36]) wishes to acquire it, he as well

may transfer ownership (of that nonexistent thing he wishes to acquire): thus two people performed formal acts of acquisition,[37] concerning a gift which one of them would receive; since whichever one would receive the gift would divide it with the other, acquisition (of the as-yet-nonexistent gift or portions thereof) has been effected. See above 176:3 for a contrary opinion.

9) If A has sold a date palm tree to B and the (nonexistent) fruit of that tree to C, he is not deemed to have reserved the space occupied by the fruit: B has effected acquisition of the tree and its fruit, C has effected no acquisition.[38]

10) If A said to B, "Acquire the date palm tree, except for its fruit," he has reserved for himself the space occupied by that fruit as well, i.e., the branches; the buyer has only the trunk of the tree when it shall be dry[39] (i.e., not in the fruit-bearing season).

210: The rule concerning transfer of ownership to one's own, or to another's, unborn. Three paragraphs.

1) One cannot transfer ownership to the unborn.[1] Therefore when one makes a fetus an owner, no acquisition has been effected,[2] even if one said, "When the fetus shall be born, it shall assume ownership."[3]

> GLOSS: This is contrary to those who hold the differing opinion and reason that if the transferor did not die or withdraw from the transaction prior to the birth, and (someone acting for the unborn) performed a formal act of acquisition by means of pulling (not by kerchief exchange since the ownership of the kerchief would revert to its owner long before the child was born, cf. *Tur* ad loc.), and the property is in fact still under the ownership of the transferor at the time of the birth, then the infant becomes the owner if the transferor stipulated that ownership shall commence at the time of birth.[4]

If the transferor was the father of the fetus,[5] acquisition has been effected even if it was not stipulated that ownership shall commence at the time of birth, provided that the transferor's wife was already pregnant at the time of the gift.[6] (A grandchild ranks as the unborn of another, not of the transferor.[7])

There are those who hold the opinion that the rule providing that one can transfer ownership to one's unborn child applies only to a transferor *in extremis*, but not to a transferor in good health.[8]

2) If A transferred ownership of part of his property to an animal or to a fetus[9] and then went back and said to B, "Effect acquisition (of the property) as does this animal," or, "as does this fetus," no acquisition has been effected.[10]

3) If A said to B, "You and this animal effect acquisition of my property[11] or such-and-such an item "(or)" You and this unborn fetus effect acquisition of my property or such-and-such an item," B has effected acquisition of half the property. (If one transfers property to a corpse, acquisition has been effected for an amount of property necessary for the grave and other requisites of a proper burial.[12])

211: The rule concerning (sale of) an item in the (seller's) lawful ownership and control, and the rule concerning the father who makes his property over to his children as a **post-mortem** gift. Seven paragraphs.

1) If an item (which is to be transferred) is not under the lawful ownership and control of the transferor, no acquisition thereof can be effected (from that transferor). The item ranks as a nonexistent thing.[1] How does this emerge in practical terms? (If A says) "Whatever I inherit from my father[2] (or any other person who may bequeath property to[3] A), is sold to you"; (or) "Whatever my net brings up from the sea is given to you"; (or) "When I buy this field, acquisition thereof shall be for you": A has said nothing of legal effect[4]; this rule applies in all similar cases.

> GLOSS: There are those who hold the opinion that this rule applies only when no explicit specification of the property has been made; if, however, the person explicitly said, "This field which I shall inherit from my father

is sold to you," acquisition thereof has been effected.[5] Cf. supra 209:5.

2) When a testator is moribund[6] (i.e., about to die, as indicated by his bringing up mucus into the throat from the lungs, which are too constricted for proper breathing), about to die, and wishes to sell a small amount of his property in order to have cash on hand for funeral expenses[7] since his son and heir is impoverished -- if such sale should be delayed until after the testator's demise, the corpse would remain unburied and improperly exposed too long; the rabbinical sages ordained that if the son and heir sells and says, "What I shall inherit from my father today is sold to you," such a sale is valid.

> GLOSS: We are not overly particular if the heir sells somewhat more than the small amount (for funeral requisites). If the heir is not successful in arranging a sale of a small portion, he may sell according to the amount of property he does successfully arrange to sell.[8]

Similarly, a poor fisherman[9] who has no food may say, "Whatever my net brings up from the sea today is sold to you." Such is a valid sale because of (his need for) sufficient sustenance.

3) If one's father were about to die, and the heir did not have the requisite items for the funeral,[10] and sold something to A and said, "What I shall inherit from my father today is sold to you for so-and-so much money," and the heir predeceases the father, and then the father dies, the heir's son (the grandson) may lawfully recover that property sold from A, and is not required to return the purchase money to A because his own father had sold something which had not yet come into his lawful ownership and possession.[11] The property is found to have remained under the lawful authority and possession of the grandfather; the grandson inherits the estate of the grandfather.

4) There is an opinion to the effect that if A borrowed money from his father, B, and then A sold some of his own property to C, and then A and B died, so that D, A's son, inherited A's note of indebtedness to B, D can seek to recover the property his father A sold to

C: D can say, "I claim my right of inheritance from my grandfather"[12] (whose loan has presumably been secured by A's property before such property has been sold to C).

5) If A writes an instrument making his property over to his son, B, after A should die,[13] the property vests in B from the date of the instrument. Any yield of the property belongs to A until A's death. B, the receiver of the property itself, cannot sell[14] the yield of that property as long as the donor, A, is living. But B may sell the property with a special conditional clause -- "as from today and after the death of A, the donor," so that the buyer assumes ownership of the property itself immediately, and of the yield of the property upon the demise of A, the donor. The buyer assumes ownership even if B, the donee, predeceases A,[15] since B did not transfer ownership of a nonexistent thing (i.e., something he did not yet own), because the property itself belonged to B: for the acquisition of the yield from the property which remained vested in A is not like the acquisition of the property itself (the acquisitions are in fact separable: one is immediate, one is yet to take effect.)

6) If A has given land to B and has also, along with it, given B the *dinars* and moveable property located on it, no acquisition has in fact been effected unless the money and moveable property were in fact under the donor's lawful control and ownership.[16] Therefore it is necessary for proof to be brought, which proof shall demonstrate that the money and moveable goods, ownership of which A transferred to B, were in fact under A's lawful control and ownership at the time[17] (of the transaction). Cf. supra 60:6.

7) One may transfer ownership of property, which he has deposited with someone, to another person by means of sale or gift because deposited property is deemed to remain under the lawful control and ownership of its legal owner.[18] The deposited property is presumed to remain in existence.[19] If the depositary denies the deposit, one is not able to transfer ownership of that property, for the transferor is like a person who has lost property; i.e., the property is no longer assumed to be subject to his authority and control.

But a loan of money, since it is given to be expended, is not deemed to exist[20] (i.e., as a specific collection of specific coins); one may not transfer ownership of loaned money unless the transfer be transacted in the presence of the three: the owner, the debtor, and the prospective owner.[21]

If there was a note of indebtedness evidencing the loan, the owner of that note may transfer his ownership of it by means of an instrument written and delivered (for that specific purpose of transferring ownership of the note) because there is then a thing which is delivered for the purpose of effecting acquisition of the obligation recorded in it[22] (i.e., the note of debt).

> GLOSS: A borrowed money from B, and A made an instrument of sale, as from now, for his (A's) field. The instrument of sale was unconditional. A deposited the instrument with C, so that if A did not repay B by the proper time, C should give the unconditional instrument to B. Before payment was due, B sold that field to D. When the loan was due for repayment, A did not repay B. C gave the instrument to B. B's sale of the property is valid even though the sale was made prior to the due date of the loan.[23] (The field was not in fact landed security for the loan.)

212: The rule concerning transfer of ownership of a right to dwell in a house or courtyard; the rule concerning consecration of a thing not yet in existence to some religious purpose. Nine paragraphs.

1) One can only transfer ownership, whether by means of sale or by means of gift, of a thing having physical substance.[1] No acquisition can be effected regarding a thing which does not have physical substance.[2] Therefore if A transfers to B the ownership of a right to eat the fruit of a certain date-palm tree, or of a right to live in a certain house, no acquisition has been effected until B effects acquisition of the house itself to live in or the tree itself to eat from its fruit.

> GLOSS: If one says, "A shall live in this house (of mine)," and did not specify a term for this occupancy,

even a single hour's occupancy may be implied.³

If a document contains the provision that A gave (leave for B) to live in A's house and that they performed a formal act of acquisition to validate that undertaking, one is to interpret that document (to show) that acquisition was effected in a legally operative manner, that A transferred to B ownership of the house itself for the purpose of B's habitation there. All the more (is the document to be interpreted in this fashion) if the parties reiterated the fact of acquisition later in that document -- for certainly (then) the (later mention that) they performed a formal act of acquisition was to emphasize (the matter of acquisition) in a legally effective manner.

If, however, the document mentioned only that they performed a formal act of acquisition regarding A's giving B leave to dwell in the house, that transaction is a nullity because then the acquisition was essentially of the right to inhabit; and the right to inhabit has no physical substance.⁴

If a document does not contain the proper formal language signifying the lawful transfer of ownership of the fruit of a tree for eating, but it merely states that A gave B the power to take the fruit according to the rabbinical ordinance thereon, (we hold that) the transferor has declared that the transfer of ownership took place according to rabbinical ordinance, which one is to interpret as a legally effective giving.⁵

2) Similarly, if A sells to B the airspace over A's ruined dwelling or the airspace over A's courtyard,⁶ such transaction is a nullity unless A transferred to B ownership of the (e.g.) courtyard for the purpose of B's bringing into it (i.e., into the airspace over that courtyard, which is included with the courtyard itself) his projecting moldings, brackets, etc.

3) If, however, A sold B a house, a ruined dwelling, a tree, or a courtyard, and reserved for himself the right of dwelling in the house, of eating the fruit of the tree, or the airspace above the

ruined dwelling or courtyard,[7] the reservation of such right is legally efective.[8] The matter stands as if the seller had explicitly stated that he reserved a place for himself (in regard to the property sold). Even if the seller did not mention such reservation at all,[9] but (merely) said, "The sale is on condition that the upper apartment (of the house) be mine," we say that the seller has reserved for himself (air) space in the courtyard (of the house) into which he can bring moldings, brackets, etc., from the upper apartment.[10]

> GLOSS: If the seller reserves a right for himself and reserves a right for another person, we say that just as the reservation for himself was done in a legally effective manner, and with a degree of liberality toward himself, in the same manner did he make the reservation for the other person, since the seller is deemed certainly to have intended (the two reservations of right) as one matter.[11] Cf. supra 209:7.

4) If one sells land for a specific, fixed period of time, such sale is valid and the buyer may enjoy the land as his own property and enjoy the produce of that land for the term of the sale.[12] At the end of the term, the land reverts to its former owner. The difference[13] between a sale of land for a specific, fixed period of time and a transfer of ownership of land for the purpose of allowing the transferee to enjoy its produce is that in the latter case the acquirer cannot change the character of the land, or build on it, or tear down existing buildings. In the former case one may build or tear down and deal with the land, during the term of the sale,[14] as he would were that land his acquisition without a specified term of ownership.

5) The difference between a sale of *this field* for the purpose of allowing the buyer to use and enjoy its produce, and the sale of *the produce* of this field to another[15] is that in the latter case the buyer can make no use of the land itself, and cannot even enter the field except at the time its produce is removed (at harvest), and the owner of the field itself makes use of that land as he sees fit. In the former case, the owner of the field may not enter it except

with the consent of the buyer of the field for its produce, and that buyer may use the field as he sees fit.

6) The difference between acquisition of the field for the purpose of allowing the acquirer to use and enjoy its produce and the lease of the field to someone[16] is that in the former case the acquirer may plant or seed whenever he wishes or leave the ground fallow. The lessee does not have this option, cf. infra ch. 320.

7) The law concerning property consecrated to a sacred purpose,[17] the law concerning property designated for the poor, and the law concerning property made subject to a vow are dissimilar to the law governing acquisition of property by an ordinary person. If a person says, "Whatever offspring my animal shall bear shall be consecrated to defray expense of repair to the Temple (in Jerusalem)"; or, "(Whatever offspring, etc.) shall be forbidden to me (to use or enjoy)"; or, "(Whatever offspring, etc.) I shall give to the poor": even though such property is not consecrated because it does not yet exist, the person is duty bound to fulfill this undertaking[18] because the Bible declares (Numbers 30:3) that a person "shall act according to everything which he utters" (in respect of vows, etc.). Since this is so, if a person *in extremis* gave the order, "Whatever this tree shall produce is for the use of the poor," or, "All the rental of this house shall be for the benefit of the poor," acquisition on behalf of the poor has been effected.[19]

> GLOSS: There is an opinion to the effect that the sacred enterprise or the charitable enterprise does not lawfully effect acquisition (on the strength of the consecrator's declaration), since one cannot consecrate property which is not yet in existence and the consecrator's assertion is in itself a nullity. If, however, one used a verbal formula such as "When my animal shall bear," or, "When my tree shall produce fruit, etc., I shall give it to a sacred purpose, or to the poor," one is duty bound to fulfill this undertaking because it is tantamount to a vow.[20] This only applies when the person making the vow is alive (when the vow can be fulfilled); but if the person making the vow has died (before the possibility of its fulfillment exists), the vow is null because the person

is not present to carry out the vow.[21]

The latter reasoning (i.e., the gloss) is the more cogent, it is the essence of this rule, and it is proper to render judgments on that basis, cf. infra 252:2. If one swore an oath to carry out a sale fully, cf. supra 209:4.

8) If one acquired land with the intent that it be consecrated to a sacred enterprise,[22] but did not orally express this intent, there are those who hold the opinion that since the acquirer had firmly resolved to give the property to charity, he is obligated to make the gift.[23] There is another opinion to the effect that even though the Bible provides (II Chronicles 29:31), "As many as were of *a willing heart* brought burnt offerings," the Babylonian Talmud clearly states the rule (*Shebuoth* 26b) that the law concerning unconsecrated property cannot be deduced or derived from the law governing consecrated property.[24] At the present time, consecrated property falls under the law governing unconsecrated property because there can presently be no actual consecration for repair of the Temple (in Jerusalem), and such consecration, if made, is simply treated as if for ordinary charitable purposes:[25] Therefore, if one does not actually state the intent to dedicate property to a sacred purpose, (mere unexpressed mental resolve) has no legal effect. (One may rule more strictly according to the first opinion advanced. Cf. *Yoreh Deah* 253:13, gloss.)

9) Similarly, if one said, "This land, when I shall acquire it, shall be consecrated to a sacred purpose,"[26] he has said nothing of legal effect because one cannot consecrate something that is not yet in existence (i.e., is not yet existent as his own property). If, however, one says, "When I shall acquire it, *I* shall consecrate it, or give it, to a sacred cause," this is tantamount to a vow undertaken by that person and he must fulfill his vow.

> GLOSS: This is the reasoning of R. Asher b. Yehiel. It differs from the view of Maimonides, who reasons that if one says, "When I shall acquire it, *it* shall be consecrated to a holy purpose," one is duty bound to fulfill that undertaking, as is written supra in para. 7 of this chapter. The view of the present compiler, which he stat-

ed without qualification above in para. 7, follows Maimonides, and the view he presents in this paragraph is the opinion of R. Asher b. Yehiel: it is not correct.[27]

213: In what manner acquisition of the yield of a beehive or a dovecote is effected. Two paragraphs.

1) When one sells the yield of a dovecote or a beehive to another,[1] acquisition is effected. This is not a sale of something which does not yet exist (as one might think) because there has been no sale of the birds which shall be born or the honey which will be present in the hive. But one is selling the dovecote for its yield[2] or the beehive for its honey, which is like the sale of a canal: the buyer benefits from everything he catches in it. So too one has transferred ownership of this dovecote for its yield, as one would sell a tree (that the buyer should have) its fruit.

2) The (new) owner of the dovecote has not acquired the eggs and young birds in the dovecote[3] as long as the young birds have not yet flown.[4] This rule is an ordinance of the rabbinical sages, based on the biblical verse (Deuteronomy 22:6) "You shall not take the mother bird with the young birds." Therefore when one wishes to transfer ownership of young birds or eggs to another, one strikes the dovecote until the mother birds fly up.[5] Afterward, ownership is transferred by means of one of the modes of effecting acquisition of moveable property.

214: An undetailed sale of a house: what is included in the sale with the house. Thirteen paragraphs.

1) When one sells a thing which has servitudes or adjunct structures, one has not sold such servitudes or adjunct structures unless he explicitly included them in the sale.[1] In practical terms, then, if one sold a house one has not sold the verandah extension which surrounds the house even though that extension opens into the house.[2] (There are those who hold the opinion that this rule applies even if the seller had noted the outer boundaries of the building[3] [for the buyer, which might be interpreted to include the verandah projecting from one wall of it].) This rule applies when the width

The Laws of Buying and Selling 157

of such a verandah is four cubits or more;[4] but if the verandah is of lesser width, it is included with the house (as part of the sale) (even if it does not open into the house.)[5] So too an upper apartment of the house[6] which opens into the house, through an opening in the paved ceiling of the house (i.e., the opening is, for instance, an aperture in the roofing of the house, which forms the floor of the upper apartment) is included in the general meaning of the term "house."

> GLOSS: This rule applies only at the time of the actual sale or gift of the house.[7] But if one has declared that he sold or gave his house to another, all adjunct structures are deemed to have been included in the sale: it being required only to mention the principal item sold or given in the declaration, not the details of those items.

2) When one sells a house, one has not sold an inner chamber of that house[8] even though the seller has noted the outer boundaries of the building (for the buyer, which would have included this separate inner apartment) (this rule has specific reference to a chamber four cubits or more wide).[9] Nor has one included in the sale a roof four cubits wide which has a parapet of ten or more handbreadths in height;[10] nor has one included pits or cisterns (a pit is excavated out of hard material and requires no masonry work to keep it watertight, but a cistern, dug from softer earth, does); pits and cisterns are not included in the sale even though the seller wrote that he did sell (with the house) the depth of earth beneath it and the airspace above it (and even though he noted the outer boundaries of the building (which would include these structures too[11]).

> GLOSS: (These structures are not included) even if the seller wrote for the buyer, "I have not, in the sale, reserved these things at all[12] (for my use)." There are authorities who differ on this point.[13]

The seller must formally acquire an easement[14] from the buyer in order to gain access to the pit or cistern which has been reserved (by the seller). If the seller said to the buyer,[15] "I have sold you the house except for the pit or cistern," it is not necessary for the seller formally to acquire an easement; similarly if one sells a pit or a cistern only, the buyer is not required formally to acquire an easement to the pit or cistern. The buyer may enter the seller's house to go to the cistern and draw water there. (This rule applies when the buyer has no other route[16] to the cistern except through the seller's property. If, however, he does have another means of access to the cistern, he cannot use the route through the seller's property.)

3) When one sells a house to another, even though the seller wrote for the buyer, "I have transferred to you the ownership (of the house and) of the subsurface soil beneath the house and the airspace above it," he is (still) required to write, "Acquire (the property) from the bowels of the earth up to the heights of the sky";[17] for the subsurface soil and the airspace are not included in the sale of a house without precise specification of them. Once one has acquired the subsurface soil and the airspace above, one has only acquired that airspace itself and the thickness of earth beneath, but one has not acquired any structures located in the subsurface soil or in the airspace. Once the seller has written for the buyer (that the sale extends) "from the bowels of the earth up to the heights of the sky," the buyer has acquired a pit or a cistern in the subsurface earth and any pavements, and any caves above such subterranean pavements.

> GLOSS: (The buyer under this last provision) has also acquired the roof even if it is furnished with a parapet of ten handbreadths in height and is four cubits in width.[18] But any roof space less than four cubits in width, or with a parapet less than ten handbreadths in height, is automatically included with the house; even without a written specification by the seller of depth of earth and airspace above, the buyer has acquired it.

4) If the seller has made no written specification that subsurface soil and airspace are sold to the buyer[19] along with the house, but has sold the house without writing out such details, the buyer

has no rights at all in the airspace above the roof of the house, or in the earth beneath the house at all: whether under or over the house itself or under or over the courtyard of the house. The buyer has effected acquisition only to the top of the courtyard walls; he has no right or permission to build into the airspace over the house or to excavate into the earth beneath it. The depth of earth and the airspace are deemed reserved (from the sale).

If the seller comes to build an apartment in the airspace over the house, such structure having support on columns, he may do so; he may not build upon the support of the (house or courtyard) walls which he did sell. Similarly if the seller came to make an excavation, starting from outside the property he sold, and running down and beneath the house he sold, he may do so provided that this excavation does not cause damage for the owner of the surface property. There is an opinion that the seller cannot excavate in the ground under the house[20] in order that no harm could (possibly) come to the owner of the surface property. On this opinion, then, the advantage gained by the reservation of subsurface earth from the sale is that if the buyer excavated cisterns, pits, or caves, they are automatically the property of the seller.

There is an authority who has written the opinion[21] that if A sells B a ruined dwelling, and A has not given written specification that he has sold the subsurface soil of the ruin or the airspace above the ruins, since (urban) ruins are ordinarily rebuilt, (the buyer has effected acquisition of and) has airspace above the ruin to accommodate the height of the rebuilt house, which height is defined as sufficient vertical space[22] for a man with an average-sized bundle on his head to enter and leave (a structure) without having to bend his head. In a field or a vineyard, (the buyer of a ruined dwelling in such a rural area) has, without specification thereof, acquired the airspace above the ruins because new structures are not ordinarily built over them and one does not (therefore) reserve (the airspace when selling a rural ruin). But the buyer (of a rural ruin) has not effected acquisition of the subsurface soil of the ruin since excavations are ordinarily made there.

When the seller has written for the buyer (in a sale of ruined property, that acquisition extends to) the earth beneath the ruin and the airspace above it, if the buyer comes to rebuild into the airspace or to excavate into the subsurface land, he may do so; but he has not effected acquisition of structures (already existing) in the subsurface land or in the airspace. If the seller wrote for the buyer the simple specification (that acquisition of the property had been effected) from the bowels of the earth to the heights of heaven, even though the seller did not specify subsurface earth and the airspace (separate), acquisition of everything has been effected[23] (by the buyer, i.e., the subsurface land, the airspace, and any structures therein).

> GLOSS: A sold a house to B. A specified in writing to B that the sale was from the bowels of the earth to the heights of heaven. A had a house adjacent to the one he sold. The latrine of A's adjacent dwelling entered partway into the house sold to B. B cannot fill in the latrine pit under his house since A did not sell that house to him, so that his own property would be endamaged (by the loss of the amenity). Cases similar to this case receive similar rulings.[24]

5) There is an opinion to the effect that (in a sale of) a courtyard, the buyer has effected acquisition of all airspace above the courtyard even though (the seller did not specify acquisition of) airspace in writing, since vertical space is not a known quantity[25] (i.e., amenable to measurement by fixed points). There is an authority who differs on this point.[26]

> GLOSS: (The difference of opinion is) as has been explained in the paragraph immediately above. The reasoning of the first authority here seems to me to be the correct one for adjudication of (disputes). A sold B a house and did not specify subsurface earth and airspace above as part of the sale: the airspace above was not acquired. Afterward A sold all his houses to C. C has not effected acquisition of the airspace above the house sold to B, even though A had specified to C that acquisition had been effected from the bowels of the earth to the heights

of heaven: in any event, since the sale to B had taken place prior to the sale to C, and A had not reserved anything for himself except airspace, which does not (by its nature) have physical substance and (thus) ownership of it cannot be transferred, as supra ch. 212. If there is a roof (of requisite size as defined above) on the house which A sold to B, since (that roof) as a separate though adjunct structure) was sold to C (along with all A's remaining houses), because it is something which does have physical substance, the law which governs the transfer of ownership of that roof also applies to the airspace above that roof: it was also sold to C. So, too, if a house stands in the courtyard of the seller, who sells the courtyard and everything in it, the airspace above it is sold with it, and the buyer of the courtyard has effected acquisition of it.[27]

6) When a seller sells a house and has not specified (inclusion in the sale of) the subsurface soil and the airspace above it,[28] if the house collapses, the buyer can rebuild it only to the extent of its original dimensions.[29] Even if the seller specified (merely) the subsurface earth and the airspace above (in the sale of the house), and there was (in the airspace above the house) an apartment resting on columns, since the buyer did *not* effect acquisition of that structure, if it collapses (the seller) may rebuild it.[30] If, however, the seller sold the structure on columns to someone, and that structure collapsed, that is the misfortune[31] of (the buyer of the supported structure) and the buyer is not allowed to rebuild it (there being nothing left but insubstantial airspace). But one who buys an apartment built upon a house can rebuild that apartment, should it collapse (since a solid foundation, physically substantial, remains -- not mere airspace).

7) When one sells someone a single apartment in a large building,[32] even though the seller indicated to the buyer the outermost property line of the structure,[33] and even though there are some people there who do call the large building simply an "apartment," acquisition has been effected only in regard to the single apartment because the seller was (only) demonstrating the widest boundaries to

him. If he had sold the entire apartment building, he would have written (the standard formula), "I have not reserved anything out of this sale at all."[34] Even if the seller wrote the formula (in the bill of sale), if no one (in that locale) does in fact call the large building simply an "apartment," acquisition of the single apartment only has been effected.[35]

> GLOSS: If everyone (in that locale) does in fact call the large apartment building simply an "apartment," and an individual dwelling in it is not called an "apartment" without some further specification of it as a single apartment, then the seller has sold the entire apartment building, even if he did not indicate that building's outermost property line.[36] If A has given B one eighth of a certain house which A possesses, and afterward it becomes known that A possesses only one half or one fourth of the house, we do not hold that A gave one eighth of his portion, but we follow the meaning of the language as people ordinarily employ it: and certainly one eighth of the whole was meant.[37] Cf. infra 218:21.

8) When one sells a house to another on condition that its upper chamber is reserved as the property of the seller, it does remain the seller's. If the seller wishes to construct moldings or brackets which project from the upper chamber, he may do so; if the upper chamber collapses, he may rebuild it; if he wishes to rebuild, he rebuilds the structure as it was formerly (i.e., without alteration).[38]

> GLOSS: The same rule applies (if the seller reserved other structures from the sale): he said, "(I sell) except for the pit, the cistern, etc."[39]

9) If there are two dwellings, one wholly inside the other,[40] and the owner of them transferred ownership of each dwelling to a different person in one simultaneous transaction, and the transfers were either both by sale or both by gift, neither new owner has an easement (to the acquired dwelling) as against the other new owner.

It goes without saying that if the ownership of the outer dwelling was transferred by means of gift and the ownership of the inner dwelling was transferred by means of sale (there is no right of easement to the inner property enforceable against the donee of the outer property); but if the original owner sold the outer property and gave the inner property (to their respective new owners), the donee of the inner property does have a right of easement against the buyer of the outer property, because a gift (is presumed to be given) with more benevolence and goodwill (which would involve the donation of the easement to the gift) than a sale (which is presumed to be more strictly defined by the seller).

10) The above rule holds good when the owner has transferred ownership of each dwelling to the two different persons in one simultaneous transaction.[41] If, however, the original owner sold or gave the inner property and afterward sold or gave the outer property, as soon as acquisition of the inner property had been effected,[42] the new owner assumed ownership of an easement to it, which right of easement is not extinguished (by the later transaction concerning the outer property). Similarly, when the ownership of the outer property is transferred by sale and the ownership of the inner property is transferred by gift: if the sale of the outer property preceded the gift of the inner property, the new owner of the inner property will assume no ownership thereafter of any right of easement.

11) When one sells a house,[43] one sells (with it) all permanent fixtures of that house:[44] for example, the door,[45] the door bolt, and the door lock,[46] the casing of a hand mill and a stationary mortar;[47] the oven, the portable stove, and the millstones,[48] if they are fixed and stationary,[49] and the door moldings, if fixed with mortar.[50] (There is an opinion to the effect that a join by means of pegs is not deemed a permanent join.[51]) One has not sold the key, even if it is fixed to the door,[52] nor a moveable mortar,[53] nor the framework under the millstone, nor moldings for bedsteads, nor window frames[54] even if set in mortar, for they are (merely) for beautification (of the house). If one said, "(I sell you) the house and everything in it, all these (aforementioned items) are sold;[55] but not the roof (if it qualifies as a separate adjunct structure),

the verandah (if it qualifies as a separate adjunct structure), the pits, cisterns, or caves[56] (i.e., adjunct structures). (There is an opinion to the effect that if the seller wrote [in the bill of sale], "[I sell you the house] and everything that is in it," it is tantamount to his writing, "I have not reserved for myself, etc."; cf. supra para. 2.)

12) If A says to B, "I give (sell)[57] you one of my (two) houses," he may give (sell) him the smaller of the houses. If one of the houses collapsed, (the seller) may show (the buyer) the one that collapsed (as the one he bought), for the possessor of the bill of sale is always at the disadvantage (i.e., the buyer must prove that a better or different property was in fact what he bought). This same rule applies when A says to B, "I sell you one of my oxen" (and one of the oxen dies, etc.).

> GLOSS: But one does not give (sell) the other an upper chamber (as a house); if, however, A said to B, "I am selling you only a house" (i.e., a dwelling place only), A may give (sell) the upper chamber because it is also styled as a house (i.e., dwelling place).[58]

13) If A sells B space on which to build a house or a cattle shed,[59] or if A receives from B space on which to build a wedding house for his son or a retirement dwelling for his widowed daughter (or if a person undertook to do so[60] [i.e., build these structures]), one constructs them (not less than) four cubits by six cubits.

If A sold B space for a large house, it is to be constructed with dimensions not less than eight cubits by ten cubits. If A sold B space for a reception hall, it is to be constructed with dimensions not less than ten cubits by ten cubits. If A sold B space for a forecourt[61] (the huge courtyard which noblemen construct in front of their palaces; the Hebrew term for it comes from the technique of using fountains there to keep the earth from blowing about)[62], it is to be constructed with dimensions not less than twelve cubits by twelve cubits (apart from the thickness of any partitions in it[63].) The height of each structure is to equal one half its length and one half its width.[64]

215: The sale of a courtyard, a press house for olive-pressing, a bathhouse, or a city: what is included in such sales. Eight paragraphs.

1) When one sells a courtyard,[1] one has also transferred ownership of cisterns, pits, and caves within it, all dwellings, both those opening directly onto the courtyard and those opening indirectly onto it, dwellings together with their adjacent sandpits, and shopfronts which open onto it. Shopfronts which do not open onto it are not sold[2] with the courtyard. Shops which open onto the courtyard and also open onto an area off the courtyard are sold if most custom and use of the shop originate within the courtyard; if not, such shops are not sold. Moveable goods in the courtyard are not sold[3] (because they are not sold with a house[4]). When the seller says to the buyer, "(I sell you) it and all which is in it," all the servitudes and equipment of the houses, even though moveable, are sold with them[5] (except for stores of wheat or barley[6] [in them]).

In any event,[7] a bathhouse or a press house for olive-pressing in the courtyard is not sold. (There are those who hold the opinion that if the seller pointed out the outer property line of the courtyard to the buyer, everything [within those boundaries] is sold, as we have mentioned in regard to pits and cisterns, above 214:2; it has already been explained that there are those who disagree with reference to pits and cisterns [as included in a sale], and the same contrary ruling would [for them] apply here.[8])

2) When one sells an olive press,[9] one has transferred ownership of the great grindstone, built into the ground, on which the olives are crushed, the two cedarwood posts on which the (beam pole[10]) is rested at the time of olive crushing, the oil tanks and the vessels in which the olives to be crushed are put, i.e., the pounding stone, (and the boards placed around the olives to keep them in place[11]). But one has not transferred ownership of the upper grindstones.[12] When the seller says to the buyer, "(I sell you) it and all which is in it," these also are sold.

In any event[13] he has not sold the presses which are used to squeeze the olives, nor the winch wheel for operating the beam, nor the beam pole itself. (There are those who hold the opinion that if the seller said to the buyer, "[I sell you] it and everything in it," all these are sold;[14] this seems to me to be the essentially correct view.) (One has) not (however) sold the sacks and packing bags (sacks are made of animal hair, the packing bags of leather[15]).

If the seller has said to the buyer, "(I sell you) the press house, and all its equipment and appurtenances do I sell you,"[16] all these things (mentioned above) are sold. If there were shops outside the[17] press house proper (but adjacent to it), where olives or sesame seeds were ground: if the seller specified the outer boundaries thereof (including these shops), the buyer has effected acquisition of all (the press house, and the shops). If the outer boundaries were not specified, the buyer has effected acquisition only of the contents of the press house proper (and the press house itself).

3) When one sells a bathhouse,[18] one has transferred ownership of the storage space for the planks on which the undressed bathers sit, the closets for the storage of basins in which water is put (i.e., small wooden basins of water set before each bather),[19] the storage space for benches, on which the clothed customers sit in the courtyard of the bathhouse, and the storage space for the towels used for drying off. But he has not sold the planks themselves, nor the basins themselves, nor the benches nor the towels themselves. When the seller says to the buyer, "(I sell you) it and everything in it," all these items are sold.

In any event he has not sold the water-collection pools which supply water, whether in the hot season or the rainy season,[20] nor the wood-storage area. If the seller said to the buyer, "(I sell you) the bathhouse, and all its accessory structures do I sell you," all of them are sold even though they are outside the bathhouse proper.[21]

There is an authority who has written[22] that this last rule applies only when the accessory structures lie within the outer property lines of the bathhouse and the seller has specified these outer property lines in writing.

4) When one sells a city,[23] one has transferred ownership of the houses, cisterns, pits, caves, bathhouses, dovecotes, press houses, the irrigated fields in it, its inhabited immediate environs, its immediately adjacent forest, the fields known to belong to it, and fish and game preserves which face it, even though at some distance

from it. One has not transferred ownership of the moveable property[24] in it. When the seller says to the buyer, "(I sell you) it, and everything in it do I sell you," all that property is sold.[25]

In any event, one has not sold end[26] portions of fields separated from the rest of the land by rocky outcroppings, steep gullies, etc., nor adjacent villages, nor forest preserves separate from it, nor a portion of it that may be on an island,[27] nor (conversely if the island portion is sold,) a portion of it that may be on the mainland, nor fish and game preserves which do not face it (i.e., are separate from it).

5) When one sells a field,[28] one has transferred ownership to the stones laid out for building a fence, the stones used for weights on the sheaves of grain, since they are necessary for the sheaves (and one has sold its boundaries);[29] he has sold the peeled canes set under the vines to support them;[30] he has sold the produce still attached to the soil even though it is ready for harvest;[31] he has sold an area of reeds[32] which area is less than that which would require a quarter *kab* of seed, even though the reeds are thick and strong; he has sold the watchman's cabin, made with mortar and stone, even though not fixed into the ground; he has sold a young carob tree which is not yet grafted and a young sycamore tree even though such trees are healthy and well foliaged; he has sold the palm trees in it (even if they stand on its boundary line).[33]

But he has not sold stones[34] which are not laid out for building fence, nor the stones which are not used for weighting sheaves though they are ready for such use. (There are those who hold the opinion that if the stones were once placed upon the sheaves, they are sold[35]). He has not sold the canes in the vineyard which are not laid out under the vines, even though they are peeled and smooth for use as vine supports. He has not sold produce uprooted from the ground, even though such produce still needs to remain in the field (for drying[36]). When the seller says to the buyer, "(I sell you) it and everything in it," all those things are sold.

In any event, one has not sold an area of reeds which area would require a quarter *kab* of seed (or more), even though the reeds are small and weak; nor has one sold a small garden of aromatics which is known by a distinct and specific name (as a separate plot), e.g., people call it "someone's roses." One has not sold the watchman's cabin when it is not made with mortar, even though it is fixed into the ground. One has not sold a grafted carob tree nor a mature sycamore tree, even though such trees are weak and fragile. One has not sold the well,[37] nor the wine press, nor the dovecote, whether such structures are in working order or not.

The seller must acquire[38] from the buyer an easement in order that the seller can go to that well, cistern, or wine press, or dovecote which remains his property in that field. If the seller explicitly said that the field was sold except for these items (or any of them), it is not necessary for him to acquire an easement.

6) The above rules hold good in reference to a seller;[39] since it was the responsibility of the buyer to secure an explicit accounting of what was included in a sale, and he did not do so, the buyer has only these things (specified as passing to his ownership together with the field, etc., in the absence of explicit statements detailing the property sold). But when one gives a gift,[40] the donee effects acquisition of everything: whether in a field, in a house, in a courtyard, in an olive press. The general rule is that when one makes a gift of land, the donee receives everything attached to that land except as explicit reservations or conditions specify to the contrary.[41]

> GLOSS: Only what is within the (boundaries of the gift) of land (passes to the donee). What may lie outside those boundaries, e.g., a verandah or a room, etc., is treated no differently in a case of gift than in a case of sale.[42]

7) Similarly, when brothers have divided an estate and one has taken ownership of a field, he has taken ownership of that field and everything within it.[43] When one has seized the property of a convert (deceased without issue), and has thereby taken ownership of a field, he has taken ownership of that field and everything within it. When one has dedicated a field to a sacred purpose, such dedication applies to the field and everything within it.

8) Even with reference to a seller and a buyer, all the above-mentioned rules, and their like, apply only when there is no prevalent custom[44] (which would supersede these rules in that locality)

nor standard and recognized terminology for each of the various items mentioned (as passing or not passing from old to new owner); but if in that locality there is an established custom that if one sells item A, item B has been sold with it, item B is deemed sold (any rule above to the contrary notwithstanding).

We rely on prevalent custom in sales of real and moveable property (to govern the description and content of property sold); this is a most important fundamental principle in commercial matters: we follow the terminology generally employed by people of the locality (to describe items, contents, etc.), and we follow (local) commercial custom[45] (in establishing the propriety and legality of transactions).

216: The rules for a sale of a field when a particular palm tree, or trees, in that field, is excepted from the sale; the rule for a sale of land to A and of the trees on that land to B. (The rules for how one should write an instrument of sale for land in order to preclude later complaints and protests regarding the sale.)[1] Fourteen paragraphs.

1) When one sells an orchard to another,[2] the seller is to write for the buyer, "Effect acquisition for yourself of palm trees, date trees, and small shrub trees." Even though the buyer acquires all these things even without such specification of them, (this language) enhances the clarity and elegance of the document.

2) Similarly, when one sells land to another,[3] the seller is to write for the buyer, "And I have reserved naught for myself in this sale," in order to preclude future lawsuits and arguments.

3) When one sells a field to another,[4] and there are palm trees in that field, and the seller says to the buyer, "(I sell the field) except for a particular tree," if that tree is a good productive one, he has reserved only that tree for himself. Other palm trees pass to the buyer. If the tree so reserved is a poor producer of fruit, the buyer has not effected acquisition of any palm trees (i.e., the seller is deemed to have reserved *even* the poor tree, thus keeping all productive trees for himself, and again, the seller is presumed to have intended to include *even* the poor trees in the

reservation, but not to have cared to specify this matter.[5])

> GLOSS: There is an opinion which holds that the buyer has effected no acquisition of the better-quality trees only, but trees of equal or poorer quality (to the one specified) have been acquired. Any tree which yields a *kab* of fruit is called a producing tree.[6]
> There is an opinion which holds that all this regulation applies to the specific kinds of tree which the seller has reserved; but the buyer effects acquisition of any tree not of that kind.[7]

4) If one sells a field to another and says, "(I sell you the field) except for the trees," if there are only date palms in the field, they have been excluded from the sale;[8] if there are only vines (which the talmudic sages here consider as trees), they have been excluded from the sale;[9] and similarly with all other types of trees. If there were vines and date palms in the field, only the vines have been excluded from the sale[10] (they are considered the more important and valuable "tree," cf. *Baer Hagolah*, n. 5). (Similarly, when there are date palms and [other] trees [not vines], the [(other) trees are excluded] from the sale.[11] If there were trees and vines, the trees have been excluded from the sale and the vines have been sold with the field[12]): because a seller will show a degree of liberality toward the buyer[13] (and therefore is presumed to make the sale more inclusive than exclusive).

> GLOSS: If the seller said to the buyer, "(I sell the field) except for this carob tree," no acquisition has been effected for any carob tree[14] in the field (cf. supra 215:5); the reason why the seller specified "except for this carob tree" was to reserve an easement to the stand of carob trees[15].

If the seller has excepted the date-palm trees in the field from the sale of that field, the exception applies only to any tall palm tree,[16] one which has to be climbed by a rope ladder (for harvesting); other (smaller) date palms pass to the ownership of the buyer. (Yet if all the date palms are short, the seller has excepted them all from the sale.)[17]

If the seller has excepted any other kinds of trees, the exception applies only to those trees which would not be bent back by the yoke borne by oxen which plow beneath the trees.[18] (The heavy wooden yoke strikes the trees and pushes them back if such trees are young and small.) Any tree which is bent back by the yoke on the oxen is acquired by the buyer and is considered as part of the field. (Yet if all the trees are bent back in this fashion, all of them are deemed weak and the exception applies to all of them.)[19]

5) If one says to another, "I am selling you land and date palm trees":[20] even if the seller owned no date palms, if the seller wished to acquire for the buyer[21] (at least) two date palm trees, the sale is valid and the buyer cannot say, "I would acquire only land which (already) has date palms on it." If one says to another, "I sell you land with date palm trees," if there are two date palm trees there, lawful sale is effected; if not, the sale is effected on the basis of an erroneous belief on the part of the buyer and he may withdraw from the transaction. If the seller said to the buyer, "I sell you a date palm field" (i.e., a field suitable for date palm trees), the buyer has no right to expect date palm trees on the field, because such language on the part of the seller implies only that the field is suitable for date palm plantation. If there are date palm trees on that field, the buyer has effected acquisition of them,

> GLOSS: (since the buyer is deemed duly and lawfully informed of them) through any of the (above) forms of language used by the seller.
> There is an opinion that if the seller says to the buyer, "I am selling you land and date palm trees," even though there are date palms on the land, if the seller owns date palms in another place, the seller must give the buyer *two more* date palms (from that other plantation); and if not, the seller need not acquire two more date palms for the buyer; but the land is acquired by the buyer: there are deemed to be two (separate) sale transactions, one for the land and one for the date palm trees.[22]

6) When one sells (a minimum) of three trees in his field,[23] even if they were small plantings or three branches of one tree[24] (which appear above ground at a distance of four cubits from each other and therefore appear as three separate trees), the buyer effects acquisition of the ground required for those trees (i.e., beneath and between them). (There is an opinion which holds that if the trees are young and fragile and are bent by the oxen's yoke, the ground between them is not acquired by the buyer of them.[25])

Even if the trees withered and died,[26] or were cut down, the buyer owns the ground required for them (and he plants others in their stead). The buyer has effected acquisition (as well) of all trees between them.

The amount of land required under, between, and around these trees is reckoned to be as much as is necessary for a harvester with his basket to pass by there[27] (comfortably). This area cannot be sown by either the buyer or the seller without the consent of the other party.[28] (But the buyer may sow the land between the trees; if the seller has excepted the land between the trees from the sale and reserved it for himself, even here the buyer owns the land the trees stand on and may plant other trees there if the purchased trees wither and die.[29])

7) These rules apply when the three trees stand like the tripod of a (portable stove):[30] two are opposite each other and the third is on a line between them, at some distance from them. Moreover (the rules apply when the tripodal configuration) shall be, between each tree, a distance of not less than four and no more than sixteen cubits, such mesaurements to be taken from the thickest roots of the trees.[31]

But if the trees did not stand in this configuration, or the trees were less than four, or more than sixteen, cubits apart from each other,[32] or acquisition of them was not effected simultaneously,[33] or one sold two trees within his field and one on the boundary line of that field, or two trees within his field and one tree (which the seller, of course, owns) situated in the (adjacent) property of a third party, or a cistern or a canal or a public roadway is located between the trees,[34] the buyer does not effect acquisition of the land between the trees. Therefore the buyer has not effected acquisition of trees standing between those he did acquire. If one of the (acquired) trees withers and dies or is cut down (the trees not standing in a tripodal configuration, etc.), that tree and its land are lost to the buyer.

> GLOSS: (There is a loss) provided that the (remaining) stump of the withered or cut tree does not sprout afresh. If the stump does sprout afresh, the growth is not deemed a new tree; it is like a sprout from the (original) trunk of the tree and belongs to the owner of the tree.[35]

8) Anyone who effected acquisition of three trees[36] (simultaneously, etc.) and (thus) owns the ground (around the trees necessary for tending them, gathering their fruit, etc.): If the trees have grown larger and branched out, the buyer is to trim them so as not to permit his tree to limit the free passage of the owner of the field itself in his property. (If the seller says that the trees have become large [enough to impede his free movement in the field], and the buyer says that they have not, the buyer has the obligation of proving his assertion[37] [since he is apparently taking property from the seller].) All vine offshoots growing upward and upper-branch growth of trees, which comes from the (acquired) trees, even directly from their roots, are the property of the owner of the trees because he owns the land (on which they grow).

9) When one acquires two trees[38] in the field of another, he does not (thereby) effect acquisition of the land (around those trees). Therefore if a tree withers and dies or is cut down, the buyer has no claim on the land where it stood.

> GLOSS: But he does have access to a patch of ground at those trees sufficient to accommodate a harvester with a basket,[39] and all the more does he have a right to use the land under the trees where their fruit is gathered. The seller has no right to sow a crop on that patch of land immediately adjacent to the trees; the buyer also has a right of easement to the tree he acquired, for the purpose of gathering their fruit.

If the two trees grew large[40] and produced offshoots or (spreading) upper-branch systems, the buyer is to trim them. Such shoots or branches could take root in the ground, and the buyer could (then attempt to) say to the seller, "You sold me three trees and therefore I own the ground (around and between them)." (If, however, the branches spread widely [in the air only], the buyer need not trim them.)[41]

10) In regard to the wood which the owner of the two trees[42] (that he acquired in another's field) cuts from them, whatever sprouted from the trunks of the trees, i.e., the visible portion of the trees, belongs to the owner of the trees; whatever sprouted from the root system directly, i.e., the underground portion of the tree, belongs to the owner of the field. In regard to the date palm tree, the owner of the tree has no ownership of any growth at all, since that tree has no trunk which produces new growth.[43]

11) When one sells land and reserves the trees on that land for himself,[44] the seller retains full half the land itself, for if he had not done so, the buyer could say to him, "Pull up your tree (and begone!)." (There is an opinion which holds that the seller retains only the amount of land required to tend the trees[45] [gather the fruit, etc.].)

12) Similarly, if a seller reserved from a sale of his land only two trees,[46] he retains the land for the trees (i.e., tending them, etc.), for if he had not done so, the buyer could say to him, "Pull up your tree -- and begone!"

13) If A simultaneously sold his land to B and the trees on that land to C,[47] and C performed a formal possessive act with the trees and B performed a formal possessive act with the land: C has effected acquisition of the trees and half the land with them, and B has effected acquisition of half the land only.

(There are authorities who disagree[48] wtih this ruling and reason that the owner of the trees owns none of the land at all; but if the trees withered and died, he would be able to plant others in their stead.)

14) If one buys olive trees for the purpose of cutting them down,[49] the buyer is to leave, close to the ground level, two shoots (of each tree), and (then) cut (the rest of the trees down). If

one buys an untrimmed sycamore tree,[50] for the purpose of cutting it down, he can cut the trunk at no less than three handbreadths (from the ground level). If one buys a mature sycamore tree for the purpose of cutting it down, he can cut the trunk at no less than two handbreadths (from the ground level). In regard to other trees, the buyer is to allow one handbreadth (from ground level as a stump, and then) he may cut them down. In regard to weeds and vines, they are to be cut down from a point above the trunk knot. In regard to date palm trees and cedar trees, one may dig them up by their roots since they do not have stumps which produce new growth.

217: The rules for selling an irrigation ditch, or a private roadway, or a publicly used roadway, or a burial plot, located in one's private property. Seven paragraphs.

1) If one sells the place of an irrigation ditch to water a field requiring irrigation,[1] which place is located in one's private property, one gives (sells) him (the buyer) space for a ditch (not less than) two cubits wide in one's property and one cubit on either side of the ditch for its banks as well.[2] If one sells (the place)[3] of a water ditch which is worked with a bucket (presumably a ditch or reservoir used for laundry, watering animals, etc.)[4] (which place is in the seller's courtyard), one gives (sells) a ditch of (not less than) one cubit in width (in one's property) and one half-cubit on either side of the ditch for its banks as well.

2) The owner of the field has the right to plant (plants) in those bank areas,[5] but he is not to sow seed there because seed (as opposed to the deep roots of plants) will keep the ground wet and (eventually) the ditch will be ruined[6] (perhaps by damp earth sliding into the water and clogging the ditch; roots of plants would possibly hold the earth in place).

3) When the banks of an irrigation ditch have deteriorated,[7] the owner of the ditch may repair them with earth from that (field[8]) (which is not the property of the owner of the ditch) because the one who sold the ditch sold it with the implicit condition that this repair could be effected, i.e., that there be (a usable) water ditch in his field.[9]

4) One may sell another a roadway through his field.[10] If he sold

a private roadway, he gives (not less than) a space of two and one-half cubits in width, sufficient room for a donkey and its load to stand along the length of the roadway. (This area is given provided that the road has no high side-fences; if it has high side-fences it is necessary to give more space[11] [so that the animal and its load would not be cramped between too-narrow boundaries].) If one sold a (private) roadway between two towns,[12] the seller gives the buyer (not less than) a width of eight cubits. If one sold a roadway for public use,[13] the seller gives the buyer a width of (not less than) sixteen cubits. If one sold a stopping place (i.e., a place on the road from a burial plot, where mourners receive consolation), the seller gives the buyer an area (not less) than is sufficient for the planting of four *kabs* of seed (50 by 33.33 cubits).

5) When one says to another, "I sell you a cistern and its walls," the seller gives the buyer (not less than) three handbreadths of wall thickness.[14]

6) When one sells another a place for a burial plot, or one receives (land) and undertakes to build (for the donor) a burial grotto, one excavates a cave, onto which eight (separate) burial chambers open:[15] three on either side and two opposite (the entrance); the cave[16] (itself) is to be (not less than) four cubits by six cubits. Each burial chamber (opening onto this cave area) is to be four cubits in length, six handbreadths wide, and seven handbreadths high. Thus, there are one and one-half cubits separating each of the side burial chambers and two cubits separating the burial chambers opposite the entrance.

7) When one sells his burial plot,[17] the roadway to that burial plot, the stopping place (for consolation) on that road, and his house of mourning, the members of his family may come and bury him (in his plot), the desire of the buyer to the contrary notwithstanding; the family gives the buyer the purchase price of the burial chamber where the seller was buried.

218: The rules for selling a tract of land sufficient for the planting of a <u>kor</u> of seed, when the plot is cut by valleys and outcroppings of rock. Twenty-five paragraphs.

1) When one person says to another, "I am selling you a tract of

land sufficient for the sowing of a *kor*[1] (of seed)" (the same rule applies if the seller simply says, "I sell you sufficient for sowing a *kor*"[2]), and there are in those fields small ravines ten handbreadths deep, even though the ravines do not have water in them,[3] or outcrops of rocks (at least) ten handbreadths high[4] (by four handbreadths wide[5]), and they do not comprise an area requiring a quarter *kab* of seed[6]) (such areas are not included in reckoning) of the area sufficient for a *kor* of seed. A man does not wish to give his money for one place which appears (in fact) to be two or three different places.[7] The buyer takes these ravines and outcrops or rocks *gratis* along with a (full) tract of land sufficient for the sowing of a *kor* of seed.[8]

> GLOSS: There are those who hold the opinion that the ravines and rocky areas remain the seller's property. In any event, the buyer must take the rest of the field (i.e., the part without rocks and ravines) provided that a plow can pass between them[9] (i.e., the untillable ravines and rocky areas).

2) If the untillable areas (*in toto*) were less than this[10] (i.e., the measurements specified above, ten handbreadths in height or depth) (even if [the ravines] were full of water[11]), they are counted in with the tillable tract of land. This rule applies when the untillable areas amount to no more than would be required to plant four *kabs* of seed and the untillable areas are spread over a surface requiring (not more than) five *kabs* of seed within the larger portion of the (tillable) field[12] (as a whole).

If, however, these untillable areas *in toto* would require more than four *kabs* of seed[13] (and they are [at least] three handbreadths high[14]) or were widespread over the field or their total area would not fit into a surface requiring five (or less) *kabs* of seed, even though they are not ten handbreadths (in depth or height), they are not included in the measurement of the tillable portion of land.

3) If most of the untillable areas were located over a small portion of the field (or)[15] (and) the smaller portion of untillable surface was located in the larger portion of tillable surface or the untillable areas were configured like a straight line, or a circle,

or a curved line (a three-sided open figure) or a stadium-like pattern, or a crooked line[16] (in all of them plowing and seeding are difficult), (in these cases) there is an unresolved doubt (in the Talmud as to whether such formations of untillable land are or are not included in the measurement of the field as a whole). In these cases, a claimant, who brings a suit to have his adversary surrender something to him, bears the burden of proof that he is entitled to what he claims.[17] (Therefore, in case of dispute, if the buyer has already paid the price, the seller must accept it -- and must prove a claim for more money; if the buyer has not yet paid the price, the seller need not accept the money, and the burden of proof is on the buyer that his payment is sufficient for the property in question.[18])

4) Similarly (as in the above cases where the configuration of the untillable land makes plowing and seeding difficult), if there was earth (less than three handbreadths in depth -- i.e., not deep enough for plowing or for some roots to grow properly) above a rock formation or conversely a (thin layer of) rock above (tillable) earth, there is an unresolved (talmudic) doubt (and a claimant who seeks, e.g., money, from another bears the burden of proof that[19] he is entitled to what he seeks).

5) If there was in the field a single, isolated rock,[20] even if it covered an area requiring a quarter *kor* of seed, it is not included in the measurement of the field.[21] If a rock was adjacent to the boundary line of the field, no matter how small that rock is, it is not included in the measurement of the field. If a (small) strip of (tillable) earth lies between a rock and the boundary of the field, there is an unresolved talmudic doubt (as to the inclusion of the rock in the measurement of the field, and therefore, as above, a claimant bears the burden of proof when he seeks to have his adversary surrender property, etc., to him). (These rules are the opinions of Maimonides; there are, however, other opinions in these matters and the *Tur* cites them.)

6) If one says to another, "I am selling you a tract of land approximately the area requiring a *kor* of seed," even if there were ravines ten handbreadths depth, or more, or rocks of ten handbreadths height, or more, all those (untillable) areas are included

in the measurement of the field.[22]

> GLOSS: There is an opinion which holds that (this rule applies) only when such untillable land does not amount to (more than[23]) an area requiring four *kabs* of seed.[24] And this rule contemplates a situation in which the buyer is not standing in that field (at the time of the transaction); if, however, he is present in the field (at the time of the transaction, the situation is held to be the same) as if the seller said, "I am selling you a tract of land sufficient for a *kor* of seed -- more or less." And (in that case -- see para. 8 infra) even if the field lacks (as much as) seven and one-half *kabs* of seeding area (one twenty-fourth of the whole), the sale is valid.[25]

7) If the seller says to the buyer, "I sell you a tract of land sufficient for a *kor* of seed," such tract to be measured precisely with a line;[26] if the land measures less than what is required for the *kor* of seed, by any amount, a deduction from the price (of the full-*kor* area is made proportionate to the amount of land lacking). If the land measures more than what is required for a *kor*, by any amount, that additional amount of land is returned to the seller.

8) If the seller says to the buyer, "I sell you (this)[27] tract of land sufficient for a *kor* of seed,"[28] the seller's statement is interpreted to imply the sense of the statement, "I sell you a tract of land more or less sufficient for a *kor* of seed." If, upon precise measurement of the field, it is found to lack,[29] or to be in excess of, not more than one twenty-fourth part of the area needed for a *kor* of seed, the sale is valid: one twenty-fourth of the whole equals an area requiring seven and one-half *kabs* of seed, or one quarter *kab* for each of the thirty *seahs* in the *kor*. (Thirty quarter *kabs* amount to seven and one-half *kabs*.) If the difference is greater than one twenty-fourth, a reckoning is conducted with him (regarding)[30] all the quarter *kabs* of lack or excess: a deduction from the price is made for each quarter *kab* of seed area lacking.

> GLOSS: There is an opinion which holds that this rule applies only when the amount of lack is small enough so

that the area may, as a whole,[31] still be styled a tract requiring a *kor* of seed. But if the area lacking is substantially more (so that the whole cannot properly be styled a tract requiring a *kor* of seed), the rule (specifying reduction in price) does not apply, since a tract requiring a *kor* was stated; and (the rule providing for deduction from the price) applies only when the seller has no more land (to make up the difference). But if the seller has sold a tract of land requiring a *kor* of seed, among his other real properties, he gives the buyer precisely that amount of land -- a tract requiring a *kor* of seed.[32]

All the excess land, beyond the amount required for a *kor* of seed, the buyer shall return to the seller.

9) The precise nature of what the buyer returns is as follows:[33] if the additional amount of land was less than a plot requiring nine *kabs* of seed (which can be reckoned as a field in and of itself), the buyer returns the price of the excess, reckoned according to the price of such land at the time of the sale: this is for the protection of the seller (in a fluctuating land market). If the additional land[34] lay adjacent to another field owned by the seller, the buyer returns the portion of land adjacent to the seller's other property; and therefore the seller loses nothing (i.e., he does not receive a small, isolated field, but his existing property is augmented).

10) If the additional amount of land[35] was (a plot requiring nine *kabs* of seed or) more, we allow (as lawful overage, which need not be returned, cf. above para. 8) a quarter *kab* area for each area requiring a *seah* of seed. If the surplus remaining after this calculation amounts to an area requiring nine *kabs* of seed (or more), all the quarter-*kab* allowance, and this surplus over that allowance, is returned to the seller (i.e., the land itself); (it is valued) at the valuation it bore at the time of the original sale. (i.e., if the buyer should choose to return the price of the excess land, he does so according to its valuation at the time of the original sale.)[36]

11) This last rule applies when the land was cheap at the time of

the sale,[37] but has risen in price by the time the additional land is to be returned. If, however, the land was expensive (at the time of the sale), but has declined in price (by the time the additional land is to be returned), we say to the buyer, "If you wish to give the seller money for all the additional land, pay him (for the land) according (to the price of land at the time of the original) sale,[38] and if you wish to give him land, give him land at its present (low) valuation (in order that the value of this land equals the amount of money the additional land cost at the former, higher valuation)."

12) With reference to a garden plot, a difference (of more land or less land) amounting to an area requiring half a *kab* of seed is treated like a difference of a nine *kabs* of seed area with regard to a field[39] (i.e., an area requiring half a *kab* of seed amounts to a separate plot). If there is (upon measurement) an excess of land (in the sale of a garden plot above the amount of land agreed upon by the buyer and seller) of less than half a *kab*'s area of seed over and above (the lawful, allowable overage of) a quarter *kab*'s area (for each area requiring a *seah* of seed), the buyer returns to the seller only the price of that overage. If the overage is an area requiring one half-*kab* of seed (or more), the buyer returns to the seller all the quarter *kabs* (per *seah* area, the allowable, lawful overage) plus any additional overage either by returning the (original) price of that amount of land or by returning an amount of land (equal in price to the original value of the additional land when) it is valued at the cheap price obtaining at the time the land is returned. (The material from para. 9[40] through para. 12 is the opinion of Maimonides, *Hilkhoth Mekhirah* 28:1-9. The commentator to Maimonides, *Maggid Mishneh*, concludes his remarks with the caution that Maimonides's opinions require further study and analysis.

The basic rule here[41] follows the opinion of those who hold that whenever the excess land does not amount to an area requiring nine *kabs* of seed, the seller has the option to take back the excess land or to take the money for the excess land. If the buyer gives the seller the price of the excess land, he gives it at the cheapest valuation of that land: whether it was cheap at the time of the original sale and rose in price, or vice versa; but if the seller owned other property adjacent to the excess land (of the sale), the buyer returns the excess of land to the seller. And as well, if the excess land amounted to an area requiring nine *kabs* of seed (or more), all the excess, both the quarter *kab* per *seah* excess and any surplus over that amount of land, is reckoned (as one parcel for return to the seller)).

13) If one sold a field which was turned into a garden plot by the buyer, or one sold a garden plot which was turned into a field by the buyer,[42] there is an unresolved talmudic doubt whether or not one considers that land (for purposes of calculating any difference, either more or less, between the actual amount of land and the amount which was to be sold) in terms of its use at the time of the original sale or its present use (i.e., the change in use instituted by the buyer).[43]

14) If the seller says to the buyer, "I sell you a tract of land requiring a *kor* of seed, measured with a measuring line, more or less,"[44] or he said to him, "I sell you a tract of land requiring a *kor* of seed, more or less, measured with a measuring line": the seller's statement is interpreted to the buyer's disadvantage and the transaction is deemed to involve a tract requiring a *kor*, more or less.[45]

15) If the seller says to the buyer, "I sell you a tract of land requiring a *kor* of seed," and the seller mentioned the tract's landmarks and boundaries:[46] If the actual extent of the tract is only one-sixth more than, or less than, a tract which would require a *kor*, the sale is valid. If the actual extent of the property lacks more than one-sixth of the *kor* tract, a deduction shall be made from the purchase price. If the actual extent of the property exceeds the area of a *kor* tract by more than one-sixth, the buyer shall either return the money value of the land or he shall return the land to the seller. What the buyer does in the case of surplus land is governed by the amount and location of the surplus land: if the additional area is less than would require nine *kabs* of seed, or a half *kab* of seed if the land is a garden plot, and was not adjacent to another property owned by the seller, the buyer returns the money value of the property.

16) If A sells B a field with which B is already familiar,[47] knowing it and its boundaries, even if A said to B that the field

contained, e.g., 200 acres, but upon survey the field was actually only 150 acres, the sale is valid because the buyer knew the property and undertook (to acquire *that* property). The seller's statement that the property contained 200 acres is to be understood as meaning that the field is equal in value to another field that does in fact contain 200 acres.[48]

17) If the seller says to the buyer, "I am selling you such-and-such a tract requiring a *kor* of seed,"[49] even though the field contains only half the specified area, the sale is valid, because the seller sold an area which is specifically styled as a *kor* tract. Therefore the seller must bring proof (in case of dispute) that that property is (in fact) specifically styled as a *kor* tract.

18) Similarly, if the seller says to the buyer, "I sell you my vineyard in such-and-such a place":[50] even though there are no vines on that property, the sale is valid, provided that the property is (commonly) styled a vineyard. Similarly, if the seller says to the buyer, "I sell you this orchard":[51] even if there are no pomegranate trees in it (i.e., it is not planted with fruit trees), the sale is valid, provided that the property is (commonly) styled as an orchard; and this rule obtains in all similar cases.

19) All these rules apply where there is no local custom[52] (in these matters); where, however, there is a local custom (in these matters), one is to follow that custom (in adjudicating disputes, determining amounts of land sold, etc.), and we recognize and maintain the usual forms of expression which the majority of people in a particular locale use (to name places, fields, etc., in settling disputes, etc., in that locale).

20) If the seller says to the buyer, "I sell you half[53] my field" (the particular half not being specified), we estimate the value of the entire field, and the seller gives the buyer the poorer part of the field up to the value of one-half of the whole field. Similarly, if the seller said to the buyer, "I sell you the southern half[54] of my field," we estimate the value of the whole field, and the seller gives the buyer the southern portion of the field up to the value of one-half the whole field.

The buyer undertakes to set aside a portion of his (newly acquired) field for a fence.[55] (There is an opinion which holds that the sel-

ler gives part of his field as the place for building the fence.[56])
Behind and adjacent to this fence there shall be dug a small
trench[57] three handbreadths wide, and one handbreadth beyond the
small trench there shall be dug another trench, six handbreadths
wide. The trenches are for the purpose of preventing small animals
from jumping the fence.

21) If one owned half a field and he said to a buyer, "I sell you
the half-field which I own," the buyer will effect acquisition of
the full half-field;[58] if he said (in this circumstance), "I sell
you half the field which I own," the buyer will only effect acquisition of a quarter of the entire field (see supra 214:7).

22) If one owned a large tract which contained many separate
fields, each marked off by boundary lines,[59] and one sold a field in
that tract and showed the buyer the (outer) boundary lines of the
(entire) tract, the buyer will only effect acquisition of one field
(in the tract) even though there may be a few people who style the
entire tract as a field (see supra 214:7; if, however, the tract is
not interrupted with field boundaries,[60] the buyer will effect acquisition of the entire tract, since an area bounded by one property
line may properly termed a field). (The assumption is that the seller would reserve the balance of the tract for himself when he sells
one field which is marked off in the tract and merely demonstrated
the outer property lines of his own holdings.)

23) If a seller says to a buyer, "I sell you Hiyya's field,"[61]
and two fields bore this designation, the buyer will only effect acquisition of the poorer-quality field of the two.

24) If a seller says to a buyer, "I sell you fields," the minimum
number of fields in the transaction is two.[62] If the seller said to
the buyer, "(I sell you) all the fields," even three or four (or
more) fields are included in the transaction but not garden plots or
orchards. (This rule applies only if the seller said "fields."[63] If,
however, he said "[all[64]] real property," all (the fields, gardens,
etc.) are included by this language, even houses.[65])

If the seller said, "(I sell you) (landed) properties,"[66] even
gardens and orchards are included in this language; if he said, "(I
sell you) all (my) properties," even buildings, slaves, and all
moveable possessions[67] known to be his, even the *tefillin* on his

head, are included in the sale. (This rule applies only when the seller said "all my properties" but [if][68] he said, "[I sell you] the property of such and such a person," which he had purchased from him, he has not sold the moveable goods he purchased, because moveable goods are not [commonly] styled by name as the property of a particular seller).[69]

25) If a seller says to a buyer, "I sell you A's field,"[70] but after the buyer came to possess and use the field, the seller declares to him, "This is not A's field; though it is called by his name, it never was his property. But this (field is the one) that belonged to A; I purchased it from him and I sold it to you": (In this case) it is the seller's duty to prove[71] (that the field purchased by the buyer was never A's); and if no proof (of that) is presented by the seller, the buyer takes lawful possession of the field which all the people (of that place) call, "A's field."

219: The rules for specifying boundary lines for real property and the rules obtaining if one did not specify boundaries. Six paragraphs.

1) If a seller says to a buyer, "I sell you such and such a field," the buyer will effect acquisition of the whole field,[1] even if it is extremely large, even though the seller did not specify its boundaries, as long as no (other) boundary line interrupts that field.

> GLOSS: If the seller specified the eastern and western property line,[2] but did not mention the northern and southern ones, the buyer effects acquisition of the entire field; we do not say that he would only effect acquisition of ridges of property along both the eastern and western property lines.

2) If a seller specified (to the buyer) the first, second, and third boundary lines (of the field he is selling), but not the fourth boundary line,[3] the buyer will effect acquisition of the whole of the field, except for (the narrow strip of land at the) fourth boundary line. ([How[4]] this occurs in practice is as fol-

lows:) if the fourth boundary line lies within the two adjacent boundary lines (i.e., if the east and west boundaries were each fifty meters long, and the north boundary intersected those lines at the fiftieth meter), and there is no stand of date palm trees on it, and the total area of the fourth boundary does not require nine *kabs* of seed, acquisition will be effected even for the fourth boundary. If the fourth boundary does not lie within the two adjacent boundary lines[5] (i.e., if the east and west boundaries were each fifty meters long, and the north boundary would intersect the other two lines just beyond the fiftieth meter), and there is a stand of date palm trees on the fourth boundary, or the total area of the fourth boundary requires nine *kabs* of seed, no acquisition of the fourth boundary line will be effected.

If the fourth boundary lies within the two adjacent boundary lines, and there is a stand of date palm trees on it, or the fourth boundary has a total area requiring nine *kabs* of seed; or if the fourth boundary does not lie within the two adjacent boundary lines, and there is no stand of date palm trees on the fourth boundary line nor does its total area require nine *kabs* of seed: (disputes over the ownership of the boundary in these two latter cases) are submitted to the rabbinical court, (which will decide the matter) according to their view of the particular case; they shall make a (lawful) judgment (in the matter), exercising judicial discretion, taking whatever course their wisdom may dictate.[6]

3) If a seller specified for the buyer two (parallel) boundary lines, one long one and one short one:[7] if the longer boundary line separates the field from property owned by only one owner, acquisition will be effected only for that portion of the field bounded by a line drawn from the end point of the shorter boundary, perpendicular to the opposite, parallel, and longer boundary line.
If the longer boundary line separates the field from two properties each owned by a different person,[8] acquisition will be effected for that portion of the field bounded by an oblique line extending from the end point of the shorter boundary line to the end point of the opposite, parallel, and longer boundary line. (Translator's Example: there is a rectangular field, abcd. The long side ab abuts two fields owned by J and K respectively. The property line between J an

K touches ab at a point z. The seller of abcd specifies the long boundary ab. The shorter specification extended only to point y along boundary cd. The amount of land sold will be the trapezoid abyd.)

(There is an opinion which holds[9] that even when the longer boundary separates the field from the property owned by only one person, acquisition will be effected for that portion of the field bounded by an oblique line extending from the end point of the shorter boundary line to the end point of the opposite, parallel, and longer boundary line.)

4) If a seller specified, to a buyer, only the corners[10] (of the field to be sold) but did not define the full boundaries of each side of the field; or (partially) specified two (sets of adjacent) boundary lines in the shape of the Greek letter gamma (one opposite the other)[11] (i.e., one "gamma" at one corner and another "gamma" at the corner diagonally opposite, so that if the lines of the "gamma" were extended, a four-sided figure would be formed); or specified only a portion of the boundary line on each side of the field: the buyer will not effect acquisition of the entire field, but only a portion thereof determined by the boundary lines actually specified and what the judges of the rabbinical court shall see in their exercise of judicial discretion to make a proper disposition of the matter.

5) If a field was bounded on the east and west by A's property[12] and on the north and south by B's property, when one sells that field one must specify for the buyer in the written instrument: A field bounded by A's property on two sides and by B's property on two sides (not just "a field lying between A's property and B's property," which does not necessarily imply the entire field).

6) If A owned a field and sold the western part of it to B while retaining the eastern part of the field for himself,[13] and A specified for B the western boundary of the field but did not specify an eastern boundary, merely writing (in the instrument) "the eastern boundary of the field (is the field) of which half is cut off," or "(is the field) of which a part is cut off": if the seller (also) wrote "and these (specifications) are its boundaries," the buyer will effect acquisition of half the field;[14] if the seller did not write (that additional language), the buyer will effect acquisition only of an area requiring nine *kabs* of seed (i.e., a minimum area

for a separate field).

220: The rule governing the sale of a ship, a cart, a yoke of oxen, a cow, an ass, and a slave-girl. Eighteen paragraphs.

1) When one sells (the hull) of a ship, one has transferred ownership of its mast,[1] its sail, anchors, all oars which direct it (i.e., rudders) (including lines used to warp[2] it to a berth), the gangplank, the ladders used to go up and down to the ship,[3] and the water butt aboard it. One has not transferred ownership of the ship's small boat, whether used for lightering people and stores to and from land or used for fishing, nor the slaves[4] who serve in the ship, nor the packing bags, nor the cargo on board. When a seller says to a buyer, "I sell you (the ship) and everything aboard her," all of these things are sold (with the ship).

2) When one sells a cart, one has not sold the mules[5] (i.e., its draft animals), when they are not hitched to the cart. When one sells the mules, one has not sold the cart.

> GLOSS: If the cart and mules are hitched together: when one sells the cart, one sells the mules; when one sells the mules, one has not sold the cart.[6]

3) There is an opinion which holds that the above rules apply only to a sale.[7] If, however, one leased out his cart, he has also leased out his mules, even though the mules are not hitched to the wagon (at the time of the transaction of hire).

4) When one sells a yoke[8] (used for oxen), one has not sold the oxen; when one sells the oxen, one has not sold the yoke, even in a locale where (some people[9]) use the word "yoke" to refer to the oxen.

> GLOSS: This rule applies only when the oxen are not harnessed to the yoke[10]; if, however, they are harnessed to the yoke, the oxen are sold (with the yoke).

5) When one sells a yoke (for a cow), one has sold the cow[11] (in it); when one sells a cow, one has not sold the yoke (for the cow).

(There are authorities who differ on this point and reason that when one has sold the yoke, one has not sold the cow[12] (in it); and thus is the correct interpretation of this rule as it appears to me.)

6) When one sells a wagon, one sells the ox[13] (which draws it); when one sells the ox (which draws a wagon), one has not sold the wagon. (And there are authorities who take issue with this rule as has been explained supra.)

7) When one sells an ass, one has sold the saddle blanket[14] (on it) and the saddle (whether a riding saddle or a pack saddle), even though these items are not on the ass (at the time of the transaction). But one has not sold the saddlebag nor a saddle for women -- even if they were on the ass at the time of the sale[15] (unless the seller said to the buyer, "It and everything on it is sold to you"[16]).

8) In all these (above-mentioned) matters,[17] an excessively high purchase price (excessive in terms of a normal standard price range for these items in the open market) is no proof (that e.g., the ox was included in the sale of the cart, etc.). If an error (as to price appears in a transaction) where a deception is a genuine possibility (i.e., an overcharge that is not inordinately excessive), one has the remedies for constructive fraud by unfair pricing practice, or rescission, available under the laws governing the transactions of any seller and buyer. If the error (as to price appears in a transaction) where deception is really not a genuine possibility[18] (i.e., an overcharge of inordinate proportion), there is no remedy of rescission, because the additional payment is deemed a gift (from buyer to seller -- it being out of the question that the buyer could ever have imagined that such a huge price was merely for the purchase of the item).

> GLOSS: This (qualification) applies only where oxen are called (specifically) "oxen,"[19] and a yoke is (specifically) called a "yoke" (i.e., there is no common use of "yoke" as a reference to a yoke with the oxen). If, however, most people (of a locality) use the term "yoke" to refer to a yoke and the oxen in the yoke, then we do hold that the amount of the purchase price is proof of whether or not the oxen were sold along with the yoke (or vice

versa). If all the people (of a locality) use the term "yoke" to refer to a yoke and the oxen in the yoke, and (in case of a sale of a yoke alone) specify that only a yoke (without oxen) is being sold, then when a "yoke" is sold, both yoke and oxen are deemed included in the transaction, without reference to the amount of purchase price as an indicator (of what specifically was sold).

There are those who hold the opinion that the rule providing that the sale of the ox does not include its yoke applies when the sale of the animal is made without specification of the purpose for which the animal is sold. In that case we say that the animal is sold for slaughter as food. If, however, the animal was sold with the specification that it was to be used for plowing, one has sold the yoke along with the ox.

9) When one sells a slave-girl,[20] one has sold the equipment and utensils upon her, even if they amount to one hundred items. But one has not transferred ownership of necklaces, bracelets, or rings (she may be wearing) nor of her decorative choker neck jewelry. If one said, "(I sell you) the slave-girl and everything upon her," (all the above-mentioned items) are included in the sale, even if she is wearing items that would fetch one hundred gold pieces (or more).

10) If one says to another, "I am selling you a pregnant slave-girl,"[21] or, "I am selling you a pregnant cow," he has also transferred ownership of the young they are carrying. There is an opinion that even if the slave-girl or the cow was sold[22] without specification of the fact that they were pregnant, but they were in fact pregnant, their young are included in the sale.

11) (If one says), "I sell you a wetnurse, or a milch-cow,"[23] ownership of their young is not transferred (by this transaction). (If one says), "I sell you a milch-ass," the young of the milch-ass is included in the sale, since an ass is not purchased as a milk-providing animal (and thus there is deemed to be no point in acquiring the milch-ass without her young).

12) If one says to another, "I sell you the head of this slave,"[24] or, "I sell you the head of this ass," one has arranged to sell half (that property). The same rule applies when the seller

undertakes to sell any portion of an animal or a slave, the removal of which would kill the animal or slave.

If one says to another, "I sell you the hand of this slave or the forefoot of this ass," they make an estimate between themselves (as to the value of the limb in reference to the performance of specific tasks, and that value becomes the purchase price). The same rule applies when the seller undertakes to sell any portion of an animal or a slave, the removal of which would not (necessarily) cause mortal injury.

13) If one says to another, "I sell you the head of a cow," he has sold only the head, since a cow's head is regularly sold (as a separate item) in slaughterhouses.[25]

14) If one sells the head of large cattle[26] (i.e., contingent upon the slaughter of the large domesticated animal), one has not sold its feet, and vice versa; if one sells the lung (of large cattle), one has not sold its liver,[27] and vice versa. But if one sells the head of a small domesticated animal (once it is slaughtered, or contingent upon its slaughter), one has included the feet of the animal in the sale; not, however, vice versa. If one sells the lung of the small animal, one has sold the liver, but not vice versa.

15) These rules (just given) apply only in localities where there is no well-known (and prevalent) custom[28] (which governs such transactions). But in a locality where there is a well-known (and prevalent) custom (which governs such transactions), all (disputes, adjudications, etc., in these matters) will follow the provisions of that custom.

16) If one sells a cistern, one has not transferred ownership of the waters in it;[29] if one sells the location of a dung heap, one has (also) transferred ownership of the manure pile on it. (There is an opinion which holds that if one has sold a cistern,[30] one has also transferred ownership of the water in it; and if one has sold water and manure, one has not transferred ownership of the cistern or the location of the dung heap, respectively.)

17) If one sells a dovecote, one has transferred ownership of its dove; if one sells a beehive, one has transferred ownership of its bees.[31]

18) There is an opinion which holds that the rule just stated al-

so applies in the converse:[32] if one has sold doves; one has also transferred the ownership of their dovecote; and if one has sold bees, one has also transferred the ownership of their hive. This converse applies when the seller has specified that he has sold all the yield of the dovecote or beehive,[33] without reserving anything (for himself from that transaction). If, however, he sold the yield of a beehive without such specification, not only has he not even transferred ownership of the beehive, he has not even transferred the ownership of all the bees in it. (In this case), however, the buyer shall take the first three swarms (of bees produced in the hive after his purchase of it): (at the beginning of the summer, the hive produces one new swarm; the buyer transfers them to a new hive; another swarm is produced about nine or ten days later, etc.). From then on, the buyer takes one (newly produced) swarm and leaves one (in the original hive[34]) so that the hive will not become depopulated.

If one has sold the yield of a dovecote[35] (without the specification that the seller reserved nothing for himself from that transaction), the buyer is not to take all the young hatched in the dovecote from the time of purchase onward, because the mother birds will flee that dovecote, and thus the buyer destroys the whole dovecote. The buyer, however, is to leave with the dovecote a sufficient number of young birds to provide for the continuing repopulation of the dovecote. The number of young (is determined as follows): If, at the time of the sale of the yield of the dovecote, there are mother birds and daughter birds, the buyer leaves in the dovecote the first broods of doves hatched by the mother birds (a dove is assumed to hatch one male and one female per month; this pair of young birds is called a brood). These birds are left in the dovecote so that the mother birds will remain in the dovecote with their first broods, and with their daughter birds which are with them. The buyer also leaves in the dovecote the first two broods of each daughter bird in order that the daughter birds remain in the dovecote with their two broods of offspring. Any birds hatched in the dovecote after the hatching of the first two broods of the daughter birds, and the first brood of the mother birds, is the property of the buyer.

GLOSS: In all these matters there is no distinction between a transaction of sale and a transaction of gift[36] (i.e., in the matter of keeping the beehive and the dovecote adequately populated, etc.). Even though in the matter of property actually joined to the ground there is a distinction (as between sale and gift transactions), see above 215:6, there is no such distinction in matters of (purely) moveable property.

221: The rule for the dispute in which the seller claims the price is two hundred zuz and the buyer claims the price is one hundred zuz. One paragraph.

1) The case is that one person desires to effect acquisition of something (moveable) which another person is selling: The seller asserts, "I sell this to you for two hundred zuz." The buyer asserts, "I will purchase it for a sum of one hundred zuz;"[1] both parties then retire to their homes (i.e., leave the scene of the transaction). Then, sometime later, the two parties come together, and, without further discussion or negotiation, the buyer effects acquisition by pulling the object. If the seller had summoned the buyer to the meeting, and gave the buyer the object, the buyer need only pay a price of one hundred zuz. If the buyer had come (without the seller's requesting it) and effected acquisition by pulling the object -- there being no further discussion or negotiation as to price, the buyer is to pay a price of two hundred zuz.

> GLOSS: If there was a prior arrangement of terms between buyer and seller,[2] and one of the parties withdrew from the arrangement (prior to the effecting of any acquisition); and then later the parties met, and acquisition was effected without further discussion or negotiation as to price, we hold that acquisition was in fact effected under the terms of the original arrangement.

222: The rule concerning disagreement between buyer and seller regarding the subject of the sale; various disputes between buyer and seller. Four paragraphs.

1) A seller's statement to the following effect is deemed trustworthy, "I sold the item to this person; I did not sell the item to that person,"[1] as long as he is in possession of the item sold. If the seller is no longer in possession of the item sold, his statement is tantamount to the declaration of one witness[2] (i.e., insufficient to prove a claim in court); and his testimony in this matter is like the testimony of any other person, since (no longer having possession of the item and therefore having no personal interest to be served) he is completely impartial. (There is no distinction to be made in this case as between the seller's receiving the purchase-price money from one person and receiving the purchase-price money from two persons,[3] when the seller says that one of the persons gave him the purchase money against his [the seller's] will.)

Therefore, if the seller took the purchase-price money from two persons,[4] from one with his (the seller's) consent and from the other against his (the seller's) will, but he does not know which person gave him the purchase money with his consent and which without his consent, the seller can give no testimony in the dispute at all, whether the object was still in his possession or the two parties were both holding on to it. Each purchaser is to swear the oath on a holy object, as the rabbinical sages have provided; each may take half the object and half (the amount of the second) purchase price (which monies the seller possesses).

2) If one purchases an object from some one of five persons,[5] and each of the five asserts a claim against him and says, "I am the seller," but the buyer does not know from whom he made the purchase, the buyer leaves the purchase-price money with the five of them and takes his leave. This money shall be deposited with the rabbinical court until they (the five) shall (individually) confess and acknowledge (which of them is entitled to the money) or until Elijah the Prophet shall come (to solve this mystery). If the buyer is pious,[6] he should give the purchase price to each of the five claimants in order to discharge his moral obligation as it would be perceived in a heavenly court (since his forgetfulness has caused the five sellers to be involved in this matter).

3) If one purchases an item from some one of five persons, then denies (having made the purchase from any of them), swearing a false

oath to that effect,[7] and then sincerely repents and desires to fulfill his obligation (to pay for the item), and each of the five persons claims (the money) and says, "I am the one you denied and against whom you swore the false oath," and the purchaser says, "I do not know (which of you is the seller)": the purchaser is obliged to pay each (of the five claimants) in full, since the purchaser committed the transgression (of denial and false oath).

4) When A raises a complaint against B, and A says, "You sold (a thing) to me"; and B says, "I did not sell (a thing) to you," or, "I sold it to you but you did not pay me for it";[8] or A claims he paid for a thing and as yet has not effected formal, legal acquisition by pulling, or "I pulled it (effecting legal acquisition), but I never saw *this* thing (i.e., the item has a defect that was not seen before)";[9] to which B responds, "I informed you of this (defect)"; or either A or B says that the sale was conditional and the other party claims it was not at all conditional: in all these suits, and in similar cases, the party claiming property or money is due him from his adversary is obliged to prove his claim, the party making the denial, from whom a recovery is sought, swears the oath prescribed by rabbinical ordinance (to the effect that the claim against him is false, and thus successfully rebuts the claimant); if, however, the party making the denial does in fact acknowledge the correctness of some aspect of the claim or the claimant can produce (only) one witness against the denying party, then the denying party (in order to avert judgment against him) shall swear the oath prescribed by biblical law, as is done in all other suits requiring an oath.

> GLOSS: One authority has written that where A says, "I sold a field, but I do not know to whom (I sold it)," and B comes and says, "I am the purchaser," B's assertion of this claim is deemed trustworthy[11] (and thus he assumes the obligations of a lawful purchaser).

223: The rule governing disposition of a dispute arising when a cow is exchanged for an ass and formal acquisition is made, and while the cow is still on the property of its first owner it calves; or of a dispute over which of two fields or slaves has been sold. Five paragraphs.

1) One exchanges a cow for another person's ass. The owner of the cow effects acquisition of the ass by pulling (thus conferring acquisition of the cow upon the former owner of the ass). But the cow is still on the property of its (former) owner, and it calves (there).[1] The (former) owner of the cow claims that the calf was born prior to his pulling of the ass to effect acquisition of it; the owner of the ass claims the calf was born subsequent to his acquisition of the cow. Similarly: One sells a slave-girl,[2] receives the purchase-price money for her, and (while still in her former owner's house) the slave-girl gives birth. The seller claims that she gave birth before he received his money for her; the buyer claims that the birth occurred after he paid the purchase price for her. Even if the buyer makes his claim with absolute assurance but the seller's claim includes some element of doubt, the buyer must bear the burden of proof for his claim[3] (against the seller) -- even if the cow, or slave-girl, was not physically on the property of the seller, but standing in a swampy area (not owned by the seller, or in a public area[4]). If the buyer does not prove his claim,[5] the seller is to take the oath (prescribed by biblical law) upon a holy object regarding the cow (and he becomes thereby the lawful owner of the calf); the seller is to take the oath prescribed by rabbinical law regarding the slave-girl's offspring[6] (and he becomes thereby the lawful owner of the child). If the buyer should be in physical possession of the cow, or slave-girl, the seller is required to prove his claim (as to the sequence of events, i.e., acquisition and birth, or else the buyer is the lawful owner of the offspring).

2) If the buyer does not know whether or not his acquisition (of the cow or the slave-girl) preceded the birth of the offspring; and the seller does not know which event preceded which; and the cow, or slave-girl, is not physically on property owned by either of them, the buyer bears the burden of proof for his claim[7] (to the offspring). (There is an opinion to the effect that [this rule applies] even if the claimant [either seller or buyer] asserts his case with absolute assurance, and his adversary [either buyer or seller] has some element of doubt in the statement of his case.[8]) (I.e., the buyer bears a burden of proof even if he is positive about the sequence of events in his favor, and all the more if he is not posi-

tive.)

There is an opinion which holds that (in this situation, the claimants) divide the offspring equally[9] (i.e., apportionments of equal value are made).

3) If one party (in this type of dispute) says, "The birth took place (while the cow or slave-girl was) under my lawful ownership," and the other party remains silent, the party making the claim assumes lawful ownership of the offspring.[10]

4) If one had two slaves, one adult and one child, or two fields, one large and one small,[11] and the buyer says, "I purchased the large one," and the seller says, "You purchased the small one": the buyer bears the burden of proof for his claims; or the seller swears an oath, prescribed by rabbinical ordinance, that he in fact sold only the smaller one. If the seller did partially admit[12] the truth of the buyer's claim, he is to swear an oath prescribed by biblical law in regard to moveable goods (at issue in the sale of the slave, e.g.) cloth for clothing the adult is claimed, while cloth for clothing the child is acknowledged by the seller), which oath is amplified in order to include the matter of the real property (and slaves are treated in this matter as real property).

5) When a buyer says, "I purchased the larger (or the adult);" and the seller remains silent, the buyer assumes lawful ownership of the larger (or adult).[13] If the seller responds to the buyer's claim by saying, "I do not know (which I sold)," the buyer must bring proof to support his claim; or the seller shall swear an oath, prescribed by rabbinical ordinance, to the effect that he does not know whether he sold the larger (or the adult) or the smaller (or the child), and the buyer becomes lawful owner of the smaller (or the child).

224: The rule for disposition of the case in which one has exchanged a cow for an ass, or acquired an ass, and the animal is found to have a perforated second stomach. Two paragraphs.

1) A burden of proof (to establish whether ownership was transferred before or after an animal is found dead or injured) is placed upon whoever had lawful possession of an animal (which died or be-

came ritually defective and was last definitely known to be in that person's lawful possession when alive).[1] How this is expressed in practical terms is as follows: A exchanges his cow for B's ass. B effects acquisition by pulling A's cow. Before A can pull B's animal, that animal is found dead. B bears the burden of proof and must show that his ass was alive at the time acquisition of the cow was effected (since if the ass was alive then, A would be its legal owner and necessarily absorb the loss of the animal). This rule applies in all similar cases.

> GLOSS: There is an opinion that the burden of proof falls upon A, the (former) owner of the cow, since he had effected acquisition (through B's act of pulling A's cow) of the ass wherever it was located; thus it was, from that moment, under the lawful ownership and control of A, who must bear the burden of proof, as will be explained shortly in the matter of the butcher.[2] If A does not bring such proof, then the seller (of the ass, i.e., B) swears an oath that he did not know of these (mortal) defects in his animal, and he bears no liability in this matter.[3] (A case:) C exchanged his horse for D's wine. When D effected acquisition of C's horse by pulling it, a non-Jew came along and seized the horse from D, asserting that the horse had been stolen from him. D wishes to retain possession of the wine which is presently in his possession:[4] If C admits that the horse was in fact stolen, the transaction was rooted in a fundamental erroneous belief (tantamount to deception) and D may retain possession of the wine. If, however, C does not admit the non-Jew's claim, we say that the non-Jew is (presumed to be) lying and D must surrender the wine to C.

2) When a needle is found (after slaughter of a meat animal) to have pierced through the second stomach of such ruminant, if a drop of (congealed) blood is found on the perforation,[5] it is certain that the animal became ritually unfit (because of this internal injury -- and therefore forbidden to be eaten by Jews) prior to the ritual slaughter of the animal. Therefore, if a scabby crust formed

over the wound, it is certain that the animal became ritually unfit three days prior to its ritual slaughter. If no scabby crust had formed, there is a doubt (as to who owned the animal when the injury occurred: before it was sold to the butcher, or after the sale but before the ritual slaughter), and the butcher bears the burden of proof that the defect originated prior to his purchase of the animal -- since the doubt came to light when the animal was under his lawful ownership and control. If the butcher can bring no such proof, the seller is to receive full payment of the purchase price.[6]

225: The rule governing a sale if the seller has undertaken to hold the buyer harmless from every accident or untoward event that affects quiet enjoyment and the rule governing a sale if the seller specifically stipulates that he assumes no undertaking of warranty against eviction. Six paragraphs.

1) Whoever sells land, slaves, or moveable goods bears no obligation to warrant[1] (the buyer against eviction from the property). How this works in practice is as follows: If one comes and seizes the items sold from the buyer because (of some prior act or omission) of the seller (e.g., the item is taken as the payment of a debt), the buyer takes back all the purchase-price money, which he paid, from the seller, because the property was taken owing to (some act or omission on the part of) the seller.

This is the rule (to be followed) in all transactions of sale, even though the buyer, at the time of effecting acquisition, did not explicitly mention this matter of warranty (against eviction).

Even if one sold land by means of a written instrument of transfer and the clause concerning warranty (against eviction) was not written into the document,[2] the seller bears the obligation to warrant (against eviction) because the omission of the clause is deemed to be a mere notarial error.

2) The above rule holds good when the item sold has been taken from the buyer through the legal process of a rabbinical court.[3] For example, the subject of the sale was moveable property which was the subject property in a theft or robbery (and its legal owners sued for its return); or land was sold and then forcibly taken (from the

buyer); or a creditor of the seller came and seized the land in payment of his claim (which predated the sale of the land): all these (seizures of property from the buyer) having been effected through the legal process of a rabbinical court. If, however, a non-Jew took the property away from the buyer, whether by royal order or through a non-Jewish legal process, the seller is not obliged (to indemnify the buyer) because of the undertaking to warrant against eviction; even though the non-Jew claims that the seller committed theft or robbery (against him to acquire) the item (he sold) and produces non-Jewish witnesses to testify to this allegation, the seller is not obliged (to indemnify the buyer) at all, because this is an unpreventable and unavoidable constraint for which the seller is not held liable.

3) The above-stated rule holds good when the seller did not stipulate[4] (to undertake a liability to indemnify the buyer against such eventualities); if, however, the seller stipulated that he would indemnify the buyer in all cases of unavoidable or unpreventable accident or constraint that might affect the land he sold, (then) even if the non-Jew came and forcibly seized the land from the buyer because of (an act or omission on the part of) the seller,[5] the seller is obliged to indemnify the buyer.

If, however, a river which irrigates the property is (later) dammed,[6] or the course of a river changes and floods the property, or the property is rendered useless by some natural disaster, e.g., earthquake, the seller is exempt from any liability to indemnify (even when he stipulated to be liable for all accidents, constraints, etc.), for these events and their like are most unusual constraints, and the seller is not deemed to have had those semi-miraculous phenomena in contemplation when he stipulated (to be liable for every accident, etc.).

This same rule applies for every stipulation in a pecuniary matter:[7] an assessment is made as to what the stipulator has contemplated (as within the scope of his liability); and those well-known phenomena, because of which the stipulation was made, and which the stipulator may have had in mind when he stipulated, are included in the scope of his stipulation.

4) In a talmudic case it was held as follows: A man hired sailors

to transport a cargo of sesame seeds to a particular place.[8] The hirer stipulated with them that they should be liable (to indemnify him) for any accident or untoward event, etc., (affecting this shipment) until the cargo of sesame seeds should reach its destination. The river on which they were transporting the cargo was dammed up (and rendered unnavigable). The rabbinical sages held that this was a most unusual type of constraint or accident, and the sailors were not obliged to secure pack animals to transport the cargo to its destination. Similar cases are treated as this case was.

5) If a seller stipulated explicitly that he should bear no obligation to warrant the buyer against eviction, even if it is known that the item sold had been taken in a robbery, and the victim of the robbery takes the item from the buyer, the seller is not obligated[9] (to indemnify the buyer); it goes without saying that (under this stipulation) if a creditor of the seller seized the property (from the buyer as payment for a debt incurred prior to the sale), the seller returns nothing to the buyer (i.e., no indemnity): every (lawful) stipulation in pecuniary matters (will be held to be) valid.

6) If A sells B a cellar of wine,[10] and they mutually stipulate that A shall bear liability only for loss (found to be due to) broken barrels or spillage and B shall only absorb any loss due to spoilage of the taste of the wine (e.g., fermentation to vinegar): If the only accident affecting the wine was ritual defilement through the handling of it by non-Jews (thus rendering it unfit for Jewish use), the liability to indemnify for this accident shall fall upon the seller.[11]

226: The rule for one who sells a field without warranting against eviction therefrom, or for one whose title is the subject of complaint and protest. Six paragraphs.

1) A sells a field to B, without any warranty against eviction. C comes and seize the property from B.[1] If A wishes to sue C (to recover the property for B) he may do so, and C will not be suffered to say, "Why should we two quarrel? You have made no warranty to B"; because A may say, "I do not wish B to have any (nonactionable) complaint against me, that he suffered loss because of me." (If,

however, A gave the field to B as a gift,[2] A cannot sue on B's behalf because the factor of [nonactionable] complaint does not exist.)

2) A sells a field to B, without any warranty against eviction.[3] A then buys the field back from B, with a warranty against eviction. A's creditor comes to seize the field. A has no recourse against B,[4] for although he undertook to furnish no warranty against eviction to B, he is deemed to have undertaken such a warranty insofar as he himself is concerned -- that he not be both the seller and the claimant of indemnity for himself. If, however, a creditor of A's (deceased) father[5] comes and seize the property from A, A may seek full restitution of the purchase price from B.

3) A sells a field to B, without any warranty against eviction.[6] A is obligated to guarantee that he personally (will not sue to retake the property from the buyer); this rule (that he personally is not to sue) has specific reference (to a suit raised owing) to any right A enjoys at the time of the sale. If, however, he acquires a new right, he may sue to retake the field under it (e.g., if B is a debtor[7] of A's father and A's father dies, A may sue to retake the field in payment of the debt).

4) Guardians (of minor orphans) who have sold the orphan's property are not held to be obliged to warrant against eviction as against themselves personally.[8]

5) If one sells land to another, and after the buyer has effected formal and legal acquisition of the property by means of one of the lawful modes of acquisition, but before he uses the property, complaints and protests are raised against the seller's title,[9] the buyer may withdraw from the transaction (without prejudice) -- for there is no greater blemish (on a title) than this: that before one can enjoy one's property, suitors come (against him). Therefore the sale may be voided; and the seller is to return the purchase price to the buyer and answer the complaints raised (against the title). If the buyer has made the least use of the field, even if (he only) tramped down a boundary ridge of it and mixed that with the earth, he cannot withdraw (from the transaction), but he answers the complaints raised (against his title) in court. If the field is taken from him through the process of the rabbinical court, he has re-

course against the seller (for indemnity) according to the rule governing all cases of such seizure.

> GLOSS: This rule applies to a complaint which has not yet been fully and openly clarified but in which the rabbinical court holds that there is plausibility to the complainant's argument. If, however, there has only been a rumor (of some flaw in the title), even if the purchase is not entirely realized (i.e., no use has been made of the field), one cannot void the purchase because of mere talk.[10]
> If the buyer withdraws (from the transaction) because of a (reasonable) complaint (against his title), even though the complaint disappears afterward, the purchase remains void, and both parties (buyer and seller) may withdraw from the transaction (without prejudice).
> If a complaint is raised against a buyer's title to a field because it is alleged that the seller owed debts to others (debts contracted before the sale), and the seller alleges that he has receipts of payment covering those debts, (this situation) is properly termed complaint or protest (as these words are used in this chapter), and the buyer may withdraw from the transaction and is not required to acquire something and to keep his (i.e., the seller's) receipt (supporting his [i.e., the buyer's] title from the seller) forever.[11]

6) It is forbidden to sell anyone land or moveable goods which are (currently) the subject of a dispute or lawsuit until the seller informs the buyer of such a circumstance.[12] Even though a seller undertakes to warrant against eviction, no one wishes to pay his money (only) to become involved in a lawsuit and be subjected to others' claims.

The Laws of Unfair Price as Constructive Fraud and Rescission Owing to a Fundamental Error in the Contract for Purchase

227: The limits of constructive fraud by means of unfair pricing; how much may be forgiven; how much requires return of the excess; an error by an agent; heirs who have made an error in the division of an estate. Thirty-nine paragraphs.

1) It is forbidden to defraud another (through unfair pricing) whether (the fraud is in terms of) the purchase one makes or the sale one makes. Whichever party, whether buyer or seller, that perpetrates such a fraud transgresses an explicit negative commandment of Scripture.[1]

2) The amount which constitutes an unfair price amounting to constructive fraud,[2] in which the defrauding party is obligated to return the excess in the price, is precisely one-sixth (either above or below the proper purchase price). How (this applies in practice is as follows): One sold an item worth six (*selas*, etc.) for a purchase price of five (*selas*, etc.) or an item worth seven for six, or worth five for six, or worth six for seven: each case is one of unfair price as constructive fraud. The acquisition of the item sold is lawful, but the defrauding party is obligated to make good the excess amount and return it to the victim of the fraud.

3) If the unfair price was less than one-sixth[3] (of the correct price) even by the smallest amount, for instance if one sold something worth seventy[4] *selas* for sixty *selas* and one *perutah*, (the buyer) is not obligated to return any of the undercharge. Any amount less than one-sixth of the price would be forgiven by any party (buyer or seller).

4) If the unfair price was greater than one-sixth (of the correct price) even by the smallest amount,[5] for example, one sold something worth sixty (*selas*) for fifty (*selas*) less (one) *perutah*, the sale is voidable (automatically) and the defrauded party is (thus) able to return the item and will effect no acquisition of it; but the de-

frauding party is not able to withdraw[6] from the transaction if the defrauded party wishes to accept (the unfair terms of the contract). (There is an opinion[7] which holds that even the defrauding party is able to withdraw [from the transaction] unless the defrauded party has one time expressed willingness [to carry through with the contract] or has kept silent [concerning the unfair price] longer than the grace period, as will be explained in paragraph 7.) If one sold something worth sixty (*selas*) for fifty-one (*dinars*) -- or the reverse (i.e., something worth fifty-one for sixty), in which there is no unfair price amounting to one-sixth the correct price: since in one case there could be a voiding of the sale, while in the other case there could be an (assumption) of forgiveness, we follow the (value) of the item sold, whether for (determining) the matter of voiding the sale or the matter of forgiveness, because people are apt to err in (pricing) an item for sale (correctly) but not in payment of the purchase-price money.[8]

(N.B. When one sells something worth sixty for fifty-one,[9] there is an overcharge of less than one-sixth of the proper price. But in the actual paying out of the price, there is more than one-sixth of an overcharge, since if fifty-one is divided by six, there are six units of eight and a half, which would mean that the nine *dinars* difference between the fair and unfair prices amounts to more than one-sixth; and the sale is theoretically voidable from a reckoning predicated on the amounts of coin involved. If one sold an item properly worth fifty-one *dinars* for sixty *dinars*, the situation is just the reverse: the excess in terms of the value of the item is nine *dinars*, while one-sixth the price paid is eight and a half *dinars*, a clear overcharge from the point of view of a reckoning based on the value of the item at sixty *dinars*.)

5) The defrauding party is not obligated[10] to return the excess in price (i.e., the sixth) unless the excess shall amount to more than one *perutah*. If the excess amounted to one *perutah* exactly, one need not return it. (There is an opinion which holds that it is to be returned [to the defrauded party].)

6) One may legitimately raise a doubt[11] as to whether or not it is permissible to charge an unfair price amounting to less than one-sixth if the excess in price amounts to (at least) one *perutah*. But with regard to a (used) coin, as long as there is no unlawful over-

charge in a transaction (involving it), one may initially spend it to get a fresh-minted one.

7) The grace period for returning (to the seller) and claiming (return of) an overcharge of one-sixth or voiding a sale for an overcharge of more than one-sixth the price[12] extends until one should (reasonably be able) to show the item to a merchant (who can offer an informed opinion as to its value) or (to one's) relative (whose opinion is trusted). If the person waited longer (than a reasonable period for seeking an informed or trusted opinion), he loses the right of withdrawal and the right to claim the excess in price.[13] If it is clear that he was not able to investigate the item within this (reasonable) time, to determine whether or not he had been the victim of a fraud, because of some untoward constraint or circumstance,[14] he is still able to withdraw from the transaction (i.e., the accident or circumstance beyond his control does not serve to extinguish his right to seek restitution). (If a buyer knew, at the time of his purchase of an item, that he had been defrauded in the matter of price, and he remained silent at that time, but immediately after the surcharge, before the [expiration of the] [time][15] in which he might show it to a merchant or a relative, he sues for return of the excess price, we do not say that he has forgiven the excess owing to the fact that he was aware [of his victimization originally].)[16]

8) This rule (above) applies to a buyer,[17] who is in possession of the item (in question) and may show it (to a merchant, etc.). But the seller may always go back (subject to the exceptions noted below) (to claim the difference in a case of) an underprice of one-sixth, and it goes without saying that in a case in which the sale could be voided (for underpricing of more than one-sixth, he may always withdraw); for he may not know the price of this thing which he has sold until he might see an item similar to this one sold in the marketplace. Therefore, if the item was something of uniform quality, and all things of this type sell for the same price, e.g., peppercorns, etc., he (the seller) may withdraw only for (a reasonable) time in which he might ask for a quotation on the market price (of the thing). Similarly, if it is known that the seller has come into possession[18] of an item like the one he sold,[19] and he becomes aware

that he erred (in regard to price) and did not claim (the payment to make up for the undercharge), he is not able to withdraw and to make his claim therefor because he (is presumed to have) forgiven (the undercharge to the buyer).

9) This rule (holds good) when the market price of the item has not fluctuated.[20] If, however, the market price of the item has fluctuated, and for that reason the seller wishes to withdraw from the transaction, he may not lawfully do so. (The new price could represent an undercharge in relation to the old purchase price.)

> GLOSS: If the defrauding party (in a case of fraud by means of unfair pricing) says that the market price has changed,[21] and the victim says it has not changed (an unchanged price would work to the victim's benefit), the victim must bring proof (that the price has not changed), because market prices customarily do in fact fluctuate.

Similarly, if one has sold an item because he is pressed (for ready cash) and has (therefore) offered an extremely low price,[22] more than one could presume to be a reasonable error (in underpricing), so that it becomes manifest that it is because of the pressure (for cash) upon the seller that he has necessarily offered the extremely low price, the seller cannot withdraw from the transaction (because of undercharges) because he knew (the circumstance of the pricing and therefore) he forgave (any undercharge he made).

10) If one sells to another something worth four *selas* for five *selas*,[23] so that the sale is clearly voidable (owing to the overcharge), and the buyer has not had sufficient time to show the item to a merchant or to a relative, and the item appreciates value to a market price of seven *selas*, the buyer can withdraw from the transaction but not the seller. The buyer can say to the seller, "If you had not overcharged me to the extent of perpetrating fraud in the price, you would not have been able to withdraw from the transaction. Now that you have committed a fraud in the setting of the price, should you indeed be able to withdraw from the transaction (by acknowledging you committed fraud and thereby regain the appreciated item? Surely not!) How is it that a sinner should reap reward from his sin?"

11) Similarly, when a seller sells an item worth five (*selas*) for four (*selas*),[24] (there being an undercharge sufficient to make the sale voidable), and the market price of the item falls to three *selas*, the seller can withdraw from the transaction (because of the undercharge), but the buyer cannot withdraw from the transaction (by asserting the new low price as a basis for an overcharge); the seller says to the buyer, "You shall not withdraw from the transaction with me, because you have taken fraudulent advantage of my undercharge."

12) If one sells an item worth five (*selas*) for six *selas*[25] (i.e., a clear case of fraudulent overpricing), and the (buyer) has not yet had time to show the item (to a merchant, etc.) before the item appreciates in value to eight (*selas*) (i.e., the buyer was theoretically undercharged if one adopts the new price), the seller is obliged to return the one (*sela*, i.e., the sixth) of unlawful overcharge (to the buyer) because the acquisition of the item had been lawfully effected (at the original price) and the seller became obliged to return the unlawful overcharge. When the item appreciated in value, it did so while in the buyer's lawful ownership and control.

13) Similarly, if one sold an item worth six (*selas*) for five[26] (*selas*), and (such items) fell in value to a market price of three (*selas*), the buyer is obliged to return the one *sela* of unlawful undercharge, because acquisition of the item was lawfully effected and the item fell in value while in the buyer's lawful ownership and control.

14) Just as the rules governing unfair price as constructive fraud apply to a layman, so do they apply to a (professional) merchant[27] even though a merchant is an expert (in the value and pricing of his wares; and he depends upon this skill for his livelihood: even so he has no special permission to withdraw from a transaction when he has underpriced or has paid too much).

15) The rules governing unfair price as constructive fraud apply to all moveable goods, even books, gemstones, and pearls. A buyer has the right to withdraw[28] (from a transaction for purchase of them) until he shall (have a reasonable time to) show them to merchants who are expert (in appraising their value), wherever such

merchants may be located; not everyone is expert in these matters. Therefore if one does not know of such an expert in his own district,[29] and he transports the purchase to another district (for an appraisal) or an expert comes to (the buyer's locale) some considerable time after (the purchase, and the expert informs the buyer) that the buyer has erred (in the price he paid), the buyer (still) retains the right to withdraw (from the transaction).

16) The rule of unfair price as constructive fraud applies to sales of coins,[30] (the amount of unlawful excess being) one-sixth. How[31] (this applies in practice is as follows): The rate of exchange was one gold *dinar* for twenty-four silver *dinars*, but one changed a gold *dinar* for either twenty or twenty-eight silver *dinars*:[32] the defrauding party returns the unlawful excess (four *dinars*, one-sixth of twenty-four). If the excess amounted to more than one-sixth, the transaction is voidable; if the excess amounted to less than this, it is (presumed) forgiven.

And similarly if a *sela* (coin) lacked one-sixth (of its correct weight of valuable metal), and the *sela* coins were paid out by (merely) counting them out,[33] not by weighing them out, the unlawful excess is returned (to the victim by the defrauding party), for if these coins were paid out by weight, (and their weight was short) by even the smallest amount, one can withdraw from the transaction.

> GLOSS: There is an opinion which holds that the unlawful excess of price in coins is one-twelfth.[34] Any lesser excess amount is (deemed) forgiven, any greater excess amount renders the purchase voidable. Whenever an excess amount is (deemed) forgiven, one may lawfully spend (such a coin if it is used) initially for a fresh-minted one, cf. above para. 6.

17) The length of the period of time during which a *dinar* or a *sela* (if sold at an unlawful excess price) is to be returned[35] (to the defrauded party) is, in urban areas, (the reasonable time until) one could show the coin to a banker. In villages where a banker is generally not present,[36] one has a period (for return of the coin which extends) to a Sabbath Eve (i.e., a Friday afternoon), when one would (normally) come to spend the coin. Only a (qualified) banker

can recognize a short-weight *sela* and (nominate) its price. After these (respective) periods have passed, the defrauding party is not obliged to take the short-weight coin back,[37] but it is a special measure of piety to take such a coin back even after a year has passed (since the transaction), if he recognized (the short-weight coin he sold), provided that such coin could be circulated with difficulty (but if not, the defrauding party must accept it back).[38]

18) If a coin has become short weight up to the point that the rule of constructive fraud could apply to it,[39] it is forbidden to keep such a coin (for circulation as money) because deception can easily be perpetrated with it. One is not to sell it to a robber or a merchant because they could deceive others with it. One is not to use it as a weight or throw it into a scrap-metal heap. One is to melt it down or pierce it in its center and make it into a necklace for his daughter.[40] One is not to pierce a coin at its edge (since such a mutilation could be filed off and the bad coin could be returned to circulation).

If a coin has lost full half its weight, for instance a *sela* weighs only a *shekel*,[41] a *shekel* weighs only a *dinar*, etc., it is permissible to keep such coins, because (with such coins) it is impossible to deceive people since their short weight is evident to everyone.

> GLOSS: A coin which is only purchased by weighing it out may (if of short weight) be lawfully kept intact because anyone buying it will (also) weigh it out.[42]

19) If one buys something for an uncounted or unweighed lump sum of cash,[43] for instance, one takes a handful of coins and says, "Sell me your cow for these coins," acquisition will be lawfully effected (for a sale, not a barter), and any unlawful excess of price is to be returned to the defrauded party. This same rule applies to one buying an uncounted or unweighed lump amount of produce for a *sela* or two *selas*: acquisition will be lawfully effected (for a sale, not a barter), and any unlawful excess of value received is to be returned to the defrauded party.

> GLOSS: There is an opinion which holds that in this case

a legitimate legal doubt exists (that this transaction is entirely free of the element of barter) and the defrauding party cannot be sued for return of the excess value.[44]

20) If one exchanges utensils for utensils or a domestic animal for a domestic animal,[45] even a needle for a suit of armor or a lamb for a horse, the law of unfair price as constructive fraud does not apply, since A has more desire for a needle than for the suit of armor. But if one exchanges agricultural produce for other agricultural produce, (i.e., fungible goods), whether these lots of produce were appraised before or after this sale, the law of unfair price as constructive fraud (will apply to the transaction).[46] (Note: presumably this last part of the paragraph proceeds on the assumption that the agricultural goods represent some equivalency of value and therefore the exchange somewhat resembles a sale.)

21) If one says to another, (in a transaction of sale), "On condition that you have no suit for unfair price against me," one retains the right to bring such a suit.[47] This rule applies when the possible amount of excess price or value received to be forgiven is as yet undetermined: it goes without saying (that the right to sue for the excess paid, etc., is not extinguished if the seller stipulates that the sale is) on condition that the sale has no element of unfair pricing, should indeed (such illegality) be present in the transaction.

But when the amount of excess price or value received to be forgiven is specified, (the parties, by accepting such a specific condition) waive the right to sue for the excess in price or value. How (this applies in practice is as follows): If a seller says to a buyer, "I know that this item tht I am giving to you at two hundred zuz is only worth one hundred zuz; I sell it to you on condition that you have no right to sue me for unfair price as constructive fraud," (if the buyer accepts the condition) he waives his right to sue on the ground of constructive fraud.

Similarly, if a buyer says to a seller, "I know that this item I am buying from you for one hundred zuz is worth two hundred zuz; I buy it from you on condition that you have no right to sue me for an unfair amount of value received as constructive fraud," (if the seller accepts the condition) he waives his right to sue on the ground of constructive fraud.

22) If one sells an item to another for one hundred *zuz* and says to him, "This item (I sell you) is only worth one *zuz*;[48] (I sell it to you) on condition that you have no right to sue on the ground of of constructive fraud," the buyer retains the right to sue. The buyer can say that once he saw that the seller said the item was worth only one *zuz*, he knew that the seller only intended to soothe his (the buyer's) mind. (The buyer retains his right) until the seller shall specify the actual amount of unlawful overpricing involved in the purchase, either with certainty or to an approximation (of certainty in which normally it is reasonable to expect that) one might (make an error[49]) (of very minor consequence); the buyer is to know the precise amount that he shall (have to) forgive.

23) If a householder sells items of his personal use and overcharges the buyer,[50] the law of unfair price as constructive fraud does not apply to this sale. If the householder had not (been able to) charge a high price, he would not (have undertaken to) sell his personal items. Even if the householder sold them because of his own need (when presumably he would take any price for them), the law of unfair price as constructive fraud does not apply. There is an authority who holds[51] that this rule applies only when the buyer knows that the seller is acting as a private householder; but if the buyer was not aware of this factor the acquisition was effected through the offices of an agent, the law of unfair price as constructive fraud applies (to the transaction).

24) The rule that a private householder can sell his personal items, overcharge the buyer, and not be liable under the rule of unfair price as constructive fraud applies only to an excess in price of one-sixth.[52] But if the price was more than one-sixth (of the proper price), the private householder is treated as any other seller. There are authorities who disagree with this ruling.[53]

25) If a buyer and a seller have expressed willingness to conclude a contract for purchase of an item[54] (at a price fixed) by the appraisal of a third party, who does in fact appraise the item at a certain price, but that appraised price turns out to have an element of unlawful over or undercharge, the rule of unfair price as constructive fraud will apply to the transaction. If it is impossible

to (seek) return of the excess,[55] for example, the defrauding party has left the locale, if the appraiser was a businessman, expert in appraisal, and received no fee for his service, he bears no liability.

26) A non-Jew has no right to sue for return of an underprice or overprice (as constructive fraud under our Jewish law),[56] for Scripture asserts, "A man, his brother," etc. Non-Jews who defraud a Jew by unfair pricing are to be sued for return of the overprice or underprice under our Jewish law so that this case of fraud not be more serious than one perpetrated by a Jew[57] (alone; i.e., if a Jew and a non-Jew were partners in the fraudulent sale, the Jew would be liable for the whole if the non-Jew were not also held liable).

27) A merchant who conducts his business on trust is not to be held liable under the rule of unfair price as constructive fraud.[58] How this applies in practice is as follows: (The merchant asserts) "I bought this item for such-and-such a price and I sell it for such-and-such a profit"; (when the buyer trusts the honesty of such a seller's statement) the rule of unfair price as constructive fraud cannot be used against the merchant.

28) A merchant who conducts his business on trust (i.e., the buyer trusts the honesty of the seller's pricing policy as noted in para. 27) is not to reckon poorer-quality goods in a lot of merchandise on trust while reckoning the better-quality goods in that same lot at their par value:[59] if he bought ten bolts of cloth for ten *dinars*, and there are some bolts in the lot worth *less* than a *dinar*, and there are some worth *more*, he is not to reckon the price of the poorer goods at an average of one *dinar* each, and the better goods at their actual value. All the goods are to be sold at the trust (price, i.e., the average of one *dinar* each), just as he in fact acquired them as one lot (at an average price for each item). He may add to the price the costs of transport and storage and include those costs in the selling price,[60] but he cannot add the cost of his labor to the selling price, and he may take from the buyer no more profit than was arranged for the buyer to give him.

29) These items are not subject to the rule of unfair price as constructive fraud: slaves, notes of debt (bought at a discount so that the purchaser can collect the amounts due), real estate, and objects consecrated to sacred purpose.[61] Even if one sold (one of

these items) worth one thousand *dinars* for one *dinar*, or vice versa, the rule of unfair price as constructive fraud does not apply.[62]

> GLOSS: (There are authorities who hold that the rule will not apply except) in a specific circumstance: (if the proper price amounts) to half (the actual purchase price, the rule does not apply), but if (the excessive price is) more than twice the proper price, e.g., if one sold one item for more than the price of two of them, the rule of unfair price as constructive fraud does apply to that transaction.[63]

30) The previous rule applies to a person who himself sells his own goods, but an agent or a guardian of orphans who has erred in a transaction (concerning the principal's or the orphan's goods) and has been defrauded by unfair pricing even by the smallest amount, whether the transaction concerned moveable property or real estate, can withdraw from the transaction.[64] If (the agent or guardian) has defrauded the buyer by unfair pricing, one authority[65] holds that the sale is voidable for any amount of excess price; another authority[66] holds that (the agent or guardian) is covered under the rule that applies to others in this matter: there is a presumption of forgiveness for up to one-sixth of the excess and the principal (or orphan) is lawfully entitled to the excess (of one-sixth).

31) The rule concerning a rabbinical court that has sold property on behalf of orphans and has erred in the transaction (in terms of proper price, value received, etc.) is set forth in ch. 109.

32) Just as the rule concerning unfair price as constructive fraud does not apply to sales of real estate, it does not apply to rentals of real estate:[67] even if one leased a great hall for (only) one *dinar* per year, or a small cattle shed for one *dinar* per day, the rule of unfair price as constructive fraud does not apply to the transaction.[68]

33) If one hires another to do work for him, whether on the hirer's land or with the hirer's moveable goods,[69] the rule of unfair price as constructive fraud does not apply to this contract because the hirer (is viewed as if he) acquired the workman (for a specific period) and the rule of unfair price as constructive fraud does not

apply to slaves (and hired workmen, who are free men, are assimilated to slaves for the purpose of this ruling).

> GLOSS: If one hired a worker along with that worker's horse or ass, even though in regard to the workman himself the unfair-price-as-constructive-fraud rule does not apply, it does apply with reference to the animal. One would estimate the amount of the total hire that has been paid out for the use of the animal and what the excessive amount is with reference to the payment for the animal, and the defrauding party is obliged to return (the excess, i.e., the sixth,) to the defrauded party.[70]

34) If one hired a person to seed his land,[71] and the hired person declares, "I sowed it with sufficient seed," but witnesses come who depose that the worker used less than a sufficient amount of seed, there is a legitimate legal doubt whether the rule of unfair price as constructive fraud applies because of the seed used (i.e., it is moveable property) or whether this rule does not apply to the transaction because it concerns real estate. Therefore the party accused of fraud cannot be required by a rabbinical court to return the excess amount (i.e., the sixth), and similarly the accused party can only be made to swear an oath prescribed by rabbinical (not biblical) law (in order to establish his innocence) because the transaction here involves real estate (to some extent).

35) If one leases utensils or a domesticated animal (from another),[72] the rule of unfair price as constructive fraud will apply to the transaction, because a lease is deemed to be a sale for a specific term. If there is an unlawful excess in price (or value) amounting to one-sixth (of the proper rental, etc.) or more, whether the lessor or the lessee is the defrauded party, the excess amount is to be returned to the victim even after a considerable length of time has elapsed (since the contract of let).[73]

36) The independently contracting artisan[74] (i.e., a craftsman engaged for a specific job, not an ordinary day laborer) is subject to the rule of unfair price as constructive fraud. How (this applies in practice is), for example, if one has undertaken to weave a garment for a fee of ten *zuzim*, or to sew a garment for two *zuzim*, the

rule applies to the transaction. Each of the parties, the contracting artisan and the owner of the garment, may always withdraw from the transaction (as a seller can in a case of improper pricing amounting to constructive fraud; thus Maimonides and *Tur*; *SMA* remarks that the owner of the garment is not subject to a time limit for the suit as is a purchaser; but the defrauding party cannot withdraw once the defrauded party signifies willingness to waive the right to sue, just like the rule in sales).

37) Brothers (i.e., heirs) or partners[75] who divide moveable property are (held analogous in the law to) buyers (as from each other): If one party acquires, in his portion of the goods, a value in excess of the value of the other party's portion, but the excess does not exceed one-sixth the value (of each portion in an equal division), the transaction is lawful and the excess is not returned (to the other party); if the excess value is more than one-sixth the value (of each portion in an equal division), the transaction is null; if the excess value amounts to one-sixth the value (of a portion in an equal division), acquisition (of each portion) is lawfully effected, but the lawful excess is to be returned to the victim of the constructive fraud.

If the parties divided real estate, even if they appraised (land) worth one hundred *dinars* for one *dinar*,[76] or vice versa, their transaction is lawful and valid. (There are authorities[77] who hold that the transaction is lawful only if (the error in appraisal) amounts to no more than half (the value of each portion of the real estate in an equal division).

If the parties deceived each other (in the transaction) with regard to measurement,[78] weight, or amount, even to the smallest degree, they may withdraw from the transaction (and seek reapportionment of the property).

If they appointed an agent who was to apportion the property between them, and that agent erred (regarding the relative values of the portions, even) to the slightest degree, the division of the property is null.

38) If (the brothers or the partners) stipulated that they would divide the property on the basis of a judicial appraisal of it[79] (i.e., an appraisal by the rabbinical court), and the judicial ap-

praisers erred in their valuation by one-sixth (the value of two exactly equal portions), the apportionment is null, because if judicial appraisers give an estimate of value which is either less or more by one-sixth (the proper value of the property), a sale made pursuant to such (an erroneous) appraisal is voidable.

39) A and B, brothers (and heirs), divided (their inheritance) on the condition that whoever of them would receive a particular house (in his portion of the estate) should construct in that house a doorway opening onto the alleyway.[80] They paid no attention to the fact that the residents of that alleyway could prevent them (from performing that construction work). A received the house. If A wishes to have the apportionment of the estate voided, he may lawfully do so (and seek a new division of the property without that stipulation).

228: The prohibition against misuse of speech to abuse or to place a person at a disadvantage; the prohibition against deceiving people and against (various) fraudulent practices in buying and selling. Twenty paragraphs.

1) Just as there is fraudulent practice through unfair pricing in buying and selling, so there is unfair advantage that can be taken by means of the misuse of speech.[1] This latter form of unfair advantage is a greater offense than fraudulently unfair pricing.[2] Unfair pricing can be reckoned in monetary terms; unfair advantage by means of misuse of speech cannot be reckoned in (mere) monetary terms. This latter unfair advantage affects the person himself; unfair pricing affects only his money. One who cries out (to God) because (he is victimized) through verbal abuse or deception receives (divine answer and aid) immediately.[3]

> GLOSS: There are those who hold the opinion that the divine commandment concerning the prohibition against taking advantage by means of misuse of speech is only addressed to very pious people,[4] and that one who has (knowingly) abused himself or placed himself at a disadvantage by means of misuse of speech may be subject to such treatment by others.[5]

2) It is necessary to be especially careful concerning verbal abuse,[6] or unfair advantage by means of misuse of speech, in respect to a convert, whether (such words refer) to his person or his property, since there are numerous scriptural warnings concerning (due care and consideration for the honor and dignity of) the convert.

3) It is necessary to be especially careful[7] concerning verbal abuse, or unfair advantage by means of misuse of speech, in respect to one's wife, since she may be easily brought to tears.

4) How verbal abuse or unfair advantage by means of misuse of speech (applies in practice is as follows): One is not to say to another, "How much do you charge for this item?" when the inquirer has no intention of buying it.[8] If donkey drivers seek to buy produce, one is not to say to them, "Go to such a one," while knowing full well that person has none to sell.[9] If one's fellow is a repentant sinner,[10] one is not to say to him, "Remember what you used to do." If one is the son of converts, one is not to say, "Remember your ancestors' (idolatrous) deeds." If one has suffered personal calamities and tragedies,[11] one is not to speak to him as Job, "Your fear of God is your confidence: Remember, please, whoever died, being innocent?" (Job 4:6 ff.). If a question which requires some special learning to answer has been posed, one is not to say to a person who does not have that learning, "What would you reply in this matter?", etc.[12]

5) One is to be careful not to apply an insulting name or epithet to one's fellow. Even when that person is used to that name or epithet, if one's intent is to cause the person embarrassment, (use of such name or epithet) is forbidden.[13]

6) It is prohibited to deceive people in matters of buying and selling, and it is prohibited to mislead them (intentionally).[14] For example, if there is a flaw in the item for sale, the seller must inform the buyer of it, even if the buyer is a non-Jew.[15] One is not to sell carrion meat as properly slaughtered kosher meat. It is even prohibited to mislead people[16] verbally by appearing to do something especially for a person when that act is not in fact done for his sake: How (this applies in practice is as follows): One is not to urge (to excess) (his friend)[17] to dine with him, knowing full well that his friend would not accept the invitation;[18] and one is not to

heap gifts upon a person, knowing full well he will not accept them; one is not to open a cask of wine which is (actually) opened (and sold) to a retailer of wine so that (one's guest) forms the impression that the cask is opened (just) for him;[19] rather it is necessary to inform the guest that the cask has not been opened for him (exclusively).

If the host's act is one which a guest should normally realize would not be done for him (exclusively), and he deceives himself to believe that the act is done for him and in his honor, it is not necessary to disabuse the guest (of his presumption).[20] For example, A meets his friend B in the street, and B is under the impression that A came out especially in honor of B -- A need not disabuse B.

7) One is not to say to a person, "Anoint yourself with oil from this flask," knowing full well that it is empty.[21] One is not to call upon a mourner and take there an empty vessel which the mourner would imagine to be full (of wine[22]). If one does this in order to do (the mourner) some honor, it is permitted.

8) One is not to sell the hide of an animal which died of natural causes as the hide of one which died by proper ritual slaughter. One is not to send someone a cask of wine with oil floating on the surface of the wine.[23]

9) One is not to alter the appearance of a person, or an animal, or utensils[24] (which are for sale, in order that they look more attractive to buyers); for example, to blacken the beard of a slave to be sold in order that he appears to be a young man.[25] (One is not) to water a cow with bran water, which causes the animal to swell (and thus appear healthier than it is), nor to brush its coat upright so that it appears fat.[26] Similarly one is not to curry it with a small tooth comb nor with a large tooth comb in order to bring the hair of its coat upright.[27] Nor (is one permitted) to paint old utensils so that they appear like new ones.[28] One is not to inflate animal entrails (which are sold as meat) so that they appear fat and broad.[29] One is not to steep meat in water so that it appears white and fat.[30]

10) One is not to mix a small amount of poor-quality produce with a large amount of good-quality produce in order to sell the lot as good-quality produce;[31] (such mixture is prohibited) even if both

types of produce are new (i.e., from the new harvest), and it goes without saying (that a deceptive mixture of new with old produce, and even[32]) (a mixture of) old with new produce, is prohibited: (such mixtures are unlawful) even when the old produce is more expensive than the new produce -- because the buyer may wish to store the new produce.[33]

11) In regard to wine, it is permissible to blend strong wine with mild wine during the pressing process only,[34] because such blending improves the wine (and all the more is a blending of mild wine with stronger wine permissible[35]). If the taste of the wine distinctive, it is permissible to blend it (with other wine) at any point, since (anything[36]) with a distinctive taste would be recognizable to a buyer of it -- therefore it is always[37] permissible to blend it.

12) Wine is not to be cut with water.[38] If one does dilute his wine with water, one is not to sell it in a wineshop unless the buyer is first informed of the dilution;[39] one is not permitted to sell diluted wine to a merchant, since the merchant may deceive others with the diluted wine.[40]

13) Where it is customary to cut wine with water during the pressing process, it is permissible to do so according to the customary amounts for such dilution.[41]

14) Where it is customary for anyone who buys wine to taste it before the purchase, it is always permissible to blend (or dilute) the wine;[42] if every (buyer) would not customarily taste the wine prior to purchase, it is not permissible (to dilute, etc.).

15) A wine merchant is not to blend the sediment of wine (in one cask) with (other) wine[43]; even if one purchased two casks of wine from him,[44] he is not to mix the sediment of one cask of wine with (the wine[45]) of the other cask. If, however, one purchased a cask of wine to be of a specific measure, when the wine is measured out, one may combine the sediment (of that wine) with the wine (itself) and sell them together (as the one specific measure of wine).

16) A merchant may take (acquire) (grain) from five threshing floors and place all of it into one storehouse,[46] or he may purchase wine from five presses and place all the wine into one barrel, because everyone is aware that (the grain or the vintage) did not all

grow in the merchant's property, and people buy from him with such a presumption (clearly understood and accepted). (The merchant may combine the grain or wine) provided that the merchant has no ulterior purpose of purchasing most of the goods from a place noted for good quality in order to gain an (erroneous reputation) that he buys all (his goods) from a place noted for good quality, while also buying goods from a locale of poor-quality production and mixing the latter with the former.

17) It is permissible to winnow out refuse matter[47] from (a lot of) split beans or split peas in order to improve their appearance (while displayed for sale), since this is a readily visible matter and a buyer may (easily) see and understand how much more the produce is worth because the refuse matter has been removed (a high price being charged for the sifted produce) -- provided that the merchant does not sift the upper portion of the goods on display while leaving the refuse matter in the produce below.

18) A shopkeeper is permitted to distribute nuts or parched corn to children in order to encourage them to trade at his shop.[48] Similarly he is permitted to sell his wares at a price lower than the prevailing market price in order to encourage his trade,[49] and other merchants in the marketplace have no right to prevent him from so doing.

19) It is forbidden to mix sediments (with good wine or oil) both in the matter of wine and the matter of oil -- even to the smallest extent.[50]

20) If one sells his fellow clarified oil, the buyer is not to accept any sediment.[51] If one sold oil without specifying (its degree of purity), the buyer is to accept one and a half *logs* of sediment for every one hundred *logs* of oil,[52] and he is to accept, with the other sediment, the muddy-appearing oil which rises above the (purer) oil, over and above the known amounts of sediment (in oil common to) that locale.[53] This rule applies when the buyer (acquires and) pays for the oil in the autumn,[54] when the oil appears muddy, and takes delivery of the oil in the spring, using the (oil) measure employed in the autumn, which is larger than the one used in the spring, because the (autumn) oil congeals (into a muddy scum) at the top of the measure; if, however, he took possession of the oil using

the springtime measure, which is smaller owing to the fact that the oil has clarified (naturally), the buyer need accept only the sediment.

> GLOSS: There is an opinion which holds that the (excess) amount of sediment is not subtracted (from the total amount of the amount of oil); but it is permissible to mix the sediment in the barrels[55] (with the oil in them). If, however, one did not mix (the oil and its sediment), he may only subtract (from the total amount of oil sold) the moldy, congealed material floating on the top of the oil (no reduction in oil being allowed for the amount of sediment). This last rule applies (only) when the oil was sold during the period when it appears muddy; if the sale is made when the oil has (naturally) clarified, no reduction in the total amount of oil is allowed even for the moldy scum on the top of it.

229: The rule governing how much refuse material a buyer is required to accept in a purchase of wheat, barley, or (other) produce. Two paragraphs.

1) If one sells wheat, the buyer is required to accept one quarter *kab* of pulse for every *seah* purchased;[1] if one sells barley, the buyer is required to accept one quarter *kab* of chaff for every *seah* purchased; if lentils, one quarter of a *kab* of sandy refuse matter for every *seah* purchased; if figs,[2] ten wormy figs for each one hundred figs (and the same rule applies to ten figs: one wormy one must be accepted in the ten). If one sold other agricultural produce, the buyer must accept one quarter *kab* of refuse material for every *seah* of produce purchased. If there is more refuse or bad fruit than these limits found in the total amount sold, (even) in the smallest degree,[3] the vendor is to sift all the produce purchased and provide sifted and entirely refuse-free produce.

> GLOSS: There is an opinion which holds that (this rule applies) only when we do not know that the seller did (not)[4] mix the produce (with the refuse material). If we

know that the seller did not mix (the refuse material with the produce), the buyer must accept (these) (above-stated) amounts (of refuse material), and any additional (refuse material) will be subtracted (from the total amount sold).[5]

There is an opinion which holds that where it is known that the seller did not mix (the refuse material with the produce), the seller must accept whatever amount (of refuse is present in the produce).[6]

There are those who interpret this rule as applying when the seller sells produce without specifying its quality or (when) the seller said "This *good* produce"; if, however, the seller said "This produce," without specifying "good," the seller must accept the produce as it is. If the seller said "Good produce," and did not specify *this* (good produce), the seller is to provide produce which is entirely good (i.e., refuse-free).[7]

2) These rules are stated to apply only where there is no prevalent custom[8] (regulating such matters). But where there is such a prevalent custom, all (matters of dispute, etc., are to be adjudicated) according to that prevalent custom in that locale. There are places where the custom prevails that all produce (to be sold) is to be clean and sifted to remove all refuse matter, and that all wine and oil (to be sold) are to be clear (i,.e., pure of dregs, sediment, etc.) and sediments are not to be sold at all. And there are places where the custom prevails that even if (wine or oil) was half sediment or produce contained dirt, straw, or other foreign matter, one could (lawfully) sell it as it is.

Therefore if one removes[9] (a pebble)[10] from someone else's threshing floor, one gives the threshing floor owner the price of wheat up to the bulk of that pebble that was removed, for if he had left it on the floor, it would have been sold with the measure of wheat. And if you should say one should replace the pebble, it has already been asserted that one is not permitted to mix the refuse matter with produce (i.e., one may not perform such an act, but sand, grit, etc., which are naturally found on the threshing floor, may be sold with the grain).

230: The rule governing the sale of a cellar of wine, and the rule for one who buys wine which goes sour.
Ten paragraphs.

1) If one says to his fellow, "I sell you this cellar of wine, for cooking purposes"[1] (i.e., for the purpose of keeping it as a source of replenishment for kitchen stores, little by little); (or one says, "I sell you this cellar for cooking purposes"[2]) or one sells another a cellar of wine without further specification,[3] the buyer is to accept (a maximum) of ten casks of bad wine in every one hundred casks, i.e., ten which have begun to sour.[4] He is not to accept more (bad wine) than this. (Anyone who declares to a wine seller that he is buying it (i.e., the wine) to drink bit by bit (over a period of time) is analogous to one who declares the purchase is for cooking purposes.

2) If a seller says, "I am selling you a cellar of wine for cooking purposes" (or he said, "I am selling you a cellar for cooking purposes"); or he says, "I am selling you a barrel of wine," he is to give him an amount of wine all of which is good and fit for cooking.[5]

3) If a seller said, "(I sell you) *this* cellar of wine," he is to deliver to the buyer a quality of wine as is sold in wineshops,[6] i.e., of intermediate quality, neither superior nor inferior. (The same rule applies if the seller said, "This barrel of wine do I sell you.")

4) If a seller said, "I sell you this cellar," the sale is lawful and valid even if all the wine therein has become vinegar.[7]

5) If one sells wine to another, and the buyer puts the wine into his own casks,[8] whereupon the wine immediately sours, the seller shall bear no liability -- even though the buyer declared at the time of purchase[9] that he needed the wine for cooking purposes (i.e., it would have to be kept for an extended period; the decanting of the wine by the buyer into containers whose quality the seller cannot warrant is held to be the crucial element in the souring process).

6) If one sells wine which is allowed to remain in the seller's casks and it sours:[12] if the buyer declared at the time of purchase that the wine was needed for cooking or was to be drunk over an ex-

tended period of time,[13] the buyer may return (the merchandise) and say, "Here is your wine and your cask" (i.e., rescission is lawful). If the buyer made no such declarations at the time of purchase, he may not return (the merchandise), since the seller may properly say, "why did you not drink it; you should not have kept it so long that it soured."[14]

> GLOSS: This latter rule applies specifically when the buyer has kept the wine longer than the normal period in which this buyer would consume that (amount and type) of wine.[15]

7) If one sells barrels of strong spirits to another, and the barrels are the property of the seller,[16] and the spirits sour within the first three days (of the purchase), the spirits are (for the purpose of determining who bears the loss due to the souring) deemed to be under the control of the seller; after this period of time, the spirits are deemed to be under the (full) ownership of the buyer.

8) If one sells barrels of wine to a retailer who will in turn sell the wine little by little[17] (the buyer to take a commission and pay for the wine from the proceeds of the retail sales), and (after some sales) a half or a third of the wine (remaining) sours, the wine is to be returned to the seller (who bears the loss).

If the buyer (the commissioned retailer) has altered the barrels' bung holes or the market day arrives and he waits and does not go out to sell the wine, the wine is deemed to be under the ownership of the buyer and he bears the loss (due to souring).

9) Similarly if one accepts a barrel of wine (on a commission) in order to transport the wine to some other place to sell it there,[18] and before he reaches that place the price of wine drops or his wine sours,[19] the wine is deemed to be under the ownership of the seller (who bears the loss) since the barrel and the wine are his property.

10) If one says to another, "I am selling you mulled (or spiced) wine,"[20] one is obligated (to deliver wine) which will remain good (at least) until the (following) time of Shavuot (late spring) (if it remains in the seller's casks[21]). If one says, "I am selling you

old wine," one is to give the buyer wine from the vintage of the year passed; (if one says, "I am selling you) very old wine," one is to give the buyer wine from the vintage of three years passed (i.e., the present year plus two more years); and the wine must remain good, and not sour, until the time of Sukkot (i.e., the autumn of the present year).22

In places where there is a well-known custom (regulating these matters), all (sales and disputes thereon are to be governed) according to that local custom.

> GLOSS: The rule governing sale of strong spirits is not the same as the rule governing sales of wine. If any strong spirits spoil within the first three days of the purchase of them, they are deemed to be under the ownership of the seller (for purposes of determining who bears the loss due to spoilage); after three days, they are deemed to be under the ownership of the buyer. If the buyer has decanted the strong spirits into his own casks, they are immediately deemed to be under the control of the buyer.23

A sued B: A said, "You sold me wine on the understanding that it was good wine." B responded, "You are to take what you tasted" (i.e., A had tasted the wine at the time of the purchase). The law is with B. If A claims that after he tasted the wine B mixed it with other wine, and B denies he did so, B is to swear an oath and thus be free of liability in this matter.24

231: The rules against deceitful practices with weights and measures. The rules governing how weights and measures are to be set up and employed. The rules requiring appointment of officers to superintend measures and market prices. Twenty-eight paragraphs.

1) If one gives short weight or short measure to another[1] (Jew) or even to a non-Jew,[2] he transgresses the negative scriptural command, "Thou shalt do not injustice in the matter of dry measure, weight, and liquid measure" (Leviticus 19:35).

2) The rabbinical court shall be obliged to appoint officers who shall visit (to inspect weights and measures in) commercial establishments.³ If any (shopkeeper) is found (to possess) a short weight or a short measure, or inaccurate scales, the court has the authority to flog him and to impose financial penalties on him as may seem appropriate to it.

3) It is prohibited for anyone to retain possession of a short-weight⁴ measure (in his house⁵) even if such short-weight measure is not used for weighing, even if it is only used as a chamber pot; perhaps someone who does not know that it is not used for measurement will come along and use it. If there is a prevalent custom in a (particular) city that measuring is effected only with a measure that is marked with a specific marking, and a particular measure is not so marked, it is permissible to retain possession of such an unmarked measure.⁶

4) The amounts in which measures are manufactured are:⁷ the *seah*, the half *seah*, and the quarter *seah*; the *kab*, the half *kab*, the quarter *kab*, half the quarter *kab*, and one-eighth the quarter *kab*. One is not to make a two-*kab* measure, that it not be confused with the quarter *seah* measure, which equals one and one-half *kabs*. Liquid measures⁸ are to be in the amounts of one *hin*, a half *hin*, a third *hin*, and a quarter *hin*; a *log*, a half *log*, a quarter *log*, an eighth *log*, and one-eighth of an eighth *log*.⁹

5) The leveling rod for a dry measure¹⁰ is not to be made of gourd because it is light and may put the seller at disadvantage; such a rod is not to be made of metal because it is heavy and may put the buyer at disadvantage. The leveling rod is to be made of nut wood, sycamore wood, or boxwood. The leveling rod shall not be thick on one side and thin on the other side.¹¹ The act of leveling a dry measure shall not be performed slowly,¹² since that may cause loss to the buyer, nor shall it be performed in one (quick¹³) stroke, since that may cause loss to the seller; it shall be performed with one deliberate stroke.

6) When one measures with a liquid measure,¹⁴ one is not to do so in such a manner that froth rises and the measure appears to be full, even if it is very small, because the froth does not amount to a *perutah*'s worth (of the liquid). It is necessary (for a seller) to

wait after the liquid has stopped flowing in order to let three
(final) drops fall from (the seller's vessel into the buyer's[15]):
this rule applies to a private person acting as the seller; a shopkeeper (who is pressed by customers[16]) is not required to wait for
the fall of the three drops.[17]

7) A wholesaler of provisions[18] who purchases (large amounts[19])
at one time, and resells to shopkeepers, is to wipe clean the liquid
measures he uses once every thirty days; a private person selling
his own produce, who does not sell in large volume, need wipe his
liquid measure clean only once every twelve months. The shopkeeper[20]
who is not required to wait for the fall of three drops (when pour-
ing from his liqiud measure), and thus much (congealed liquid) would
cling to his measure, is to wipe it clean twice each week.

8) In a locale where the mercantile custom is to employ a smaller
unit of measure, one must not use a larger one,[21] even if one could
give (a buyer) three large measures for four smaller ones. Similarly, where the mercantile custom is to employ a larger unit of measure, one must not use a smaller one. Where the prevalent custom is
to heap the measure, one is not to level it, even if the seller is
willing to provide the buyer with three level measures for two
heaped ones.[22] It is prohibited (to depart from local mercantile
custom) even where merchants sell a heaped *seah* for three *dinars* and
(a buyer) says, "Give me a leveled *seah* for two *dinars*.[23]

Similarly, where the mercantile custom is (to level the measure,
one is not to leave it heaped.[24])

9) Weights are to be made in units of one pound, a half pound,
and a quarter pound.[25] They are not to be made in units of a third
of a pound, a fifth of a pound, or three-quarters of a pound, because such weights can be used to deceive (buyers).

10) Weights are not to be made of metal[26] (which may become
lighter through friction, oxidation, etc.) but from smooth stone.
There is an authority who holds that weights (used for measurement)
of silver, gold, and dry materials may, if one wishes, be made of
metal.[27]

> GLOSS: And such is the custom. In regard to the small
> weights used for measurement of silver and gold, one
> keeps them in a leather pouch (when not in use) because

even a small amount of friction can cause significant damage (to them).[28]

11) It is forbidden to steep weights in salt (which presumably makes them slightly heavier and thus there could be fraud in purchasing).[29]

12) A shopkeeper who weighs out moist or wet goods (e.g., meat) must wipe the weights clean once each week[30] and wipe the scale balances clean after each use of them.[31]

13) (The various types) of scale balances must be (constructed to hang) level -- each acording to the type of balance it is (i.e., what it is used to measure). How (this is carried out in practice is as follows): sellers of large metal bars, etc., must have lines suspending the scale, in which the weights are hung, that provide a clearance of three handbreadths from the ceiling and three handbreadths from the ground; the length of the beam at the two ends of which the scale pans are hung is to be twelve handbreadths. The length of the lines suspending the scale pans is to be twelve handbreadths.[32]

The scale of a wool or glass merchant is to be suspended to a clearance of two handbreadths from the ground, and the length of the line on which the scale is suspended (from the ceiling is to provide a clearance of) two handbreadths.[33] The lengths of the scale beam and the lines suspending the scale pans are to be nine handbreadths. The keeper of a (small) shop or one selling his own products is to have a scale with a clearance of one handbreadth from the ground, and a length of line suspending the scale to a clearance of one handbreadth (from the ceiling); the scale beams and the lines suspending the scale pans are to have lengths of six handbreadths. A gold or silver merchant, or a merchant of purple dyestuff or other fine stuffs, is to have a scale with a clearance of three fingerbreadths from the ground and a suspending line providing the same ceiling clearance. The lengths of the balance beam and the lines suspending the scale pans have no specific (length) requirements: they are constructed as the merchants wish.[34]

14) Where the prevalent custom is to allow the scale to dip slightly (thus allowing the buyer a slight advantage of overweight), the scale pan must dip to the extent of one handbreadth.[35] Where the

prevalent custom is not to allow the scale pan to dip, and exact weight is given, (a seller) must allow (the following) minor surplusages (to the buyer's advantage): one one-hundredth (of the weight) in liquid measure and one four-hundredth of the weight in dry measure.

If one asked for ten pounds' weight, one is not to say, "Weigh each pound separately, with the (allowable) surplus weight."[36] One is to weigh the entire amount together and allow one surplusage for the entire amount.

If one was weighing three-quarters of a pound (of meat), one is not to say (to the merchant), "Weigh each quarter pound separately," but one is to weigh by placing a pound weight in one scale pan and a quarter-pound weight with the meat in the other scale pan:[37] for if you should say that a half-pound weight and a quarter-pound weight should be put in one scale pan, it is possible that the quarter-pound weight (which is clearly small) might slip from the scale pan and the buyer not be aware that it has fallen.

15) The people of a district who have mutually agreed to increase (standard) weights and measures are not to raise the standard of such weights and measures by more than one-sixth.[38] If the *kab* contains five (units) and they make the *kab* measure contain six (units), they may lawfully do so. They may not lawfully go beyond an increase to six (units).

16) In the measurement of land, whether in the case of brothers (dividing an estate) or partners (dividing their joint assets -- and of course in sales), it is necessary to be most precise[39] in the reckoning of land measurement according to the principles explained in mathematical treatises,[40] for even a finger-length in matters of real estate can be seen as if it were to be a garden for saffron.[41]

17) The four cubits of land adjacent to a canal are not measured with great care[42] (since land close to a canal could not be sown). The four cubits of land adjacent to a river are not to be measured (in private transactions) at all because they are public domain.

18) One is not to measure real estate (for one party, e.g., in a division of an estate) in the summer and for another party (to that division) in the winter,[43] because the measuring line shrinks in the summer. Therefore if one measures with a (wooden) rod or with a

chain, etc. (which are not affected by weather), there is no objection (to measurements for the parties at different seasons of the year).

19) The (divine) punishment is serious indeed in the matter of (employing false) weights and measures,[44] for it is impossible for one using false weights and measures to effect full and proper repentance (which can involve an element of restitution):[45] such a person (using false weights, etc.) is like one who denies (the verity) of the Exodus from Egypt (which represents divine providence, since the transgressor does not act as though he believes divine account is taken of his acts).

20) The rabbinical court is obliged to appoint officers to superintend market prices,[46] so that each individual not make whatever profit he wishes. One is not to profit in sales of basic foodstuffs,[47] i.e., wine, oil, and grain, beyond one-sixth (as a margin of profit in the price). This rule applies to one who sells his merchandise in one lot, (a transaction) with little (attendant) effort;[48] but in the case of a shopkeeper who sells his merchandise little by little, we estimate the (value of) his labor and all his expenses (to advertise, perhaps), and he may charge a profit of one-sixth in addition to his overhead expense. The (latter) rule applies when the market price (of his goods) is not high; when it is high he shall sell at that high price,[49] (thus covering both overhead and profit in the high price itself).

These rules apply when the rabbinical court has made it clear to all merchants to set prices in this fashion; if, however, each merchant sells for whatever he can get, one individual merchant is not to be obliged to set a low price.[50]

21) If anyone disrupts market conditions[51] by selling at a price higher than the allowable one, the court has the authority to flog him and to impose financial penalties on him as may seem appropriate (to it).

22) Double profits cannot be made on (sales of) eggs,[52] but the first merchant sells them at a profit, while the person buying them can resell them only for his cost. There is a (talmudic) authority who holds that profit on eggs can be as much as double (their cost to the seller) but no more (than that).[53]

23) In the Land of Israel, it is forbidden to engage (in large or wholesale) commercial traffic in basic foodstuffs.[54] Each person is to bring the grain from his threshing floor and sell it, in order that basic foodstuffs be sold inexpensively. Where oil is plentiful, it is permissible to profit on sales of oil.[55]

24) One is not to stockpile basic agricultural commodities in the Land of Israel[56] or in any other locale where the majority of the population is Jewish.[57] This rule applies to one who purchases (such foodstuffs, presumably for speculation) from the marketplace, but one may (store a portion of the crop) grown on his land.[58] In time of food shortage, one may not store more foodstuffs than are required for the sustenance of his household for one year.[59]

25) Anyone in the Land of Israel, or in a place where the majority of the population is Jewish, who disrupts market conditions (by an inflated price) or by keeping large quantities of basic foodstuffs off the market, is analogous to a usurer.[60]

26) Basic foodstuffs may not be shipped outside the Land of Israel, or to Syria, or from the dominion of one king to another king in the Land of Israel.[61]

27) The inhabitants of a city may set their own market price[62] for any item they wish to and may stipulate that anyone who transgresses (the ordinance setting the price) will be liable to such-and-such penalties.

28) The members of a particular trade or craft are permitted[63] (to enact regulations pertaining to their particular trade or craft,[64] e.g.,) to agree among themselves that A will not practice the trade on the day that B is practicing it, etc., and that they shall institute such-and-such punishment for anyone who shall transgress (their) regulations.

> GLOSS: This [rule that members of a trade or a craft are able to regulate themselves applies] when all members [of such a group do so], but two or three members of such a group may not validly [institute such regulations[65]].

This rule applies in a district where no competent rabbinical authority is appointed to superintend the community.[66] Where such an authority (does hold an appointment), the trade association's agreement (or any general community agreement[67] [e.g., on a fixed price for something]) has no legal effect, nor can (the association or community) institute penalties or punishments against anyone not fulfilling such agreement unless such agreement has been made with the knowledge and consent of the rabbinical authority.

> GLOSS: But if (such agreement) would cause no pecuniary loss to others (i.e., a purely internal matter that would not put a financial burden on members or non-members of the association or community), they may make among themselves whatever regulations they wish to make.[68]

232: The rule concerning one who sells something by weight or measure and errs in the weight or measure, or one who errs in the counting out of money, and the rule concerning one who sells a thing which is found to be defective. Twenty-three paragraphs.

1) If one sells something requiring weighing, measuring, or counting out to another, and has erred even in the slightest degree in the weighing, measuring, or counting, the amount of error is always to be made good, because (the rules for remedy of constructive fraud by unfair pricing apply) only to money[1] (paid as purchase price), but in the calculation (of the amount of goods bought and sold, any shortage or surplus is always) to be made good.[2] How (this rule applies in practice is as follows): one sells another one hundred nuts for a *dinar*, and the number of nuts is found to be one hundred and one or ninety-nine; the purchase is lawful and valid, and one (either the buyer or the seller as the case may be) returns the surplus, even after a number of years have passed (since the transaction).

Similarly if the number of coins (actually paid as the price) is found to be less or more than the number the parties agreed upon[3] (the surplus is returned or the shortage made good). Even after (e.g., partners) have performed a formal act of acquisition as a legal declaration that neither party owes the other any money (and it turns out that one does in fact owe the other some money), that money is to be returned, because the formal act of acquisition (declaring the absence of any debt) was done under an erroneous assumption.[4]

2) If one receives coins from another, whether in a transaction of sale, of loan, or of repayment of a loan,[5] and there is a surplus (in the amount of money) delivered, the receiver is obligated to return that surplus, if it is of such an amount that an error in counting is indicated, even if no claim for such a return has been made.[6] (An error in counting is determined as) e.g., if the surplus money can be divided for spending into units of ten (coins each) or five (coins each), and there are not one or two surplus coins that are not included in a set of five (or ten).[7] One may (then) say that there has been an error in counting: if the (surplus) amounts to ten coins, there has been a counting error as between fifty and forty, or forty and thirty. If the surplus coins can be divided into groups of five coins, there are those who are accustomed to count out coins in groups of five; if there were fifty-five coins, one may have erred in the counting of units of ten, as will be explained. With a surplus of five coins, there may be a counting error as between three and four units of five. If the surplus amounts to fifteen or twenty-five, the error has been repeated three or five times in the (counting of) units of five.

If, however, there are in addition one, two, three, or four coins of surplus that (clearly) do not make up (another) surplus unit of five coins, all the surplus is deemed a gift, provided that the additional coins found do not equal the number of units of five or ten coins[8] (into which the correct purchase price is divisible, i.e., four coins -- four units of ten, a purchase price of forty); for if they do represent the number of units of five or ten coins (divisible into the number of coins of the correct purchase price), one is obligated to return them, since perhaps the additional coins were used as counters in the process of paying out the money in units of five or ten coins each and the counter coins became mixed into the purchase money. (N.B. As a person counts out a pile of five, or ten, coins, another coin is put down to represent one pile of five; thus five coins are put down for five piles of ten; and the counting error of fifty-five -- one counter coin for each pile of ten, mentioned above, becomes reasonable if the counter coins become confused with the payment.)

> GLOSS: In a locale where the customary mode of counting out coins is one by one or two by two,[9] etc., what is called a counting error (to be returned is appropriately adjusted) according to the customary counting procedure. (N.B. In other words, a different counting procedure naturally requires an appropriate means of determining what is a returnable error in account.)

3) If one sells another land, a slave, a domestic animal, or other moveable property, and a defect, which the buyer did not know if, is found in the purchase,[10] the buyer may return it (to the seller and get his money back) even if a number of years (have passed since the transaction), since this transaction was based upon fundamental error, provided that the buyer did not continue to use the item after he became aware of the defect. If, however, the buyer continued to use the item after he saw (or became aware of) the defect, he has (by his conduct) renounced (his right of rescission) and cannot return[11] (the defective item to the seller and get his money back).

4) We do not reckon the decrease in an item's value due to a defect in it.[12] Even if one sold an item worth ten *dinars* and one discovered a defect in it that reduced its price by a *issar* (i.e., by one-sixth its price), the buyer returns the item to the seller and the seller cannot say, "Here is an *issar*, the value of the decrease in price owing to the defect (in the item)." The buyer can say, "I want an item without defects." Similarly, if the buyer wants to take the money value of the defect (along with the defective item), the seller has the right to say, "Either take the item as it is (with its defect and without any refund), or take your money and give me back the item."[13]

5) A sold B house which A owned in another city.[14] Before the sale became final, some non-Jews entered the houses and vandalized some of the places, caused smoke damage to walls, and tore out doors and windows. B wishes to withdraw from the transaction, while A pleads that since the defect (in the property) is of a temporary nature (it can be repaired), he would subtract the amount necessary

to restore the houses to their former condition from the purchase price and the sale could become final. The law is with A.

> GLOSS: For after all, A sold a house and the (property) may still properly be called a house.
> Similarly, a defect that is not a basic defect in the house, e.g., an easement in the property for a path, or a drainage ditch, may be removed so that the sale of the house can become final. If, however, there is a basic structural defect in the house, e.g., the seller said that a wall was sound and it is found to be tottering, (the seller) is not allowed to build a solid wall[15] (i.e., to effect basic structural repairs to satisfy the requirements of the sale), etc.

6) Whatever the inhabitants of a particular locale agree to term a defect in regard to an item sold, which defect shall be grounds[16] for rescission shall in fact constitute grounds for rescission (in that place). Whatever the inhabitants of a particular locale agree is not a defect (in regard to an item sold, etc.) shall not be grounds for rescission unless (a right of rescission for such a defect was) explicitly mentioned (in the transaction); for anyone who conducts business without specifying (any exceptions or special regulations in his transactions is held to) adhere to the (commercial custom of that district).

7) Every buyer, in the absence of a specific exception to the contrary, is held to buy something which is free of all defects.[17] If the seller made a stipulation and said, "(I sell) on condition that you shall not withdraw from the transaction because of a defect (in the item)," the buyer retains the right to seek rescission until the seller shall explain exactly what defect is in the item and (the buyer, thus informed) shall renounce his right of rescission, or (the buyer) shall say to (the seller), "I have accepted (every defect)[18] which may be present in this item purchased, which defect(s) diminishes the item's value up to such-and-such an amount, for one renouncing his right of rescission must know the (value) of the thing he is renouncing. (A seller) is to explain whatever is renounced just as he is (required) to specify the amount of overcharge

in a purchase price (in order for that overcharge to be accepted by the buyer and for the buyer thus to renounce any of his rights and remedies).

> GLOSS: If one sold an item of wood and told the buyer it was an item of gold, since the buyer (is present) to see it, the seller may say, "I said it was good as gold (and thus bear no liability for fraud)."[19]

8) If one sells a cow to another, and says to him, "The cow has such-and-such defects (e.g., it is lame) which are discernible," and among them he mentioned one defect which is not discernible,[20] and the nondiscernible defect is in fact present in the cow, while the other, discernible, defects are not, the sale is deemed to be based on a fundamental error (and rescission may be sought). How (this applies in practice and the reasoning behind it are as follows): For example, the seller said to the buyer, "This cow is lame, blind, a habitual biter, and it breaks down under a load," and in fact the cow is only a habitual biter, the sale is deemed to have been based on a fundamental error, for the buyer may say, "When I saw that the cow was not lame or blind, I said (to myself) that just as these (obvious) defects are not present, so too nondiscernible defects are not present in it, (and the seller spoke of the cow as he did only) to soothe my mind (regarding any reservations I might have had about the cow)." (If[21]) however, the cow does have discernible defects, whether all or some of those mentioned (by the seller), and also a nondiscernible defect, e.g., the cow is lame and it bites, or it is blind and it bites, the sale is not deemed to have been based on a fundamental error: since (one may assume) that just as the buyer renounced (right of rescission regarding) the discernible defect, so also did he do so regarding the nondiscernible defect.

9) If the cow possessed a discernible defect which the seller pointed out to the buyer, and the seller said, "The cow has such-and-such a defect and such-and-such a defect which are not discernible,"[22] and the cow does in fact have the nondiscernible defects mentioned, the sale is not deemed to have been based on a fundamental error, even if the cow has all the mentioned defects, for the seller did not mislead the buyer; he only mentioned the defects of the cow

which are (actually) present[23] (i.e., since the bill of particulars on the cow was in fact truthful, the buyer cannot argue that the seller was overstating matters and thus attempting to deceive).

10) If one sells a male slave or a female slave, the buyer cannot return the slave (i.e., seek rescission) because of defects which do not affect the performance of the slave's duties,[24] which defects are termed *simpon* (i.e., a bodily defect which is not mentioned in the contract). If such a *simpon* was discernible (on the exposed portions of the slave's body), the buyer has (presumably) seen it (and renounced his right of rescission because of it); if the defect is not manifestly disfiguring, e.g., it is a wart or mole on the skin (but not a bony growth) or a dog bite, or malodorous breath at the mouth or nose, etc., since these do not affect the slave in the performance of his or her duties, there is no right of rescission (because of them): slaves are not for sexual intercourse but for labor.

If a slave has a serious eruption on the skin, or some illness that saps bodily strength,[25] or is subject to fits which cause collapse, or is mentally incompetent, such are defects (for which there is a right of rescission) because they affect performance of duties. Similarly, if the slave is leprous or has any other repulsive condition, there is deemed to be a defect (for which there is a right of rescission) because a person would grumble and complain of them and thus could not be served well by such a servant in the kitchen or at the table. Similarly, if the slave turns out to be an armed brigand,[26] this is deemed a defect which entirely negates the slave as a useful servant (and rescission is proper), since the crown would seize and execute the slave; and also if the slave were part of a royal levy, this ranks as a defect for which rescission may sought because the crown may seize the slave at any time. If, however, the slave is found to be a common thief or cutpurse or kidnapper or a constant runaway or a glutton or a drunkard,[27] etc., these conditions are not grounds for rescission of the sale of the slave because all slaves are presumed to be characterized by all (these and similar) evils, unless a stipulation was made (which specifically provides for one of these conditions or the like to be grounds for rescission).

GLOSS: There is an opinion which holds that a kidnapper is tantamount to a person registered in the royal levy[28] (i.e., it is a ground for rescission); but (habitual) gambling is not a defect (for which rescission can be sought).

11) If one sells another a cow for slaughter[29] and the buyer performs ritual slaughter on it, but the animal turns out to be ritually unfit (for consumption by Jews): if it can be certainly determined (after the slaughter) that the animal had been unfit (for consumption by Jews) when it was purchased, e.g., upon postslaughter examination it appears that the second stomach of the animal had been pierced and a scab had formed on the wound, so that it is then evident that the wound (that rendered the animal ritually unfit) had existed for (at least) three days[30] (prior to the slaughtering process), if the animal had been purchased within three days of slaughter, the sale is deemed to be based on a fundamental error (i.e., that the animal was kosher, which in fact it was not), and the seller is required to return the buyer's money.

If the animal had not been purchased within three days prior to slaughter, or if the animal had been purchased within three days prior to slaughter but upon postslaughter examination no scab was found on the wound, then there is a legitimate doubt (as to) whether or not the wound occurred within three days prior to slaughter: (in this case) the buyer must bring proof; he shall bear the loss and pay the purchase price if he has not already done so[31] (if the money is still in the buyer's hand).

12) In cases of ritual unfitness of meat animals owing to adhesions of the lung, the same law applies: the sale is voidable; but there are authorities who disagree.[32]

GLOSS: Since (ritual unfitness by reason of lung adhesions) is a common occurrence, the buyer should (have been aware of the likelihood of such adhesions and should) have made a stipulation[33] (that such adhesions in the lung shall render the sale voidable, and in the absence of such a stipulation the sale remains valid.) Even cases of ritual unfitness, in which the meat is declared prohibited for Jewish consumption by reason of some doubt (as to the condition of internal organs, the previous health of the animal, etc.), a sale is voidable (as based on a fundamental error); and a seller cannot say (to a buyer), "Bring proof that the animal is (certainly) ritually unfit."[34]

13) If one sells a defective piece of merchandise, and the buyer damages it before he becomes aware of its original defect,[35] if the damage done by the buyer was part of the normal and proper use of the item (e.g., cutting cloth or melting metal), the buyer is free of any liability for the damage to the merchandise other than through the normal use of the item, such damage being caused before he becomes aware of the original defect; he returns the item to its (previous owner -- the seller) and pays for the damage he caused. (The buyer could, of course, get back any portion of the price remaining after the cost of the damage was made good).

14) If one buys linen cloth and cuts it to make a shirt, and a defect in the cloth becomes manifest because of the cutting of the cloth,[36] the buyer returns the cut pieces to the seller (and receives his money back). If the buyer sewed the shirt and the defect in the cloth became evident after the sewing, if the sewing has improved the cloth, the buyer takes a payment for such improvement of the goods from the seller (along with his purchase price -- the sale is voided). All cases of a similar nature are decided in this fashion.

15) If one sells land to another, and the buyer enjoys the produce of that land, and sometime later a defect in that land becomes manifest,[37] if the buyer wishes to return the land to its (previous) owner (i.e., to seek rescission), the buyer is to return all the produce he enjoyed (i.e., the value thereof, in order to seek rescission); if one had leased a courtyard and lived in it (and the defect in the living quarters became manifest later), the tenant is to pay the rental (for the period he actually occupied the premises).

16) A sold B (three) cheeses.[38] After three days B opened them and found them rotted with a (large)[39] amount of moldy material. Inquiries are to be made of cheesemakers: How much time is required

for this amount of mold and rot (to form)? If the cheesemakers say that the mold had to have formed while the cheeses were on the seller's premises, the sale has turned out to be one based on a fundamental error (and rescission may be sought). If the matter (of the time required for the decay to set in) is in doubt, the party seeking the voiding of the sale (i.e., the buyer) shall bear the burden of proof (of the matter).

17) A sold B a flask of oil. B did not open it (at first) but had confidence in A's statement that the oil was good.[40] When B did open the oil, he found it was muddy. A is to swear an oath (prescribed by biblical law) to the effect that he fulfilled his stipulation and gave good oil to B.

If A does not wish to take this oath, B is to swear an oath (prescribed by biblical law) that A stipulated to deliver good, clear oil and that this (muddy) oil was in fact delivered, and B then returns the (muddy) oil (and receives the price he paid out); or, an estimate is made of how much less than good oil this (muddy) oil is worth,[41] and if B wishes to take (the muddy oil), A shall return the difference in price to B.[42]

18) If one sells to another an item which has a defect that is not discernible, and the item is ruined because of that (nondiscernible) defect,[43] the seller is to return the buyer's money to him. How (this applies in practice is as follows): One sells to another an ox that has no teeth[44] (presumably a nondiscernible defect). The buyer leaves the ox with his herd and places feed before all his oxen, which eat the feed. But the buyer cannot tell that this one ox is not eating until the ox in fact dies of hunger. The buyer returns the carcass (to the seller), and (the seller) returns (the buyer's) money. All cases of a similar nature are decided in this fashion.

If the seller was a cattle broker,[45] who buys from one and sells to another, (i.e.) who does not keep animals in his possession, and who (therefore) does not know of a (nondiscernible) defect in an animal (and the ox's sale and death by starvation take place as noted above), the broker is to take an oath as prescribed by rabbinical law to that effect, and the broker shall bear no liability (for the cost of the dead animal to the buyer). It was the buyer's duty to examine the ox himself and return it to the seller before it would die (of starvation, and get his money back). The broker would (then) return it (to its previous owner,[46] the first seller, and get his money back). It was the buyer's responsibility (to examine the ox purchased from the broker), and since he did not do so, he bears the loss of the dead animal himself.

> GLOSS: There are authorities who disagree (with this last rule) and reason that even the broker must indemnify[47] the buyer. Even though there was unfair advantage taken of the broker (by the seller who sold him the toothless ox), the broker has (therefore) no right to take unfair advantage of others, and this (type of) ruling should apply to all cases of a similar nature.[48] This appears to me to be the correct (rule, which is to be followed). How much the more (is unfair advantage not to be taken) in a case in which the buyer is innocent of any fault, e.g., one sells a ring on the assumption that it is gold; after a while the buyer breaks it, and it is found (in fact) to be tin; the seller is obliged to return the buyer's money even though the seller was defrauded (when he bought the ring on the assumption that it was made of gold). If the seller does not believe that the (so-called gold ring) was found to be tin, the seller is to swear an oath (prescribed by biblical law) to the effect that he knows nothing of any tin content in the ring (i.e., that he did not order the ring to be made with a core of tin, since he could not very well swear about the tin content of a ring he purchased, when he does not believe it had a tin content: a person cannot swear about something that is doubtful to him).[49] The seller shall (then) bear no liability in the matter of the ring.[50]
>
> If a broker purchased something on the assumption that it was tin, and after he sells it, the item turns out to be gold or silver, the person buying (from the broker) is the legal owner of the item, since the broker never did (actually) own such an item as an object of gold or silver, since he had no knowledge of its (true) metal con-

tent.[51] Cf. infra ch. 268.

19) If one sells eggs to another and the eggs are (in fact) fertilized, and the chick has begun to grow in them, so that the eggs are unfit for food,[52] the sale is deemed to be based on a fundamental error; the seller returns the buyer's money. (This rule) is not customarily followed now, and the custom (to ignore this rule) supersedes this rule of traditional Jewish Law.

20) If one sells vegetable seeds to another, which seeds are not themselves fit for food,[53] and (the buyer) sows them but they do not grow, the seller is liable for them and is to return the buyer's money which he took, because the presumption[54] (underlying the purchase of) these (seeds) is that they will be (viable) for planting (and since they are not, the sale was based on a fundamental error). This rule holds good when the seeds do not grow because of some defect in the seeds; but if the seeds were (sown) and damaged by a hailstorm,[55] etc., that battered the earth, (the seller) is not liable for them, since perhaps the seeds did not grow owing to the (damaging) hail; and thus (we are to be guided) in any similar case.

21) If one sells another seed grain, which could also be used for food,[56] e.g., wheat or barley, and (the buyer) sows the seed, but it does not grow, (the seller) is not liable (for the loss to the buyer), even if the sale was of flax seed, which most people acquire for the purpose of sowing: since (flax seed) could be eaten, the seller is not liable (for the buyer's loss if the seed does not grow). (If, however, the buyer has not yet paid the seller the money of the purchase price, there is an authority who holds that [if the seed has not sprouted] the buyer can say to the seller, "I bought it for sowing" [and thus make the seller liable].[57]) If the buyer informs the seller that he is acquiring (the seed grain) for and as seed, (the seller) is liable (if the seed does not grow). This same rule applies for items sold as medicines and dyestuffs, etc.

If one purchases something from another and the buyer informs the seller that he is going to transport the merchandise to such-and-such a place[58] to resell it there, and after he has transported the merchandise there it is found to be defective, the seller cannot say, "Return the item purchased to me here," but the seller is to effect the return of the buyer's money to him. The seller is to attend to the return transport of the merchandise or to its sale wherever it is. Even if the merchandise was lost or stolen (after the buyer has informed the seller)[59] (of the intent to transport the goods), the merchandise is deemed to be under the lawful ownership and control of the seller. If the seller knew (at the time of the sale) that his merchandise was defective, the seller shall also be liable (to indemnify) the buyer for the costs of transport to such-and-such a place incurred by the buyer;[60] if the seller was (at the time of the purchase) unaware of the defect in his merchandise, he shall bear no liability for the cost of transport incurred buy the buyer; he shall be liable only for the cost of return transport (for the merchandise).[61]

If the buyer did not inform the seller that he would transport the merchandise to another country,[62] and he did transport it, whereupon it was there found to be defective, the merchandise is deemed to be under the lawful ownership and control of the buyer until he shall return the defective merchandise to the seller.

22) If one purchases an item, which is found to be defective, and that item is afterward lost or stolen,[63] the item is deemed to be under the lawful ownership and control of the buyer until he shall return (the defective) merchandise to the seller.

If the item became decayed or was (a loss due to) damage because of its defect, the item (once it is retrieved) is deemed to be under the lawful ownership and control of the seller.[64]

If the buyer should have informed the seller (and it was clearly opportune to apprise the seller of the defect in the goods -- i.e., the flaw came to the buyer's attention soon after the purchase and he should have informed the seller so as not to lose his money[65]), and he did not do so, the item is deemed to be under the lawful ownership and control of the buyer.

23) If one sells another an ox, and that ox turns out to have the defect of being a gorer:[66] If it cannot be definitively shown that the ox was purchased for plowing, or, alternatively, that the ox was purchased for slaughter, e.g., the buyer acquires animals for both purposes; and the purchase price of the animal does not indicate for which purpose it was acquired, e.g., the price of a meat (animal)

has risen to a point of parity with the price of a draft animal, (the sale) is not (voidable as a sale based on) a fundamental error, since the seller can say, "I sold you the animal for meat" (and goring is clearly not a defect in such a case). (This rule holds) even if most people (there) acquire oxen for draft purposes; we do not follow the practice of the majority (as an indication of purpose or intent in pecuniary matters) in order to require the seller to surrender the price paid (to the buyer); if, however, the buyer is still in possession of the purchase money, it goes without saying (that he need not pay for a goring ox) in a place where most people acquire oxen for draft purposes,[67] but even if both purposes of purchase are equally present there, the one (i.e., the seller) who seeks the payment from another (i.e., the buyer) bears the burden of proof (in this case, that the animal was sold for meat).

If the buyer customarily acquires oxen only for draft purposes, and the seller is aware of this fact, (this sale of a goring ox) is deemed a sale based on a fundamental error.[68]

If the buyer customarily acquires oxen only for slaughter, it is (then properly) presumed that he acquired this ox for slaughter[69] (there being no contrary indication in the case).

If the buyer customarily acquires oxen for both draft purposes and for slaughter,[70] if the price paid for the animal gives an indication (of the purpose of the purchase, (i.e.) if the buyer gave the (going) price of a draft animal, we say that the buyer acquired the animal for draft purposes, (and a sale of a goring ox is deemed) a sale based on a fundamental error: if the buyer gave the (going) price for a meat animal, we say that the buyer acquired the animal for slaughter.

> GLOSS: Whenever there has been a sale based on a fundamental error and it is required that money be returned (to the buyer) and (the seller) has cash money, he is required to give back cash money -- as to an ordinary creditor;[71] this rule is contrary to the authorities who hold that one may return (the value of the money in) land.[72]

233: The rule regarding the sale of one type of produce which turns out to be another type or the sale of a poor type of produce which turns out to be a good type. One paragraph.

1) If one contracts to sell one type of produce, but delivers another type (though a similar one), there is no lawful sale and both parties can withdraw from the transaction.[1] How (this works out in practice is as follows): One contracted to sell white wheat that turned out to be red wheat, or vice versa; or one contracted to sell wine that turned out to be vinegar, or olive wood that turned out to be sycamore wood, or vice versa.

If, however, one contracted to sell good wheat that turned out to be bad,[2] the buyer can withdraw from the transaction even if there was no (constructive fraud by reason of) unfair price in the total amount (of the price). The seller cannot withdraw from the transaction even if the merchandise (delivered) rose in value.[3] If one contracted to sell poor goods and they turned out to be of good quality, even if there was no (constructive fraud by reason of) unfair price in the total amount (of the price), the seller can withdraw from the transaction, but the buyer cannot withdraw from the transaction even if the merchandise (delivered) fell in value.[4]

If one sold another poor-quality merchandise which was in fact of poor quality,[5] or if one sold good-quality merchandise which was in fact of good quality, even though there might be a better-quality merchandise than the good merchandise, and a poorer-quality merchandise than the poor merchandise, and there is (constructive fraud owing to) an unfair price amounting to one-sixth (of the correct price), neither party can withdraw from the transaction: acquisition has been effected and the amount of the fraud is to be returned (to the defrauded party).

> GLOSS: If one sells another meat with the presumption that the meat comes from a gelded ram, and it turns out that the ram was not gelded, the purchase is valid, and the amount of unfair price (i.e., the sixth) is returned (to the defrauded party) unless it was known that the buyer was of a delicate physical constitution and cannot eat the meat of a ram which has not been gelded. The

principle of this rule applies in all cases similar to this.

If one sells another silver with the presumption that it is pure silver, and it turns out to be alloyed with a base metal, the purchase is valid, and the amount of unfair price (i.e., the sixth) is returned (to the defrauded party) because the item in point only involves) one type (of material): silver.[7]

234: The rule concerning one who sells a (ritually) forbidden thing and the buyer who consumes (or enjoys) it. Four paragraphs.

1) If one slaughters the firstborn[1] (of a kosher meat animal, which cannot lawfully be slaughtered for meat unless properly certified as a blemished, imperfect animal) and sells it, and it becomes known that the butcher did not show the animal to an expert (in order to get certification that the animal was blemished and fit for ordinary slaughter for meat), whatever has been (sold and) eaten, has been eaten. The butcher is to return the money the buyer paid for the meat. Whatever meat remains unconsumed in the possession of the buyer is to be buried, and the butcher is to return the money the buyer paid (for the unconsumed portion of meat).

2) Similarly, if one butchers a cow and sells it, and it becomes known that the cow was ritually unfit,[2] whatever portion of ritually unfit meat has been consumed, has indeed been consumed, and the butcher is to return the buyers' money (paid for the consumed portion) to the buyers: The buyers are to return the unconsumed portion of meat to the butcher, and the butcher is to return to the buyers their money (they paid for the unconsumed portion of meat).

If the buyers resold[3] the ritually unfit meat to non-Jews or they fed it to dogs, they are to reckon with the butcher the price of the unfit meat (which they received for the resale) and the butcher is to return the additional amount to them (i.e., the difference between the lower cost of unfit meat and the more expensive kosher meat.)

This is the rule governing all who sell items, the eating of which is prohibited by biblical law.[4]

3) If one sells another an item, the eating of which is prohibited by rabbinical ordinance,[5] if the (unfit) produce still exists one is to return such produce and take one's money back. If one has consumed it, then it is gone, and the seller is not required to return any (money) at all to the buyer.

> GLOSS: If one has sold the meat of a cow that was not properly examined (for evidence of unfitness after proper ritual slaughter), (the meat of such a) cow is as if forbidden pursuant to rabbinical ordinance, because the process of post-slaughter examination is a provision of rabbinical law.[6]

4) (In the matter of) all things forbidden for the use, benefit, or enjoyment by Jews,[7] whether pursuant to biblical law or rabbinical ordinance, (any price paid for such goods) is to be returned (to the buyer) and they are not subjects of lawful sale at all (among Jews).

235: The rule concerning the minor, the deaf-mute, the mentally incompetent, and the inebriate: when such as these sell moveable goods; and the rule concerning the effecting of acquisition on the Sabbath and on the holy days. Twenty-eight paragraphs.

1) A minor, up to the age of six years, cannot validly cause others lawfully to acquire (his property) at all.[1] From the age of six until majority, if the minor understands the nature of commerce (i.e., the minor [until age ten] has been examined and found sufficiently knowledgeable, and after age ten, any minor who is not manifestly mentally incompetent), the rabbinical sages have ordained, in regard to moveable goods, that a sale, purchase, or gift effected by a minor shall be lawful and valid,[2] whether the transaction is large or small, whether the gift is made by a minor donor of sound health or the gift is *mortis causa*. (There are authorities who hold that since [the minors' right (to sell and to grant)] rests only on the basis of a rabbinical ordinance, therefore where they have [clearly] acted improperly, e.g., they have sold the small amount of

[moveable] property which minor female orphans owned [as their only source of income and support], such sale is a nullity.[3])

In regard to real estate, however, a minor cannot sell real property,[4] nor grant it as a gift, until majority is reached (i.e., age thirteen for males; age twelve for females; plus the onset of puberty for both).[5] (This rule holds good) even if the land had been granted to the minor as a gift,[6] or the minor's legal guardian acquired it for the minor. If the minor does grant a gift of real estate, even if the gift is *mortis causa*,[7] the gift is a nullity, even if the land had been a gift to the minor and even though the minor understands the nature of commerce. (But as long as [in this case] the minor remains desirous of doing what he has done, and neither his relatives nor the rabbinical court explicitly declare the minor's transaction void, the person taking the land [from the minor] is under no obligation to indemnify the minor for what he took[8] [and enjoyed].)

If a minor inherited a (collectable) note of debt (against a debtor) from his father,[9] such a note is legally like any other type of moveable property; and the minor (if competent to do so) can lawfully sell it or give it to another person.

2) The (above) rule holds good when the minor has no legal guardian.[10] If, however, the minor has a legal guardian, the minor's transactions are null, even in respect of moveable property, unless they are done with the consent of the guardian. If the guardian wishes to confirm the minor's purchase, sale, or gift of moveable property, such transaction becomes valid.

> GLOSS: The same rule (governing transactions by minors) applies if the minors are supported by a private person, who is treated at law as a (lawfully appointed) guardian, as will be explained infra ch. 290.
> Once the minor has reached majority, even though he has a guardian appointed by his (deceased) father, (the minor's) purchase or sale is lawful.[11] Even though a guardian must fulfill the requests of the (deceased father who appointed him), and may be prohibited from giving (property) to an heir or to a purchaser until the time stipulated by the decedent, in any event, a purchase (from the minor)

is valid; and if the buyer seizes the property he bought, he cannot be sued for return of that property in a rabbinical court.[12]

3) If a minor, who understands the nature of commerce and who has no legal guardian, engaged in commerce and erred (in such a manner that another party has become the victim of a constructive fraud), he is, at law, treated the same as an adult:[13] there is renunciation of any amount (of fraudulent gain) up to one-sixth (of the correct price, etc.); (a fraudulent gain) of one-sixth (of the correct price) is to be returned to the defrauded party; (a fraudulent gain) in excess of one-sixth (of the correct price) renders the sale voidable.[14]

4) A minor's purchase or sale of moveable goods becomes lawful and valid only if acquisition has been effected by pulling (and the money price is also paid, cf. supra 199:4).[15] If, however, a minor has (only) paid a purchase price (without the act of pulling), and then withdraws from the transaction, he does not take upon himself the formal rabbinical condemnation of "He who punished."[16] If other parties (i.e., adults) withdraw from a transaction (with the minor), they do take upon themselves the formal rabbinical condemnation.

5) Similarly, if others (i.e., adults) have effected acquisition (of moveable goods) from a minor,[17] or the minor has leased to them (the adults) the place where the goods are located[18] (lease being tantamount to a sale of real property for a term), and the minor withdraws from the transaction, the purchaser is not deemed to have effected a lawful and valid acquisition. We do not permit a rabbinical court to entertain a suit to divest a minor (of that moveable property); and we do not effect lawful acquisition of something directly from the hand of a male minor (i.e., acquisition by kerchief), for such an act of acquisition is tantamount to an instrument of acquisition (which is in writing), and witnesses do not sign such an instrument unless it be an adult's instrument.[19] (No witnesses means the instrument is not valid, and by extension, there can be no acquisition by kerchief directly from the hand of a minor, which acquisition is tantamount to acquisition by instrument.)

6) Similarly if a male minor is acquiring moveable goods, and an act of acquisition (i.e., by kerchief) has been effected directly

from the male minor,[20] and the minor rented the location of the goods, no lawful acquisition has been effected until the minor shall pull (the goods), because a minor's courtyard[21] (i.e., the one leased to him, the lease being a sale for a term) effects no acquisition, since acquisition by courtyard is an extension of the law of agency, and a minor male cannot lawfully appoint an agent. Neither the act of (kerchief) acquisition nor the lease of the location of the moveable goods could be of greater (legal import) than the (principle that) his courtyard (effects no acquisition).

But a minor female,[22] who does have the right to effect legal acquisition by means of "courtyard," as an extension of the rule which permits her lawfully to acquire by direct means of her hand (i.e., kerchief acquisition), may acquire moveable goods if the formal acquisition was effected (by kerchief) from her hand, or by the lease to her of the location of the goods. (N.B. the direct acquisition by the female's hand is deemed biblical, cf. Deuteronomy 24:1.)

7) If a minor acquires land,[23] and has paid a purchase price for it, and has taken possession of it, it shall remain in his possession, since a person who is not present may be granted a benefit,[24] (i.e., the benefit is conferred without the minor's participation in the transaction; a minor is "not present" owing to his tender years -- he is not deemed fully competent yet, but in this case that is immaterial.)

8) Once a child has reached majority and the onset of puberty is manifest,[25] thirteen years of age for males and twelve years of age for females, even though (these persons) do not understand the nature of commerce, any sale, purchase, or gift by them of moveable property is lawful and valid. But their transactions in respect to real property[26] are not valid until, having attained majority, they understand the nature of commerce.

> GLOSS: All this (above-stated rule) applies to a private transaction[27] of the minor. The rabbinical court, however, may sell a minor's land to pay the debts of his (or her) (deceased) father, etc., cf. infra para. 26.

9) The above rule applies to a minor's real property which he acquired (by means of purchase) or which was granted to him as a gift

inter vivos.[28] Land which he inherited from his ancestors, however, or which was bequeathed to him by others,[29] or which was granted to him as a gift *mortis causa*, he cannot lawfully sell until he is a full twenty years old and signs of puberty are manifest in him.

Before twenty full years, even though signs of puberty are manifest (in the person), and the person understands the nature of commerce, the person cannot (lawfully sell inherited lands or lands acquired by a gift *mortis causa*);[30] perhaps he will sell the lands cheaply because he is only thinking of the cash proceeds of the sale, and he is still not really very sophisticated (in commercial matters).

When a person is full twenty years of age, the signs of puberty being present, the person may sell his moveable property and his real property, whether his or whether (inherited from) his father, even if the person does not understand the nature of commerce. (This rule is contrary to the view of other[31] [authorities].)

10) If a person makes a gift (of land), the person being more than thirteen years of age and less than twenty years of age,[32] the signs of puberty being present, whether that gift is *inter vivos* or *mortis causa*, such gift shall be valid. (We reason that) if (this act) did not afford the donor substantial pleasure (or benefit), he would not have made the gift. This is (moreover) an occurrence which is not common, and the rabbinical sages declared that the person's gift should be valid in order that his statements and declarations be given weight and credence (by others).

11) This rule, that the person shall have the lawful power to sell land (inherited from) his father, applies when the person is twenty years of age,[33] the onset of puberty having become manifest, or the signs of physiological retardation of adult sexual development having become manifest.[34] If, however, neither of these physiological phenomena is evident, the person is deemed (still) to be a minor and may make no lawful and valid sale (of land) even from his own property until he shall reach a full half[35] (of a normal lifespan) of years: i.e., thirty-six years.

12) If a person sells (real estate) before it has become clear that he has in fact reached majority, i.e., prior to age twenty, the onset of puberty not being manifest, and no sign of physiological

retardation of adult sexual development being manifest, and sometime later the onset of puberty does become manifest,[36] so that it is now clear that he has reached majority, his sale previously made is null. But with the appearance of signs of physiological retardation of adult sexual development in a person of twenty years of age (or after), majority for that person is deemed to be retroactive to age thirteen years and one day;[37] since it is now clear that the person was in fact naturally without adult sexual potential from birth, the nonappearance of normal puberty was due to this cause; and the matter becomes clear that majority had in fact been reached at thirteen years of age plus one day (normal puberty being an impossibility), and the person's previous sale was valid.

13) If a person has sold either his (real) property or his inherited (real) property, and thereafter dies, and his relatives complain that he was at the time of the sale still a minor,[38] and his relatives complain (that his sale was invalid) and wish to make a (*post-mortem*) examination of the body (to determine whether or not puberty had begun): we do not listen (to the relatives who complain in this fashion; i.e., the court will not hear their suit).

> GLOSS: The legal presumption is that witnesses would not sign a document (i.e., a bill of sale) unless they know that the seller had in fact reached majority[39] (such a bill of sale being assumed to be customary in sale of real property), and moreover signs of puberty may undergo physiological change *post mortem*, and further, a dead body is not to be subjected to degrading examination.[40]

14) If a person of less than twenty years of age has sold land (inherited) from his father,[41] he (can) lawfully seek to have the buyer return that land, either before (the seller) reaches twenty years of age or immediately upon his reaching twenty years of age. The person can also lawfully seek return of all the produce (of that land or its value, presumably) which the buyer enjoyed. If the buyer spent money on that land (e.g., to till it) or planted seed in it, an estimate (of his outlay) is made, and the remainder (of the crop or its value) is returned (to the seller after a deduction to cover the buyer's expenses).[42]

If, however, when the person became twenty years of age, the person did not raise a protest (in the matter of the sale of inherited land immediately), his right to so is extinguished, even if he had made the sale when he was a minor.[43]

15) If a minor has borrowed money from others: one authority holds that he is liable for repayment of the debt upon reaching majority,[44] one authority exempts him from repayment.[45] One authority makes a distinction: if it is known that the debt was incurred in order to provide necessary food (to sustain himself), the debt is to be repaid; if it is not known that the debt was for this purpose, he is exempt from repayment.[46]

> GLOSS: There are authorities who hold the opinion that even though a minor cannot sell property, he may in any event mortgage it.[47] Even in the case of a sale of land by a minor, which transaction is a nullity, it is necessary for the minor to return the purchase money he took. If the minor does not have the ready money, the purchaser may collect his money due from the minor's unencumbered real property.

16) If a minor has acted as a surety for others, he is exempt from paying such surety even when he reaches majority.[48]

17) The deaf-mute, or the completely deaf person, may sell and buy moveable goods (in transactions carried on by means of) signs and gestures.[49] They may not buy and sell real property; even in regard to moveable property, their transactions shall not be valid until they are fully and completely examined (as to mental competence) and the examiners, after full discussion of the case, are satisfied in the matter.

18) The mute or the person who has (temporarily) lost the power of speech (can) make lawful and valid purchases, sales, and gifts, whether of moveable goods or of real property, provided that such person be examined (for mental competence and understanding of the transaction in question) as he would be in a matter of a bill of divorce; or he can transact the business in writing.[50]

19) One who cannot hear unless he is addressed in a loud voice is not considered to be deaf; he is deemed to be in full possession of

his faculties for all purposes.[51]

20) The mentally incompetent person can make no lawful and valid sale, purchase, or gift, neither of moveable property nor of real property.[52] The rabbinical court is to establish guardians for the mentally incompetent (where necessary) as it does for minor (orphans). (The mentally incompetent person cannot take lawful possession of anything by himself.[53])

21) A person who experiences episodes of mental incompetence and episodes of sound mental state, e.g., the epileptic, makes lawful and valid transactions during his periods of sound mental state;[54] he takes possession lawfully on his own behalf or on behalf of others as can any other person of sound mind. Witnesses (to a transaction by such a person) must take special pains to examine the matter (i.e., the transaction they bear witness to) very thoroughly: (to preclude the possibility that) perhaps the person engaged in the transaction (during the transitional period) either at the beginning of an episode of incompetence or at the end of an episode of incompetence.

> GLOSS: If two (witnesses) state that a person sold something while he was in an episode of mental incompetence, and two (other witnesses) state that that person sold something while he was in a period of mental competence: if the sale was of real property, the real property is deemed to be in the legal possession of the seller; if the sale was of moveable goods, they are deemed to be in the legal possession of the one who is (in fact) in possession of them.[55]

22) The person under the influence of alcoholic beverages lawfully and validly buys, sells, or grants by gift[56] (real or moveable property). If such a person has reached a state of intoxication as severe as that of Lot, i.e., he has no idea of what he is doing (cf. Genesis 19:33), his acts are null and he is deemed to be like a mentally incompetent person.

23) If one sells real property or moveable goods, and has transferred (legal title) to such property to the buyer without the buyer's knowledge, the buyer shall enjoy the position of advantage[57]:

if he wishes to take the goods, the seller cannot withdraw from the transaction; if he does not wish to do so, the property reverts to its (previous) owner.

24) Similarly, if a slave has acquired (property) or sold property or granted any property as a gift, or a gift was given to the slave, the slave's master shall enjoy a position of advantage.[58] If the master wishes to confirm the slave's transactions, they are (by the master's confirmation) confirmed; if he does not wish to do so, all the slave's transactions are void. The master may confirm the transactions verbally; it is not necessary to effect any (further) acquisition from him at all.

25) The rule governing the sale of a wife's property by her husband and a sale by a wife is found in *Even Haezer* 85:90.

26) A rabbinical court which has sold or purchased property with the property of minor orphans (i.e., wards of the court), whether such transactions concerned real or moveable property, has made lawful and valid sales or purchases[59]. Similarly, a guardian of minor orphans, whether appointed as guardian by the rabbinical court or by the orphan's (deceased) father, who has sold or purchased property with the property of his ward, has transacted a lawful and valid sale or purchase. Neither the rabbinical court nor a legal guardian can make a lawful gift (of the orphan's property) because a man cannot make a gift of that which he does not own.

27) The necessities for which sales (of orphans' property by the court or the guardian) are lawful and permissible are explained in ch. 290.

28) If one sells (property) or effects formal and legal acquisition of property on the Sabbath, the Day of Atonement, or any holy day,[60] even though the person is liable to a flogging for such a transgression of rabbinical law, his act is valid, and documents (necessary for the transaction) are indited after that day[61] (of special religious observance).

236: The rule concerning the non-Jew who takes land from a Jew by force or by means of false accusations.
Nine paragraphs.

1) If non-Jews exercise force against a Jew and threaten to kill him,[1] unless and until he shall redeem himself from their power by

means of his field or his house which he must give to the extortionist, so that afterward he would be left alone: When the extortionist should wish to sell that (extorted) real property, if the (lawful Jewish) owner is in a position to purchase it from the extortionist, he shall enjoy first option (to do so). If he is not in a position to purchase the property, or the extortionist has held the property for (at least) twelve (consecutive) months (the lawful Jewish owner, having the resources to buy the property but showing no inclination to do so), whoever (of the Jewish people) comes first to purchase the property (from the extortionist) shall be able lawfully so to do (under Jewish law). (This shall be the rule) provided that the (Jewish) purchaser shall give the original (Jewish) owner one-fourth the land itself or one-third the money price paid for the land, since the extortionist would sell the property for less than its value: the property not lawfully being his own, he (chooses) to sell it. He would sell the land for one-fourth, or approximately one-fourth, (of its actual value), and this one-fourth (difference between the actual price and the selling price) shall belong to the (original, lawful, Jewish owner), since because the land is (rightfully) his, (the extortionist) sells it cheaply. Therefore the party purchasing from the extortionist for thirty (selas) gives the (original owner) ten (selas -- or one-quarter the actual price of forty selas in cash money) or gives him one-quarter of the land (itself), after which the party (purchasing from the extortionist) shall effect acquisition of the whole (of the property). If the quarter is not given (to the former Jewish owner), that quarter (in land or money) is deemed the proceeds of robbery in the possession of the party (who purchased from the extortionist).

> GLOSS: If the (original owners) state that they had the resources to purchase (the real property extorted from them), and the party (who purchased from the extortionist) states they did not have such resources, the previous owner shall bear the burden of proving (that he could have purchased the property), because real estate (in this case shall be) presumed to be (under the lawful ownership) of the purchaser.2
>
> There is an opinion that this rule applies when the

(original lawful) owner surrenders the land himself in order to avert a death threat; if, however, the extortionist took the land by force (but without a threat of death), the land shall be returned (by the party purchasing from the extortionist *gratis*), and that party is to receive (from the original owners an amount to represent) the benefit and pleasure[3] (they have received -- the return of their property -- which covers any expenses incurred by the purchaser in order to secure the property from the extortionist the property itself being returned *gratis*) as will be explained infra para. 8.

If Jews seize a fellow Jew and threaten to kill him unless and until he gives them (some real estate), this rule (above) does not apply, because (victims) should know that Jews are not killers[4] and will not carry out death threats. These extortionists are deemed to be as if without the power to kill, as will be explained infra para. 8.

2) If (the purchaser from the non-Jewish extortionist) is not believed (when he states) how much (he paid when) he bought the property, and there are no (proper Jewish) witnesses[5] (who can support the purchaser's claim), the purchaser shall swear an oath (prescribed by biblical law) as to how much (he paid when) he bought the property (in order to confirm his assertion).

3) If (the purchaser) bought the land from the (non-Jewish extortionist within twelve months (of the extortion): if the (original lawful) owners wish, (the purchaser) must return the land to them, in return for the (full price) the purchaser paid to the non-Jewish (extortionist); or the (original lawful) owners may leave the property with the purchaser who will give the original owners a third (of the cash price) given to the non-Jewish[6] (extortionist).

4) Even within twelve months (of the extortion by the non-Jew), if one acquires the property first (from its original lawful owners) and afterwards acquires the property from the (non-Jewish) extortionist, the purchase is lawful and valid[7] (the property being lawfully transferred by its true owner first). If, however, (within twelve months) one acquires the land first (from the) non-Jewish

(extortionist) and afterward acquires the land from (the original and lawful owners), the purchase is null (it being assumed that the acquiescence of the lawful owner to the sale by the extortionist was not of the owner's free will), even if a (formal) instrument of sale is prepared:[8] unless the (lawful owner sold the property and) undertook (to provide) warranty of title; or he explicitly acknowledged (of his own free will that he received an adequate price) from him[9] (the buyer).

5) If one purchased real property from a (non-Jewish) extortionist, and that land remained in the buyer's possession[10] (without challenge by the original owner) for three years, and afterward he sold the land to another (a Jew), the original owners have no claim against the second (Jewish) buyer, since the (rabbinical court) advances the claim for him that the first buyer had (in fact) bought the land from them and (that first buyer) had given them the third (of the purchase price, a quarter of the land's full value).

This same rule applies if the purchaser from the extortionist had kept the land for but one day (before selling the land) to the (Jewish) second buyer (who held the land for) three years.[11]

> GLOSS: There is an authority who holds that (the above rule applies) only when the first buyer is not Jewish, and this non-Jewish buyer sells the property to a Jew; the rule governing the second buyer is the same as if the second buyer had purchased directly from the extortionist.[12]

6) Similarly, this rule applies if the buyer held the land (after purchase from the extortionist) for three years (unchallenged by the original owner), whereupon the buyer dies and bequeaths the property to his heirs.[13] (The rabbinical court) advances the same claim for the heir (as for the second buyer).

7) If a non-Jew, known for his violence, takes the real property of a Jew by force, and enters the Jew's (e.g.) field because the non-Jew was (in fact) the (lawful) creditor of the owner of the field, or because he had some (lawful) claim for damage or loss against the Jew;[14] and after seizing the land, the non-Jew sold it to a Jew, the original owner has no right (to sue) to take the land

away from the purchaser. This rule applies when the (original) owner acknowledges that the non-Jew's claim is truthful.[15]

Similarly, if there is a king or a nobleman in that place who is able to compel the non-Jew to go to law[16] (to answer for his act against the Jew's property), and the owners (of the seized property) do not sue the non-Jew, they are not able to file a suit (in a rabbinical court) to take the land away from the (Jew) who purchased the land from the non-Jew, even though the owners do not acknowledge the truth of the non-Jew's claim, nor do any (proper Jewish) witnesses testify to the truth of the non-Jew's claim. The purchaser can say to the (original) owners, "If the non-Jew is a robber, why did you not sue him under non-Jewish law?"

8) If a non-Jew tricks or swindles a Jew out of his field, but the Jew was in no fear of his life from the non-Jew,[17] and the non-Jew (then) sells or gives the field to another Jew, the Jewish buyer or donee is required to return the field to its owner, even if he had been in possession of the field for a number of years. It is not, however, necessary to return the field *gratis*;[18] we estimate how much the owner would give to the non-Jew to return the field, and he is to give that amount to the Jewish (buyer or donee).

If the buyer has incurred expenses in order to get the land from the non-Jew (e.g., legal fees), the owners are to reimburse the buyer (for his expenses) up to the value of the property, if the owners wish to take the property back from the buyer.[19] It is (also) not necessary to give the buyer more than he spent, e.g., if the non-Jew was the buyer's friend and the non-Jew gave the property to him cheaply, the original owners are required to give (the buyer) only what he gave to the non-Jew:[20] even though the original owner would not have been able to secure the return of the property from the non-Jew for the same small amount; even if the non-Jew gave it to the Jew *gratis*, the property is to be returned to its owner *gratis*.

If, while the property is in the possession (of the buyer or donee, the buyer or donee) improves the property by building on it, (the buyer or donee) is deemed to be tantamount to a person who enters another's property without permission and effects improvements therein: the owner can say to him, "Take your wood and your stones away[21] (I'll not pay for them!)."

GLOSS: (The above applies) only to real property whose owners do not despair (of regaining it if it is taken from them by force or guile). But with regard to moveable goods,[22] which are despaired of, one is not required to return such items to their owners -- except for (Jewish) books, the return of which is not despaired of since we know they are only sold to Jews (thus there is always a good chance that such books, which would only have value to Jews, will be returned to their Jewish owners).

9) The (above-stated) rule applies when there is no (system of courts and) judges that could be employed to recover the field from the non-Jew.[23] If, however, there is (a system of courts and) judges in the land, and it would be possible to recover (the land) from the non-Jew by means of that legal system: (if) one has not made use of that system, certainly (this is proof) that the owner (of the property) has despaired (of ever getting it back); and the property shall (in this case) lawfully remain in the buyer's possession and the buyer need not give the (original) owner (of the property) anything (for it).

GLOSS: All this (chapter) concerns an extortionist, one who acts without any lawful authority. But a nobleman or a ruler, who becomes angry with his servants and ministers, and takes the house of one of them (is, as far as rabbinical law is concerned, held to be acting in compliance with the rule that) the law of the kingdom is law (and the nobleman's act of confiscation is justifiable thereunder). (Therefore) a purchaser (of the property from that nobleman) is not required to give (the former Jewish) owner (of the property) anything.[24]
If a Jew has mortgaged his land to a non-Jew, and set a specific time at which he will redeem the land, and does not redeem the land (at that time), and (then) the non-Jew sells it to someone else: if he sold the land for its proper value, the sale is lawful and valid, because he sold the property according to legal provisions (for that sale). If, however, he sold the property for less

than its proper value, even by the smallest amount less, the [25] (mortgagor) can seek rescission.

237: The rule concerning one who acquires a thing which another person is negotiating to acquire. Two paragraphs.

1) If one is in the process of negotiating to acquire or lease a thing -- whether real property or moveable property[1] -- and (during this process) someone else comes and lawfully acquires it, this latter person is deemed wicked (his transaction, however, is valid).

This same rule applies when one wishes to hire himself out to an employer[2] (and during the course of negotiations, another person comes and takes the position).

There are authorities who hold that if one comes to take title to ownerless property or one is (presumably) receiving a gift from someone, and another person comes (in the meanwhile) and takes title or receives the gift first,[3] this other person is not deemed wicked, since the item in question is not something that is (readily) available in another place.

(If A is in the process of acquiring real property adjoining the property of another person, even though the right of first option enjoyed by an adjoining landholder B does not apply to this property [e.g., it belongs to a non-Jew], [B may preempt A][4] and acquire the land [while A is still negotiating for it] and not be deemed wicked -- because [the availability of this land] is like a [rare] find[5] [i.e., it is not available elsewhere]. Similarly, if A is in the process of acquiring something, and B comes and is able to acquire the thing more cheaply here than would be possible in any other place, the case is tantamount to one of a [rare] find [for B], and B shall be able to acquire it as long as A has not acquired it.)[6]

There are authorities[7] who hold that there is no difference (between the cases of sale and hire and the cases of ownerless property and gift; if A is about to take title and B comes to take title first, B is deemed wicked, even in matters of ownerless property, etc.).

GLOSS: The first line of reasoning appears to be the

basic (and correct) one. Even in regard to the second line of reasoning (i.e., no difference as among sale, hire, gift, etc.), it applies only to the poor, but not to the rich (i.e., a poor man who acquires, while the rich man is coming to take title, is not deemed wicked), unless the (item[8] in question) is not (elsewhere) available, in which case (the person taking title first) is deemed wicked even when the other person is wealthy.[9] Cf. supra 156:5.

All the above only treats the case in which a price between parties (to a sale) has been mutually agreed upon, and only the act of formal acquisition is lacking (to complete the sale). If, however, no price has yet been agreed upon, the seller wants so and so much, and the buyer wants to pay less, it is permissible for another party (to break into those negotiations) to acquire the item, whether the seller is a non-Jew or a Jew[10] (i.e., no unfair advantage can be taken of a merchant by permitting the bargainer for the lowest possible price to assert a right to exclude other potential purchasers). There is an authority[11] who has written that there is an ordinance, with a penalty of excommunication, attributed to R. Gershom, that it is forbidden to take unfair advantage or to encroach upon the rights (of a Jew) in the matter of renting buildings from a non-Jew (i.e,. if a non-Jewish landlord has evicted a Jewish tenant, no other Jew is to rent those premises even though the non-Jew no longer owns them): and this same (prohibition applies where it is customary for a Jew to acquire (as by a contract of hire) the right to loan money (at interest) -- to non-Jews. (I.e., no other Jewish banker is to encroach upon that lender's territory.)

2) It is forbidden for a tutor to hire himself to a householder (to teach the children of that household) if that householder (already) has a tutor in his household, unless the householder declares, "I do not wish to retain my (present) tutor."[12] If, however, a householder has engaged a tutor, another householder may engage

that same tutor.[13]

238: The rule providing that a written record of a sale be indited for the seller, but not for the buyer. Three paragraphs.

1) A record of sale is written for a seller who has sold his field to such-and-such a person, even though that specific person is not present[1] (at the writing of this document). (This holds good) provided that (the seller) has already transferred ownership[2] of the field to him (the buyer) by means of a formal and legal act of acquisition or (the seller) bears witness upon himself that (the buyer) has already effected acquisition by means of one of the lawful modes of effecting acquisition; and provided that the witnesses to the document personally know the principals[3] whose names appear in the document, that this person is such-and-such a one, and that person is such-and-such a one.

A written record of sale is not, however, indited for a buyer, except with the consent of the seller.[4]

There is an authority[5] who holds that even if a formal act of acquisition is effected by the seller, to validate (the seller's assertion that) he has transferred ownership (of his field, lawfully and formally) to such-and-such a person -- buyer not being present, and that buyer comes to request that a record of the sale be written for him, that that record is not written (i.e., we do not listen to him), because the principle that a lawful act of acquisition is normally recorded in writing only applies when (the seller) is present (at the writing).

> GLOSS: If one comes to (two) witnesses and declares, "I make a gift of my house, located in such-and-such place, to such-and-such person," even though the witnesses do not know whether or not the donor has a house in that specified place, they are permitted to write (and witness the deed of gift) because they only bear witness to the fact that a gift (is granted), and if the donor does not (actually) have (the property specified)[6] the gift itself is a nullity (i.e., the witnesses do not support the

claim that the donor has the property, only that he is giving it).

2) The buyer bears the cost of the scribe's fee, even when the seller is selling his field because of its poor quality[7] (and he wants very much to sell the property).

3) There is an authority who holds that the rule that a record of sale is written for the seller even if the buyer is not present applies only when witnesses attest that the seller has in fact already received the purchase-price money from the buyer.[8] If this matter (of price) has not been written into the record of the sale, when the seller should sue the buyer for the purchase price, the seller must show proof that the sale was with the consent of the buyer.

There is an authority who holds that even if the witnesses attest that the seller (already) received the purchase-price money, if the record itself reflects the fact that the purchase was by the mutual consent of seller and buyer, (the notation of payment of price) is not[9] written (into the document).

There is an authority who holds that it (such a notation of payment) is written into the record of the sale, even if witnesses did not attest that (the seller) (in fact) received the purchase price.[10]

> GLOSS: (This last is based on the notion that) this document does not oblige the buyer to acquire (anything); it has evidentiary value only. Therefore the buyer is also deemed trustworthy to say that he has (in fact) paid the purchase price.[11]
>
> A record of a sale which does not contain the amount of the sale (price, etc.) but only records the matter of the sale is a valid document[12] (as a record of the sale).

239: The rule concerning how another instrument of acquisition is prepared for a person who claims the original document has been lost. Two paragraphs.

1) If one comes and says, "A document, which I had, (showing) that I acquired a certain field from such-and-such a person, has be-

come lost," we accept this statement (i.e., we listen to him), and another document is prepared for him.[1]

> GLOSS: The same rule applies at the outset; when one has effected acquisition [of real property], one can have two or three copies of the instrument of sale made in this fashion.[2]

And they write:[3] "This document is not to be used to enforce any collection, either from encumbered or unencumbered property, and it is written for the sole purpose of establishing that this field may not be (lawfully) taken away from the buyer by the seller or the seller's heirs."

There is an authority who holds that (this rule can) only (mean that the duplicate shall have validity) from the date of the first document, not the date of the second, duplicate, one, because one apprehends that after (the original sale) the buyer sold the land back to the seller;[4] yet after (that transaction) the original buyer produces this second (document)[5] which postdates the (lawful) resale, whereupon the original buyer declares, "I repurchased it from you" (thus cheating the original seller with a postdated document and a bogus claim).

2) Even though postdated bonds of indebtedness are valid,[6] postdated instruments of sale are invalid documents unless such a postdated document specifically states that it is indeed postdated.[7]

240: The rule for the situation in which there are two instruments of sale, each bearing the same date, which relate to the same real property. Four paragraphs.

1) There are two instruments relating to the same field; both instruments give the name of the same acquirer, but each bears a different date.[1] If the earlier document was an instrument of gift and the later one an instrument of sale, the latter does not nullify the former, because one can say that the (previous owner) indited the latter instrument as a sale to add a warranty (against eviction) even though such warranty is not specifically included, (it is presumed to exist in a sale; its omission) being a (mere) notarial er-

ror.[2]

Similarly, if the first document is an instrument of a sale and the second is an instrument of gift, the field has been lawfully acquired as of the date of the former document, since the instrument of gift was indited for the sole purpose of strengthening the position of the acquirer in the matter of the adjoining neighbor's right of preemption[3] (which does not apply to a gift of land).

> GLOSS: Or (it is to strengthen the acquirer's position) in other matters in which acquisition by gift is more advantageous to him than acquisition through sale;[4] and it is necessary (then) for the acquirer to present only the latter document (i.e., the instrument of gift) in court, since if he should present both records, the first one is deemed to be the essence (of the acquisition, i.e., a sale).
> There is an authority who holds[5] that if the latter document was an instrument of sale, even though both documents are presented to the court, both documents are valid (the second document being a matter of strengthening the position of the acquirer by warranty of title).

2) There are two instruments of sale or two instruments of gift (referring to the same property). If the one bearing the later date (in either the case of the sale or the case of the gift) adds any provision to the first one, the first document is valid, since the second was written only for the purpose of including that additional provision[6] (not as the instrument of the gift or sale *per se*).

If the document bearing the later date adds nothing (to the first document), the second one invalidates the first one, and warranty (against eviction) runs only from the later date.[7] Therefore, the buyer (or donee) is to return all produce (or the value thereof) of that land, which he enjoyed between the date of the first document and the date of the second document.[8] If this field (sold or donated) was to provide a fixed amount (of produce) for the king each year, the donor or seller is to provide that share (*pro rata*) up to the date of the second document.

> GLOSS: If the first document specified an entire field and the second document specified half a field (for the sale or gift), how much the more would the second document invalidate the first one.[9]
> If a person close to death says, "Give a *maneh* to such-and-such a person," and then repeats the order, that person is to receive only *one maneh* because the donor did not say, "Give again a *maneh* . . . "[10]

3) There are two instruments, either both of sale or both of gift, both bearing the same date and both relating to the same field.[11] If it is (not[12]) the practice of the people of that place to include the hour of the day in the date (so that the sequence of the documents could be determined by that means), the matter is given over to the rabbinical court:[13] whomever the judges in their wisdom and discretion shall incline toward (as the lawful owner) of this field, that person shall they establish as the owner thereof.

> GLOSS: There is an authority who holds that discretionary judgment shall be invoked only when there is an expert (judge present) and only in regard to (disputes involving) real property.[14]
> There is an authority who holds that discretionary judgment shall also apply in suits (involving) moveable property, whenever no one party is in fact in possession of that moveable property.[15]

4) The above rule applies to an instrument which has in it no formula of acquisition other than "Acquire this field by means of this instrument," and it is not known which of two (recipients of such instruments) received his instrument first.[16] If, however, each instrument has a (proper) formula of acquisition, whoever first received[17] such (instrument of) acquisition gains lawful title (to the field), and the witnesses (to the documents) will be questioned (on the matter of the sequence of the documents).

Similarly, if there were witnesses there (who can verify) that this (particular) person's deed of gift reached him first, that first (recipient) has effected lawful acquisition[18] (of the property).

GLOSS: If one has given a gift to another and gave details of that gift, e.g., he gave land or a seat in the synagogue and specified the boundaries or limits thereof, and afterward the donor gave someone else a seat in the synagogue, or land, without further specification: one authority[19] holds that the first gift is valid, since perhaps the donor gave some other seat or some other land to the second donee; and another authority holds that certainly the donor only intended (to give) the seat or the land known to be his: since it is not known that the donor (in fact) has another seat or other land, the second donee has effected lawful acquisition (of the property). This rule applies specifically to a gift *mortis causa*, which the donor can retract (from one donee and give to another), but in regard to a gift *inter vivos*, the first donee has in any event effected lawful acquisition.[20]

Notes

Notes to Introduction

1. *RLS*, p. 1.
2. B. *Bava Mezia* 47a.
3. *RLS*, pp. 2f.
4. Gaius 3, 135-7; Inst. 3, 22.
5. Ibid.
6. *RLS*, p. 5.
7. Ibid.
8. Gaius 3, 135-7; Inst. 3, 22.
9. *RLS*, pp. 5, 9; Inst. 3, 15.
10. Pomp. 19, 1, 6, 8; U. 4, 3, 9 pr.; Jul. 30, 84, 5.
11. *RLS*, p. 9; cf. Inst. 4, 6, 30.
12. Ibid.; cf. Flor. 18, 1, 43, 1; U. 4, 3, 37; 21, 1, 19 pr.
13. Ibid. P. Sent. 2, 17, 2; U. 21, 1, 31, 20; 19, 1, 11, 1.
14. Ibid.
15. *RLS*, p. 10; cf. Gaius 3, 139; Inst. 3, 23 pr.; U. 18, 1, 2, 1; P. 18, 1, 34, 1. Inst. 3, 19.
16. Inst. 3, 19, 2; Pomp. 18, 4, 1.
17. Ibid.
18. *RLS*, pp. 14 f.; Pomp. 18, 1, 8, 1; U. 19, 1, 11, 18; cf. Jul. 18, 1, 39, 1.
19. U. 18, 1, 2, 1.
20. U. 18, 1, 7, 1; 19, 1, 13, 24; Inst. 3, 23, 1, 2.
21. Ibid.
22. U. 18, 1, 2, 1.
23. Ibid.
24. Ibid.; cf. P. 19, 2, 20, 1; U. 46.
25. *RLS*, pp. 19 f.; C. 4, 44, 2, 8; cf. C.T. 3, 1, 1 (319); 4 (383); 7 (396).
26. *RLS*, p. 20; Gaius 3, 139; Inst. 3, 23, pr.
27. *RLS*, pp. 21, 23.
28. *RLS*, p. 22; C. 4, 21, 17 (528); cf. Inst. 3, 23 pr.
29. Ibid.
30. *RLS*, pp. 22 f.; Gaius 3, 139.
31. *RLS*, p. 23; Gaius, 3, 139.
32. *RLS*, p. 31; C. 2, 3, 20 (293); Inst. 3, 23, 3., 3a; P. 18, 6, 3. Cf. *RLS*, p. 2.
33. Ibid.
34.- Ibid.
35. Ibid.
36. *RLS*, pp. 34 f.
37. D. 19, 1, 11 pr. - 13, 18.
38. U. 19, 1, 11, 13; Pomp. 3 pr.
39. Ibid.

40. Ibid.
41. Pomp. 19, 1, 9.
42. *MPM*, pp. 264 f.
43. Ibid.
44. Ibid.
45. *MPM*, p. 265; cf. J. A. C. Thomas, *The Institutes of Justinian*, p. 233, on the aedilician edict. This edict is clearly the Roman root and basis for these medieval provisions.
46. Ibid.
47. Ibid.
48. Ibid., p. 267.
49. Ibid., p. 268.
50. Ibid., pp. 268 f.
51. Ibid., p. 262.
52. Ibid.
53. Ibid., pp. 262 f.
54. Ibid., p. 263.
55. Ibid., p. 263.
56. Gaius 3, 141; Inst. 3, 23, 2.
57. Ibid.
58. Ibid.
59. *RLS*, p. 18; D 19, 4, 1, 2.
60. Inst. 3, 23, 3, 3a; P. 18, 6, 3.
61. Cf. n. 20 above.
62. Cf. *RLS*, p. 10.
63. Ibid.; cf. Inst. 3, 19, 12.
64. Cf. n. 18 above.
65. Cf. *RLS*, p. 50, and Buckland, *Main Institutions of Roman Private Law*, 1st ed., p. 272; cf. also Thomas, *The Institutes of Justinian*, p. 233.
66. *MPM*, p. 265.
67. Ibid.
68. *RLS*, p. 19; cf. n. 25 above.
69. *RLS*, pp. 19 f.; cf. n. 25 above.
70. *MPM*, pp. 267 f.
71. Cf. Herzog, *Main Institutions of Jewish Law*, vol. I, p. 117.
72. *MPM*, p. 269.
73. Ibid., p. 264; D. 4, 3, 1, 2.
74. Ibid.; cf. n. 10 above.
75. *MPM*, pp. 264 f.
76. Ibid.
77. U. 19, 1, 1, 1; 11, 5; 13, 6.
78. P. 18, 1, 34 pr.
79. U 18, 1, 9, 2; P. 19; Marcian 45: U. 19, 1, 11, 5.
80. Ibid.
81. *RLS*, p. 47; Flor. 18, 1, 43, 1; U. 19, 1, 13 pr. 2; cf. Thomas, op. cit., p. 233.
82. *RLS*, pp. 47 f.; cf. *RLS*, p. 9.

83. *RLS*, p. 49.
84. P. Sent 2, 17, 2; 21, 2, C. 8, 44 6 (222); cf. also U. 19, 1, 11, 8. 21, 1, 31, 20.
85. U. 19, 1, 11, 15-18; Pap 21, 2, 68 pr.
86. *RLS*, p. 28.
87. Ibid., pp. 29 f.; P. 18, 6, 8 pr.; U. 18, 2, 4 pr.; P. 41, 4, 2, 2, 3., cf. also de Zulueta's n. 11.
88. *RLS*, p. 30; U. 18, 2, 2 pr.; U. 18, 2, 6 pr.; 16.
89. Ibid.
90. *RLS*, p. 36; U. 18, 1, 25, 1. 19, 1, 11, 2., cf. also de Zulueta's n. 5.
91. Ibid.
92. *RLS*, p. 59., Inst. 3, 23, 4; U. Mela 19, 5, 20, 1; U. 18, 1, 3; U. 21, 1, 31, 22.
93. Ibid. U. 21, 1, 31, 11-12.; C, 4, 58, 4.
94. *RLS*, p. 22; cf. n. 28 above.
95. Cf. *B. Gittin* 10b; there is an extensive literature on this basic maxim of Jewish law; e.g., L. Landman, *Jewish Law in the Diaspora; Confrontation and Accommodation* (Philadelphia: Dropsie College, 1968).

No. 189 Notes

1. *Tur, HM* 189; cf. *B. Bava Mezia* 49a.
2. In this case, both contracting parties must acknowledge that there was a transaction; cf. *Baer Hagolah*, n. 2, and *B. Qiddushin* 65b.
3. Israel Isserlein, *Terumath Hadeshen*, no. 311, and Responsa of Isaac B. Sheshet, no. 510.

No. 190 Notes

1. *B. Qiddushin* 26a, cf. also *B. Qiddushin* 3a.
2. Cf. *Tur, HM* 190:1.
3. *B. Qiddushin* 6b and *SMA*, n. 2 ad loc.; a stipulation to return the gift to its original owner does not negate its full legality or the donee's rights in it during the term of the gift.
4. *B. Qiddushin* 7a; Maimonides, *Mekhirah* 1:6.
5. This is cited from the *Tur, HM* 190:5; cf. also *B. Qiddushin* 7a.
6. Ibid.
7. *B. Qiddushin* 7a; Maimonides, loc. cit.
8. Cf. *B. Qiddushin* 67a.
9. Cf. *B. Qiddushin* 8a.
10. This opinion is found in *Hilkhoth Mordecai*, end of tractate *Ketubot*; cf. also *Tur, HM* 190:7.
11. *B. Qiddushin* 26a.
12. Ibid.
13. Thus *MM* to Maimonides, *Mekhirah* 1:5.
14. *B. Qiddushin* 8b.
15. *B. Qiddushin* 8a.

16. Cf. Tosafot, *Qiddushin* 8b, s.v. *maneh*, and *Mordecai*, 483, to ch. 1 of *Qiddushin*. See also infra, ch. 204:5 and ch. 207:17.
17. Maimonides, *Mekhirah* 8:1, and *MM* thereto. See also *B. Bava Mezia* 77a f.
18. Cf. *B. Bava Mezia* 77b.
19. Maimonides, *Mekhirah* 8:2, and *B. Bava Mezia* 77a f.
20. The phrase beginning "at the current" appears in the text in the Rashi script and in parentheses. There are numerous parenthetical clauses and provisions that appear in this fashion. They are first found in the Cracow 1580 edition of *Shulhan Arukh*, which has Isserles' annotations. The parenthetical material is not formally marked as a gloss, but clearly the information it provides is a most valuable and necessary amplification of Karo's text.
    See Rabbenu Nissim to ch. 1 of *Qiddushin*, *MM* to *Mekhirah* 8:2 citing Nahmanides, and *BY* to *Tur*, *Hoshen Mishpat* 190, citing Rabbenu Asher.
21. Cf. *B. Bava Mezia* 78a ff. On the portion of this provision set off in parentheses, see note 20 above in this chapter.
22. Ibid.
23. Cf. *Tur*, *HM* 190:12, and *BY* ad loc., n. 12.
    The *SMA*, n. 13, explains: once the balance has been charged as simple loan to the buyer, to be repaid as an ordinary loan, the sale is completed even if the buyer does not repay the loan at the agreed-upon time; it is as if the buyer made a simple loan to be repaid, and it is not repaid. The remainder of the purchase price is no longer the essence of the matter outstanding between buyer and seller.
24. See *Ba'er Hetev*, n. 16.
25. See *SMA*, n. 15.
26. See *SMA*, n. 16; see infra ch. 218, end.
27. *B. Bava Mezia* 77a-b. Cf. also *SMA*, n. 17.
28. Ibid.
29. Tosafot, s.v. *d'ayel*, and *B. Bava Mezia* 77b.
30. Cf. *Tur*, *HM* 190:14, citing Meir Abulafia.
31. This rule and the one following (no. 14) are based on variant readings of the same text, *B. Bava Mezia* 78a (see *SMA*, n. 18). Karo first gives the rule on the basis of Maimonides' reading, which presents the seller's position as a matter of unresolved doubt: i.e., if the seller sold the field for two hundred *zuz* when it was worth one hundred *zuz*, received part-payment, and repeatedly called on the buyer for the balance, one could say that the seller may well be unwilling to see the buyer come to his senses over the inflated price since he may well have second thoughts about buying such a valuable property in the first place. Thus there may be doubt as to the resolve of the parties to see acquisition effected, and the seller, because of his eagerness to get the money, might be analogous to the person who sold a field because of its poor quality and wants his money before the buyer has second thoughts about the transaction. The *MM* to *Mekhirah* 8:5 points out that Maimonides had a variant talmudic text which permitted him to assert a matter of unresolved doubt. The *Maggid Mishneh* and the *SMA* both call attention to Rashi's different reading of the same *Bava Mezia* material. Both *MM* and *SMA* tell us that Rashi's text is the version found in the standard editions of the Talmud.

In rule 13, based on Maimonides, the acquisition is effective, as in cases of sale of land owing to its poor quality, but the element of unresolved doubt relieves the seller of liability to a lawsuit if the seller takes back the portion of the property not yet paid for. Yet neither party may withdraw from the transaction.

In rule 14, based on Rashi's (and our) text, the material allows the ruling that acquisition has not been effected and either party may withdraw from the transaction when the seller has not been able to find a buyer for the one hundred *zuz* field and has therefore sold a two hundred *zuz* field, receiving part of the purchase price for it. Presumably the seller did not really wish to part with so valuable a property and is eager to get the buyer's money in order to purchase other land (see SMA, n. 21). This element of reluctance on the part of the seller is apparently sufficient to keep the acquisition from taking effect.

If, however, the seller did not put forth sufficient effort to find a buyer for the cheaper property, and therefore sold the more expensive property (and received partial payment), there may be grounds to suspect that the seller, for reasons of his own, did not care for the more expensive property and sold it. Thus there is doubt: did the seller really want to sell or not? This element of doubt in regard to the seller permits the ruling that neither party may withdraw from the transaction: the buyer because he is getting value, and the seller because he may really want to be rid of that land. Yet, because there is only a reasonable doubt as to the seller's motive, if the seller should take back the part of the land not yet paid for, he is not liable to a lawsuit. See SMA, n. 22.

In rule 13 and the latter part of 14, it is therefore possible to see the seller as a party analogous to one who sells land because of its poor grade or quality.

32. See note 31.
33. *SMA*, n. 21. In these circumstances, the seller is thought to have acted against his own desires in this matter; he did not care to sell so much land and repeatedly seeks the full price in order to buy more land. Since he was, as it were, without any option but to sell the more costly property, presumably he did not enter the transaction unreservedly.
34. *SMA*, n. 21. The doubt is whether or not this seller is the same as a seller who was trying to get rid of poor land. One could assume that the seller, for reasons of his own, did not want the land any longer; he certainly took the path of least resistance.
35. *Tur, HM* 190:15, citing Rabbenu Asher; cf. also *MM* to *Mekhirah* 8:1.
36. *Tur, HM* 190:17, citing Meir Abulafia.
37. *SMA*, n. 25, suggests the understanding of the text conveyed in this translation. The commentator asserts that "the day they set" cannot refer to the day of the sale since such an interpretation would mean that "the day close to it" is the day *after* it (since the day *before* the sale is a patently impossible time for the demand for payment); but the day after is already too late for the seller to establish ground for withdrawal from the transaction, as the text goes on to say. Thus the *SMA* understands the day they set as the day specified

for the actual payment of the purchase price; i.e., the sale is made on Monday with a condition that money change hands a day or so later. Therefore the seller visits the buyer on the day set for payment *or* on the day close to it -- the day prior to it -- to urge the buyer to have the cash ready. *SMA* refers to the wording of his version of the *Tur* in support of his interpretation, *Tur*, *HM* 190:17. His text of the *Tur* apparently read: ". . . on the day they set for the transaction or the day close to it for payment." *SMA*, also the author of the *Perishah* commentary to *Tur*, ad loc. (n. 17), explains that the phrase "for payment" refers also to "the day set for the transaction" -- as if one said, "the day set for payment of the transaction." *SMA*'s comment depends upon the presence of the word "close" in the text, and clearly his copy of the *Tur* had the word and so did Karo's. (Karo's complete familiarity and profound grasp of the *Tur* goes without saying: his *BY* commentary to *Tur* is proof of his mastery of it.) The word "close," however, is in parentheses in the Vilna 1900 edition of *Tur*; the preferred word is "one fixed," *qabha'* rather than *qarov*. Conceivably these words could have been confused in a manuscript. The Vilna edition of the *Tur* then reads," the day they set for the sale or the day one fixed for the payment." If "close" is dropped and "one fixed" used instead, the meaning is perfectly clear: the visit has to be made on the day of the sale, presumably because the money changed hands at that time, under ordinary circumstances, or on the day set for that actual payment. In any case, the seller had to visit on the day of payment. The presence of the word "close," however, requires *SMA* to understand "for payment" as modifying "the day set."

Alternately, one could simply say that the day set for the transaction does indeed mean the day of the sale when the money would ordinarily change hands, or on the day just prior (i.e., "close") to it, when the parties might be expected to urge each other to have everything ready for the forthcoming transaction. After all, we are dealing with sales of real property, and one is entitled to assume that such matters were not taken lightly or arranged on the spur of the moment. The important element in the rule appears to be that the seller's visits indicate his desire to have all his money as soon as possible; on any interpretation, he cannot withdraw from the transaction if he has allowed the sun to set on the day of the transaction, whether or not it is also the day of the sale, without calling on the buyer for the cash.

38. Rabbenu Nissim to ch. 1 of *Qiddushin* and *Nimmuke Joseph* to ch. 6 of *Bava Mezia*.
39. *MM* to *Mekhirah* 1:5.
40. *Tur*, *HM* 190:19; *Mekhirah* 8:4 and *MM* thereto.
41. Rabbenu Nissim and Nimmuke Joseph to ch. 6 of *Bava Mezia*.
42. B. *Qiddushin* 47a; cf. Maimonides, *Mekhirah* 8:6 and *MM* thereto.
43. *SMA*, n. 30, explains that the victim is afraid his land will be seized as a consequence of the calumny against him.
44. Cf. *BY* to *Tur*, *HM* 190, end, citing Simon b. Zemah Duran.

No. 191 Notes

1. B. *Qiddushin* 26a.

2. Ibid.
3. Cf. *BY* to *Tur*, *HM* 191:3. The opinion is cited in the name of various authorities: e.g., Solomon b. Adret, Nahmanides. These authorities differ from Rabbenu Asher, who holds that the instruments are merely evidentiary.
4. Rabbenu Nissim to ch. 1 of *Qiddushin* and *MM* to *Mekhirah* 1:7.
5. *BY* to *Tur*, *HM* 191:3, in the name of Solomon b. Adret. Cf. *B. Ketuboth* 110a.
6. The phrase "has said to him . . . acquisition shall be effective" (as rendered here) does not appear in the text of the gloss until the publication of the Cracow edition of 1618-19. Cf. next note.
7. Cf. *BY* to *Tur*, *HM* 191, end, citing Tosafot to *Yebamot* 93a, s.v. *Qenuyah*. Cf. also *Nimmuqe Joseph* to *Bava Mezia*, ch. 1.

No. 192 Notes

1. Mishnah *B. Bava Bathra* 42a, cf. *Mekhirah* 1:8. Cf. also *B. Qiddushin* 26a.
2. Ibid.
3. *B. Gittin* 77b.
4. Maimonides, *Mekhirah* 1:10 and *MM* thereto; cf. *Tur*, *HM* 192:3 and *BY* thereto, citing *inter alios*, Tosafot *Bava Bathra* 52b, s.v. *na'al*. See also *SMA*, n. 5, the fact that the new owner can unlock the door as well as lock it clearly demonstrates possession of the house.
5. Cf. *Tur*, *HM* 192:2 and *BY* thereto. *B. Bava Bathra* 42a, 43a, 53a.
6. Cf. *Tur*, *HM* 190:1 and *BY* thereto; cf. also Maimonides, *Mekhirah* 1:11 and *Bava Bathra* 42a, 43a, 53a.
7. *B. Bava Bathra* 42a ff.; Maimonides, *Mekhirah* 1:11.
8. *B. Bava Bathra* 43a; Maimonides, *Mekhirah* 1:12.
9. The three earliest Venice editions of *Shulhan Arukh* (1565-67) have the word *hkhr* instead of *hbhr* rendered "conserved." The word *hbhr* is first found in the *Shulhan Arukh* in the Amsterdam 1664 edition; Maimonides uses *hbhr*, *Mekhirah* 1:12; the Gemara, *Bava Bathra* 53a, has *tsmd*, "to dam up, to retain." The early Venice editions clearly have a misprint, since *hkhr*, meaning "to farm on shares," is meaningless here. The word could be a misprint for *hbhr* or *skhr*, another word found in *Bava Bathra* 53a, with a meaning virtually the same as *tsmd*. The early Cracow editions (and even early Venice editions, from 1574 onward) have *skhr* or *skhur*.
10. Cf. *Tur*, *HM* 192:7; cf. also *B. Bava Bathra* 53a. The remark is a paraphrase of the *Tur*. The earlier editions all use the phrase *yizovu hamaim* for "water running off the land"; the change to the reading of *sheyetzu hamaim* first appears only with the Amsterdam 1664-66 edition. The modern reading is merely a modification of the *Tur*'s text.
11. Maimonides, *Mekhirah* 1:13. Cf. *MM* thereto and Alfasi to *Bava Qamma*, 9a.
12. *B. Bava Bathra* 100a; see also 101a.
13. Ibid.
14. Cf. *Tur*, *HM* 192:8.
15. *B. Bava Bathra* 29b; Maimonides, *Mekhirah* 1:15, Rabad and *MM* thereto. Cf. also *Ba'er Hagolah* ad loc., n. 1.
16. *B. Bava Bathra* 53b; cf. *BY* to *Tur*, *HM* 192:10.

17. Cf. *BY* to *Tur*, *HM* 192:10, end, citing Rabbenu Asher.
18. *BY*, loc. cit.
19. Maimonides, *Mekhirah* 1:16 and *MM* thereto.
20. Ibid.
21. Cf. *SMA*, nn. 17 and 18. Cf. Rabad to Maimonides, *Mekhirah* 1:15. Cf. also Rabbenu Nissim to *Qiddushin*, ch. 1.
22. Cf. *Mordecai* to *Bava Bathra*, as cited by Isserles in *DM* to *Tur*, *HM* 192, n. 2.
23. *B. Qiddushin* 26b f.; Maimonides, *Mekhirah* 1:19 and *MM* thereto.
24. Cf. *B. Bava Bathra* 67a.
25. *B. Qiddushin* 26b f.
26. The conclusion of Maimonides, *Mekhirah* 1:20.
27. *Tur*, *HM* 192:17, Rabbenu Asher is cited.
28. *Nimmuqe Joseph* to *Bava Bathra*, ch. 4.
29. Cf. n. 26 of this chapter.
30. *BY* to *Tur*, *HM* 192:14.
31. *BY* to *Tur*, *HM* 192:15.
32. *Tur*, *HM* 192:14.
33. Cf. Maimonides, *Mekhirah* 1:20 and *MM* thereto. Cf. also *BY* to *Tur*, *HM* 192:14.

No. 193 Notes

1. *B. Shebuoth* 43a; cf. Maimonides, *Mekhirah* 1:17.
2. Cf. *MM* to Maimonides, loc. cit.; cf. also *B. Bava Bathra* 84b, 87a.
3. The concept of constructive fraud in pricing is the subject of Chapters 227-240, below.
4. *Tur*, *HM* 193.

No. 194 Notes

1. Cf. Maimonides, *Zekhiah U'mattanah* 1:14 and *MM* thereto. Cf. also *B. Bava Bathra* 54b and *Tur* 194.
2. The parenthetical phrase "or by money payment" first appears in the Cracow edition of 1580; cf. Maimonides, *Zekhiah U'mattanah* 1:14.
3. Cf. *BY* to *Tur*, *HM* 192, end, and 194:1.
4. *B. Bava Bathra* 54b.
5. Cf. *Baer Hagolah* ad loc., n. 3, citing Rabbenu Samson and Rabbenu Hananel.
6. *Tur*, *HM* 194:1, citing Solomon b. Adret, and *MM* to Maimonides, *Zekhiah* 1:14. Cf. also *Mordecai* to *Bava Bathra*, ch. 6, cvited by Isserles in *DM* to *Tur*, *HM* 194, n. 2.
7. The phrase "on all Jewish legal views" first appears in the early Cracow editions of *Shulhan Arukh*; cf. *Mordecai* to *Bava Bathra*, ch. 3.
8. Maimonides, loc. cit. and *MM* thereto. Cf. also Hai Gaon's *Sefer Meqah Umemkar*, ch. 14.
9. *SMA*, n. 11, explains that this holds goods despite the fact that B may already have paid the price to A.
10. *BY* to *Tur*, *HM* 194:6.
11. *Tur*, *HM* 194:6, in the name of Rabbenu Asher; cf. also *BY* ad loc.

Notes

12. B. *Bava Bathra* 54b.
13. Responsa of Solomon b. Adret, no. 1032, and *BY* to *Tur, HM* 194:1, citing Rabbenu Yeruham.
14. *Tur, HM* 194:4 and *BY* ad loc., which cites *inter alios* Rabbenu Asher and Maimonides as sources.
15. *Tur, HM* 194, end; cf. also *Tur, YD* 320.

No. 195 Notes

1. Maimonides, *Mekhirah* 5:5; cf. B. *Bava Mezia* 47a.
2. *Tur, HM* 195:2.
3. *Tur, HM* 195:1.
4. *Tur, HM* 195:2. Cf. Maimonides, *Mekhirah* 5:9.
5. Responsa of Rabbenu Asher, sec. 66, no. 8.
6. B. *Bava Mezia* 47a.
7. *Tur, HM* 195:9.
8. B. *Bava Mezia* 45b.
9. See infra ch. 203.
10. B. *Bava Mezia* 45b.
11. Maimonides, *Mekhirah*, 5:7; cf. B. *Qiddushin* 6b and *Baer Hagolah* ad loc., no. 10.
12. Cf. *Tur, HM* 195:6; cf. Tosafot to *Qiddushin* 26b, s.v. *hakhi*.
13. Maimonides, *Mekhirah* 5:7.
14. *Tur, HM* 195:6.
15. Responsa of Jacob Weil, no. 14.
16. B. *Bava Mezia* 7a; Maimonides, *Mekhirah* 5:7 and *MM* thereto.
17. Ibid.
18. *MM*, loc. cit.; Rabbenu Nissim to *Nedarim*, ch. 4, end; *By* to *Tur, HM* 195:5, citing Ittur; *Nimmuke Joseph* to *Bava Mezia*, ch. 1.
19. Cf. *Hagahot Asheri* to *Bava Mezia*, ch. 4; cf. also sources given in n. 18.
20. Responsa of Solomon b. Adret, no. 1018, and Responsa of Nahmanides, no. 101; cf. also *Mordecai* to *Bava Bathra*, ch. 5, end, and *Bava Mezia*, ch. 4, no. 299.
21. B. *Nedarim* 48b and Rabbenu Nissim thereto.
22. Ibid.
23. Pesaqim of Israel Isserlein, *Terumath Hadeshen*, no. 176, cf. no. 173.
24. B. *Bava Bathra* 114a f.
25. Maimonides, *Mekhirah* 5:10 and *MM* thereto. Cf. B. *Bava Bathra* 86b. Cf. also *BY* to *Tur, HM* 195:12, citing Rabbenu Asher.
26. Cf. *Tur, HM* 195:12.
27. B. *Bava Qamma* 79a; Maimonides, *Mekhirah* 1:18.
28. Cf. supra ch. 190 and *BY* to *Tur, HM* 195:13.
29. *Tur, HM* 195:13 and *BY* thereto, citing Tosafot to *Qiddushin* 27a, s.v. *mikomo*.
30. *SMA*, n. 21: the creditor enjoys the right to the produce of the land in exchange for a periodic deduction from the amount of the debt, a transaction which is also treated as a sale for a term; see *Tur, YD* 172. Cf. *BY* to *Tur, HM* 195:13, end, citing *Sefer Haterumoth*, sec. 64.
31. Cf. infra ch. 204:10.

32. *BY* to *Tur*, *HM* 195:14, no. 15, citing Rabbenu Yeruham.

No. 196 Notes

1. B. *Qiddushin* 22b; Maimonides, *Mekhirah* 2:1. Cf. *Tur*, *HM* 196:1.
2. Maimonides, *Mekhirah* 2:2, 3 and *MM* thereto.
3. Maimonides, *Mekhirah* 2:2.
4. Maimonides, *Mekhirah* 2:3.
5. Ibid. and *MM* thereto.
6. Maimonides, *Mekhirah* 2:2.
7. Ibid. and *MM* thereto.
8. Ibid.
9. Ibid.; cf. also *Tur*, *HM* 196:5.
10. B. *Qiddushin* 22b and Rashi thereto.
11. Ibid.

No. 197 Notes

1. B. *Qiddushin* 25b; *MM* to Maimonides, *Mekhirah* 2:5.
2. *Hagahot Maimuniot* to *Mekhirah*, ch. 2, n. 2, citing Eliezer b. Joel Halevi.
3. *SMA*, n. 2; cf. *BY* to *Tur*, *HM* 197:7, citing Tosafot, s.v. *'ahaza*, and Rabbenu Tam to *Qiddushin* 25b, s.v. *behemah*.
4. *Tur*, *HM* 197:10.
5. B. *Qiddushin* 22a; Maimonides, *Mekhirah* 2:5 and *MM* thereto. Cf. also B. *Bava Bathra* 84b.
6. B. *Bava Bathra* 84b, cf. also 76a.
7. Maimonides, *Mekhirah* 2:6.
8. B. *Qiddushin* 22b; cf. *Tur*, *HM* 197:1, 2.
9. The parenthetical clause first appears in the Cracow 1580 edition, cf. *Tur*, *HM* 197:2.
10. Maimonides, *Mekhirah* 2:6 and *MM* thereto.
11. Ibid.; cf. B. *Bava Qamma* 52a f.
12. Maimonides, *Mekhirah* 2:7 and *MM* thereto.
13. The parenthetical phrase first appears in the Cracow 1619 edition.
14. *Teshubot Maimuniot* to *Sefer Qinyan*, no. 18. The *Hagahot Maimuniot* to *Mekhirah*, ch. 5, are also cited as a source, but the matter is not discussed there. The *SMA*, no. 10, provides a citation of the *Hagahot Maimuniot* material. Cf. *BY*, *Tur*, *HM* 197:11.
15. *BY* to *Tur*, loc. cit.
16. B. *Bava Mezia* 9a; Maimonides, *Mekhirah* 2:10 and *MM* thereto.
17. The parenthetical phrase first appears in the Cracow 1580 edition, cf. *Tur*, *HM* 197:12.
18. The parenthetical phrase first appears in the Cracow 1580 edition, cf. *Tur*, *HM* 197:12.
19. B. *Bava Mezia* 9b.
20. Ibid. and Rashi thereto.
21. Maimonides, *Mekhirah* 2:8 and *MM* thereto.

22. *Tur, HM* 197:13, citing Maimonides.
23. Maimonides, *Mekhirah* 2:9; *B. Ketubot* 82a.
24. Ibid.
25. Maimonides, *Mekhirah* 2:9 and *MM* thereto.
26. Ibid; cf. *B. Qiddushin* 60a.

No. 198 Notes

1. *B. Bava Mezia* 47b.
2. *B. Bava Bathra* 86a.
3. Maimonides, *Mekhirah* 3:2 and *MM* thereto; cf. also *B. Bava Bathra* 86b.
4. *Tur, HM* 198:6.
5. Tosafot to *Bava Mezia* 9b; cf. *Sifte Cohen*, n. 3, and *SMA*, n. 4. Cf. also Hagahot Mordecai ad loc. and *Hagahot Maimuniot, Mekhirah*, ch. 2, n. 1, citing Rashi. *Tur, HM* 198:2-4 and *BY* ad loc.
6. *B. Bava Bathra* 75b; cf. *Tur, HM* 198:8, and Maimonides, *Mekhirah* 3:3 and *MM* thereto.
7. *Tur, HM* 198:8; *B. Bava Mezia* 9a.
8. *B. Bava Mezia* 47b; Maimonides, *Mekhirah* 3:5.
9. *B. Bava Mezia* 49b; Maimonides, *Mekhirah* 3:6 and *MM* thereto.
10. Maimonides, *Mekhirah* 3:7; *B. Bava Mezia* 11b.
11. Cf. *BY* to *Tur, HM* 198:16.
12. *Mordecai* to *Bava Mezia*, ch. 4; cf. *BY* to *Tur, HM* 198:1.
13. Rabbenu Nissim to *Bava Mezia*, ch. 4, cites the opinion.
14. Maimonides, *Mekhirah* 3:3; *B. Bava Bathra* 76b.
15. Ibid.
16. *B. Bava Bathra* 75b.
17. Maimonides, *Mekhirah* 3:3 and *MM* thereto, citing Solomon b. Adret.
18. Maimonides, *Mekhirah* 4:3; *B. Bava Bathra* 84b.
19. Rabbenu Nissim to *Qiddushin*, ch. 1.
20. Maimonides, *Mekhirah* 3:3 and *MM* thereto.
21. Ibid.
22. Ibid., citing Solomon b. Adret and Joseph ibn Migash.
23. *Tur, HM* 198:11, citing R. Jonah.
24. Maimonides, *Mekhirah* 4:4.
25. Ibid. and *MM* thereto.
26. Maimonides, *Mekhirah* 7:3 and *MM* thereto, who calls attention to the geonic opinions in this matter.
27. Ibid.
28. *Tur, HM* 198:18.
29. Ibid.

No. 199 Notes

1. *B. Bava Mezia* 46b f.; cf. *Tur, HM* 199, beginning.
2. *BY* to *Tur*, loc. cit.
3. Maimonides, *Mekhirah* 5:3, 4; cf. Alfasi to *Bava Mezia* 46b.

4. *MM* to *Mekhirah* 5:3, 4; Rabbenu Nissim to *Bava Mezia*, ch. 4; cf. *Tur*, *HM* 199:1.
5. *B. Hullin* 83a.
6. Ibid.
7. Cf. *DM* to *Tur*, *HM* 199:2, citing R. Jacob Moellin.
8. *B. Gittin* 52b.
9. *Mordecai* to *Gittin* ad loc., no. 3a, 4; cf. *BY* to *Tur*, *HM* 199:2, citing Tosafot to *Gittin* ad loc., s.v. *da'ato*.
10. *B. Gittin* 52b.
11. *Mordecai* to *Gittin* ad loc., no. 394, and Rabbenu Nissim to *Qiddushin*, ch. 1. Cf. also *SMA*, n. 11.

No. 200 Notes

1. *B. Bava Bathra* 85a; *B. Bava Mezia* 11a.
2. *BY* to *Tur*, *HM* 200:1.
3. *Mordecai* to *Bava Mezia*, ch. 1.
4. *B. Bava Bathra* 85a.
5. Maimonides, *Gezelah* 17:8 and *MM* thereto; *B. Bava Mezia* 11a.
6. *B. Bava Bathra* 85a.
7. *B. Bava Bathra* 86a.
8. Cf. *BY* to *Tur*, *HM* 200:16:[2].
9. *B. Bava Bathra* 85a.
10. Ibid.
11. See *SMA*, n. 4.
12. *Tur*, *HM* 200:4 and 5.
13. *BY* to *Tur*, *HM* 100:2, 3, 4, citing Maimonides and *MM* to Maimonides, *Mekhirah*, 4:6; cf. *SMA*, n. 6.
14. *B. Bava Bathra* 84b; Maimonides, *Mekhirah* 4:1.
15. *Tur*, *HM* 200:6; cf. *BY* thereto, citing Rabbenu Asher, and Tosafot *Bava Bathra* 84b, s.v. *madad*; cf. also *Hagahot Maimuniot*, *Mekhirah*, ch. 4, n. 1.
16. *MM* to Maimonides, *Mekhirah* 4:1.
17. Ibid.
18. Ibid.
19. Maimonides, *Mekhirah* 4:2 and *MM* thereto. Cf. *B. Bava Bathra* 85b.
20. *Tur*, *HM* 200:8, citing R. Jonah, and *BY* thereto, citing Rabbenu Asher.
21. *BY* to *Tur*, *HM* 200:9, citing Tosafot to *B. Bava Bathra* 85b, s.v. *lo*, and Rabbenu Asher.
22. *Tur*, *HM* 200:10; cf. *B. Bava Bathra* 8b f. Cf. also Maimonides, *Mekhirah* 4:12, 13.
23. *B. Bava Bathra* 85b f.
24. Maimonides, *Mekhirah* 4:12 and *MM* thereto. Cf. also *BY* to *Tur*, *HM* 200:10, citing Rabbenu Asher *inter alios*.
25. *BY* to *Tur*, *HM*:10, citing Alfasi to *Bava Bathra*, ch. 7, end.
26. Cf. Maimonides, *Mekhirah* 4:7, and *B. Bava Bathra* 86b.
27. *B. Bava Bathra* 86b.
28. *Tur*, *HM* 200:11 and *BY* thereto.
29. *B. Bava Bathra* 86b and *MM* to Maimonides, *Mekhirah* 4:7.

There is a curiosity in the text. The phrase "*each seah*" appears in parentheses in the modern editions. The first edition, Venice 1565, has the phrase without parentheses, where it is no doubt based on the style of Maimonides, *Mekhirah* 4:7. The parentheses do appear in the early Cracow editions of 1580 and 1593, where the phrase *pasku damim al* comes at the end of page 81a. Page 81b begins *kol seah sheyagbiha*, thus omitting what presently appears in parentheses. No doubt the omission of the phrase was only a typographical error owing to the change in the page.

30. *SMA*, n. 22, explains that the vendor's statement may foster some legitimate doubt about his intentions. If the vendor says he is selling "a *kor* for thirty (*selas*), a *seah* for a *sela*;" is one to understand that the vendor is emphasizing the first part of the statement, and therefore the sale is not complete until the whole *kor* has been measured out, or indeed does the second part of the statement govern the transaction, and therefore as each *seah* is measured out, the sale for it is complete? Since one may be in doubt as to which part of the statement is crucial, the acquisition of each *seah* depends upon the actual physical possession of it as it is measured out. This opinion presumes, of course, that the transaction occurs in the locations specified above: the recessed alcove, etc. Cf. *Tur*, *HM* 200:11, citing Rabbenu Asher and Meir Abulafia.
31. Responsa of Rabbenu Asher 102:1.
32. Cf. *Tur*, *HM* 200:13.
33. Ibid. in the name of Rabad.
34. Responsa of Isaac b. Sheshet, no. 222.
35. B. *Bava Bathra* 85b and Tosafot thereto, s.v. *mashakh*; cf. *Tur*, *HM* 200:13.
36. Maimonides, *Mekhirah* 4:8 and *MM* thereto; cf. B. *Bava Bathra* 87a; and also 85b.
37. Maimonides, *Mekhirah* 4:9 and *MM* thereto; B. *Bava Bathra* 86b, 87a.
38. Maimonides, *Mekhirah* 4:10; B. *Bava Bathra* 86b.
39. *Tur*, *HM* 200:14.
40. B. *Bava Bathra* 88a; Maimonides, *Mekhirah* 4:14.
41. Ibid. and *MM* to the Maimonides citation. Cf. Rashi to *Bava Bathra*, loc. cit., and *Baer Hagolah* to *Shulhan Arukh*, 200:11 n. 20: the reference is to small items of a standard price.
42. B. *Nedarim* 31b and *MM* to Maimonides, *Mekhirah* 4:14.
43. *Tur*, *HM* 200:16, citing Meir Abulafia for the opinion that the buyer is an unpaid bailee; cf. B. *Nedarim* 31b, the opinion of Samuel.
44. B. *Bava Mezia* 8a ff.; Maimonides, *Mekhirah* 4:15.

No. 201 Notes

1. Maimonides, *Mekhirah* 7:6; cf. B. *Bava Mezia* 74a.
2. See below, ch. 204, for the rules concerning this condemnation.
3. Maimonides, *Mekhirah* 7:6 and *MM* thereto, citing Solomon b. Adret. B. *Bava Mezia* 74a. Cf. also *Baer Hagolah* n. 4.
4. *Tur*, *HM* 201:3, citing Rabbenu Asher.
5. Ibid. 201:2, citing Rabbenu Hananel.
6. *Hagahot Maimuniot*, *Mekhirah*, ch. 7, no. 5; *SMA*, n. 6, explains that this provi-

sion is not contrary to chapter 192, in which it is laid down that acquisition of land is not effected by delivery of the key to it. The storeroom where the goods are located is not acquired by delivery of the key, only the goods stored there, if that is the prevailing mercantile custom.

No. 202 Notes

1. B. *Qiddushin* 27a; Maimonides, *Mekhirah* 3:8. Cf. II Chronicles 21:3, which describes moveable property given along with land, i.e., cities.
2. B. *Qiddushin* 27a and *MM* to Maimonides, loc. cit.
3. Cf. *DM* to *Tur*, *HM* 202, n. 1, citing Rabbenu Yeruham.
4. Maimonides, *Mekhirah* 3:9.
5. *Tur*, *HM* 202:2, in the name of Rabad; cf. Rabad to Maimonides, *Mekhirah* 3:9.
6. Cf. Rabbenu Nissim to *Qiddushin*, ch. 1, commenting on Rashi to *Qiddushin* 26a. Cf. *BY* to *Tur*, *HM* 202:2.
7. Maimonides, *Mekhirah* 3:10 and *MM* thereto.
8. Rabbenu Nissim to *Qiddushin*, ch. 1. Cf. also *BY* to *Tur*, *HM* 202:4. Cf. *SMA*, nn. 7 and 8: an unresolved talmudic matter involving money is for practical purposes resolved in favor of the person in possession of the goods.
9. Rabbenu Nissim, loc. cit. Cf. *MM* to Maimonides, *Mekhirah* 3:10.
10. *SMA*, n. 13, the biblical verse II Chronicles 21:3 is held to exclude land from items, ownership of which passes "as a consequence of land." Cf. Tosafot to *Bava Qamma* 12a, s.v. *ba'inan*.
11. B. *Bava Qamma* 12a; *Tur*, *HM* 202:3. See M. *Peah* 3:6, the opinion of R. Akiba.
12. *BY* to *Tur*, *HM* 202:1.
13. Responsa of Solomon b. Adret, 934, 935.
14. Maimonides, *Mekhirah* 3:11; *Tur*, *HM* 202:7; B. *Bava Qamma* 12a.
15. B. *Bava Qamma*, loc. cit.
16. Maimonides, *Mekhirah* 3:12.
17. *Tur*, *HM* 202:8; cf. Tosafot to *Bava Qamma* 12a, s.v. *wehilkhata*. The slave is deemed a "moving courtyard" which cannot effect acquisition for its owners. The slave, as an animate human being, while the owner's property, may still move about and thus frustrate the requirement that the "courtyard" be under the owner's absolute and conscious supervision. See *SMA*, n. 19.
18. *Tur*, *HM* 202:5; Maimonides, *Mekhirah* 3:15; B. *Gittin* 22a. Cf. also *MM* to Maimonides ad loc.
19. Ibid.
20. Ibid.
21. *SMA*, n. 22, explains that the acquisition is as a consequence of acquiring the land.
22. Rashi to *Gittin* 7b.
23. Tosafot to *Gittin* 7b, s.v. *'atzitz*.
24. *Tur*, *HM* 202:9, 10; Maimonides, *Mekhirah* 3:13; B. *Bava Mezia* 9b.
25. B. *Bava Mezia*, loc. cit.
26. *Tur*, *HM* 202:10.
27. Maimonides, *Mekhirah* 3:14; *Tur*, *HM* 202:9.
28. *Tur*, *HM* 202:10, and Tosafot to *Bava Mezia* 9b, s.v. *meshokh*.

Notes

1. *B. Bava Mezia* 44a; Maimonides, *Mekhirah* 5:1; *Tur, HM* 202:1.
2. Cf. *Shulhan Arukh*, ch. 195.
3. *B. Bava Mezia* 47a; *SMA*, n. 3, explains that agricultural produce includes items that are not manufactured utensils or animals. The comment also refers to ch. 195, in which geonic authority declares that acquisition is effected by agricultural produce in a value-for-value barter, but such produce cannot be used to effect a kerchief style of exchange and acquisition. Cf. also *B. Bava Mezia* 45b.
4. *B. Bava Mezia* 46a; cf. *SMA*, n. 4; the parties are deemed to be exchanging the image stamped on the coin, which image is easily defaced.
5. *Tur, HM* 203:1; Maimonides, *Mekhirah* 5:14; *B. Bava Bathra* 3a f.
6. *Hagahot Maimuniot, Mekhirah*, ch. 5, n. 7.
7. Responsa of Solomon b. Adret, no. 1033.
8. *B. Bava Mezia* 47a.
9. *B. Qiddushin* 28a f.
10. Cf. n. 3; *BY* to *Tur, HM* 203:1.
11. *B. Bava Mezia* 47a.
12. *Tur, HM* 203:2.
13. Israel Isserlein, *Responsa Terumath Hadeshen*, no. 311.
14. *B. Bava Mezia* 45b; Maimonides, *Mekhirah* 6:2.
15. Cf. *MM* to Maimonides, loc. cit.
16. See *SMA*, n. 7: the three separate rulings given here are explored; coinage cannot be acquired by means of exchange, coinage given as the purchase price of goods does not effect acquisition *per se*, and a coin is not to be used as a means of effecting acquisition by exchange.
17. *Tur, HM* 203:4.
18. Maimonides, *Mekhirah* 6:2, 3, and *MM* thereto.
19. *MM*, ibid.; cf. *B. Bava Mezia* 44a.
20. *Tur, HM* 203:3.
21. Maimonides, *Mekhirah* 6:3.
22. *B. Bava Mezia* 45b.
23. Maimonides, *Mekhirah* 6:5 and *MM* thereto.
24. *BY* to *Tur, HM* 203:5, citing R. Yeruham.
25. *Tur, HM* 203:5, the views of R. Isaac and Rabbenu Asher respectively; cf. *MM* to Maimonides, *Mekhirah* 6:3; *B. Bava Mezia* 44b. Cf. also *BY* to *Tur* ad loc.
26. *Tur, HM* 203:7, 8; and *BY* thereto, citing R. Yeruham, Rabbenu Asher, Rabbenu Nissim, and other authorities. Cf. also *MM* to Maimonides, *Mekhirah* 6:2.
27. Maimonides, *Mekhirah* 6:6 and *MM* thereto. Cf. also *B. Bava Mezia* 44a and Rashi thereto.
28. Ibid.; and *B. Bava Mezia* 46b f.
29. *Tur, HM* 203:6 and *BY* thereto, citing *Nimmuke Joseph* to *Bava Mezia*, ch. 4, and *MM* to Maimonides, *Mekhirah* 6:6.
30. Maimonides, *Mekhirah* 6:7 and *MM* thereto. Cf. *B. Bava Mezia* 46a and *B. Bava Bathra* 77b.
31. See *Shulhan Arukh* 211:7.

32. Maimonides, *Mekhirah* 6:7.
33. Responsa of Solomon b. Adret, no. 1227; cf. *BY* to *Tur*, *HM* 203:2, which cites the responsum as no. 1226.
34. *Mordecai* to *Bava Bathra*, ch. 9. Cf. *SMA*, n. 19, which reviews the background of the three separate views; cf. *DM* to *Tur*, *HM* 203 n. 3.
35. Responsa of Isaac b. Sheshet, no. 263.
36. Israel Isserlein, *Responsa Terumath Hadeshen*, no. 311.

No. 204 Notes

1. B. *Bava Mezia* 44a.
2. *Tur*, *HM* 204:1; Maimonides, *Mekhirah* 7:1.
3. B. *Bava Mezia* 48b and Rashi thereto.
4. Maimonides, *Mekhirah* 3:6; *Tur*, *HM* 198:14.
5. *Tur*, *HM* 204:10; cf. Tosafot, *Bava Mezia* 47b, s.v. 'i.
6. Maimonides, *Mekhirah* 7:2; B. *Bava Mezia* 44a. cf. *BY* to *Tur*, *HM* 204:2.
7. *BY* to *Tur*, *HM* 204:2.
8. *Mordecai* to *Bava Mezia*, ch. 4.
9. Maimonides, *Mekhirah*, 7:5 and *MM* thereto. Cf. B. *Qiddushin* 8b.
10. Maimonides, *Mekhirah* 7:6.
11. Maimonides, Ibid., 7:8; B. *Bava Mezia* 49a.
12. Maimonides, *Mekhirah* 7:9; B. *Bava Mezia* 49a.
13. B. *Bava Mezia* 49a.
14. Cf. *Shulhan Arukh*, *YD* 228.
15. *BY* to *Tur*, *HM* 204:12, end, citing the early notes to *Mordecai*, *Bava Mezia*, ch. 6.
16. Maimonides, *Mekhirah* 7:4 and *MM* thereto.
17. Rabad to Maimonides, ibid. Cf. *Tur*, *HM* 204:7, 8, citing Rabbenu Asher.
18. *BY* to *Tur*, *HM* 204:1., citing notes to *Mordecai*, *Ketubot*, ch. 1.
19. *Tur*, *HM* 204:9-12.
20. *BY* to *Tur*, *HM* 204:11, citing numerous authorities.

No. 205 Notes

1. Maimonides, *Mekhirah* 10:1 and *MM* thereto. Cf. B. *Bava Bathra* 47a ff.
2. B. *Bava Bathra*, loc. cit.
3. *MM*, loc. cit.
4. Rabad to Maimonides, *Mekhirah* 10:1, and *Tur*, *HM* 205:5.
5. *BY* to *Tur*, *HM* 205:2, citing Rabad, Alfasi, and Rabbenu Asher.
6. B. *Bava Bathra* 40b, 48b; cf. *Tur*, *HM* 205:5.
7. Maimonides, *Mekhirah* 10:2.
8. B. *Bava Bathra* 40b.
9. Maimonides, *Mekhirah* 10:3 and *MM* thereto; B. *Bava Bathra* 40a; *Tur*, *HM* 205:12. *SMA*, n. 9, explains that in the case of gift or of forgiving of a debt, the stated intent of the donor, etc., is sufficient to void the transaction, since there is no value received as there is in a sale.
10. Maimonides, *Mekhirah* 10:3 and *MM* thereto; cf. also *SMA*, n. 9.

11. Isaac b. Sheshet, Responsa, no. 250.
12. *Tur, HM* 205:1, citing R. Jonah. On the meaning of the remedy of a postsale price adjustment, see infra chs. 222-240.
13. *Tur, HM* 205:1 and *BY* thereto.
14. Isaac b. Sheshet, Responsa, no. 127.
15. *Tur, HM* 205:10, citing R. Jonah.
16. *BY* to *Tur, HM* 205:10.
17. Maimonides, *Mekhirah* 10:3.
18. Maimonides, *Mekhirah* 10:4 and *MM* thereto.
19. Joseph Colon, Responsa, no. 186.
20. *B. Bava Bathra* 40b.
21. Maimonides, *Mekhirah* 10:4 and *MM* thereto.
22. Maimonides, *Mekhirah* 10:5 and *MM* thereto. Cf. *B. Bava Bathra* 47b.
23. Cf. Maimonides, *Mekhirah* 10:5 and *Kesef Mishneh* thereto. *Ba'er Hagolah* cross-references this material to *HM* 149:13 and 151:3.
24. *B. Bava Bathra* 48b f.; Maimonides, *Mekhirah* 10:6 and *MM* thereto.
25. Ibid.
26. This is Isserles' own opinion, based on an old text of the *Mordecai*, cf. *DM* to *Tur, HM* 205, n. 1.
27. Maimonides, *Mekhirah* 10:7 and *MM* thereto.
28. Maimonides, *Mehirah* 10:8 and *MM* thereto.
29. Ibid.
30. *Tur, HM* 205:16, citing Rabbenu Asher.
31. Cf. *BY* to *Tur, HM* 205:15, citing Rabbenu Nissim.
32. *BY* and *Tur, HM* 205:16; Joseph Colon, Responsa, no. 118.
33. *BY* to *Tur, HM* 205:16, citing a responsum of Solomon b. Adret.
34. *Tur, HM* 205:6.
35. *BY* to *Tur, HM* 205:6, citing the *Ittur*.

No. 206 Notes

1. Maimonides, *Mekhirah* 8:7 and *MM* thereto; *B. Avodah Zarah* 72a.
2. *Tur, HM* 206:3 and *B. Avodah Zarah*, loc. cit.
3. *B. Avodah Zarah*, loc. cit.
4. Joseph Colon, Responsa, no. 20.
5. Notes on *Mordecai, Bava Mezia*, ch. 5, and *MM* to Maimonides, *Mekhirah* 1:5.
6. Maimonides, *Mekhirah* 8:8 and *MM* thereto.
7. Rashi to *B. Avodah Zarah* 72a.
8. Maimonides *Mekhirah* 8:8 and *MM* thereto.
9. Ibid., cf. also *Tur, HM* 206:5. *B. Avodah Zarah* 72a.

No. 207 Notes

1. Maimonides, *Mekhirah* 11:1 and *MM* thereto.
2. *B. Bava Mezia* 94a.
3. *Tur, HM* 207:2, citing Rabbenu Asher; *DM* ad loc., n. 2, citing *Hagahot Mordecai, Bava Mezia*, ch. 5; *BY* to *Tur*, loc. cit., citing the pupils of

Solomon b. Adret, and Tosafot, *Bava Mezia* 65b, s.v. *lo'*.
4. Maimonides, *Mekhirah* 11:2 and *MM* thereto; cf. *B. Bava Mezia* 65b.
5. Maimonides, *Mekhirah* 11:8 and *MM* thereto; cf. *B. Qiddushin* 50a and *B. Ketubot* 97a.
6. The reference to a "particular place" may, of course, simply be the Land of Israel, because settlement there was a particularly treasured desire of the pious. *B. Qiddushin* 50a specifically mentions the Land of Israel.
7. *B. Qiddushin*, loc. cit.
8. Ibid.
9. *Tur, HM* 207:5, citing Rashi to *Qiddushin* 49b; cf. also *SMA*, n. 9. The point is made that one does not sell real estate, which is presumed to be the basis of livelihood, if one is not really serious about resettlement.
10. Maimonides, *Mekhirah* 11:9 and *B. Qiddushin* 49b.
11. *MM* to Maimonides, *Mekhirah* 11:9. Cf. *Tur, HM* 207:5.
12. Cf. *DM* to *Tur, HM* 207:5, n. 4, citing Rabbenu Asher, Responsa, no. 85, and Tosafot to *Ketubot* 97a, s.v. *zabin*.
13. Maimonides, *Mekhirah* 11:10 and *MM* thereto.
14. Ibid.
15. Cf. rule 6 of this chapter.
16. *Tur, HM* 207:9; *B. Bava Mezia* 65b.
17. Maimonides, *Mekhirah* 11:11; *B. Bava Mezia* 65b.
18. *Kesef Mishneh* to Maimonides, *Mekhirah* 11:11.
19. *B. Bava Mezia* 67a.
20. *Tur, HM* 207:13; *B. Bava Mezia* 65b.
21. *BY* to *Tur, HM* 207:13.
22. The parenthetical phrase "shall be mine" does not appear in the earliest Venice editions. It is an amplification of the text in the spirit of its talmudic source, *B. Bava Mezia* 65b; it is first found in the early Cracow editions.
23. *Tur, HM* 207:13.
24. Maimonides, *Malweh Weloweh* 6:5 and *MM* thereto.
25. Cf. *BY* to *Tur, HM* 207:13, citing Rabbenu Asher, Rabad, and Tosafot, *Bava Mezia* 67a, s.v. *pera*.
26. *Mordecai* to *Bava Mezia*, ch. 5, as cited in *DM* to *Tur, HM* 207:13, n. 7.
27. Rabbenu Asher, Responsa, 72:1 and Isaac b. Sheshet, Responsa, no. 335.
28. Maimonides, *Mekhirah* 11:4 and *MM* thereto; see *SMA*, ad loc., nn. 24, 25, the matter of acquiring security is detailed. But cf. also *Ture Zahav*, ad loc., where security is identified as earnest money.
29. *BY* to *Tur, HM* 207:15, citing Rashi and Rabad to Maimonides, *Mekhirah* 11:4.
30. Maimonides, *Mekhirah* 11:5 and *MM* thereto.
31. Maimonides, *Mekhirah* 11:6 and *MM* thereto. *B. Bava Mezia* 67b.
32. *BY* to *Tur, HM* 207:16, 17, 18. Karo identifies four types of aleatory forfeiture in an extensive analysis of the transaction.
33. Cf. *HM* 321:2.
34. Rabbenu Asher, Responsa, 66:8; *Tur, HM* 207:17; cf. *SMA*, n. 33.
35. *Mordecai* to *Sanhedrin*, ch. 3, no. 691.
36. *Hagahot* to *Mordecai*, loc. cit.

Notes

37. Tosafot to *Sanhedrin* 24b, s.v. *kol*, end. Cf. *DM* ad loc., no. 10, and *Mordecai* to *Sanhedrin*, ch. 3, no. 691.
38. *BY* to *Tur*, *HM* 207:16, 17, 18, citing the Responsa of Solomon b. Adret (pt. I, no. 833).
39. *Tur*, *HM* 207:17; *Mordecai* to *Bava Mezia*, ch. 5, citing Rabbenu Tam; cf. *DM* ad loc., n. 8.
40. *SMA*, n. 35: The commentator sets the various disagreements among rabbinic authorities in order. First, there is an opinion that asserts that there is aleatory forfeiture even if the gamblers make mutually exclusive stipulations and the outcome of the wager is independent of them. Second, the subject of the verb "are required" is an ambiguous "they." The *SMA* clarifies the ambiguity. The "they" is necessarily interpreted as referring to two separate groups. The requirements for finding other reasons for the permissibility of gambling applies only to those who claim an aleatory forfeiture is present, even with mutually exclusive stipulations and an outcome of the wager independent of the wagering parties. Clearly the view that denies aleatory forfeiture in these circumstances requires no other reason to establish the legality of a wager. This is the first sense of "they." Yet both sides of the disagreement over aleatory forfeiture when there are mutually exclusive stipulations, etc., are required to find another reason for the permissibility of penalty clauses in proposals of matrimony. On either view, there is forfeiture if the parties can control the outcome of the future event, which is certainly the case in a marriage proposal and its fulfillment, thus the necessity for some reason to permit what appears to be unlawful applies to both sides of the disagreement. This is an additional meaning of the "they" in "they are required."
41. Maimonides, *Mekhirah* 11:7 and *MM* thereto.
42. Cf. *DM* to *Tur*, *HM* 207, n. 14, citing Rabbenu Asher.
43. *BY* to *Tur*, *HM* 207:19, citing Maimonides.
44. *BY* to *Tur*, *HM* 207:19, citing Responsa of Solomon b. Adret, nos. 908, 1149. Cf. *SMA*, n. 41.
45. Maimonides, *Mekhirah* 11:13 and *MM* thereto; *B. Nedarim* 27b.
46. Responsa of Rabbenu Asher 72:5.
47. *Mordecai* to *B. Bava Mezia*, ch. 4, and *MM* to Maimonides, *Mekhirah* 11:13, citing Solomon b. Adret.
48. The phrase "note of debt" appears first in the Cracow 1607 edition. Prior to that edition, the phrase *shetar tov*, a "good (perhaps "properly executed") note" was the phrase adopted in the glosses. Both versions of the phrase continued to appear. Given the context of this rule, in which the possibility of some ambiguity is present in the demand that the note be indited, "good note" may indeed be as good a reading as "*shetar hov*, "note of debt."
49. *Hagahot Maimuniot* to *Mekhirah*, ch. 11, n. 7, and *Teshubot Maimuniot* to *Kinyan*, no. 4. The phrase "note of debt" appears in the *Hagahot Maimuniot*.
50. *B. Nedarim* 27b.
51. Maimonides, *Mekhirah* 11:14.
52. Cf. *BY* to *Tur*, *HM* 207:19, citing Rabbenu Asher.
53. Maimonides, *Mekhirah* 11:14, and *B. Nedarim* 27b.

54. BY to Tur, HM 207:24.
55. Maimonides, Mekhirah 11:18 and MM thereto.
56. Cf. Shulhan Arukh, Even Hazer 50:7.
57. Cf. Tur, HM 207:21, citing Rabbenu Asher.
58. Cf. DM to Tur, HM 207, n. 14, citing Mordecai to Bava Mezia, ch. 4.
59. Cf. BY to Tur, HM 207:21.
60. Cf. Tur, HM 207:22 and BY thereto, citing Tosafot to Qiddushin 8b, s.v. maneh, and Rabbenu Asher to Qiddushin.
61. Ibid.
62. Tur, HM 207:23, citing Rabbenu Asher, Responsum no. 72, and Ittur, as well as Hagahot Asheri to Bava Mezia, ch. 4.
63. Tur, HM 207:23. Cf. SMA, n. 51: the mere assertion that something is not an aleatory forfeiture has no standing when the transaction clearly does involve one, but the document strongly suggests intent to transfer ownership without reservation.
64. Cf. Mordecai to Bava Qamma, ch. 4.
65. Isaac b. Sheshet, Responsa, no. 387.
66. Maimonides, Mekhirah 11:16, and Tur, HM 207:27. See SMA, n. 60: there is some mystery as to who disagrees with Maimonides on this matter.

No. 208 Notes

1. B. Bava Mezia 65a and Rabbenu Asher thereto; Tur, HM 208:1. Cf. MM to Maimonides, Malweh Weloweh 8:15, citing Nahmanides and Solomon b. Adret.
2. BY to Tur, HM 208, end.
3. MM to Maimonides, Mekhirah 8:15.
4. BY to Tur, HM 208:1, citing the pupils of Solomon b. Adret.
5. BY to Tur, HM 208, end.

No. 209 Notes

1. Maimonides, Mekhirah 21:1 and MM thereto. B. Bava Bathra 95a.
2. Ibid. and cf. Kesef Mishneh to Maimonides, loc. cit., and B. Bava Mezia 46b.
3. Maimonides, Mekhirah 21:3 and Kesef Mishneh thereto.
4. Cf. Isserlein, Terumath Hadeshen, no. 320.
5. Maimonides, Mekhirah 21:4 and MM thereto. B. Bava Mezia 60a.
6. Maimonides, Mekhirah 22:1 and MM thereto. B. Yebamot 93a and B. Qiddushin 62b.
7. MM to Maimonides, Mekhirah 22:1.
8. Cf. Tur, HM 209:8.
9. Cf. Baer Hagolah, n. 9, citing Tosafot to Qiddushin 62b, s.v. w'amar.
10. Cf. B. Bava Mezia 66b and Rashi thereto.
11. Maimonides, Mekhirah 22:2 and B. Bava Mezia 66b.
12. B. Bava Mezia 66b and Rashi thereto.
13. Iserlein, Terumath Hadeshen, no. 320, and Hagahot Maimuniot, Mekhirah, ch. 22, n. 1. Cf. also SMA: the final parenthetical remark is partly based on the comment of note 13. Once the goods exist, the instrument of sale is delivered, and the property is as good as held by the buyer. In any case where the buyer seizes the goods, the assumption must, of course, be that the goods do in fact exist.

Notes

14. Tur, HM 209:5; B. Bava Bathra 147b.
15. Mordecai to Gittin, ch. 6, no. 415.
16. DM to Tur, HM 209:3, citing Mordecai to Bava Bathra, ch. 8.
17. Ibid. and DM cites Mordecai to Bava Bathra 9, citing R. Meir of Rothenburg.
18. Tosafot to Bava Bathra 159a, s.v. lamru.
19. Cf. Nimmuke Joseph to Bava Mezia, ch. 5, citing the pupils of Solomon b. Adret. SMA, n. 17, explains that the disagreement concerns the party who wishes to withdraw from such an obligation before the goods come into existence. But after the goods exist, even those who disagree acknowledge that one cannot lawfully withdraw from the obligation. See also the Sifte Cohen ad loc., n. 8.
20. DM to Tur 209, n. 6.
21. Isaac b. Sheshet, Responsa, nos. 335, 345, and 387.
22. Rabbenu Nissim, Responsa, no. 23; cf. SMA, n. 21, which gives the background of the responsum.
23. Isserlein, Responsa, no. 320.
24. B. Bava Mezia 63a; Maimonides, Mekhirah 22:3 and MM thereto.
25. Nimmuke Joseph to Bava Mezia, ch. 5.
26. Tur, HM 209:7; B. Bava Bathra 148a.
27. Ibid.
28. BY to Tur, HM 209:10, citing Rabbenu Nissim, Rabad, and Solomon b. Adret; cf. infra 212:3.
29. Tur, HM 209:8; B. Bava Mezia 63a.
30. Tur, HM 209:9 and B. Bava Mezia 63a.
31. Tur, HM 209:10 and B. Bava Mezia, 63a.
32. Tur, HM 209:10, and BY, citing Nahmanides.
33. Tur, HM 209:11.
34. Ibid. 209:12, and DM to Tur, HM 209, n. 8, citing Mordecai to Bava Mezia.
35. DM to Tur, HM 209. Cf. Baer Hetev, n. 25: Once one actually becomes the owner of the thing, the formal act for relinquishment is, of course, necessary, words are not enough.
36. The parenthetical phrase "he also" first appears in the Cracow 1619 edition, cf. next note.
37. Cf. DM to Tur, HM 209, n. 8, citing Hagahot Mordecai to Bava Bathra, ch. 3.
38. Tur, HM 209:13.
39. Ibid. 209:14

No. 210 Notes

1. B. Bava Bathra 141b.
2. B. Bava Bathra 142a f.
3. Tur, HM 210:1, citing R. Meir Abulafia; cf. B. Bava Bathra 142a f.
4. Tur, loc. cit., citing Rabbenu Hananel and Rabbenu Asher.
5. Maimonides, Mekhirah 22:10; B. Bava Bathra 140b and 142b.
6. B. Bava Bathra 142b.
7. Responsa of Rabbenu Asher 82:4.

8. Maimonides, loc. cit., and *MM* thereto.
9. Maimonides, *Mekhirah* 22:12.
10. *MM* to ibid., cf. *B. Bava Bathra* 142b f.
11. Ibid.; *Kesef Mishneh* to *Maimonides, Mekhirah* 22:12.
12. Responsa of Solomon b. Adret, no. 375.

No. 211 Notes

1. Maimonides, *Mekhirah* 22:5.
2. *B. Bava Mezia* 16a.
3. *BY* to *Tur, HM* 21:1, citing the pupils of Solomon b. Adret.
4. *B. Bava Mezia* 16a.
5. *Tur, HM* 211:1, citing Rabbenu Tam.
6. *B. Bava Mezia* 16b; Maimonides, *Mekhirah* 22:6.
7. *SMA*, n. 3: Rabbenu Asher in Responsum 76 includes the gravestone as a proper item in the funeral expenses.
8. Cf. *BY* to *Tur, HM* 211:1, citing Rabbenu Nissim; *MM* to Maimonides, *Mekhirah* 22:b, in the name of R. Hai Gaon, and the pupils of Solomon b. Adret.
9. *B. Bava Mezia* 16a f.
10. *B. Bava Bathra* 158b; cf. *BY* to *Tur, HM* 211:2.
11. Maimonides, *Mekhirah* 22:7.
12. *Tur, HM* 211:3, in the name of R. Hai Gaon.
13. *B. Bava Bathra* 136a.
14. *Tur, HM* 211:4, Maimonides, *Zekhiah Umattanah* 12:13.
15. *B. Bava Bathra* 136b. Cf. Maimonides, *Zekhiah Umattanah* 12:13.
16. *B. Qiddushin* 27a; Maimonides, *Mekhirah* 23:8 and *MM* thereto.
17. *MM* to Maimonides, *Mekhirah* 23:8, citing Solomon b. Adret.
18. Maimonides, *Mekhirah* 23:9; *B. Bava Qamma* 70a and 104b.
19. *B. Bava Qamma*, loc. cit.
20. Maimonides, *Mekhirah* 6:7; cf. supra 203:9. Cf. *B. Bava Bathra* 77b.
21. Cf. *Shulhan Arukh, Hoshen Mishpat* 126, entire.
22. Cf. *Shulhan Arukh, HM* 66:1.
23. Cf. *Tur, HM* 54:13, citing Rabad.

No. 212 Notes

1. Maimonides, *Mekhirah* 22:13.
2. *MM* to Maimonides, loc. cit.; cf. *B. Bava Bathra* 147b.
3. *Hagahot Mordecai* to *Bava Bathra*, end. Cf. *BY* to *Tur, HM* 212:1.
4. Nahmanides, Responsa, no. 68.
5. *DM* to *Tur, HM* 212 n. 2, citing *Mordecai* to *Bava Bathra*, ch. 9.
6. *Tur, HM* 212:2, and *BY* thereto, citing *B. Bava Bathra*, ch. 3, and Rabbenu Asher thereto.
7. *Tur, HM* 212:4.
8. Cf. above 209:7.
9. *B. Bava Bathra* 63a.
10. Ibid., R. Samuel b. Meir's commentary thereto; and Maimonides, *Mekhirah* 24:16.

11. Nahmanides, Responsa, no. 18. Cf. also B. Bava Bathra 63a and Tosafot thereto, s.v. 'al.
12. Maimonides, Mekhirah 23:5 and MM thereto.
13. Maimonides, Mekhirah 23:6.
14. MM to ibid.
15. Maimonides, Mekhirah 23:7 and Kesef Mishneh thereto.
16. Maimonides, Mekhirah 23:8.
17. Maimonides, Mekhirah 22:15.
18. Maimonides, Arakhin Veharamim 6:32, 33, and Rabad ad loc.
19. Maimonides, Mekhirah 22:15 and MM thereto.
20. Tur, HM 212:10, 11.
21. Mordecai to B. Bava Bathra, ch. 9; cf. DM to Tur, HM 212, n. 5.
22. Tur, HM 212:12, 13, citing a responsum of Rabbenu Asher.
23. Cf. Shulhan Arukh, YD 258:13, end. gloss, citing Mordecai thereto; also, Joseph Colon, Responsa, no. 185, inter alios.
24. The opinion of Rabbenu Asher in the responsum cited in Tur, cf. note 22 above.
25. Ibid.
26. Tur, HM 212:14.
27. SMA, n. 22, clarifies the apparent contradiction. The view of Maimonides, expressed in 212:7, specifically refers to matters which in the normal course of events will come to pass: the cow will produce a calf, the tree will bear fruit; in these cases the element of vow is present and a dedication of the calf must be performed. When, however, the item dedicated would not necessarily become the dedicator's property, as in the case of land -- which he may or may not be able to acquire -- no element of vow to be fulfilled can be said to exist, presumably even according to Maimonides. If the dedication is made without the assertion of a certainty regarding the property, the dedication has to be performed. That is, one should say, "When I acquire, I shall . . . " rather than, "When I acquire, it shall be . . . "

No. 213 Notes

1. Maimonides, Mekhirah 23:9 and MM thereto. B. Bava Bathra 80a.
2. Cf. Kesef Mishneh to Maimonides, loc. cit.
3. Maimonides, Mekhirah 23:10 and MM thereto. B. Hullin 141b.
4. Cf. MM to Mekhirah 23:10.
5. Cf. Kesef Mishneh to Maimonides, Mekhirah 23:10.

No. 214 Notes

1. Maimonides, Mekhirah 25:1 and MM thereto, B. Bava Bathra 61a f.
2. Ibid.
3. Tur, HM 214:1, citing Rabbenu Asher; B. Bava Bathra, loc. cit. SMA, n. 3, explains that the seller specified the boundaries of the house as is usual, but the verandah is built, e.g., on the south wall. The seller did not write for the buyer, " . . . from the south side of the house is a verandah," but he noted only the southern boundary of the house or the courtyard there to the

south. We do not say that the verandah within the boundary was sold; we do say that the seller must specify a recognized boundary, which the verandah is not taken to be.
4. *Tur*, loc. cit.
5. Ibid.
6. Ibid., citing Maimonides, loc. cit.
7. *BY* to *Tur*, *HM* 214:10, citing Solomon b. Adret.
8. Maimonides, *Mekhirah* 25:2 and *Maggid Mishneh* thereto. *B. Bava Bathra* 61a f.
9. *Tur*, *HM* 214:1, citing Rabbenu Asher, and *BY* thereto, citing Nahmanides.
10. *MM* to Maimonides, *Mekhirah* 25:2.
11. *B. Bava Bathra* 64a.
12. *Tur*, *HM* 214:1.
13. *BY* to *Tur*, *HM* 214:1, citing *Nimmuke Joseph* to *Bava Bathra*, ch. 4.
14. *B. Bava Bathra* 64a.
15. Ibid.
16. Isaac b. Sheshet, *Responsa*, no. 248.
17. Maimonides, *Mekhirah* 24:15; *B. Bava Bathra* 63 f.
18. *BY* to *Tur*, *HM* 214:1, citing Rabbenu Nissim; Nahmanides also holds this view, citing R. Joseph Halevi (ibn Migash). Nahmanides is the clearer source.
19. *BY* to *Tur*, *HM* 214:2; *MM* to Maimonides, *Mekhirah* 24:15.
20. *MM* to *Mekhirah* 24:15, ibid., citing R. Joseph ibn Migash. Cf. *Tur*, *HM* 214:3.
21. *MM* to *Mekhirah* 24:15. Cf. *Tur*, *HM* 214:5, citing Solomon b. Adret.
22. *MM* to *Mekhirah* 24:15.
23. Ibid., citing geonic authorities. Cf. *BY* to *Tur*, *HM* 214:5, citing Nahmanides, Rabbenu Nissim, and Rabbenu Asher, *inter alios*.
24. *BY* to *Tur*, *HM* 214:10:2, citing R. Judah, son of Rabbenu Asher.
25. *Tur*, *HM* 214:5, citing R. Jonah and Rabbenu Asher.
26. Ibid., citing Solomon b. Adret.
27. *BY* to *Tur*, *HM* 214:10, citing a responsum of Solomon b. Adret.
28. *Tur*, *HM* 214:6, citing Nahmanides.
29. *BY* to ibid.
30. *SMA*, n. 29, explains: the seller has the right to rebuild, but only if the second-story apartment collapses, while the buyer's house underneath remains intact. The buyer, having no ownership of the airspace above his dwelling, cannot prevent the seller from rebuilding the upper apartment on the columns.
31. *SMA*, n. 30, explains: The buyer of the second-story apartment is left with nothing except insubstantial air, and he cannot rebuild. His ownership extended only to the physical materials of the dwelling, not its airspace. The seller, as just pointed out above, would retain the airspace, above the lower dwelling, which airspace he had legally retained when he sold the lower dwelling; the seller could therefore rebuild if he owned the upper dwelling.
32. Maimonides, *Mekhirah* 21:17; *B. Bava Bathra* 61b.
33. *MM* to Maimonides, *Mekhirah* 21:17.
34. *B. Bava Bathra* 61b.
35. *MM* to Maimonides, *Mekhirah* 21:17.
36. *Tur*, *HM* 214:10.
37. *DM* to *Tur*, *HM* 214 n. 2, citing *Mordecai* to *Bava Bathra*, ch. 6.

Notes 295

38. Maimonides, *Mekhirah* 24:16; *B. Bava Bathra* 63a. This rule is assumed to hold good only if there had been such an upper chamber before, cf. *Baer Hetev*, n. 29.
39. This is a citation of the *BY* quoting Nahmanides. The source may be Nahmanides, Responsa, no. 18, since the principle involved is that if one reserves something for himself he does so with a proper degree of liberality and leniency toward himself, so that he is assumed to reserve an easement, etc., to the thing reserved. Cf. also *BY* to *Tur*, *HM* 209:10, citing Nahmanides. The extensive citation of Nahmanides in *BY* to *Tur*, *HM* 214:11 does not specifically say that "the same rule applies."
40. Maimonides, *Mekhirah* 25:4 and *MM* thereto. *B. Bava Bathra* 65a. Cf. *Tur*, *HM* 214:16.
41. Ibid.
42. *MM* to *Mekhirah* 25:4.
43. *B. Bava Bathra* 65a.
44. *Tur*, *HM* 214:17.
45. *B. Bava Bathra* 65a.
46. *B. Bava Bathra* 6b.
47. *B. Bava Bathra* 65a f.
48. Maimonides, *Mekhirah* 25:5 and *MM* thereto.
49. *MM* to *Mekhirah* 25:5.
50. Maimonides, *Mekhirah* 25:5; cf. *B. Bava Bathra* 69a.
51. Cf. *BY* to *Tur*, *HM* 214:17.
52. *B. Bava Bathra* 65a f.
53. Ibid.
54. *B. Bava Bathra* 69a.
55. *B. Bava Bathra* 65a f.
56. *Nimmuke Joseph* to *Bava Bathra*, ch. 4. Cf. *BY* to *Tur*, *HM* 214:17.
57. *B. Menahot* 108b f. Maimonides, *Mekhirah* 21:19. The word "sell" is found in Gemara, *Hilkhot Mekhirah*, and the *Tur*, *HM* 214:18. The word "give" appears in the *Shulhan Arukh*, for no apparent reason, except that in this context it could perhaps be construed as "to give for money," i.e., a sale.
58. *Tur*, *HM* 214:18, citing Rabbenu Asher.
59. *B. Bava Bathra* 98b. Cf. *SMA*, n. 49. The better reading of this paragraph is found in the *Tur*, which uses the word "space," so that it can easily be understood in reference to each structure; i.e., one sells space for a specific structure. Maimonides, *Mekhirah* 21:5, has the same sort of reading. The word "space" has, accordingly, been adopted in the translation of this section where necessary.
60. Cf. *Tur*, *HM* 214:20.
61. The Hebrew is "a garden court of a courtyard." The word "of" is found in the first Venice edition but it drops out in the di Cavalli edition, Venice 1567. It is present in almost all of the other early Venice editions. The word does not appear in the early Cracow editions. It appears for the first time outside a Venice edition in the Amsterdam 1664-66 edition.
62. Cf. R. Samuel b. Meir's commentary to *Bava Bathra* 98b.
63. Maimonides, *Mekhirah* 21:5.

64. The dimensions refer to the situation where A sells B space for a particular structure, or where one undertakes to build one of them. But if A simply sells a house to B, the structure can be only four cubits by four cubits. Cf. *BY* to *Tur, HM* 214:20, and *Baer Hetev*, n. 34.

No. 215 Notes

1. Maimonides, *Mekhirah* 25:6; *B. Bava Bathra* 67a; cf. *MM* to Maimonides ad loc.
2. *B. Bava Bathra*, loc. cit.
3. Ibid.
4. *Tur, HM* 215:1.
5. Ibid., cf. *B. Bava Bathra* 150a.
6. *Tur, HM* 215:1.
7. *B. Bava Bathra* 67a; see also *Darke Moshe* to *Tur* 215, n. 1, citing *Nimmuke Joseph* to *Bava Bathra*, ch. 4, who cites Solomon b. Adret.
8. Cf. *SMA*, n. 7.
9. Maimonides, *Mekhirah* 25:7; *B. Bava Bathra* 67b.
10. The phrase in parentheses does not appear in the first Venice editions of the *Shulhan Arukh*. This phrase is found inserted parenthetically in the earliest Cracow editions; cf. *Tur, HM* 215:4.
11. *Tur, HM* 215:4.
12. *B. Bava Bathra* 67b.
13. Ibid., cf. also *MM* to Maimonides, *Mekhirah* 25:7.
14. *Tur, HM* 215:4.
15. Cf. *MM* ibid. In this instance the explanation of obscure wording is useful in the translation; on many occasions, however, there is no need to give the explanatory remark for a Hebrew or Aramaic term as found in the text because the English word is sufficiently clear without necessity for further comment.
16. *B. Bava Bathra* 68a.
17. Ibid.
18. Maimonides, *Mekhirah* 25:9; *B. Bava Bathra* 67b.
19. Cf. *MM* to Maimonides, *Mekhirah* 25:9.
20. *B. Bava Bathra* 67b.
21. *B. Bava Bathra* 68a.
22. *Tur, HM* 215:5.
23. Maimonides, *Mekhirah* 26:1; *B. Bava Bathra* 68a.
24. *B. Bava Bathra* 68a.
25. Maimonides, *Mekhirah* 26:1; *B. Bava Bathra* 68a.
26. Ibid.
27. Ibid.
28. Maimonides, *Mekhirah* 26:2; *B. Bava Bathra* 68b.
29. The parenthetical phrase does not appear in the earliest Venice editions. It appears first in the earliest editions published in Cracow. The phrase is taken from the language of the *Tur, HM* 215:7.
30. *B. Bava Bathra* 68b.
31. Ibid.
32. Maimonides, *Mekhirah* 26:3; *B. Bava Bathra* 69a. An area requiring at least a

source, worked with a bucket and presumably used for laundry, etc., cf. *SMA*, n. 2.
5. Maimonides, *Mekhirah* 21:8; *B. Bava Bathra* 99b.
6. Cf. *B. Bava Bathra* 99b and Samuel b. Meir thereto.
7. Ibid.
8. The word "field" is placed in parentheses here because it appears in parentheses in modern editions. The first Venice edition has the word in the body of the text. The edition published by the House of Griffio (Venice 1567) also has the word. The edition produced by the House of Cavalli (also Venice 1567) does not have it. One might conclude, therefore, that the Cracow editions, which placed the word in parentheses, followed the Cavilli text. The Cavilli text appeared in July of 1567; the Griffio text had appeared in April of 1567.
9. *B. Bava Bathra* 99b.
10. Maimonides, *Mekhirah* 21:9; *B. Bava Bathra* 100a ff.
11. Cf. *SMA*, n. 8; cf. also *MM* to Maimonides, *Mekhirah* 21:9, citing Joseph ibn Migash.
12. *B. Bava Bathra* 99b.
13. Ibid.
14. Maimonides, *Mekhirah* 21:12; *B. Bava Bathra* 17b.
15. Maimonides, *Mekhirah* 21:6; *B. Bava Bathra* 100b.
16. Cf. *MM* to Maimonides, *Mekhirah* 21:6.
17. Maimonides, *Mekhirah* 24:17; *B. Bava Bathra* 100b. Cf. *Tur, HM* 217:8.

No. 218 Notes

1. Maimonides, *Mekhirah* 28:1, cf. *MM* ad loc.; *B. Bava Bathra* 102b.
2. Cf. *Tur, HM* 218:2 and *BY* ad loc., citing Isaac of Dampierre and Rabbenu Asher.
3. *B. Bava Bathra* 102a.
4. *B. Bava Bathra* 102b.
5. *Tur, HM* 21.
6. *Tur, HM* 218:3.
7. *B. Bava Bathra* 103a.
8. Cf. *MM* to Maimonides, loc. cit.
9. *Tur, HM* 218:1, citing Samuel b. Meir and Rabbenu Asher; cf. also *BY* ad loc., citing Rabbenu Nissim.
10. *B. Bava Bathra* 102b.
11. *Tur, HM* 218:2.
12. *B. Bava Bathra* 103a.
13. Ibid.
14. *Tur, HM* 218:3.
15. Cf. Maimonides, *Mekhirah* 28:2; the word "or" appears in parentheses; the word is found in brackets or not at all in modern editions, but occurs in all the editions up to Amsterdam 1664-66, in which it is strangely missing. This is most curious, since this edition includes many corrections and clarifications of the text, some of which first appear in this edition. The word "or" does occur in the Maimonidean text.
16. *B. Bava Bathra* 103a f.
17. Ibid.

18. This is the essence of the explanation provided by *SMA*, n. 19.
19. Maimonides, *Mekhirah* 28:3, and *MM* ad loc.; B. *Bava Bathra* 103b; cf. also *BY* to *Tur*, *HM* 218:4.
20. Maimonides, *Mekhirah* 28:3; B. *Bava Bathra* 103b.
21. B. *Bava Bathra* 103b.
22. Maimonides, *Mekhirah* 28:4; B. *Bava Bathra* 102b.
23. The parenthetical phrase "more than" does not appear in the text until the Amsterdam edition of 1664-66. The *Baer Hetev*, n. 12, credits the *SMA* with the introduction of the phrase into the text, but the author of the *SMA*, Joshua Falk, died in 1614; it is curious indeed that a textual note by so famous a commentator did not find its way into editions published in the first half of the seventeenth century. Cf. *SMA*, n. 24, end, where Joshua Falk suggests the parenthetical phrase.
24. *Tur*, *HM* 218:3; cf. *BY* ad loc., citing *inter alios* Rabbenu Asher and Rabbenu Nissim.
25. *Tur*, *HM* 218:6.
26. Maimonides, *Mekhirah* 28:5; B. *Bava Bathra* 103b. Cf. *MM* to Maimonides ad loc.
27. The word "this," which appears in parentheses, is first found in the earliest Cracow editions; cf. B. *Bava Bathra* 103b f.
28. Maimonides, *Mekhirah* 28:6; B. *Bava Bathra* 104a and *MM* to Maimonides, ad loc.
29. B. *Bava Bathra* 104a.
30. The word "regarding" appears in parentheses when it occurs in modern editions. It is in all the earlier editions up to the one of Amsterdam 1664-66, which, curiously, does not have it. Cf. n. 15.
31. Cf. *SMA*, n. 31: the translation given here follows the sense of *SMA*'s interpretation.
32. Cf. *SMA*, n. 32: a deduction in price is not a satisfactory disposition of the matter.
33. Maimonides, *Mekhirah* 28:7; B. *Bava Bathra* 103b.
34. B. *Bava Bathra* 104b.
35. Maimonides, *Mekhirah* 28:7 and *MM* thereto.
36. Cf. *SMA*, nn. 35, 36.
37. Maimonides, *Mekhirah* 28:8.
38. The rather complex translation of these complex points is based upon *SMA*, nn. 35, 36.
39. Maimonides, *Mekhirah* 28:9.
40. The material in parentheses was first published with the previous paragraph; the present placement of the gloss with para. 12, and its present text, dates from the Amsterdam 1664-66 edition.
41. *MM* to Maimonides, *Mekhirah* 28:7; cf. *Tur*, *HM* 218:8.
42. Maimonides, *Mekhirah* 28:10; B. *Bava Bathra* 104b.
43. Cf. *SMA*, n. 39: the buyer may use the land as he wishes.
44. Maimonides, *Mekhirah* 28:11; B. *Bava Bathra* 105a.
45. B. *Bava Bathra* 105a; cf. *MM* to Maimonides, *Mekhirah* 28:11. The seller has the advantage because he is in possession of the land when he offers the land for sale by using this equivocal language.
46. Maimonides, *Mekhirah* 28:12; B. *Bava Bathra* 106a.

Notes

47. Maimonides, *Mekhirah* 28:13; *B. Bava Bathra* 106b.
48. Cf. *Tur, HM* 218:13.
49. Maimonides, *Mekhirah* 28:14; *B. Bava Mezia* 104a.
50. Ibid.
51. Ibid.
52. Maimonides, *Mekhirah* 28:15.
53. Maimonides, *Mekhirah* 21:22; *B. Bava Bathra* 107b.
54. *B. Bava Bathra* 107b and *MM* to Maimonides, *Mekhirah* 21:22.
55. *B. Bava Bathra* 107b.
56. *Tur, HM* 218:18.
57. *B. Bava Bathra* 108a.
58. Maimonides, *Mekhirah* 21:23; *B. Bava Bathra* 62b f.
59. *B. Bava Bathra* 61b.
60. *Tur, HM* 218:20 and *BY* ad loc., citing Rabbenu Asher.
61. Maimonides, *Mekhirah* 28:20; *B. Bava Bathra* 61b.
62. Maimonides, *Mekhirah* 28:18; *B. Bava Bathra* 61b.
63. *Tur, HM* 218:22, citing R. Jonah.
64. Cf. *SMA*, n. 61; the word "all" appears in brackets in the text. It does not appear in the earlier editions. The first occurrence of this word, which certainly improves the sense of the text, is in the Amsterdam 1664-66 edition.
65. *Tur, HM* 218:22.
66. Maimonides, *Mekhirah* 28:18 and *MM* thereto.
67. Ibid.
68. The word "if" appears in brackets; it does not appear in some texts at all, e.g., Vilna 1883-84. It first appears as a parenthetical insertion in the Amsterdam 1664-66 edition.
69. *Tur, HM* 218:23, citing R. Jonah.
70. Maimonides, *Mekhirah* 28:21; *B. Bava Bathra* 30a.
71. Ibid.

No. 219 Notes

1. *B. Bava Bathra* 62b; cf. *Tur, HM* 219:1 and *BY* ad loc., citing Rabbenu Asher to *Bava Bathra*, ch. 4.
2. Ibid.
3. Maimonides, *Mekhirah* 21:15; *B. Bava Bathra* 62b.
4. The word "how" appears in parentheses. It is inserted into the text in the earliest Cracow editions. Cf. the reading of Maimonides, *Mekhirah* 21:15.
5. Maimonides *Mekhirah* 21:15; *B. Bava Bathra* 62b.
6. *B. Bava Bathra* 62b.
7. Maimonides, *Mekhirah* 21:13; *B. Bava Bathra* 62a.
8. Ibid.
9. *Tur, HM* 219:1, citing R. Meir Abulafia and R. Jonah.
10. Cf. *B. Bava Bathra* 62a and *MM* to Maimonides, *Mekhirah* 21:16.
11. The parenthetical explanation of the configuration as "one opposite the other" first appears in the earliest Cracow editions; the parenthetical insertion is based on *Tur, HM* 219:1.

12. Maimonides, *Mekhirah* 28:14; *B. Bava Bathra* 62a.
13. *B. Bava Bathra* 62b f., and Samuel b. Meir's commentary thereto.
14. Cf. *SMA*, n. 14: the basic notion is that the inclusion of the additional language, which was unnecessary, places the buyer in the more advantageous position. The additional language is deemed to have been used for the purpose of construing the matter in the buyer's favor.

No. 220 Notes

1. Maimonides, *Mekhirah* 27:1; *B. Bava Bathra* 73a. This chapter has a number of parenthetical explanations of Hebrew words which may be considered technical or obscure. The translation has omitted these explanations in almost all cases because the English terms are commonly used and understood.
2. *MM* to Maimonides, *Mekhirah* 27:1.
3. *B. Bava Bathra* 73a.
4. The traditional meaning for "slaves," i.e., the crew, those who work the ship, is given here because that is the meaning which Karo and others have preserved. Another meaning, "slaves for sale," is reasonable in the context of the original talmudic source, *B. Bava Bathra* 73a; cf. S. M. Passamaneck, "Traces of Rabbinical Maritime Law and Custom," *Tijdschrift voor Rechtsgeschiedenis*, XXXIV, Leiden, 1966.
5. Maimonides, *Mekhirah* 27:2; *B. Bava Bathra* 77b.
6. *Tur, HM* 220:2; the gloss, based on the opinions given in the *Tur*, properly comes with paragraph 2 of this chapter. It was, however, appended to paragraph 3 in all the early editions, until the appearance of the Hanau edition of 1627-28. The shift of the material from the third to the second paragraph was maintained in almost all later editions, but see the edition of Fuerth 1691.
7. *Tur, HM* 220:4.
8. Maimonides, *Mekhirah* 27:2; *B. Bava Bathra* 77b.
9. The word for "some people" appears in brackets; this insertion, based on Maimonides, *Mekhirah* 27:2, first appears in the *Shulhan Arukh* in the Amsterdam 1664-66 edition.
10. *MM* to Maimonides, *Mekhirah* 27:2; *Tur, HM* 220:6, citing R. Joseph Halevi.
11. Maimonides, *Mekhirah* 27:3; cf. Rabad ad loc.
12. *Tur, HM* 220:7, citing Rabad, loc. cit.
13. Maimonides, *Mekhirah* 27:3.
14. Maimonides, *Mekhirah* 27:4 and *MM* thereto, citing Joseph ibn Migash.
15. *B. Bava Bathra* 78a.
16. *Tur, HM* 220:9, citing Alfasi and Rabbenu Asher *inter alios*.
17. Maimonides, *Mekhirah* 27:5; *B. Bava Bathra* 78a.
18. Ibid.
19. This entire gloss is based upon *Tur, HM* 220:6, citing R. Meir Abulafia.
20. Maimonides, *Mekhirah* 28:6; cf. *MM* ad loc.
21. Maimonides, *Mekhirah* 27:7; cf. *MM* ad loc.
22. *Tur, HM* 220:10, citing Rabbenu Asher.
23. Maimonides, *Mekhirah* 27:7; cf. *MM* ad loc.; *B. Bava Bathra* 78b.
24. Maimonides, *Mekhirah* 27:8.

25. Ibid.
26. Maimonides, *Mekhirah* 27:9; *B. Bava Bathra* 83b.
27. Ibid.
28. Maimonides, *Mekhirah* 27:11; *Tur, HM* 220:14.
29. Maimonides, *Mekhirah* 27:10; *B. Bava Bathra* 78b.
30. *Tur, HM* 220:16; citing R. Samuel b. Meir and Rabbenu Asher.
31. Maimonides, *Mekhirah* 28:10; *B. Bava Bathra* 78b.
32. *Tur, HM* 220:19; cf. *BY* ad loc., citing Rabbenu Asher.
33. *Tur, HM* 220:20.
34. This translation follows the explanation of *SMA*, n. 25.
35. Maimonides, *Mekhirah* 28:13; *B. Bava Bathra* 80a.
36. *Tur, HM* 220:15, citing R. Samuel b. Meir.

No. 221 Notes

1. Maimonides, *Mekhirah* 20:1, based on Alfasi's epitome of *Qiddushin*, ch. 1.
2. *DM* to *Tur, HM* 221:1, n. 1, citing *Nimmuke Joseph* to *B. Bava Mezia*, ch. 6.

No. 222 Notes

1. Maimonides, *Mekhirah* 20:4; *B. Qiddushin* 73b f.; cf. *B. Bava Mezia* 2b.
2. Tosafot to *Qiddushin* 73b, s.v. *bame devarim amurim*.
3. *Tur, HM* 222:1.
4. Maimonides, *Mekhirah* 20:4 and *MM* ad loc.
5. Maimonides, *Mekhirah* 20:2 and *MM* ad loc.; cf. *B. Yebamot* 118b.
6. *Kesef Mishneh* to Maimonides, *Mekhirah* 20:2 and *B. Bava Mezia* 27a.
7. Maimonides, *Mekhirah* 20:3 and *MM* ad loc.; *B. Bava Qamma* 103b.
8. Maimonides, *Mekhirah* 20:5 and *MM* ad loc.
9. The translation follows the explanation of *SMA*, n. 8.
10. Maimonides, *Mekhirah* 20:6.
11. *Hagahot Maimuniot* to Maimonides, *Ishut*, ch. 9, n. 4.

No. 223 Notes

1. Maimonides, *Mekhirah* 20:10; *B. Bava Mezia* 100a; cf. also *Tur, HM* 223:1.
2. Maimonides, loc. cit., *MM* ad loc., who explains that title to a non-Jewish slave is acquired by payment of the purchase price, which is the same rule that applies in sales of real property.
3. Cf. *Baer Hetev*, n. 1, citing Tosafot to *Bava Mezia* 100a, s.v. *welihaze*.
4. Maimonides, loc. cit.; *Tur, HM* 223:1.
5. Ibid.
6. The *SMA*, n. 4, reminds the reader that the oath prescribed by biblical law does not apply in respect of oaths concerning slaves.
7. *Tur, HM* 223:1.
8. Ibid.
9. Maimonides, *Mekhirah* 20:11; *B. Bava Mezia* 100a. Cf. also *B. Bava Mezia* 71a.
10. Maimonides, *Mekhirah* 20:11; cf. *MM* thereto.

11. Maimonides, *Mekhirah* 20:12; *B. Bava Mezia* 100a.
12. *B. Bava Mezia* 100a; Maimonides, *To'en Ve'nitan* 5:2; *Tur, HM* 223:2.
13. Maimonides, *Mekhirah* 23:13 and *MM* thereto.

No. 224 Notes

1. Maimonides, *Mekhirah* 20:14; *B. Ketubot* 76a f. The translation of this text clearly departs from the word order and syntax of the Hebrew original. A strict and literal translation of the material would yield a misleading and ambiguous text. Therefore the idiomatic sense is preferable for purpose of translation.
2. *Tur, HM* 224:1, citing Rabbenu Asher.
3. Cf. *DM* to *Tur, HM* 224, n. 1, citing *Mordecai* to *Ketubot*, ch. 7, which cites a a responsum of Meir of Rothenburg.
4. *BY* to *Tur, HM* 224:2, citing *Mordecai* to *Bava Mezia*, ch. 4; cf. *Teshuvot Maimuniot* to *Qinyan*, no. 6.
5. Maimonides, *Mekhirah* 20:15; *B. Hullin* 50a f.
6. *MM* to Maimonides, *Mekhirah* 20:15, and *B. Hullin*, loc. cit.

No. 225 Notes

1. Maimonides, *Mekhirah* 19:3; *B. Bava Mezia* 15b; cf. *MM* to Maimonides ad loc.
2. Cf. *BY* to *Tur, HM* 225:1, citing *Nimmuke Joseph*.
3. Maimonides, *Mekhirah* 19:4; *B. Bava Bathra* 45a f.
4. Maimonides, *Mekhirah* 19:4, 5, 6.
5. Ibid.; cf. *MM* thereto.
6. Maimonides, *Mekhirah* 19:4, 5, 6; *B. Gittin* 73a.
7. Cf. *MM* to Maimonides, *Mekhirah* 19:4, 5, 6.
8. Maimonides, *Mekhirah* 19:7; *B. Gittin* 73a.
9. Maimonides, *Mekhirah* 19:8 and *MM* ad loc.; *B. Bava Bathra* 44b.
10. *Tur, HM* 225:7, citing a responsum of Rabbenu Asher, 102:2.
11. Ibid.

No. 226 Notes

1. Maimonides, *Mekhirah* 19:9; *B. Bava Qamma* 8b.
2. *BY* to *Tur, HM* 226:3, citing a responsum of Solomon b. Adret.
3. Maimonides, *Mekhirah* 19:10; *B. Ketubot* 91a ff.
4. *B. Ketubot* 92a.
5. Ibid. and Maimonides, *Mekhirah* 19:10.
6. *B. Ketubot* 97a.
7. This parenthetical remark follows the sense of *SMA*, n. 8.
8. *B. Ketubot* 97a; cf. *Shulhan Arukh, HM* 147:2, and *Responsa* of Isaac b. Sheshet, 244.
9. Maimonides, *Mekhirah* 19:2; cf. *B. Bava Qamma* 91; *B. Bava Mezia* 14a, and *B. Ketubot* 92 ff.
10. *Tur, HM* 226:3, citing Rabbenu Asher.
11. *Tur, HM* 226:6, citing a responsum of Rabbenu Asher, sec. 97, end.

12. Maimonides, *Mekhirah* 19:1; *B. Shebuot* 21a; cf. *MM* to Maimonides ad loc.

No. 227 Notes

1. *Tur, HM* 227:1; cf. Leviticus 25:14 for the biblical basis of all these rules.
2. Maimonides, *Mekhirah* 12:2 and *MM* thereto. Cf. *B. Bava Mezia* 49b.
3. Maimonides, *Mekhirah* 12:3.
4. *MM* to ibid.
5. Maimonides, *Mekhirah* 12:4 and *MM* thereto.
6. Ibid.
7. *Tur, HM* 227:6, citing R. Jonah and Rabbenu Asher.
8. *Hilkhoth Mordecai, Bava Mezia*, ch. 4, no. 304.
9. Cf. *SMA*, n. 9, which is the basis for this explanatory material.
10. Cf. *SMA*, n. 12; cf. Maimonides, *Mekhirah* 12:4 and *MM* thereto; cf. *B. Bava Mezia* 55a.
11. *Tur, HM* 227:5; citing Rabbenu Asher.
12. *Tur, HM* 227:8; cf. also Maimonides, *Mekhirah* 12:5 and *B. Bava Mezia* 49b and 90b.
13. *B. Bava Mezia* 50b.
14. *Tur, HM* 227:9.
15. The word "time" appears in brackets in modern texts. It does not appear in the earliest Cracow editions of the glosses and amplifications. Its first appearance in the text is in the Cracow 1619 edition.
16. *Mordecai* to *Bava Mezia*, ch. 4, no. 307.
17. Maimonides, *Mekhirah* 12:6; cf. *B. Bava Mezia* 50b, and *SMA*, n. 19.
18. *B. Bava Mezia* 51a.
19. Cf. *SMA*, n. 20. It must be perfectly clear that the merchant has a true duplicate of the item he sold.
20. *Tur, HM* 227:11, citing a responsum of Rabbenu Asher, no. 102:7.
21. *DM* to *Tur* 227, n. 2, citing *Mordecai* to *Ketubot*, ch. 7.
22. *Tur, HM* 227:11, citing Rabbenu Asher, op. cit.
23. Maimonides, *Mekhirah* 12:13 and *MM* thereto. Cf. *B. Bava Bathra* 83b f.
24. Maimonides, *Mekhirah* 12:14 and *MM* thereto.
25. Maimonides, *Mekhirah* 12:15 and *MM* thereto.
26. Ibid.
27. Maimonides, *Mewkhirah* 12:8; *B. Bava Mezia* 51a.
28. Maimonides, *Mekhirah* 12:11; cf. *B. Bava Mezia* 52b.
29. Cf. *MM* to Maimonides, *Mekhirah* 12:11.
30. *B. Bava Mezia* 52a.
31. Maimonides, *Mekhirah* 12:9.
32. Ibid.
33. *MM* to ibid., and *Mekhirah* 12:10 and *MM* thereto.
34. *Tur, HM* 227:16, citing Rabbenu Asher, and *MM* to Maimonides, *Mekhirah* 12:10, citing Nahmanides; cf. also *SMA*, n. 34.
35. *B. Bava Mezia* 52b.
36. Ibid.
37. *Tur, HM* 227:18; *B. Bava Mezia* 52b.

38. This last phrase is to be construed as a continuation of the rule relieving the defrauding party of responsibility after a specific period of time has elapsed. But this relief is only good if the coin can pass as currency, albeit with difficulty. The statement of this rule in Maimonides, *Mekhirah* 12:12, is far clearer.
39. *Tur, HM* 227:19; cf. *B. Bava Mezia* 52a f.
40. Ibid.
41. Ibid.
42. *BY* to *Tur, HM* 227:16, citing Rabbenu Yeruham.
43. Maimonides, *Mekhirah* 13:2.
44. *Tur, HM* 227:21, citing Rabbenu Asher; cf. *B. Bava Mezia* 46b f.
45. Maimonides, *Mekhirah* 13:1.
46. Ibid. and *Kesef Mishneh* thereto. The basic point is that unfair price as constructive fraud applies in sales, where there is some sort of price, not in barter.
47. Maimonides, *Mekhirah* 13:3; *B. Bavia Mezia* 51b.
48. Maimonides, *Mekhirah* 15:11.
49. The word for "make an error," *to'ah*, appears in brackets in the body of the text; in the early Venice and Cracow editions, however, the word *notah*, clearly a misprint, is found. The early-seventeenth-century commentary *SMA* (n. 41) already draws attention to the necessary change to *to'ah* as the better reading for the Karo text. The reading is based on *Mekhirah* 15:11. Cf. Amsterdam edition of 1664–66.
50. *Tur, HM* 227:27; cf. *B. Bava Mezia* 51a. Cf. Responsa of Rabbenu Asher, sec. 102.
51. *Tur, HM* 227:27, citing Rabbenu Asher.
52. Ibid., citing R. Isaac.
53. Cf. Maimonides, *Mekhirah* 12:2.
54. *Tur, HM* 227:30, citing the Responsa of Rabbenu Asher 102:3.
55. *Tur, HM* 227:33.
56. Maimonides, *Mekhirah* 13:7 and *MM* thereto; cf. *B. Bekhoroth* 13a f.
57. *MM* to Maimonides, *Mekhirah* 13:7; cf. also *B. Avodah Zarah* 71b.
58. Maimonides, *Mekhirah* 13:6; cf. *B. Bava Mezia* 51b.
59. *B. Bava Mezia* 51b.
60. Ibid.
61. *B. Bava Mezia* 56a.
62. Maimonides, *Mekhirah* 13:8 and *MM* thereto.
63. *Tur, HM* 227:41, citing Rabbenu Tam and Rabbenu Asher.
64. Maimonides, *Mekhirah* 13:9 and *MM* thereto; cf. *B. Qiddushin* 42b.
65. Rabad to Maimonides, *Mekhirah* 13:9, and *Tur, HM* 227:49, citing R. Hai.
66. *Tur, HM* 227:49, citing R. Jonah and *MM* to Maimonides, *Mekhirah* 13:9.
67. Maimonides, *Mekhirah* 13:14 and *MM* thereto; cf. *B. Bava Mezia* 56b. Cf. also, supra, para. 29 in Isserles' gloss, for another opinion on the matter of grossly excessive prices or rents.
68. The lease of property is viewed as a sale of that property for a specific period. Therefore, a rule against constructive fraud by means of excessive price in the sale of real property applies as well to the rental of real property.
69. Maimonides, *Mekhirah* 13:15 and *MM* thereto.

70. Israel Isserlein, *Terumath Hadeshen*, no. 318. This gloss appeared with para. 36 in printed editions until the Amsterdam edition of 1664-66, in which it was shifted to its present position in the text.
71. Maimonides, *Mekhirah* 13:16.
72. Ibid., 13:17.
73. Cf. *MM* to ibid.
74. Maimonides, *Mekhirah* 13:18 and *MM* thereto; cf. also *Tur, HM* 227:46.
75. Maimonides, *Mekhirah* 13:12; cf. *B. Qiddushin* 42b.
76. Cf. supra, para. 32.
77. *Tur, HM* 227:51.
78. Ibid., cf. also Maimonides, *Mekhirah* 15:1, and *B. Qiddushin* 42b.
79. *Tur, HM* 227:51; Maimonides, *Mekhirah* 13:12, and *B. Qiddushin* 42b.
80. *Tur, HM* 227:52, citing a responsum of Rabbenu Asher, 98:5.

No. 228 Notes

1. *B. Bava Mezia* 53b; Maimonides, *Mekhirah* 14:12; *Tur, HM* 228:1.
2. *B. Bava Mezia*, loc. cit.
3. Ibid.
4. *Nimmuke Joseph* to *Bava Mezia*, ch. 4.
5. Cf. *Ba'er Hetev*, n. 1; cf. *Nimmuke Joseph*, loc. cit.
6. *B. Bava Mezia* 58b, and Maimonides, *Mekhirah* 14:13.
7. *B. Bava Mezia* 59a; *Tur, HM* 228:1.
8. *B. Bava Mezia* 58b.
9. Ibid.
10. Ibid.
11. Ibid.
12. Maimonides, *Mekhirah* 14:14 and *MM* thereto.
13. *B. Bava Mezia* 58b. Cf. *Tur, HM* 228:4.
14. Maimonides, *Mekhirah* 18:1; cf. *B. Bava Mezia* 58b and *B. Hullin* 94a.
15. Ibid.
16. *B. Hullin* 94a.
17. The word for "his friend" appears in brackets in the text. In the first edition the word is "with him." The phrase "his friend" replaces "with him" for the first time in the Amsterdam edition of 1664-66. The alteration makes the clause conform to its talmudic source, *Hullin* 94a.
18. Cf. *SMA*, n. 8. The commentator emphasized the notion of excessive invitation. It is, however, quite proper to ask someone once or twice to come to dine, but if the invitation is refused one should not pursue the matter.
19. Cf. *Baer Hagolah*, loc. cit.
20. *B. Hullin* 94b.
21. Ibid. Cf. *Tur, HM* 228:7.
22. The word "wine" appears in brackets in the text. Its first appearance in this paragraph occurs in the edition of Amsterdam 1664-66.
23. *B. Hullin* 94b; *Tur, HM* 228:7 and *BY* ad loc. Oil is more costly than wine, so therefore one might suppose that he has received a costly cask of oil, which is not really the case.

Notes

24. B. *Bava Mezia* 60a; and Maimonides, *Mekhirah* 18:2.
25. B. *Bava Mezia* 60b.
26. Ibid.
27. Ibid.
28. B. *Bava Mezia* 60a f.
29. B. *Bava Mezia* 60b.
30. Ibid.
31. B. *Bava Mezia* 5b f.
32. Ibid.; cf. *Tur*, *HM* 228:9.
33. B. *Bava Mezia* 60a.
34. Maimonides, *Mekhirah* 18:5; B. *Bava Mezia* 60a.
35. *Tur*, *HM* 228:10 and *BY* thereto.
36. B. *Bava Mezia* 60a. The assumption is that the customer would in fact taste the wine before the purchase.
    The word "anything" appears in brackets. The editions up to that of Cracow 1619 have the word *maqom* in place of *dabhar*, a possible reference to distinctive taste as a function of the region in which the wine grapes were grown. The Cracow 1619 edition is the first to use the phrasing found in the modern editions. Cf. Maimonides, *Mekhirah* 18:5.
37. The word "always" first appears as the final word in this paragraph in the Prague edition of *Shjulhan Arukh*, 1628. In the prior editions, it was the first word of the following paragraph, which also yields good sense: "one is never . . . . " The inclusion of the word with the eleventh paragraph was no doubt an attempt to make the phrasing of *Shulhan Anukh* conform to that of the *Tur* 227:10, end.
38. Maimonides, *Mekhirah* 18:6; B. *Bava Mezia* 60a.
39. Ibid.
40. The merchant would quietly sell the watered wine.
41. Maimonides, *Mekhirah* 18:6; B. *Bava Mezia* 60a.
42. *Tur*, *HM* 227:12; B. *Bava Mezia* 60a, but cf. *Ba'er Hagolah ad loc.*, which explains that the *Tur* expands upon the basic sense of the talmudic provision, which refers to blends of wine with wine, to include mixtures of wine and water.
43. B. *Bava Mezia* 60a; Maimonides, *Mekhirah* 18:8.
44. *Tur*, *HM* 228:13.
45. The words "the wine" appear in brackets. The modern phrasing dates from the Amsterdam edition of 1664-66. Slightly different phrasing using the word for wine, but yielding precisely the same sense, appears in the editions of Cracow 1619 and Prague 1628. Up the Cracow 1619 edition the word for wine did not appear explicitly in the phrase, which followed the wording of the *Tur*, *HM* 228:13.
46. B. *Bava Mezia* 60a; Maimonides, *Mekhirah* 18:7; *Tur*, *HM* 228:14.
47. B. *Bava Mezia* 60a.
48. B. *Bava Mezia* Ibid.
49. Ibid.; cf. *Shulhan Arukh*, *HM* 156:5.
50. Maimonides, *Mekhirah* 18:8; B. *Bava Mezia* 60a.
51. Maimonides, *Mekhirah* 18:9; B. *Bava Mezia* 40a.

52. *B. Bava Mezia* 40a f.
53. Ibid.; cf. Maimonides, *Mekhirah* 18:9.
54. *MM* to Maimonides, *Mekhirah* 18:9.
55. Cf. above para. 15; cf. *B. Bava Mezia* 60a and Maimonides, *Mekhirah* 18:8; cf. also *Tur*, *HM* 228:19 and 20.

No. 229 Notes

1. Maimonides, *Mekhirah* 18:11; *B. Bava Bathra* 94a.
2. *B. Bava Bathra* 93b; Maimonides, loc. cit.
3. *B. Bava Bathra* 94a and *MM* to Maimonides, loc. cit.
4. The word "not" is in brackets; it first appears in the text in the Cracow edition of 1619; cf. *Tur*, *HM* 229:1.
5. *Tur*, *HM* 229:1.
6. Ibid., citing R. Samuel b. Meir.
7. Ibid., citing R. Meir Abulafia.
8. Maimonides, *Mekhirah* 18:13 and *MM* thereto.
9. *B. Bava Bathra* 93b.
10. The word for pebble appears in the first edition, Venice 1565. The modern editions have it in brackets. The word is present in the Venice 1567 edition of Giovanni Griffio but not in the Venice 1567 edition of di Cavalli. The word is absent from *Shulhan Arukh* editions appearing in Cracow until the publication of the Cracow 1619 text. The word appears in the Gemara, *B. Bava Bathra* 93b; Maimonides, *Mekhirah* 18:13; and *Tur*, *HM* 229:2.

No. 230 Notes

1. *B. Bava Bathra* 95b; Maimonides *Mekhirah*, 17:7; cf. *B. Bava Bathra* 93b.
2. *Tur*, *HM* 230:1; cf. also *MM* to Maimonides, *Mekhirah* 17:8, citing Nahmanides.
3. *B. Bava Bathra* 95b.
4. Cf. *MM* to Maimonides, *Mekhirah* 17:8.
5. Maimonides, *Mekhirah* 17:8 and *MM* thereto, and *Tur*, *HM* 230:1. Cf. *B. Bava Bathra* 95a; cf. *SMA*, n. 7, where the noun "barrel" is clearly in the singular.
6. Ibid.
7. Ibid.
8. Maimonides, *Mekhirah* 17:3; *B. Bava Bathra* 97b f.
9. Ibid.
10. Ibid.
11. *Tur*, *HM* 230:1, end.
12. Maimonides, *Mekhirah* 17:3 and *MM* thereto; cf. *B. Bava Bathra* 98a.
13. *MM* to Maimonides, *Mekhirah* 17:3, citing Solomon b. Adret.
14. Maimonides, *Mekhirah* 17:3.
15. *Tur*, *HM* 230:1, citing R. Hai Gaon.
16. Maimonides, *Mekhirah* 17:4 and *MM* thereto. *B. Bava Bathra* 96a.
17. Maimonides, *Mekhirah* 17:5; *B. Bava Bathra* 98a.
18. Ibid.
19. Ibid.

20. Maimonides, *Mekhirah* 17:6, according to Maimonides' reading of the Mishnah, *B. Bava Bathra* 97b f. Cf. also *Tur, HM* 230:2.
21. *Tur, HM* 230:2.
22. *B. Bava Bathra* 97b f.; Maimonides, *Mekhirah* 17:6 and *MM* thereto.
23. Cf. above para. 7.
24. *Mordecai to Bava Mezia*, ch. 4, no. 310; cf. *DM* to *Tur, HM* 230.

No. 231 Notes

1. Maimonides, *Genevah* 7:8; cf. *B. Bava Qamma* 113a and *B. Bava Mezia* 61b.
2. Maimonides, loc. cit., and *MM* thereto; *B. Bava Qamma*, loc. cit.
3. *B. Bava Bathra* 89a; Maimonides, *Genevah* 8:20.
4. *Tur, HM* 231:3; Maimonides, *Genevah* 7:3; *B. Bava Bathra* 89b.
5. The phrase "in his house," which appears in the *Tur* and Maimonides, and which is based on the wording of the Gemara, is not found in the printed text of the *Shulhan Arukh* until the Amsterdam 1664-66 edition.
6. Maimonides, *Genevah* 7:4; *B. Bava Bathra* 89b.
7. Maimonides, *Genevah* 7:7; *B. Bava Bathra* 89b.
8. Ibid.
9. *B. Bava Bathra* 90a; Maimonides, *Genevah* 7:7.
10. *B. Bava Bathra* 89b; Maimonides, *Genevah* 8:5.
11. Ibid. Cf. *SMA*, n. 6: a thick rod could benefit the buyer; a thin one, the seller.
12. *B. Bava Bathra* and Maimonides, *Genevah* 8:5; *Tur, HM* 231:6.
13. The word "quick" appears in the *Tur, HM* 231:6, but it does not appear in the *Shulhan Arukh* until the Amsterdam 1664-66 edition. It does not, however, occur in all subsequent editions.
14. *B. Bava Bathra* 896; Maimonides, *Genevah* 8:7; *Tur, HM* 231:7.
15. *B. Bava Bathra* 87a; *Tur, HM* 231:7.
16. Cf. *SMA*, n. 9, and *B. Bava Bathra* 87b.
17. *B. Bava Bathra* 87b and *Tur, HM* 231:7.
18. *B. Bava Bathra* 88a; Maimonides, *Genevah* 8:18.
19. The word for "large amounts" appears in brackets and is an interpolation from the *Tur, HM* 231:8. It is found in the Amsterdam edition, 1664-66, but in no prior edition. It is also missing in several post-1666 editions.
20. *B. Bava Bathra* 88a f.; Maimonides, *Genevah* 8:18.
21. *B. Bava Bathra* 88a f.; Maimonides, *Genevah* 8:16.
22. *B. Bava Bathra* 89a.
23. *Tur, HM* 231:10.
24. The parenthetical phrase appears in several versions. The earliest editions have "where the custom is to heap, we do not level," i.e., just the reverse of the modern version. The Venice 1598 edition has "to level, we do not heap." The Cracow 1619 edition has "leveling, one is not to heap." The Amsterdam edition, 1641-42, is the same as the Venice 1598 edition. The Prague 1628 edition gives the wording now commonly found, which is consistently used from the Amsterdam 1664-66 edition onward.
    The Mishnaic text of *B. Bava Bathra* 88b has "to level, one is not to heap, one

is not to level"; Maimonides, *Genevah* 8:10, gives only the second phrase; the *Tur*, *HM* 231:10, gives "to level, we do not heap," as in the Venice 1598 and Amsterdam 1641-42 editions of *Shulhan Arukh*.

Clearly the Mishnah gives both the heaping and leveling alternatives. The various editions of the *Shulhan Arukh* mention only one of them. Karo's first edition uses the second phrase of this part of the Mishnah for the ruling, following Maimonides' reading. The more modern texts follow the *Tur* in emphasizing the first phrase of this part of the Mishnah. The precise phrasing of the rule is not consistent in regard to the use of participles or infinitives.

25. B. *Bava Bathra* 89a; *Tur*, *HM* 231:11.
26. B. *Bava Bathra* 89b; Maimonides, *Genevah* 8:4.
27. Cf. *Tur*, *HM* 231:14, citign Rabbenu Tam.
28. *BY* to *Tur*, *HM* 231:14.
29. B. *Bava Mezia* 61b; Maimonides, *Genevah* 8:7; *Tur*, *HM* 231:15.
30. B. *Bava Bathra* 88a: Maimonides, *Genevah* 8:18; *Tur*, *HM* 231:16.
31. Ibid.
32. B. *Bava Bathra* 89a and commentaries thereto; *Genevah* 8:8-11; *Tur*, *HM* 231:17, 18, and *BY* and *BaH* thereto. The talmudic source is interpreted by some to mean that the *total* length of the beam and the two lines suspended from it is to be twelve handbreadths, cf. *Bava Bathra*, ed. Soncino, p. 367.
33. B. *Bava Bathra* 89a; Maimonides, *Genevah* 8:8-11 and *Tur*, *HM* 231:17, 18. In some modern editions, the ceiling clearance is said to be twelve, rather than two, handbreadths. The correct reading is "two"; this is based on the texts of both Maimonides and *Tur*, as well as the Gemara. Cf. also the Vilna 1883 edition of the *Shulhan Arukh*.
34. *MM* to Maimonides, *Genevah* 8:8-11.
35. B. *Bava Bathra* 89b; Maimonides, *Genevah* 8:13, 14; *Tur*, *HM* 231:19.
36. B. *Bava Bathra* 89a; Maimonides, *Genevah* 8:15.
37. B. *Bava Bathra* 89a; Maimonides, *Genevah* 8:19.
38. B. *Bava Bathra* 90a; Maimonides, *Genevah* 8:17.
39. B. *Bava Mezia* 107b; Maimonides, *Genevah* 8:1.
40. Maimonides, *Genevah* 8:1 and *MM* thereto.
41. Maimonides, *Genevah* 8:1; B. *Bava Mezia* 107b.
42. B. *Bava Mezia* 107b; Maimonides, *Genevah* 8:2.
43. B. *Bava Mezia* 61b; Maimonides, *Genevah* 8:3; cf. also *MM* to Maimonides, ad loc.
44. Maimonides, *Genevah* 7:12; *Tur*, *HM* 231:25; cf. B. *Bava Bathra* 88b.
45. B. *Bava Bathra* 88b.
46. B. *Bava Bathra* 89a; Maimonides, *Genevah* 7:20.
47. Maimonides, *Mekhirah* 14:2; cf. B. *Bava Bathra* 90a f.
48. *Tur*, *HM* 231:26; cf. *BY* ad loc., citing Rabbenu Asher on this matter.
49. Maimonides, *Mekhirah* 14:1-2; *Tur*, *HM* 231:26 and *BY* thereto, citing Samuel b. Meir and Rabbenu Asher.
50. *Tur*, *HM* 231:26, citing Meir Abulafia.
51. *Tur*, *HM* 231:27; cf. Maimonides, *Genevah* 8:20, and B. *Bava Bathra* 89a.
52. B. *Bava Bathra* 91a; Maimonides, *Mekhirah* 14:3; *Tur*, *HM* 231:28.
53. *Tur*, *HM* 231:28.

54. Maimonides, *Mekhirah* 14:4; *B. Bava Bathra* 91a.
55. Ibid.
56. *B. Bava Bathra* 91a; Maimonides, *Mekhirah* 14:5; *Tur, HM* 231:29.
57. Ibid., cf. *B. Bava Bathra* 90b.
58. Maimonides, *Mekhirah* 14:5; and *B. Bava Bathra* 90b.
59. Cf. *BY* to *Tur, HM* 231:29, citing Samuel b. Meir.
60. *B. Bava Bathra* 90b; Maimonides, *Mekhirah* 14:6.
61. *B. Bava Bathra* 90b; Maimonides, *Mekhirah* 14:8.
62. *B. Bava Bathra* 9a; Maimonides, *Mekhirah* 14:9; *Tur, HM* 231:30.
63. Maimonides, *Mekhirah* 14:10 and *MM* thereto, citing Tosefta *Bava Mezia* 11:23 (ed. Zukermandel).
64. *Tur, HM* 231:30.
65. *MM* to Maimonides, *Mekhirah* 14:10, citing Nahmanides, who cites Albargeloni; cf. also *BY* to *Tur, HM* 231:30.
66. *B. Bava Bathra* 9a; Maimonides, *Mekhirah* 14:11; *Tur, HM* 231:30.
67. *Tur, HM* 231:30.
68. *BY* to ibid., citing Rabbenu Nissim.

No. 232 Notes

1. *B. Qiddushin* 42b; Maimonides, *Mekhirah* 15:1; *Tur, HM* 232:1.
2. Cf. *MM* to Maimonides, loc. cit.: the amount of surplus or lack is to be made good; the sale remains valid and binding.
3. *B. Qiddushin*, loc. cit.; cf. also *B. Gittin* 14a.
4. Cf. *B. Gittin*, loc. cit. Cf. Maimonides, *Mekhirah* 15:1.
5. *B. Bava Mezia* 63b f.; *Tur, HM* 232:2.
6. Ibid.
7. Cf. Rashi to *B. Bava Mezia* 64a.
8. Maimonides, *Malweh Weloweh* 4:10 and *MM* thereto.
9. *MM* to *Malweh Weloweh* 4:10.
10. Maimonides, *Mekhirah* 15:3 and *MM thereto*; cf. *Tur, HM* 232:4.
11. *MM* to Maimonides, *Mekhirah* 15:3.
12. *B. Bava Mezia* 80a; Maimonides, *Mekhirah* 15:4 and *MM* thereto.
13. Ibid.
14. Responsa of Rabbenu Asher, sec. 96, end. Cf. *Tur, HM* 232:5.
15. *BY* to *Tur, HM* 232:5 and *DM* ad loc., n. 1.
16. Maimonides, *Mekhirah* 15:5.
17. Maimonides, *Mekhirah* 15:6 and *MM* thereto.
18. The phrase "every defect" appears in brackets. The word for "defect" does not occur in the earliest Venice editions. It does appear from the first Cracow edition, 1580, until the Amsterdam 1664-66 edition.
    The phrase "every defect," which is the wording of Maimonides in *Mekhirah* 15:6, is adopted in the Amsterdam 1664-66 edition.
19. *Nimmuke Joseph* to *Bava Bathra*, ch. 7; cf. *BY* to *Tur, HM* 232:6, 7.
20. *B. Bava Mezia* 80a; Maimonides, *Mekhirah* 15:7; *Tur, HM* 232:8.
21. The word "if" appears in brackets. It is present in the earliest Venice editions, but it does not occur in the early Cracow editions and the other early

Notes

editions until the publication of the text in Prague 1628, although not every post-1628 edition has it. The phrasing with "if" is based on the *Tur*, *HM* 232:8.

22. *B. Bava Mezia* 80a; *Tur*, *HM* 232:8; cf. Maimonides, *Mekhirah* 15:9 and *MM* thereto.
23. Cf. *SMA*, n. 19.
24. *B. Qiddushin* 11a; Maimonides, *Mekhirah* 15:12 and *MM* thereto.
25. Cf. *MM* to Maimonides, *Mekhirah* 15:13, and *B. Bava Mezia* 80a; *Tur*, *HM* 232:9. Cf. also *B. Gittin* 86a.
26. *B. Bava Bathra* 92b and *B. Qiddushin* 11a; Maimonides, *Mekhirah* 15:13 and *MM* thereto; *Tur*, *HM* 232:9.
27. Ibid.
28. *Tur*, *HM* 232:9, citing Rabbenu Hananel.
29. *B. Hullin* 50b; Maimonides, *Mekhirah* 20:15; *Tur*, *HM* 232:10; cf. Maimonides, *Mekhirah* 16:6.
30. *B. Hullin* 50b; *Tur*, *HM* 232:10; Maimonides, *Mekhirah* 20:15.
31. Cf. Tosafot to *Hullin* 51a, s.v. *hamotzi*.
32. Cf. Maimonides, *Mekhirah* 16:6; *Tur*, *HM* 232:10.
33. *Tur*, *HM* 232:10.
34. Rabbenu Nissim to *Hullin*, ch. 3.
35. Maimonides, *Mekhirah* 16:6; *Tur*, *HM* 232:11.
36. Maimonides, *Mekhirah* 16:7; *Tur*, *HM* 232:11, cf. *SMA*, n. 32.
37. Maimonides, *Mekhirah* 16:8; cf. *B. Bava Mezia* 66b; *Tur*, *HM* 232:12.
38. *Tur*, *HM* 232:13, a responsum of Rabbenu Asher 102:7, on the word "three," which appears in some texts, cf. *SMA*, n. 34.
39. The word "large" appears in brackets although it does occur in the *Tur*'s version of the responsum, *Tur*, *HM* 232:13. The word does not appear in the text of the *Shulhan Arukh* until the Prague 1628 edition.
40. *Tur*, *HM* 232:14, a responsum of Rabbenu Asher 102:7.
41. Ibid.
42. Ibid.
43. *B. Bava Mezia* 42b; Maimonides, *Mekhirah* 16:9-10. *Tur*, *HM* 232:15.
44. *B. Bava Mezia* 42b.
45. Ibid. and Maimonides, *Mekhirah* 16:11 and *MM* thereto. *Tur*, *HM* 232:15.
46. Maimonides' version says that the party that bought from the broker should have examined the animal and returned it to the broker, who would in turn return it to *the first seller*, i.e., its previous owner. The *Tur*'s version of Maimonides says that the broker should, in these circumstances, return the animal to the previous owner.
The *Shulhan Arukh* has the broker returning the animal to the *first purchaser*, which makes no sense unless one interprets that party to be the original seller, the previous owner, who sold the animal to the broker. The version of the *Tur* appears to be the clearest statement.
47. *Tur*, *HM* 232:15, cf. RAshi to *Bava Mezia* 42b and Tosafot ad loc., s.v. *dene*.
48. Ibid.
49. The talmudic rule which precludes a person from swearing to something he may doubt is part of the commentary of *SMA* to this provision, *SMA*, n. 43.
50. *DM* to *Tur*, *HM* 232, n. 4, citing *Mordecai* to *Bava Mezia*, ch. 3, and *Bava Bathra*, ch. 5.

51. *Hagahot Asheri* and *Mordecai* to *Bava Mezia*, ch. 2, no. 258.
52. *Tur, HM* 232:16, a responsum of Rabbenu Asher 102:10.
53. *B. Bava Bathra* 9a-b; Maimonides, *Mekhirah* 16:1 and *MM* thereto; *Tur, HM* 232:18.
54. The word for "presumption (underlying, etc.)," *hezqatan*, first appears in this form in the Venice 1593-94 edition, cf. Maimonides, *Mekhirah* 16:1. In the earlier Venice and Cracow editions the form is *hizqan*, which can be taken to mean "he presumed them (to be, etc.)."
55. *MM* to Maimonides, *Mekhirah* 16:1, and *Tur, HM* 232:18.
56. *B. Bava Bathra* 93a; Maimonides, *Mekhirah* 16:2; *Tur, HM* 232:18.
57. *Tur, HM* 232:18, citing Meir Abulafia.
58. Maimonides, *Mekhirah* 16:3; *Tur, HM* 232:19.
59. The clause "after the buyer has informed the seller" appears in both Maimonides, *Mekhirah* 16:3 and *Tur, HM* 232:19. It does not appear in the text of the *Shulhan Arukh*, however, until the Amsterdam 1664-66 edition, and even then it is not found in all post-1664 editions. Cf. *SMA* ad loc., n. 51; Karo remarks on this very clause in both *BY*, *Tur*, ad loc., and in this *Kesef Mishneh* to Maimonides, ad loc.
60. *Tur, HM* 232:20, citing Meir Abulafia.
61. Ibid.
62. Maimonides, *Mekhirah* 16:3; *Tur, HM* 232:19.
63. Maimonides, *Mekhirah* 16:4 and *MM* thereto; *Tur, HM* 232:20.
64. Ibid.; cf. *Kesef Mishneh* to Maimonides, *Mekhirah* 16:4.
65. Cf. *SMA*, n. 56, for the basis of this parenthetical remark.
66. *B. Bava Bathra* 92a f.; Maimonides, *Mekhirah* 16:5; *Tur, HM* 232:21.
67. *Tur, HM* 232:21, citing Meir Abulafia.
68. Ibid. and *BY* thereto.
69. Ibid.
70. *Tur, HM* 232:22.
71. *Nimmuke Joseph* to *Bava Bathra*, ch. 6.
72. *Teshuvot Maimuniot* to *Mishpatim*, no. 13.

No. 223 Notes

1. *B. Bava Bathra* 83b; Maimonides, *Mekhirah* 17:1 and *MM* thereto; *Tur, HM* 233:1.
2. *B. Bava Bathra* 83b and Maimonides, *Mekhirah* 17:1; *Tur, HM* 233:2.
3. *B. Bava Bathra* 84a; *Tur, HM* 233:2.
4. *Tur, HM* 233:2.
5. Maimonides, *Mekhirah* 17:1; *Tur, HM* 233:3.
6. Israel Isserlein, *Terumath Hadeshen*, no. 322.
7. *Mordecai* to *Bava Bathra*, ch. 5; and *Hagahot Maimuniot* to *Mekhirah*, ch. 17, n. 1. But cf. *Sifthe Cohen* ad loc., n. 1.

No. 234 Notes

1. *B. Bekhoroth* 37a; Maimonides, *Mekhirah* 16:12; *Tur, HM* 231:1.
2. Ibid.
3. *B. Bekhoroth* 37a and *Tur, HM* 231:1; Maimonides, *Mekhirah* 16:13.

4. B. *Bekhoroth* 37a; Maimonides, *Mekhirah* 16:14; *Tur*, *HM* 234:2.
5. Maimonides, *Mekhirah* 16:14, and *Tur*, *HM* 234:2. Cf. to Maimonides ad loc.
6. Isaac b. Sheshet, Responsa, no. 499.
7. Cf. *MM* to Maimonides, *Mekhirah* 16:14.

No. 235 Notes

1. B. *Gittin* 59a, 65a; Maimonides, *Mekhirah* 29:16; *Tur*, *HM* 235:1. Cf. also *MM* to Maimonides ad loc.
2. B. *Gittin* 59a, 65a.
3. Responsa of Rabbenu Nissim, no. 49.
4. B. *Bava Bathra* 159b; cf. Maimonides, *Mekhirah* 29:6; *Tur*, *HM* 235:1 and 3, citing a responsum of Rabbenu Asher, sec. 1, end, and sec. 85, end.
5. Maimonides, *Mekhirah* 29:12; *Tur*, *HM* 235:12, citing Rabbenu Asher; cf. B. *Bava Bathra* 155b.
6. *Tur*, *HM* 235:1 and 3, and the responsum of Rabbenu Asher, sec. 85, end.
7. Ibid.
8. Nahmanides, Responsa, no. 5.
9. *Tur*, *HM* 235:4, citing a responsum of Rabbenu Asher, sec. 85, end.
10. B. *Ketubot* 77a; Maimonides, *Mekhirah* 29:7; *Tur*, *HM* 235:1.
11. Isaac b. Shesbet, Responsa, nos. 141, 168.
12. Rabbenu Nissim to *Ketubot*, ch. 6, end. Some modern editions have, in the last line of this gloss, literally "from his hand . . . from his hand," others have "from hand . . . from his hand." The latter text appears in all earlier editions of the gloss; the Ran text on which it is based uses different wording. The latter version also gives the sense of an immediate seizure of the property, which is not in point. The matter under notice is simply that if the buyer has taken the goods, they cannot be retrieved through the rabbinical legal process. The former phrasing, i.e., "his hand . . . his hand," appears to be the preferable reading. The *Darke Moshe* commentary has a version of this provision which also demonstrates the preferability of the former reading. *DM* to *Tur*, *HM* 235, n. 1.
13. B. *Gittin* 59a; Maimonides, *Mekhirah* 29:8.
14. Ibid.; cf. also Rabad to Maimonides ad loc.
15. Maimonides, *Mekhirah* 29:8; *Tur*, *HM* 235:5.
16. Cf. *MM* to Maimonides, *Mekhirah* 29:8.
17. Maimonides, *Mekhirah* 29:9.
18. Cf. *MM* to ibid.
19. Maimonides, *Mekhirah* 29:9.
20. Maimonides, *Mekhirah* 29:10.
21. *MM* to ibid.; cf. B. *Bava Mezia* 10b.
22. B. *Bava Mezia* 10b; *Tur*, *HM* 235:9 and Maimonides, *Mekhirah* 29:10.
23. Cf. B. *Qiddushin* 42a; Maimonides, *Mekhirah* 29:11; *Tur*, *HM* 235:10.
24. B. *Bava Bathra* 137b; cf. *MM* to Maimonides, *Mekhirah* 29:11.
25. Maimonides, *Mekhirah* 29:12; cf. B. *Bava Bathra* 155b.
26. Ibid.
27. *Hagahot Mordecai* to *Bava Mezia*.

28. Maimonides, *Mekhirah* 29:13; *Tur*, *HM* 235:13; cf. Samuel b. Meir to *Bava Bathra* 155a and Tosafot ad loc., s.v. *mokher*.
29. Maimonides, *Mekhirah* 29:13 and *MM* thereto; *Tur*, *HM* 235:13.
30. *Tur*, *HM* 235:13, citing Meir Abulafia.
31. *MM* to Maimonides, *Mekhirah* 29:13; *Tur*, *HM* 235:13 and *BY* thereto. The opinion of others is ascribed to the Geonim, who presumably require a degree of common sense even if age twenty has come and gone, cf. *Ba'er Hagolah* ad loc., and *BY*, citing Yom Tov Ashbili.
32. *B. Gittin* 59a; Maimonides, *Mekhirah* 29:14 and *MM* thereto.
33. *B. Bava Bathra* 155a; Maimonides, *Mekhirah* 29:15.
34. Ibid.
35. Ibid.
36. *Tur*, *HM* 235:14, citing Meir Abulafia, cf. para. 13.
37. Cf. *BY* ad loc., citing a responsum of Isaac b. Sheshet, no. 468.
38. *B. Bava Bathra* 154a; Maimonides, *Mekhirah* 29:16 and *MM* thereto.
39. *B. Bava Bathra* 155a; Maimonides, *Mekhirah* 29:16.
40. Maimonides, *Mekhirah* 29:16.
41. Maimonides, *Mekhirah* 29:17; *Tur*, *HM* 235:16.
42. Maimonides, *Mekhirah* 29:17; *Tur*, *HM* 235:16.
43. Maimonides, *Mekhirah* 29:17, cf. *MM* thereto; *Tur*, *HM* 235:16.
44. *Tur*, *HM* 235:18, citing Meir Abulafia.
45. Ibid., citing R. Jonah.
46. Ibid., citing Rabbenu Asher.
47. *BY* to *Tur*, *HM* 235:13, citing responsa of Solomon b. Adret.
48. *BY* to *Tur*, *HM* 235:18, citing R. Yeruham.
49. *B. Gittin* 59a; Maimonides, *Mekhirah* 29:2 and *MM* thereto, cf. *Gittin* 67a; *Tur*, *HM* 235:19.
50. *B. Gittin* 71a; Maimonides, *Mekhirah* 29:3 and *MM* thereto; *Tur*, *HM* 235:19.
51. *Tur*, *HM* 235:20, citing a responsum of Rabbenu Asher, sec. 85.
52. *B. Bava Bathra* 155a; Maimonides, *Mekhirah* 29:4 and *MM* thereto; *Tur*, *HM* 235:21, 22,; cf. *B. Hagigah* 3a.
53. *Mordecai* to *Bava Mezia*, ch. 9.
54. *B. Ketubot* 20a; Maimonides, *Mekhirah* 29:5.
55. Cf. *BY* to *Tur*, *HM* 235:23, citing Rabbenu Asher and Tosafot to *Ketubot* 21a, s.v. *weoge*.
56. *B. Eruvin* 65a; Maimonides, *Mekhirah* 29:18 and *MM* thereto.
57. Cf. *B. Bava Bathra* 167a; Maimonides, *Mekhirah* 30:1.
58. Maimonides, *Mekhirah* 30:2 and *MM* thereto, citing Hai Gaon.
59. Maimonides, *Mekhirah* 30:6 and *MM* thereto; cf. *B. Gittin* 52a.
60. Maimonides, *Mekhirah* 30:7 and *MM* thereto.
61. Maimonides, *Mekhirah* 30:7; cf. supra 195:11.

No. 236 Notes

1. *B. Gittin* 55b, cf. *B. Gittin* 58b.; Maimonides, *Gezelah* 10:3 and *MM* thereto; *Tur*, *HM* 236:1.
2. Rabbenu Nissim to *Gittin*, ch. 5.

3. Isaac b. Sheshet, Responsa, no. 290; Israel Isserlein, *Pesaqim Uketabim*, *Pesaqim*, no. 69.
4. *Mordecai* to *Gittin*, ch. 5.
5. *Tur*, *HM* 236:1.
6. *B. Gittin* 55b; *Tur*, *HM* 236:1.
7. *B. Gittin* 55b; *Tur*, *HM* 236:2.
8. On the matter of the acquiescence, cf. *SMA*, n. 8; *B. Gittin* 58a; *Tur*, *HM* 236:2.
9. *Tur*, *HM* 236:2; cf. *B. Bava Bathra* 48a; cf. *SMA*, n. 9.
10. *B. Gittin* 58b; *Tur*, *HM* 236:3.
11. *Tur*, *HM* 236:3 and *BY* thereto, citing Nahmanides.
12. Isaac b. Sheshet, Responsa, no. 207.
13. *B. Gittin* 58b; *Tur*, *HM* 236:3.
14. *B. Gittin* 58b f.; Maimonides, *Gezelah*, 10:1, 2, and *MM* thereto.
15. Ibid.
16. *B. Gittin* 58b and Maimonides, *Gezelah* 10:1, 2.
17. *Tur*, *HM* 236:8.
18. Ibid., citing Rabbenu Gershom.
19. *Tur*, *HM* 236:6, citing a responsum of Rabbenu Asher, sec. 95, end.
20. Ibid.
20. Ibid.
21. *Tur*, *HM* 236:7, the responsum of Rabbenu Asher continues into this paragraph (cf. n. 19).
22. *Mordecai* to *Bava Qamma*, ch. 6; *Hagahot Mordecai* to *Bava Mezia*.
23. *Tur*, *HM* 236:5.
24. *Mordecai* to *Bava Mezia*, ch. 6, no. 341; cf. Maimonides, *Gezelah* 5:13.
25. Cf. *BY* to *Tur*, *HM* 190, end.

No. 237 Notes

1. *B. Qiddushin* 59a; *Tur*, *HM* 237; cf. Maimonides, *Ishut* 9:17.
2. *Tur*, loc. cit.
3. *Tur*, *HM* 237, citing Rabbenu Tam.
4. The verb for "come forward," or "precede," appears in brackets. In this context, it is rendered as "preempt." In more modern editions, the verb is suffixed with the third-singular masculine pronominal object, i.e., "to precede him." The earliest editions omit the word; a form of it without suffix first appears in the Cracow 1618-19 edition; the modern form with suffix first appears in the Amsterdam 1664-66 edition. The rule is based on *BY* to *Tur*, *HM* 237; *Mordecai*, *Bava Qamma*, ch. 1, citing Meir of Rothenburg.
5. Cf. n. 4, end.
6. David Cohen, Responsa, no. 31.
7. Rashi to *Qiddushin* 59a; cf. *BY* to *Tur*, *HM* 237, Rabbenu Nissim citing Nahmanides to *Qiddushin*, ch. 3.
8. The word "item" appears in parentheses. It appears in the *Shulhan Arukh* text in the Prague 1628 edition. The insertion is based on the reading of *Tur*, *HM* 237.
9. Cf. note 7.

10. *BY* to *Tur, HM* 237, citing *Mordecai*; cf. *DM* to *Tur*, ad loc., n. 1.
11. Meir of Padua, Responsa, no. 41 (40); cf. Louis Finkelstein, *Jewish Self-Government in the Middle Ages* (New York: Feldheim, 1964), pp. 95, 304-406, see especially p. 304, n. 1, where Finkelstein cites R. Meir's responsum no. 40.
12. *BY* to *Tur, HM* 237, citing Tosafot to *B. Qiddushin* 59a, s.v. *oni*.
13. Ibid.

No. 238 Notes

1. *B. Bava Bathra* 167b; *Tur, HM* 238:1. Cf. Maimonides, *Malweh Weloweh* 24:1.
2. *B. Bava Mezia* 13a; *Tur, HM* 238:3 and 5.
3. *B. Bava Bathra* 167b; *Tur, HM* 238:1.
4. Ibid.
5. *Tur, HM* 238:2, citing Nahmanides.
6. *Mordecai* to *Bava Bathra*, ch. 6, end.
7. *B. Bava Bathra* 167b; *Tur, HM* 238:2; cf. Maimonides, *Malweh Weloweh* 24:2.
8. *B. Bava Bathra* 167b. *Tur, HM* 238:4, citing Joseph Halevi.
9. *Tur, HM* 238:5, citing Meir Abulafia.
10. *Ibid.*, citing Nahmanides.
11. Ibid., cf. Solomon b. Adret, Responsa, no. 1136.
12. Solomon b. Adret, Responsa, no. 981.

No. 239 Notes

1. *B. Bava Bathra* 168b, cf. Maimonides, *Malweh Weloweh* 23:11 and *MM* thereto; *Tur, HM* 239:1.
2. *BY* to *Tur*, loc. cit., citing Solomon b. Adret.
3. *B. Bava Bathra* 169b; *Tur*, loc. cit.
4. *Tur*, loc. cit., citing R. Isaac.
5. The word "document" appears in brackets. The word first appears in *Shulhan Arukh* in the Prague 1628 edition. The insertion is based both on the reading of *Tur* 239:1 and on *B. Bava Bathra* 169b.
6. *B. Bava Bathra* 171b, cf. Maimonides, *Malweh Weloweh* 23:7 and *MM* thereto; *Tur, HM* 239:2.
7. *MM* to *Malweh Weloweh* 23:7, citing Nahmanides and *Ittur*.

No. 240 Notes

1. *B. Ketubot* 44a; Maimonides, *Zekhiah Umattanah* 5:8; *Tur, HM* 240:1.
2. Cf. *B. Bava Mezia* 14a.
3. *Tur, HM* 240:2; Maimonides, *Zekhiah Umattanah* 5:8.
4. *Tur, HM* 240:2, citing Rabbenu Asher.
5. Ibid., citing Meir Abulafia.
6. *B. Ketubot* 44a; Maimonides, *Zekhiah Umattaneh* 5:9 and *MM* thereto; *Tur, HM* 240:1.
7. *B. Ketubot* 44a; Maimonides, *Zekhiah Umattaneh* 5:9; *Tur, HM* 240:1.
8. *B. Ketubot* 44a; Maimonides, *Zekhiah Umattaneh* 5:9.
9. Rabbenu Nissim to *Ketubot*, ch. 4, cf. *DM* to *Tur, HM* 240, n. 1.
10. *Mordecai* to *Ketubot*, ch. 4, no. 153; *Hagahot Mordecai* to *Bava Bathra*.

11. *B. Ketubot* 94b; Maimonides, *Zekhiah Umattanah* 5:6.
12. The word "not" appears in brackets. It does not occur in the Venice editions of 1565, 1567, 1574, or 1578. This rather important insertion, which is based on Maimonides' text, *Zekhiah Umattanah* 5:6, shows up in the first Cracow edition, 1580, and has appeared in all subsequent editions.
13. Maimonides, *Zekhiah Umattaneh* 5:6 and *MM* thereto.
14. *Tur, HM* 240:3, citing Rabbenu Hananel.
15. Ibid., citing R. Isaac; cf. also Tosafot to *Ketubot* 94a, s.v. *shne*, and *Mordecai* to *Ketubot*, ch. 10, n. 243.
16. Maimonides, *Zekhiah Umattanah* 5:7.
17. *MM* to ibid.
18. Cf. *B. Ketubot* 94b.
19. Cited in the name of R. Yom Tov Ashbili in *BY* to *Tur, HM* 240:2.
20. Cf. *BY* to *Tur, HM* 253:11, citing Solomon b. Adret, *Toledot Adam*, no. 272; cf. also *DM* to *Tur, HM* 240, n. 2.

Index

acquisitions (see *kinyan* this index)
adverse possession 124
agents 76, 131, 213, 214, 217, 252
aleatory contract 60, 61, 71, 72
aleatory forfeiture 128, 129, 131, 132-141
animals
  barter of 64
  constructive fraud 212, 216
  dead 197
    time of death 197-199
  deceptive practice 220
  defective 236, 238-243, 245, 246
  draft 188
  firstborn 248
  form of acquisition (see *kinyan* this heading and this index)
  future offspring 143, 156, 190, 196
  implements for 188, 189
  kinyan (see also *kinyan* this index) 75, 81, 94-97, 108, 111, 113, 148
  ritually defective 197-199, 248
  sale of portion 190, 191
  transfer of 57
  unfair price 212, 216
  utensils on 113
  yokes 183-190
apartments 162
appraisals 217
appraisers 106, 127, 128, 212-214, 217
appurtenances (see also fixtures, servitudes, this index)
  to land, acquisitions of 87
  to leases 98
  to presshouses 166
artisan's objects 216, 217 *kinyan* (see also *kinyan* this index) 109
Asher b. Yahiel, R. 155, 156
asmakhta (see aleatory contract, conditions, this index)
assessors (see appraisers this index)
airspace 152, 158-161
Babylonian Talmud 5, 24, 155
bailments 65
barter 14, 20, 211, 212
  ancestor of true sale 20
  Jewish law 21, 22
  kerchief exchange 31
  kinyan (see also *kinyan* this index) 21, 22, 36, 44
  Roman law 21
bathhouses 165, 166
beehives 191-193
  yield of 156
biblical law 36, 97, 98, 102, 103, 132, 195-197, 216, 227, 242, 243, 248, 249, 252, 259
bill of particulars 239
bill of sale 164
bonds 267
books 262
boundaries 182, 184-188, 270
Boyden, E.A. 2
burden of proof 178, 185, 196-199, 208, 241, 242, 258, 266
burial plot 175, 176
buyer present 238, 265
  duty to inspect 238, 239, 242, 243
  duty to notify seller of defects 245
  reasonable reliance (see duty to inspect this heading)
capacity (see also various classes of individuals, this index)
  to consent 38-40
  to sue 41
carts 188, 189
caveat emptor 57
caves 158, 159, 164-166, 176
charity 141, 154, 155

cisterns 157-159, 164-166, 176, 191
city 166, 167
Code of Jewish Jurisprudence 2
coins
   constructive fraud 210, 211
   counting 50, 210, 211, 234-236
   located on land 150
   payment in 50, 114, 115, 234-236
   transfer of 49, 116, 117, 206, 207
   unfair price 210, 211
   weight 210, 211
collateral security 77
commandments 205, 218, 227
commercial custom 44
compromise settlement 122, 123
concealment (see fraud this index)
conditions (see also conditional
   contract this index) 14, 15, 44,
   62, 76, 128-131
   aleatory 60, 61, 71
   defined 59
   expressed 61, 130, 131
   failure of 60, 129, 130, 138
   money matters 61
   option to repurchase 61
   reserved rights 146, 162
   resolutive 59-61
   suspensive 59-61
   unstated 130
conditional contract (see also conditions this index)
   defined 59
   non-existent subject matter 61
   Roman law 59
consecration 154-156, 214, 215
consent
   bilateral 38
   capacity (see various classes of
      individuals, this heading)
   contract, required for 14, 16, 17,
      22, 38, 52, 53
   duress 53
   erroneous 52
   formal forms 17
   fraud 52
   good faith 40

   inadequate price 52
   Jewish law 22, 29, 38, 52-54
   kinyan, required for (see also
      kinyan this index) 29, 38, 40,
      260
   negotiation of 38, 52-57, 59
   negotiation for 40
   Roman contract 17, 22, 29, 54, 55
   withdrawal 54
   written 17
consideration (see price this index)
contract conditions (see conditions,
   conditional contract this index)
contract promises 15
contract of sale, requisites
   bilateral 14, 15, 38
   capacity 38, 39
   consent 14, 16, 17, 22
   good faith 15, 16, 26
   Jewish law 22, 23, 26
   kinyan (see *kinyan* this index)
   mutuality 14, 15
   price 16, 41
   res 16, 41
   Roman contract 14-17, 22, 25
converts 86, 88, 168, 219
corpse 148
counting 81, 234
courtyards 165, 168
craft regulations 233, 234
custom, local 53, 55, 59, 67, 68,
   77, 83, 87, 110, 120, 165, 168,
   169, 183, 191, 221, 222, 224, 227-
   231, 233, 236, 237, 246, 269
date palms 147, 170, 171, 174, 175,
   186
deaf-mutes 255, 256
debt
   fictional 138, 139
   for food 255
   gambling 135
declaration of protest 122-125
defective products (see also various
   subject matter headings this in-
   index) 53, 54, 169, 236-246
   animals 64

buyer unaware 55
discernible 238-240, 242, 243
failure to reveal 53
latent 238-240, 242, 243
notice of 55
non-discernible 238-240, 242, 243
patent (see also patent defects this index) 238-240, 242, 243
reparable 236, 237
remedy for 236-238
ritually unfit 64
temporary 54, 236, 237
defective title, curing 111
demand for payment 78-80
repeated demands 78-81
Denburg, Dr. Chaim 2
dicta promissave 15, 58
divisible transaction 171
dovecote 191-193
included with city 166
included with field 168
duress 53, 122-126
defined 124, 126
negating consent 53
dying person (see *in extremis* this index)
earnest money 78, 81
easements 157, 158, 162, 163, 168, 170, 173, 237
extinguishment 164
of necessity 158, 163
Elijah the Prophet 194
emptio venditio 140, 18, 26, 29, 34, 52, 58, 60
employment contracts 216, 263
English law 13
ethical business practices (see also rabbinical condemnation this index) 6, 7, 15, 20, 24-26
excavations 159, 160
excommunication 140, 264
expectancies 148, 149
express terms 15
extortion (see also extorted property, non-Jews this index) 67

extorted property (see also non-Jews this index) 67, 259-262
restitution of 259-262
restitution of additional damages 261
faithless persons 120, 121
fields (see also land this index) 167-173, 175, 177-179, 182-185
description of 185-188
irrigated 166
warranties 201, 203
fixtures (see also appurtenances, servitudes this index)
house 163
leased property 98
food 244, 245, 255
contracts for 51, 52, 190
hoarding 51
inclusion of refuse material 53
kinyan for (see also *kinyan* this index) 102, 149
price regulation 51, 52, 232, 233
warranties 59
forgiving of obligation 123, 124, 141
formal contract
verbal contract 22
verbal contract, unenforceable in Jewish law 22
requirement for *kinyan* (see also *kinyan* this index) 23
found property 113
fraud 1
buyer, duty to inspect 239
concealment as constituting 56
constructive (see also unfair price this heading) 52, 54, 55, 67, 70, 123, 142, 247, 248, 251
deceit 218-224, 238, 239
defective goods 53
duress 53, 123
implied (see constructive fraud this heading)
incidental 19
intentional 19, 52, 53, 217, 219

kinyan, effect of 209
   measuring 217, 230
   medieval law 19
   mistake of fact 19, 52
   non-Jews 67
   ona'ah (see *ona'ah* this index)
   price, unfair (see unfair price this heading)
   remedies 19, 52, 205
   unfair price 50, 70, 142, 189, 205-218, 234, 247, 248
   unintentional 52
   waiver of 206-208, 212, 213
   weights 217
frauds, statute of (see also instruments, written this index) 65, 66, 77, 166, 255, 256
freedom of bargaining 19
fruit 143, 147
futurus 40, 42, 43
gambling 135, 136, 142
gardens 181, 182, 184, 231
Gershom, R. 264
gifts 86, 91, 110, 120-124, 126, 130, 132, 133, 141, 143, 145-147, 151, 157, 162, 163, 168, 189, 193, 202, 220, 249, 250, 252, 253, 257, 263, 265, 266, 268-270
   causa mortis 143, 145, 249, 253, 270
good faith
   coins 49
   contract requisite 15, 16, 26
   defined 15, 40
   kinyan after (see also *kinyan* this index) 41
   price, as affected by 41
   Roman contract 15, 16
   showing of 145
   withdrawal, allowing for 41
guardians 214, 250, 251, 256, 257
handshake
   evidencing consent 140
   evidencing *kinyan* (see also *kinyan* this index) 140

Hanukah, The Laws of 2
heirs (see also inheritance this index) 146, 149, 217, 218, 231, 260, 267
hoarding 51, 233
holy days 36, 38, 102, 257
houses 156-159, 161-164, 166, 168, 184
   defined 156, 157
humiliation 139
hypothec 132
illegal contract 141, 203
immediate payment
   defined 80
implied terms 15
incentives to purchase, distribution by shopkeeper 222
incompetents 39, 249, 252, 253, 255, 256
inebriates 39, 256
in extremis 148, 154, 269
inheritance (see also heirs this index) 250, 253-255
institutions, sacred and charitable 103, 111
instruments, written (see also frauds, statute of, *kinyan* this index) 77, 257, 265
   boundaries 270
   conditions, setting forth 129
   consent of seller required for 265
   duplicate 267-269
   evidence of *kinyan* (see also *kinyan* this heading and this index) 151
   extorted property 260
   kinyan (see also *kinyan* this index) 82, 143, 151, 169, 265, 269
   land transfers 169, 199
   lost 266, 267
   minors 251, 257
   multiple copies 267-269
   mutes 255
   non-existent subject matter 143

non-Jews 87-89
paid for by buyer 266
postdated 267
post mortem 150
transfers upon death 150
when written 257, 265
intent
  expression of 155
  kinyan (see also *kinyan* this index) 142
  transfers 131, 134
  transfers of indeterminate amounts 142
Israel 233
Jewish history 11
Jewish jurists 11
Jewish moral attitudes 6, 7
Justinian's law 55, 65
Kadushin, Rabbi J. L. 2
Kaplan, Aryeh 2
kerchief exchange (see also *kinyan* this index) 22, 31, 72, 73, 114, 141, 144, 147, 251, 252
  abating forfeiture 140
  barter 31
  conditions placed thereon 32, 59
  land 27, 31, 75
  moveables 31, 37
  nullification of 32
  requirements for 31, 47
  Sabbath 37
  simultaneous acquisitions 32
kinyan (see also courtyard, handshake, kerchief exchange, oath, price, payment of, instrument, written, various subject matter headings this index)
  agents 38, 39, 109, 131
  aleatory contract 71
  animal, to an 148
  bailment 65
  barter 36
  benefit to acquiree 102, 105, 121
  Biblical rules 36
  bilateral 26
  buyer present 31, 38, 91, 179
  buyer in possession 34, 35
  capacity 38, 39
  charitable institutions 103
  consent 29, 32, 38, 40, 60-62
  converts 86, 88
  conveyance, act of 23, 62
  corpse, to a 148
  custom, local controlling 110
  defined 72, 73
  effected by (see forms of this heading)
  effect of 75
  form of, generally 22, 23, 26, 27, 30, 34, 35, 59
  formal contract 26
  forms of, particular
    by agreement 34, 35
    by courtyard 252
    by custom, mercantile (see by mercantile custom this subheading)
    by delivery 94, 99
    by deposit in acquiree's property 101-109
    by good faith showing 145
    by grasping 33
    by handshake 37, 110, 140
    by kerchief exchange 27, 30-32, 37, 72, 73, 114, 251, 252
    by leading animal 33, 95
    by lifting 33, 34, 64, 65, 94, 95, 97-100, 104, 106, 109, 113
    by mark of buyer, placing 37, 109, 110, 120
    by measuring 107-109
    by measuring vessels 108, 109
    by mercantile custom 37, 120
    by oath 37, 140
    by payment 24, 27, 28, 30, 31, 35-37, 87-89, 93, 97-99, 101-103
    by payment, part 29, 45, 80, 81
    by possession, taking 27, 29, 50, 51, 77, 83-87, 89, 93, 94, 107, 109, 113

by pulling 33, 34, 94-100, 104, 106, 109, 113, 251, 252
by pulling, measuring as 107, 108
by repeated demands for part payment 29, 45, 80, 81
by riding animal 33, 95, 96
by symbolic exchange (see also by kerchief exchange this sub-heading 89, 93
by vow (see by oath this sub-heading)
by words 128
by written instrument 27, 29, 82-89, 93, 151, 169, 251, 265, 268-270
fraud, control of 209
functions of 26, 27
gift 35
good faith 25, 26, 40, 41
holy days 36, 38, 102
inclusions 161
in extremis, transferor in 148
intent 131, 142, 108
knowledge of transferee 256, 257
minors 249-252
mistake, under 234, 235
mistake of quality, under 247
non-Jews 67, 87-89
of (see subject matter this heading)
orphans 36, 103
perfecting obligation to perform 23, 26, 116, 127
physical substance required 151
place, determined by 96, 99, 100, 102, 104, 105, 107, 108, 112, 162
possession, transferring 23
price, disputed 193
price, specified 106-109, 127
price, unfair 205-206
quantity, specified 106-109
rabbinic ordinance 151
requirements of 29, 31, 32, 38, 40, 42, 60-62, 83, 91, 95, 106-110, 121, 127, 131, 142, 151
res, specific 42
retroactive 60, 62, 97, 127-129, 132, 136, 137
risk of loss, shifting 25, 63
Sabbath, 38, 93
sacred institutions 103
seller, presence of 83, 95, 110
slaves 257
stipulations controlling 28-33, 37, 39, 59, 60, 98, 99, 110, 112, 113, 120
subject matter, particular, *kinyan* of (see also various subject matter headings this index)
of abandoned property 144, 145
of airspace 152
of animals 33, 75, 81, 94-97, 108, 113
of animals, lead 95
of apartments 162
of beehives, yield of 154-156
of box contents 113
of coins 116, 117
of consecrated property 154
of deposited property 150
of diverse property as lot 112, 113
of dovecotes, yield of 154-156
of easements 158
of expectancies 148, 149
of found property 113
of houses 156-159, 161
of kosher meat 36
of land 24, 27-31, 75-77
of land by boundaries 186-188
of land by trees 172-174
of lost property 150
of money located on land 150
of money, uncounted 211
of moveables 24, 25, 31, 33, 35-37, 75, 81, 97-109, 113, 156
of moveables connected with land 35, 110, 111, 117, 118, 150
of non-existent property 61,

144, 148, 150, 154, 156
of notes, promissory 151
of ownerless property 89
of poor, property designated for 154
of security 28, 77, 133
of sellers, property not within control or ownership of 148
of separable property 150
of ships 33, 34
of slaves 32, 93, 94, 112
of vow, property subject to 154
of wagers 136
of wine 143
successive sales 35, 36
symbolic exchange, objects useable for 90-92, 114-118
third party, through 27, 28, 38-40
title, transferring 23, 62
transferring possession (see possession, transferring this heading)
transferring title (see title, transferring this heading)
unborn persons 147-148
unilateral contracts 37
warranties 26
withdrawal, time to 92
witnesses 29, 31
Kosher Code, The 2
kosher meat 219, 240, 248, 249
laches 122, 206-208, 255, 258, 260-262
laesio enormis 46, 47
in Jewish law 47, 48
land and land transfers
acquired for use and produce 154
adjoining 263, 268
appurtenances 87, 110, 111
attachments to 87, 110, 111
boundaries 182, 185-188
coins included with 117, 118
conditions, subject to 130-132
constructive fraud 123, 214, 216, 217

damages, in lieu of money 246
deaf mute 255
defective 236, 237, 241
descriptions 185-187
dwelling, for 164
extorted 258-262
fluctuating price 181
gardens, for 181, 182
gifts 168
hypothecation 132
included with trees 172-174
incompetents 256
inebriates 256
kinyan (see also *kinyan* this index) 75-87, 122, 128, 131
landmarks 182
lease of 154
limited duration 153
local custom 169
measurement 177-179, 182, 231, 232
measurement, determining price 179-182
measurement, return after 179-182
minors 250-255, 257
money combined with 150
mortgaged 262
moveables combined with 150
non-Jews 65, 87-89
orphans 257
ownership 258
planting, for 176-178, 182
poor quality 78, 79, 82, 266
portion, sale of 183, 184
possession 258
purpose of buyer's use 153
reserving trees 174
return of (see measurement, return of after this heading)
slaves included with 112
subject to dispute 203
subject to lawsuit 203
survey 185-187
trees, included with 172-174
unfair price 214, 216, 217
untillable 176-181

Index

valuation of 181-183
warranty against eviction 199
wicked persons 263
written instruments 169, 265-270
landmarks 182
language
    local 169, 183, 189, 190
    ordinary people's 162
leases 76, 86, 88, 93, 99, 110, 153, 154, 188, 215, 216, 241, 251, 252, 263, 264
Levin, S.I. 2
limitations (time to bring suit)
    coins, in event of sale of 49
    error, in event of fundamental 236
    error, in event of in price 48
    repurchase from extortionist 258, 259
    rescission 48, 206-210, 236
    underpayment 48, 206-210, 216
loans 131, 264
    money 150, 151
    secured 131
local custom (see custom, local this index)
Maggid Mishneh 181
Maimonedes 5, 22, 141, 155, 156, 178, 181, 216
manuscript transmission 4
mark, buyer's (see also *kinyan* this index) 37, 120
market conditions, description of 232, 233
matrimonial proposals 139
non-matrimonial proposals 138
measures (see also weight this index) 227-232, 234
measurement (see also *kinyan* this index)
    deceit regarding 217
merchantability (see also warranty, this index) 220-227, 236-245, 247
    buyer, duty to inspect 238, 239, 242, 243
    remedy for lack of 223, 224, 237, 238, 241, 242
medieval law
    civil law 12, 13, 47, 54, 55
    contracts 19
    incidental fraud 54
    mistake of fact 54
minors (see also orphans this index) 249-256
    capacity 39, 40
    unfair price 49
    transfers by 257
mistakes 18, 52, 55, 171, 198, 217, 334, 247
    fundamental 198, 236-238, 240-242, 244, 246
money
    Biblical law 21
    collateral security 28
    counting error 81
    holy days 38
    instrument of transfer, in lieu of 28
    Jewish law 21
    kinyan, use of as (see also *kinyan* this index) 14, 24, 28
    land exchanged for 75-83
    moveables exchanged for 89
    partial payment 77-79
    payment, as form of *kinyan* (see *kinyan* this heading and this index)
    Sabbath 38
    use of, as form of *kinyan* (see *kinyan* this heading and this index)
moral obligations 194
mortgages 144, 255, 262, 263
mourners 220
moveables
    constructive fraud 123, 209, 214, 216, 217
    deaf mutes 255
    defective 236
    description of 185
    disputed price 193

extorted 262
gift of 193
incompetents 256
inebriates 256
instruments of transfer, duplicate 269
instruments of transfer, multiple 269, *kinyan* (see also *kinyan* this index) 75, 97-118, 122, 128, 155, 184
local custom controlling 169
located on land 110, 111, 150, 165, 167
located on slaves 112
notes 250
oath for 197
orphans
sale of 193
slaves acquired with 112
slaves, on 112
subject to dispute 203
subject to lawsuit 203
unfair price 209, 214, 216, 217
warranty against eviction 199
wicked persons 263
mutes 255
nonactionable complaint 201, 202
non-Jews (see also extorted property, land, *kinyan* this index) 236
adjoining land owners 263
contracts with 65-67, 87-89, 227
constructive fraud 214
extortion 257-262
fraud upon 219, 227
mortgages to 262
non-Jewish law controlling 89, 138
presumed to lie 198
seizure of property by 200
transfers from 262
transfers to 260
unfair advantage 264
unfair price 214
notarial error 58, 199
notes (of debt) 122, 137, 151, 214, 215, 250

notice
of defect in property 55
oaths (see also *kinyan*, vows this index) 140, 141, 144, 155, 194-198, 216, 227, 242, 243, 259
oil 108, 222-224, 232, 233, 242
olive press 165, 166, 168
ona'ah (see also fraud, price, speech this index) 46-52, 69, 70
defined 46
option to repurchase 61
orchards 183, 184
orphans (see also minors this index) 214, 250, 256, 257
capacity 39, 40
constructive fraud 214
guardians of 202
kinyan (see also *kinyan* this index) 36, 103, 111
unfair price 214
warranties 202
ownership 62, 64, 243
ownerless property 89, 263
partners 217, 218, 231, 234
patent defects (see also defective property this index) 55, 57
buyer's responsibility 57
obvious 58
slaves 57
pavements 158
performance
contracts
Roman law 18, 19
time of 19
prevention of 138
pits
defined 157
easement to 158
included with city 166
included with courtyard 165
included with house 163
reserved 158, 159
planting 176-180, 182
pledge 78, 81, 120, 131, 132, 139, 140, 144

Poland 139
poor
  property designated for 154
possession, taking (see *kinyan* this index)
postdating 267
predated instrument 82
press house 165, 166
pretium iustum 46, 47
price
  adequacy 16, 20, 46-52, 123
  ascertainable 16, 45
  assessors setting 127, 128
  certainty 45, 46
  constructive fraud (see unfair price this heading)
  control by rabbinical court 51, 52, 232
  custom, local regulating 51
  disputes 193
  excessive 189
  fixing 234
  fluctuating 181, 208, 209, 233, 247
  former agreement to 193
  fraud, constructive (see unfair price this heading)
  good faith effected by 41
  inflation causing 233
  instrument, written 266
  kinyan (see also *kinyan* this index) 26, 29, 34, 77, 78, 106, 127, 141, 251
  local custom regulating 51
  measurement setting 179-182
  money, to be in 16, 46
  obligation to pay 18, 22, 34, 37
  part payment as constituting *kinyan* (see also *kinyan* this heading and this index) 29, 34, 77, 78
  payment as *kinyan* (see *kinyan* this heading and this index)
  payment giving rise to rabbinical condemnation 119-121
  payment prior to *kinyan* (see also *kinyan* this heading and this index) 41, 97, 98
  purpose indicated by 245, 246
  rabbinical condemnation 119-121
  rabbinical court controlling 51, 52, 232
  regulation by rabbinical court 51, 52, 232
  regulation by local custom 51
  requirement of contract 16, 45, 106
  restoration of 125
  restoration of for forbidden subject matter 248, 249
  Roman contract of sale 16, 22, 46, 50
  setting 22
    assessors 127, 128
    measurement 179-182
    third party 50, 106
  specificity 38, 106, 127, 141
  third party setting 50, 106
  time for payment of 66
  unfair 46-52, 55, 142, 189, 205-218, 234, 247, 248, 251, 263
    exemptions from 49
    waiver of rights regarding 49
  valuation 191
  written instruments 266
profits of sellers 232
proof, burden (see burden of proof this index)
quiet enjoyment, warranty of (see also warranty this index) 41, 42
rabbinical condemnation 37, 40, 109
  form of 119
  minors 251
  withdrawal from transaction 119-121, 142, 143, 245, 251
rabbinical court 1, 6, 51, 52, 67, 119, 122, 124, 131, 135, 137, 138, 143, 144, 194, 199, 200, 202, 203, 214, 216, 217, 250-252, 256, 257, 260, 261, 269

330

  date palms 170, 171
  defective subject matter 169
  failure to specify 192
  for another 153
  gift 168
  implied 159, 160, 176
  land between trees 172
  pits 157
  poor quality property 169, 170
  structures 162
  subsurface 159
  trees 169, 170, 172
  vines 170
restitution
  effected by *kinyan* (see also *kinyan* this index) 209
  false weights and measures 232
  right to 207, 212
risk of loss 63, 226, 227, 240, 245
  animals 64
  artisan's objects 64
  aspect of ownership 63, 198, 199, 226, 227
  defective goods 64
  money paid prior to *kinyan* (see also *kinyan* this index) 101
  passage of 63, 64, 98, 198
  Roman law
  warranty 65
roadway 175
Roman Catholic canon law 12, 13, 19, 45-47, 51
Roman contract of sale 14
  enforceable *ex bona fide* 19
  fundamental requisites 14-17, 22, 38
Roman law of sale 12-14, 54-59, 61-63, 65
  contrasted with barter 21
ruins 159, 160
Sabbath 93, 210, 257
sacred purpose (see also charity, consecration this index) 154-156, 168, 214, 215
sale, defined 14

sample, sale by 56, 227
security 133, 135, 136, 139, 140, 150, 151
seller, obligation of liberality 170
servitudes (see also appurtenances, fixtures, this index) 156-158, 165
Shavuot 226
ships 99, 100, 188
Shulhan Arukh
  commentary on 13
  contents of 1, 13
  history of 4, 5
  translations of 2
simpon 239
slaves 257
  acquired with land 112
  acquired with moveables 112
  acquisition of 93, 94, 112, 184
  capacity 39
  constructive fraud 214-216
  contracts for 46, 57, 58, 190
  deceptive practices 220
  defective 236, 239, 240
  future offspring 143, 190, 196
  included with 190
  included with ship 188
  patent defects 57
  portion of, sale 190
  real property, treated as 197
  unfair price 214-216
  warranty against eviction 58, 199
Spain 138, 139
speech (see also *ona'ah* this index)
  abusive 70, 71
  misuse of 218-220, 223, 224
standing to sue 41
stipulations (see also conditions, expressed this index)
  between wagerors 136
  constructive fraud 212, 213
  controlling transaction 81, 157, 158, 237-239, 244, 245
  describing subject matter 157-171, 176-179, 182-192

disclaimer of warranties 201
grounds for rescission 237-239
limitation of warranties 201
quality, describing 224-226, 238, 239, 242, 244, 247
quantity, describing 229, 231
unfair price 212, 213
witnessed 133
written 133, 166
stipulationes 14, 15, 37, 58
as independent undertakings 15
stones, included with field 167
subject matter (see also price, consideration, *res*, various subject matter headings this index)
abandoned 144, 145
airspace 152, 158
animals 186-192, 197-199
bathhouses 165, 166
beehives 156, 191-193
books 262
burial plots 175
carts 188
caves 158, 166
cisterns 166, 191
city 166
consecrated 214, 215
courtyards 165, 166
date palms 170, 171, 174
defective 169. 170, 236-247
deposited 150
disputed 195-197
ditches 175
dovecotes 156, 166, 168, 191-193
dung 191
easements 157
extorted 258-261
fields 167, 169, 170
  irrigated 166
  produce of 153
forbidden to Jews 249
garden 181, 182, 184
houses 156, 162-164, 166, 184
household goods 213
indeterminate 142

land 185-188, 214, 215
  attached to 193
  dwelling, for 164
  fence, for 183, 184
  gardens, for (see gardens this heading)
  planting, for 176-180, 182
  portion of 183, 184
lost 150
manure (see dung this heading)
mistake as to 247
moveables 193
necessities 257
nonexistent 143, 144, 146-148, 150, 154, 156
  in future 146, 147
notes 151, 214, 215
olive press 165
orchard 183, 184
pavements 158
physical substance required 151, 161
poor, designated for 154
poor quality 169
presshouse 165, 166
rare 263
rights to property 151, 152
roadway 175
ruins 159, 160
sacred purpose 214, 215
seller's ownership and control 144, 145, 148, 150
separable 150
servitudes 156
ships 188
slaves 190, 191, 197, 214, 215
stolen 258
subsurface 158
vines 170
vow, subject to 154
water 191
winepress 168
yokes 188-190
subsurface 158-161
Sukkot 227

surety 27, 28, 255
synagogue seats 112, 270
Talmud 178
teachers 139
tefillin 184
Temple 154, 155
third party, consideration to 76
title, challenged 202
trees 147, 167-175
trust, business on 214
Tur 5, 178, 216
tutors 264
unborn 147, 148
unfair advantage 243, 264
unfair price (see price this index)
unilateral promises 15
usury 61, 131-133, 233
  indirect 132
Venetian Hebrew books 4
verbal agreements
  unenforceable 75
  withdrawal from 120
vines 170, 173, 175, 183
vows (see oaths this index)
  charity, to 140
  described 154
  evidencing consent 140
  evidencing *kinyan* (see also *kinyan* this index) 140
  property subject to 154
wager (see gambling, *kinyan* this index)
wagons (see carts this index)
warranties
  accidents, against 201
  disclaimers 201, 202
  eviction, against 58, 62, 63, 71, 88, 123, 199, 201-203, 267, 268
  express 5, 58, 62, 200
  extorted property 260
  fitness for us, of 225, 226, 244-246
  foreseeable risks, against 200
  guardians 202
  implied 55, 58, 59, 199, 202

latent defects, against 56, 57
quality of the thing, of 15, 55-59
quiet enjoyment, of 15, 58
risk of loss 65
Roman law 58
title, of 260, 268
unavoidable constraints, against 58, 200
unusual constraints, against 201
waiver of 58, 62, 201
water 191
weight, deceit re 217
weights (see also measures this index) 44, 45, 227-232, 234
wells 86, 87, 168
wicked persons 263, 264
wilderness 88
wine 220-222, 224-227, 232, 247
  defilement, ritual 201
  kinyan (see also *kinyan* this index) 59, 201
  non-Jews 201
  proceeds of sale of 143
  ritual defilement 201
  warranties 59, 201
winepress 168
witnesses 137, 194, 195, 251, 256, 259, 261, 265, 266, 269
  declaration of protest, to 125
  duress, to 53, 122, 123
  incompetents 39
  kinyan, to (see also *kinyan* this index) 29, 31, 82, 90, 122
  sale, not required for 40
  seller as 194
  stipulations 133
  verbal agreement, to 75
written instruments (see instruments, written this index)
yokes
  cows' 188, 189
  oxen 188-190